W9-AEZ-533

An Introduction to Poetry

An Introduction to Poetry

LOUIS SIMPSON

University of California · Berkeley

ST. MARTIN'S PRESS
NEW YORK

13381

Preface

I WANTED to make a book that would serve as an introduction to poetry for beginning readers and at the same time interest people who had read many poems. The trouble with introductions is that the writer usually treats poems as though they were exercises in meter or diction or figures of speech. But the first object of poetry is to give pleasure, not to illustrate rules. So the main part of this book is an anthology, where the poems stand by themselves; and in the opening chapters where I do undertake to explain, especially in the chapter titled "Reading the Poem," I have not tried to explain everything. I believe that the tide is turning against the kind of close reading that interprets every word of a poem. C. S. Lewis says, "The main task of an interpreter is to begin analyses and to leave them unfinished," and in *The Critical Quarterly* Mr. Charles Tomlinson recently said, "The critic should stop supposing that we like being in the classroom the whole time or that, outside of it, he must keep rushing to our aid, eternally and infernally helpful where we did not ask for help, explaining (to adopt Dr. Johnson) 'what no reader has found difficult' . . . . The trouble with the disease is that it leaves poet and reader with nothing to do." I have left the reader something to do, and it may be that protests such as these show that changes in critical method are on the way. I hope that critics will stop turning every line of a poem into prose, and will find ways of considering the quality of feeling and the importance of ideas in a poem.

The anthology represents authors and movements in the order of their occurrence—though of course it does not represent them all or show every side of an author—and also there is a variety of types and forms. Many of the poems are famous, but beginning readers do not know them, and readers who do may want to have them again. I can sympathize with the man who has seen Sidney's sonnet to the moon once too often, but it is a great poem and it has not yet palled on me.

In coming down to modern times I might have been as whimsical as I liked, for the reading of poetry has lagged behind production, and scholars who are sure of the meaning of poems written three hundred years ago cannot understand poems written in their own day. Nevertheless, in choosing modern poems I have tried to be as impartial as in selecting from early periods. I have chosen the best and the most representative poems. Finally, I have added and subtracted from the anthology so that it would have a structure like that of a poem, one part fitting to another. Keat's nightingale calls to Williams' sparrow. The collection ranges from simple lyrics to narrative and discursive poems, such as *Mauberley*, that raise important questions about the nature of poetry.

The third part of the book is a Glossary. I hope that this will be particularly useful. Besides definitions the Glossary contains statements about poetry by poets and critics, for a bright remark is more useful than a dim definition. If these quotations encourage readers to look up the original texts, then the Glossary is also an introduction to criticism.

This book is a labor of love. It must be, for it has grown out of all proportion to the original idea. At first I thought of simply putting together all the poems I liked. But then I had to consider what poetry is and try to explain my ideas to other people, and there are aspects of poetry that cannot be explained. Poetry remains fundamentally mysterious, like life itself. The rational mind can go only so far toward understanding poetry, and then the reader must make a leap in the dark, as the poet does when he is writing.

I am most grateful to Helene Margrethe Knox, who worked on the Glossary, and Moffett Beall Hall, who helped to revise the manuscript.

Contents

viii

ix

x

An Introduction to Poetry

The Art of Poetry

RHYTHM

POETRY IS thought expressed in rhythm. Poetry incorporates images and ideas that can also be found in prose, but poetry begins with a vital rhythmic movement. The rhythm is the way the poet's personality really comes into the poem. This is the difference between poetry and prose. There are rhythms in prose, but these are not essential; the words could be placed in a different order without changing the effect. But a line of poetry is like dancing—the words have definite positions in time and space.

A poem, Coleridge said,

> is that species of composition, which is opposed to works of science, by proposing for its *immediate* object pleasure, not truth; and from all other species (having this in common with it) it is discriminated by proposing to itself such delight from the *whole*, as is compatible with a distinct gratification from each component part.

The second part of the statement is questionable, for several works of prose fiction have the unity between the parts and the whole that Coleridge speaks of. The novelist Flaubert wrote sentences as carefully as poets write lines; *Madame Bovary* rises on a structure and accumulation of details.

The pleasure of poetry lies in the rhythm of the poem. Also it is in the choice and arrangement of words, for poetry, as Ezra Pound said, must be at least as well written as prose; but poetry is more than this, and the *more* is rhythm, expressed in lines of verse. Prose writers think in sentences; poets think in lines.

IMITATION

Poetry is thought that is felt. Aristotle says, "There is nothing in the intellect that is not first in the senses." To make us grasp his thought, the poet uses figures of speech and creates images—imitations of life, words that evoke mental pictures and appeal to our senses of hearing, touching, smelling, and tasting. The poet does not merely talk about things, he represents them. He makes us feel and see. When we have experienced his thought, we know it.

Though poetry is an imitation of life, it is not photography, for the poet wishes to communicate ideas. Therefore he selects, concentrates, and arranges matters to this end.

In the *Poetics* Aristotle says,

> The greatest thing by far is to be a master of metaphor. It is the one thing that cannot be learned from others; and it is also a sign of genius, since a good metaphor implies an intuitive perception of the similarity in dissimilars.

Let us see how this works, in a song by Burns:

> My luve is like a red, red rose
> That's newly sprung in June:
> My luve is like the melodie
> That's sweetly played in tune.

"Like a red, red rose" is a simile, a form of metaphor, comparing one thing to another. Burns is describing a Scottish girl. Thinking of her fresh beauty and "redness"—perhaps it is her mouth he is thinking of—he thinks of the redness of a rose.

Why does our attention move from one thing to another that is like it? There seem to be instincts that make us look for "similarity in dissimilars," searching for a unity in different things. We want our experiences to be unified, so that they will have a meaning.

As the poet imagines a rose, thoughts associated with roses come into his mind. Roses are symbolic; over the centuries they have gathered an aura of passion. Roses grow in gardens and climb up castle walls. A beautiful woman is looking down from a window; a troubadour is singing beneath the trellis. And so on.

The poet returns to the Scottish girl, transferring his thoughts back to her. Now she is enriched with associations of the rose and adorned in romance. She *is* the rose. Then, in the second simile he compares her to music, and she becomes music.

Consider the opening lines of Hamlet's soliloquy:

> To be, or not to be: that is the question:
> Whether 'tis nobler in the mind to suffer
> The slings and arrows of outrageous fortune,

4

> Or to take arms against a sea of troubles,
> And by opposing end them?

These are metaphors. In a metaphor the poet likens one object to another by speaking of it as if it were that other, omitting words of comparison such as "like" and "as." Thus, in Hamlet's speech mental suffering is not merely compared to, it is translated into, the picture of a man being shot at with stones and arrows. In the second metaphor, suffering is pictured as a man fighting against the waves. The metaphors have translated ideas into scene and drama. From these metaphors we get a more vivid impression than we would get from abstract words. Suppose Hamlet said:

> To be, or not to be: that is the question:
> Whether 'tis nobler in the mind to suffer
> The insults and misfortunes of our life,
> Or make a strenuous effort to resist,
> And by opposing end them?

How dull this is! Having no metaphorical power, the words do not affect our senses; they do not rouse the instincts that make us sympathize with what we think we see, hear, taste, or touch.

What are these instincts, and why do men, particularly poets, speak in metaphors? This is a large question, but it may be useful to explore the ideas of one writer on the subject. Vico, in *The New Science*, 1744, says that in primitive ages men ascribed their own human characteristics to everything. Then they terrified themselves with these beliefs; the phenomena seemed supernatural. When the sky thundered, it was the anger of Jove. Everything was permeated with one divine spirit, and then with many spirits that were related, making a great whole. Nothing was perceived in isolation, but in relation to the rest, and one perception led to another.

> The most luminous and therefore the most necessary and frequent [trope] is metaphor. It is most praised when it gives sense and passion to insensate things, in accordance with the metaphysics above discussed, by which the first poets attributed to bodies the being of animate substances, with capacities measured by their own, namely sense and passion, and in this way made fables of them. Thus every metaphor so formed is a fable in brief.

5

Vico also says:

> It is noteworthy that in all languages the greater part of the expressions relating to inanimate things are formed by metaphor from the human body and its parts and from the human senses and passions. Thus, head for top or beginning; eyes for the looped heads of screws ... mouth for any opening; lip for the rim of a vase or of anything else; the tooth of a plow, a rake, a saw, a comb; ... a neck of land; handful for a small number; heart for center ... foot for end; the flesh of fruits; a vein of water, rock or mineral ... the bowels of the earth. Heaven or the sea smiles; the wind whistles; the waves murmur; a body groans under a great weight.

One power of metaphorical writing, then, is to make us experience thought as sense-perception, and so understand it. The other effect is to unify our experience.

Metaphor is a process of comparing and identifying one thing with another. Then, as we see what things have in common, we see the general meaning they have. Now, the ability to see the relation between one thing and another is almost a definition of intelligence. Thinking in metaphors—and poetry is largely this—is a tool of intelligence. Perhaps it is the most important tool.

In the following passage from *Biographia Literaria*, 1817, where Coleridge is talking about imagination, it is clear that he means the ability to think in metaphors:

> The poet, described in ideal perfection, brings the whole soul of man into activity ... He diffuses a tone and spirit of unity, that blends, and (as it were) *fuses*, each into each, by that synthetic and magical power, to which I would exclusively appropriate the name of Imagination ... This power ... reveals itself in the balance or reconcilement of opposite or discordant qualities: of sameness with difference; of the general with the concrete; the idea with the image; the individual with the representative ...

Several writers have described the unifying power of metaphors. In *The Advancement of Learning*, 1605, Francis Bacon said:

> Neither are these only similitudes, as men of narrow observation may conceive them to be, but the same footsteps of nature, treading upon several subjects or matters.

Owen Barfield, in *Poetic Diction*, 1928, says that the relationships of one object with another, and between objects and ideas, that we perceive through metaphor, have an existence independent of the individual thinker. They are reported in the language of primitive men as "direct perceptual experience." To primitive men, and children, everything is infused with the same life. But we have lost the ability to perceive the unity of things. Only through poetry, or through science, may we regain this power.

> Our sophistication, like Odin's, has cost us an eye; and now it is the language of poets, in so far as they create true metaphors, which must *restore* this unity conceptually, after it has been lost from perception.

So, not only does poetry give pleasure, but also it unifies our experience and enables us to see the meaning of things.

STYLE AND TONE

Critics used to make elaborate general descriptions of styles of writing. There was plain style, middle style, grand style, and as many variations as the critic could find examples of. There is a list of this kind by Scaliger:

> We recognize three kinds of style, the grand or lofty (*altiloqua*), the humble (*infima*), and the mean of the two, which I please to call the moderate (*æquabilis*). Some properties are common to all of these, some are particular. Common properties are perspicuity (*perspicuitas*), refinement (*cultus*), propriety (*proprietas*), elegance or grace (*venustas*), and rhythm (*numerositas*). These qualities should inhere in every poem. Of the other common properties some are not invariably used, but subject to occasion, as smoothness (*mollitia*), winsomeness (*suavitas*), rapidity or spirit (*incitatio*), purity or unadornedness (*puritas*), acumen (*acutum*), sharpness or raillery (*acre*), fullness (*plenum*), and ornateness (*floridum*). As of the common properties, so of the particular, some should be employed always, others only on occasion. In the grand style those to be observed always are dignity (*dignitas*) and sonorousness (*sonus*); those to be used on occasion, ponderousness (*gravitas*) and fervency

(*vehementia*). In the lowly style that to be observed always is plainness or artless purity (*tenuitas*); on occasion, simplicity (*simplicitas*) and negligence (*securitas*). Those to be invariably observed in the moderate style are roundness (*rotunditas*) and fluency (*volubilitas*). Such is our classification, and it is complete and invariable.

Poetics, 1561

He might as well have said that poets write in every conceivable manner.

Poets are original. Each poet has, to some extent, his own diction and his own ways of using figurative and rhetorical devices, tones, and patterns of sound. Of course some writers are mere imitators, in the bad sense of the word, but they need not concern us. As Horace said, "Neither gods nor men nor publishers can tolerate a mediocre poet."

Though poets are original, however, they share certain characteristics, and within a historical period we can see definite resemblances among poets that set them off from the poets who precede them and the poets who follow. That is why we speak of Elizabethan, Augustan, or romantic poetry. Though there are differences between Augustan poets such as Pope and Swift, they have similar styles of writing that set them off sharply from Wordsworth and Keats, who wrote in the romantic period.

In literary generations, style swings like a pendulum from simple to elaborate, and back again. At the beginning of the nineteenth century Wordsworth argued against the farfetched words and circumlocutions of eighteenth-century verse, the idea that it was unpoetic to call things by their common names. Writing such as this, by Samuel Johnson, was too far removed from the language in which men thought and spoke:

> Turn on the prudent Ant thy heedless eyes,
> Observe her labors, Sluggard, and be wise;
> No stern command, no monitory voice,
> Prescribes her duties, or directs her choice.

This, Wordsworth says, is a hubbub of words. He compares it with the original in Scripture:

> Go to the Ant, thou sluggard, consider her ways, and be wise: which having no guide, overseer, or ruler, provideth her meat in the summer, and gathereth her food in the harvest.

Wordsworth's liking for simplicity enabled him to write lines of his own that have a Biblical grandeur:

> The silence that is in the starry sky,
> The sleep that is among the lonely hills . . .

However, later in the century Browning is anything but simple:

> While Paul looked archly on, pricked brow at whiles
> With the pen-point as to punish triumph there,
> And said "Count Guido, take your lawful wife
> Until death part you!"

The eccentricities of Gerard Manley Hopkins would have puzzled Wordsworth:

> In a flash, at a trumpet crash,
> I am all at once what Christ is, since he was what I am,
>   and
> This Jack, joke, poor potsherd, patch, matchwood, im-
>   mortal diamond,
>   Is immortal diamond.

Before the First World War, the American poet Ezra Pound was living in London. Thinking that the current styles of poetry were vapid and unreal, he formulated ideas for new writing and launched the imagist movement, which included the critic T. E. Hulme and the poets Richard Aldington, F. S. Flint, and H. D. (Hilda Doolittle). The ideas of the school are described in the six "common principles" listed in the preface to *Some Imagist Poets*, 1915. These ideas have had a strong influence on modern poetry and on prose as well:

1. To use the language of common speech, but to employ always the *exact* word, not the nearly exact, nor the merely decorative word.

2. To create new rhythms—as the expression of new moods—and not to copy old rhythms, which merely echo old moods. We do not insist upon "free-verse" as the only method of writing poetry. We fight for it as a principle of liberty. We believe that the individuality of a poet may often be better expressed in free-verse than in conventional forms. In poetry, a new cadence means a new idea.

3. To allow absolute freedom in the choice of subject. It is not good art to write badly about aeroplanes and automobiles; nor is it necessarily bad art to write about the past. We believe passionately in the

artistic value of modern life, but we wish to point out that there is nothing so uninspiring nor so old-fashioned as an aeroplane of the year 1911.

4. To present an image (hence the name: "Imagist"). We are not a school of painters, but we believe that poetry should render particulars exactly and not deal in vague generalities, however magnificent and sonorous. It is for this reason that we oppose the cosmic poet, who seems to us to shirk the real difficulties of his art.

5. To produce poetry that is hard and clear, never blurred nor indefinite.

6. Finally, most of us believe that concentration is of the very essence of poetry.

It is in accordance with these principles that T. S. Eliot writes:

> They are rattling breakfast plates in basement kitchens,
> And along the trampled edges of the street
> I am aware of the damp souls of housemaids
> Sprouting despondently at area gates.

This is "hard and clear," but a generation later, in these lines by Dylan Thomas, the pendulum has swung the other way. Thomas is "cosmic."

> And I must enter again the round
> Zion of the water bead
> And the synagogue of the ear of corn.

Writing such as this is not easy to understand, but it can be understood, with a dictionary and a little patience.

There is an important consideration that affects the poet's style: decorum, or suiting the style to the subject. The song by Robert Burns, "My luve is like a red, red rose," is made of familiar words and simple, declarative sentences. The passage from *Hamlet* is somewhat more complicated. In each instance the poet's style is fitted to his purpose: for Burns, a song; for Shakespeare, a soliloquy in which the speaker meditates on life and death.

Also, style is determined by the necessity to make the reader see and feel. In the following passage from Milton's *Paradise Lost*, Moloch, one of the angels who have been driven out of heaven, describes the battle in which they fell. Moloch argues that as there is a kind of gravity that draws spirits upward, it will not be too hard for the fallen angels to fly up again:

> Who but felt of late
> When the fierce foe hung on our broken rear
> Insulting, and pursued us through the deep,
> With what compulsion and laborious flight
> We sunk thus low?

In the lines:

> With what compulsion and laborious flight
> We sunk thus low?

the words "compulsion" and "laborious," due to the plosives *p* and *b*, the following vowel sounds, and the ponderous length of the words, give a sense of wings pushing back against a pressure that is forcing them downward, a pressure greater than the strength of wings but not irresistible.

Coleridge said, "What is Poetry? is so nearly the question with what is a poet? that the answer to the one is involved in the solution of the other." And the American poet Wallace Stevens says, "Poetry is a process of the personality of the poet." These remarks serve to remind us that, in any discussion of style, there is a quality that cannot be accounted for by analysis of the use of language, or by reference to historical influences. This quality is personality.

Some modern critics, reacting against a sentimental kind of writing about poets that was prevalent in the nineteenth century, have made an effort to eliminate from the reading of poetry such matters as speculation about the poet's life or his intention in writing the poem. The New Criticism performed a useful function; it focused attention on the poem itself, where it should be. However, other critics have taken this to mean that any expression of the poet's life as it appears in the poem, or of his ideas, is irrelevant. To such critics, a poem is a machine without emotion, and the reader another machine constructed to have no emotions. This way of thinking about poetry is not only boring, it is impossible.

To suggest the ways in which personality appears, we speak of the poet's "voice," or the "tone" of his writing. By these words we mean qualities of humor or pathos, sincere feeling or irony. These qualities are not additions, they are intrinsic to the poem; they are what holds the poem together and makes it convincing. The only way to discern these qualities is by reading intelligently, as whole men, open to all possible shades of meaning.

It helps to see what devices the poet uses, and to be aware of how much his voice is the voice of the age. For example, in reading Donne, we need to know that when, in "The Autumnal," he writes lines to a woman in her forties, describing her wrinkles:

> Call not these wrinkles, graves: if graves they were,
> They were love's graves . . . .

he is not being tactless. He is being witty, developing a paradox in the manner of a popular genre, *capitoli*. The paradox here is that it is better to love an older woman than a young girl. Donne is exhibiting his ingenuity. The lady about whom he is writing would have been amused and flattered. Though we should be aware of particular circumstances, however, we should also be aware of the poet's voice, that is, his personality. This requires that we extend ourselves. As Wordsworth said, we must love the poet before he can seem worthy of our love. There is no doubt that some poets—Donne, Hopkins, and Dylan Thomas, for example—need the extension, for they can be exceedingly difficult.

Sometimes the poet is struggling with a difficult idea. In order to make distinctions, or bring strange thoughts together, he chooses unusual words and puts them in an unusual order. Or he may wish to surprise the reader with a compression of ideas, and write in a kind of shorthand, leaving out the usual connecting words of prose. In an attempt to express original ideas, or old ideas in an interesting manner, the poet may develop a style that is nearly impenetrable, and draw upon himself the ridicule of the public, until they grow accustomed to his way of writing.

The question "Why is modern poetry obscure?" is one that all poets who read their works in public may expect to be asked. The answer is that poetry changes, as does everything else, and new ways of writing demand an effort on the reader's part. The great poets of the past were not simple. Much of Shakespeare does not yield its meaning at a glance, and Milton can be difficult. If we can read and understand these poets today, it is because we have learned to do so. A similar effort is necessary in order to understand new poetry. If we do not wish to learn, we must be content with what we already know.

> And there will I keep you forever,
> Yes, forever and a day,
> Till the walls shall crumble to ruin,
> And moulder in dust away!
>
> Longfellow, "The Children's Hour"

PLEASURE AND/OR TRUTH

When Coleridge said that a poem "is that species of composition, which is opposed to works of science, by proposing for its *immediate* object pleasure, not truth," he put his finger on a harmful misconception, the idea that poetry "teaches a lesson."

In ancient times, when there was hardly any writing, many kinds of information were put into verse, for verse was memorable and portable. Advice about farming or shipbuilding would be conveyed in poetry. This practice continued into literary times. The *Georgics* of Virgil, for example, include a good deal of practical advice about farming. However, this is not the kind of lesson that Coleridge had in mind, for in his time such information was placed, as it is nowadays, in books of prose. Coleridge was thinking of didactic writing, the aim of which is to give moral instruction.

Many great poems do give moral instruction. Dante's *Divine Comedy* and the *Book of Job* are full of wisdom. But these poems instruct us by pleasing; as we read we are delighted by the episodes, imagery, and language, and we are persuaded rather than argued into virtue. But writing that is primarily didactic does not please. There have been sermons that are a pleasure to hear or read—those of Donne, for example—but they are exceptions. Most didactic writing is tedious, and poems that set out to teach a lesson are bad poetry.

If we read Poe's essay, "The Poetic Principle," or better still, Baudelaire's explanation of Poe's ideas, we see how alert poets are to the dangers of didacticism. In the following passage Baudelaire begins with a stiff bow in the direction of Science and Morality, then turns on his heel and makes off as fast as possible in the other direction:

> I do not mean that poetry does not ennoble manners—let there be no mistake about it—that its final result is not to raise man above the level of vulgar interests; that would obviously be an absurdity. I say that, if the poet has pursued a moral aim, he has diminished his poetic force; and it is not rash to wager that his work will be bad. Poetry cannot, under penalty of death or failure, be assimilated to science or morality; it does not have Truth as its object, it has only Itself. The means for demonstrating truth are other and are elsewhere. Truth has nothing to do with songs.

Yet many people still believe, as they did in Baudelaire's day, that poetry should be functional, a kind of moral chair, and they search out poems that have a "message" that can be applied. The effect of this on the young is disastrous, for children regard poetry as a task, and when they grow up they will not read it. Not only are moralizing poems boring, but if poems are only messages about how to be "good," that is, how to get along with people and succeed in life, then children can learn more from textbooks or from experience.

Many people know Kipling's "If":

> If you can dream—and not make dreams your master;
>   If you can think—and not make thoughts your aim . . .
>
> If all men count with you, but none too much:
> If you can fill the unforgiving minute
>   With sixty seconds' worth of distance run—
> Yours is the Earth and everything that's in it,
>   And—which is more—you'll be a Man, my son!

According to this advice, we are always to keep cool and not to attach ourselves wholeheartedly to any cause or person. In fact, we are to be ready to cut and run. This may be practical advice, but I doubt it. A man who was so calculating would not be trusted, and I doubt that he would succeed. He would always be taking second place to someone with imagination. But the main thing to be said

14

about "If" is that it is not true. There is no guarantee—and the poet is presumptuous to offer one—that if we comply with these rules, we will own the earth.

In the schoolroom we learn to dislike these poems; we sense the hypocrisy. The moralizing poet tells only a part of the truth, not the whole. The message in his writing is a platitude, and he aims to make us satisfied with a platitude. But we will not be talked down to. A moralizing poet asks for a horse laugh or a snicker, and gets it in the form of parody.

The following poem called "The Bee" was written by Dr. Isaac Watts.

> How doth the little busy bee
> Improve each shining hour,
> And gather honey all the day
> From every opening flower!
>
> How skillfully she builds her cell!
> How neat she spreads the wax!
> And labors hard to store it well
> With the sweet food she makes.
>
> In works of labor or of skill
> I would be busy too;
> For Satan finds some mischief still
> For idle hands to do.
>
> In books, or work, or healthful play,
> Let my first years be past;
> That I may give for every day
> Some good account at last.

In England in the eighteenth century, when commerce and industry were on the rise, it was in the interest of employers to hire children who would work long hours for low pay. Poems such as this became popular, among employers. Children who hated working all day and part of the night in shops and factories might well be persuaded, or terrified—note the threat of Hell-fire—into keeping their noses to the grindstone. The virtue that the poem recommends is work done out of fear, not love. It is doubtful that such work made the children virtuous; it is certain that it made their employers rich.

In *Alice's Adventures in Wonderland*, Lewis Carroll wrote a parody of "The Bee" called "The Crocodile":

> How doth the little crocodile
> Improve his shining tail,
> And pour the waters of the Nile
> On every golden scale!
>
> How cheerfully he seems to grin,
> How neatly spreads his claws,
> And welcomes little fishes in,
> With gently smiling jaws!

Carroll has seen the results of Dr. Watts' advice. As Dryden says, "A satirical poet is the check of the layman on bad priests."

When we have seen that moralizing poems are bad poetry, and that the aim of poetry is not to teach a lesson, it would nevertheless be wrong to think that poetry is only a luxury, having no real use. To the contrary, poetry is a necessity. In the first place it gives us pleasure, and without pleasure human beings cannot live. Also poetry enlarges our imagination, and without imagination men cannot live together in society.

Sometimes it is difficult to feel the pleasure in poetry, for the poet may be describing painful things. Poetry is an imitation of life, and the ways may be subtle and difficult. Yet as we are changed by living, so we are changed by poetry. We are delighted, our imagination is roused, we have a stronger apprehension of things.

In "A Defense of Poetry," Shelley argued that without poetry society cannot function. If men live without imagination, only for selfish aims, then the country decays:

> The rich have become richer, and the poor have become poorer; and the vessel of the state is driven between the Scylla and Charybdis of anarchy and despotism. Such are the effects which must ever flow from an unmitigated exercise of the calculating faculty.

In another place, Shelley says that his aim is to fill the imagination of his readers with "beautiful idealisms of moral excellence." When, through poetry, the individual is changed for the better, then society will change—for society is composed of individuals.

The difference between Shelley's moral "idealisms" and the kind of moralizing found in Kipling's "If" may not be clear at first. But as we read we see the difference. It is in the largeness of imagination and the narrowness of morality. Poets tell us all they know—though, of course, they do not know everything. The moralizing writer, on the other hand, tells only a part of what he knows, and this is less than we know ourselves.

Though I admire Shelley's moral imagination, and hope that poetry acts in the long run to improve men's minds and change the world, I am not aware of these matters while reading a poem. The better the poem, the less I am conscious of any aim beyond reading it. The poem is a world in itself. Perhaps there is a fundamental contradiction between the world of poetry and the world of everyday. Men of action have always suspected that there is, and on occasion have tried to put down poetry. Long ago Plato said that poets were liars, and recommended that they be crowned with laurel, led to the frontier, and told not to come back to the country. But when he wrote *The Republic*, Plato was trying to reform Athens. The perfect Republic, as he describes it, is a place so grimly functional that only drill instructors could live there happily. Poets would not have to be escorted to the border; they would flee, along with all the other sensible men and the pretty girls.

The Technique of Verse

POETS ARE "makers"; they know how poems are put together, and though they may not know the names for technical devices, they use them all the time. If we wish to discuss poetry, some knowledge of these things is necessary.

METER

In English, meter is the pattern of stressed and unstressed syllables.

Prosodists distinguish between syllables with heavy and syllables with light stresses, but I shall not do so. Prosody, the "science" of poetical forms, is not an exact science, and if we attempt to make it so, it disappears. If we mark half-stresses, there is no reason that we should not mark quarter-stresses, and so on. But when we think we hear half- and quarter-stresses, we can be sure that other people do not hear them. At that point, either we must impose our own way of hearing upon others, which is impossible, or agree that it is up to the individual to say exactly how he hears the beat of verse. The only system we can agree upon is the division of meter into stressed and unstressed syllables.

As we read lines of verse, each stressed sound combines with one or two unstressed sounds. This combination is called a foot. In the following line I have separated the feet by putting a virgule (/) between them. I have marked each stressed syllable: — . Unstressed syllables are marked: ◡. (Quantities in Greek and Roman verse are also marked with these signs, but I am using them to mark stresses, not quantities):

Rŏmān/tĭc Īre/laňd's dēad/ aňd gōne.

Here each foot consists of an unstressed syllable followed by a stressed. A foot of this kind is called an iamb, and verse in which such feet predominate is iambic. In the line above there are four feet. A line with four feet is called a tetrameter. Therefore, the complete description of the meter of the line above is iambic tetrameter.

Besides the stresses, or accents, of meter, there are rhetorical accents. Rhetorical accent is the emphasis given to a word because of its importance in the sentence. The meter of verse, the regular pattern of stressed and unstressed sounds, is sometimes wrenched by a rhetorical accent. It would be a rare poem that followed its meter exactly, without variation, and a poem like that would sound mechanical.

Though the poem by Yeats from which I have taken the line above is in iambic tetrameter—that is, most of the lines are in iambic tetrameter—there are places where the rhetorical accent wrenches the meter, substituting irregular feet and giving the line a more passionate, natural sound, as though a man were thinking and feeling:

> Wās ĭt/ fŏr thīs/ thĕ wīld/ gēese sprēad
> Thĕ grāy/ wĭng ŭp/ŏn ēv/erў tīde;
> Fŏr thīs/ thăt āll/ thăt blōod/ wăs shēd,
> Fŏr thīs/ Ēdwărd/ Fĭtzgēr/ald dīed,
> Ănd Rōb/ert Ēmm/ĕt ănd/ Wōlf Tōne,
> Āll thăt/ dĕlīr/iŭm ŏf/ thĕ brāve?

I am not sure that Yeats would have stressed the sounds as I have done, for everyone reads in a different way, but I think he would have played as many variations, of one kind or another, upon the basic meter.

Meter is like waves of the sea, and rhetorical accents are like cross-currents. The waves come on at a regular pace. They are crossed by the currents, and writhe, and seem to break. Then they resume their pace.

In English the basic feet are:

> the iamb (adjective, iambic) ⌣ —
> trochee (trochaic) — ⌣
> anapest (anapestic) ⌣ ⌣ —
> dactyl (dactylic) — ⌣ ⌣

Less common are:

the spondee (spondaic) — —
pyrrhus (pyrrhic) ◡ ◡
amphibrach (amphibrachic) ◡ — ◡

And there are other feet so rarely used that we do not need to know them.

Lines of verse are named for the number of feet they contain.

A line of one foot is a monometer
two feet   dimeter
three feet   trimeter
four feet   tetrameter
five feet   pentameter
six feet   hexameter
seven feet heptameter

and so on.

Or else the line may be named for the number of syllables in it. A line of eight syllables is called octosyllabic; a line of ten syllables, decasyllabic.

Unrhymed iambic pentameter, the line in which Marlowe and Shakespeare wrote plays, is often called blank verse (not to be confused with free verse). The iambic hexameter is sometimes called an Alexandrine. In the following couplet, Pope shows the difference between a line of iambic pentameter and an Alexandrine:

Ă nēed/lĕss Āl/ĕxand/rĭne ēnds/ hĭs sōng,   (*iambic pentameter*)

Whĭch,/ lĭke ă wōund/ĕd snāke,// drăws ĭts/ slōw lēngth/ ălōng.
    (*iambic hexameter*, or *Alexandrine*)

In this Alexandrine I have marked the caesura—that is, a "cutting" or pause in the line—with a double bar. Here the caesura is in the middle of the line, dividing it into two equal parts, each of which contains three feet. But a pause may occur anywhere in a line.

Here are other lines and meters. The first two examples are not very good poetry, but they are good enough for our purpose:

Whĕn thrēads/ căn māke   *iambic dimeter*
A heartstring shake,

Philosophy
Can scarce deny
Thē soūl/ cōnsĭsts/ ŏf hārm/ŏnў.   *iambic tetrameter*

Nŏ, thĕ heārt/ thăt hăs trū/lў lŏved nēv/ĕr fŏrgēts,
                                           anapestic tetrameter

        Bŭt ăs trū/lў lŏves ōn/ tŏ thĕ clōse,   *anapestic trimeter*
As the sunflower turns on her god when he sets,
        The same look which she turned when he rose.

    Lōng-ĕx/pēctĕd/ ōne ănd/ twēntў,   *trochaic tetrameter*
    Ling'ring year, at last is flown;
    Pomp and pleasure, pride and plenty,
    Great Sir John, are all your own.

    Mīdnĭght hăs/ cōme, ănd thĕ/ grēat Chrĭst Chŭrch/ Bēll
                                   dactylic tetrameter

    Ănd/ mānў ă/ lēssĕr bēll/ sōund thrŏugh thĕ/ room.

Though meter may reinforce the meaning of poetry, it cannot
be the meaning. As I have said, poetry is an expression of thought;
it is composition.

Reading these lines by Tennyson, we may think we feel the gallop of horses:

            Half a league, half a league
                Half a league onward,
            All in the valley of Death
                Rode the six hundred.
            "Forward, the Light Brigade!
            Charge for the guns!" he said:
            Into the valley of Death
                Rode the six hundred.

But if we think we feel the pace of a cavalry charge, it is because
the words tell us it is a cavalry charge. The meter alone does not
call up the scene. A poet could write lines with the same meter but
with different words that would make us think of something entirely different. Once we have a meaning, meter can support it; but
without meaning, meter drifts in a void.

In his *Life of Pope*, Samuel Johnson argues against the fallacy of thinking that meter alone can represent meaning. Johnson says that through meter:

> Motion . . . may be in some sort exemplified; and yet it may be suspected that in such resemblances the mind often governs the ear, and the sounds are estimated by their meaning.

He shows that Pope uses the same meter when describing a running girl, and, in another place, a slow march. Pope himself says, "The *sound* must seem an *echo* to the *sense*." But this is a far cry from saying that sound is sense. Poetry has both meaning and meter, and in a good poem they are so closely related that they seem one thing.

Though meter and sound cannot by themselves represent the subject, frequently they represent the author's feelings about it—in Pope's phrase, the sound echoes the sense. If the poet wishes to express a heroic mood, he may choose a long, slowly moving line. To express lyrical feeling, he may write in short lines with tripping meters. But there are no standard correlations between lines and feelings. A long, slow line may be humorous, and a tripping line satirical.

There is no end to descriptions of meter. *Secondary stress* and *hovering accent*, and other kinds of rhythmic organization—*cadence* and *syllabic* verse—are described in the Glossary. We could go on talking about prosody, but it makes more sense, and it is certainly more enjoyable, to read poems than to try to think of all the kinds of poems there might possibly be.

RHYME, STANZA, AND SOUND

Poems used to be called rhymes, and some people think that anything that rhymes is a poem. The commonest kind of rhyme is repeating sounds at the ends of lines. It is not a necessary part of poetry, though if a poem is constructed with rhymes, then rhyme should seem essential to that poem. The ancient Greek, Hebrew, and Latin poets did not use rhyme. It was invented by monks in the Middle Ages as a memory aid; they found it easier to memorize chants if the ends of lines had the same sound. Then rhyme was taken up by Italian poets and their imitators, and by the time of Chaucer (c. 1340-1400) we find it ensconced in English.

In comparison with other languages, English does not have a variety of rhyming words. This is evident if we read the poems of an English rhymer such as Pope, who is frequently compelled to use the same terminal words. Rhyme schemes that in other languages are easy—*terza rima*, for example—are hard to find rhymes for in English.

In the history of verse there has been a running quarrel between men such as Samuel Daniel (1562-1619) who *would* rhyme, and men such as Thomas Campion (c. 1566-1620) who *wouldn't*. Daniel defended rhyming on the ground that it was customary (though it was not customary with the ancients); Campion called rhyme, together with the English system of meter, a "vulgar and easie kind of Poesie." Milton, who had written several poems in rhyme, broke with it scornfully:

> rhyme being no necessary adjunct or true ornament of poem or good verse, in longer works especially, but the invention of a barbarous age, to set off wretched matter and lame meter.

The defenders of rhyme say that the sound is pleasing. Moreover, searching for rhymes makes the poet have thoughts he would not otherwise have had. Those who attack rhyme say that in searching for a rhyme the poet loses the thought he had to start with. As for sound, there are other, more subtle devices than the correspondence of terminal sounds. And besides, writing without rhyme is more *natural*. To this the defenders of rhyme reply that all art is artificial, and a poet is free to do as he likes. The argument continues, but in fact rhyme is used less and less by good poets, and some day may be used only for light verse and commercials.

In scansion, rhymes are marked by placing the same letter of the alphabet after words that rhyme with each other. I have marked the following couplets from Pope's *The Rape of the Lock* in this manner:

The hungry Judges soon the Sentence sign,	*a*
And wretches hang that Jurymen may dine;	*a*
The Merchant from th'*Exchange* returns in Peace,	*b*
And the long Labors of the *Toilet* cease.	*b*

Actually, in this instance the letters *a a b b* are not needed to describe the lines, for the word "couplet" means two consecutive lines that rhyme with each other. But if we wish to describe other rhyme schemes, letters are useful. Here is a ballad stanza:

> It is an ancient Mariner,   *a*
> And he stoppeth one of three.   *b*
> "By thy long gray beard and glittering eye,   *c*
> Now wherefore stopp'st thou me?   *b*

We could describe this rhyme scheme simply by saying, "a ballad stanza rhyming *a b c b*." This would differentiate the stanza from others—for example, stanzas rhyming *a b a b*.

At the same time we could describe the meter by placing numbers after the letters to show the number of feet in each line: $a^4\ b^3\ c^4\ b^3$.

A stanza is a group of lines forming a unit of a poem. It is recurrent, with a regular pattern of lines, meter, and rhyme—though the pattern may vary. Some of the stanza forms—quatrain, *rime royal, ottava rima*, Spenserian stanza, and so on—are described in the Glossary.

Before rhyme came into English, there was an entirely different system of sound-correspondence, by alliteration, the repetition of initial consonants or vowels in words placed close together. William Langland, a contemporary of Chaucer, wrote in this manner:

> In a somer seson, whan soft was the sonne,
> I shope me into shroudes, as I a shepe were;
> In habite as an heremite unholy of workes
> Went wide in this world, wondres to here.
>
> *Piers Plowman*

Though alliteration is no longer used as a system, in most poetry there is some alliteration:

> Now the old come out to look,
>   Winter past and winter's pains,
> How the sky in pool and brook
>   Glitters on the grassy plains.
>
> A. E. Housman, "Spring Morning"

In this quatrain the initial consonant *w* occurs twice, in "Winter" and "winter's," the initial *p* occurs three times, and the *g* twice.

Besides alliteration, in this quatrain there is another sound device: assonance, the repetition of vowel sounds within different words placed close together. "Past" and "pains" are assonant; so are "pool" and "brook."

On the other hand, repetition of consonants within words placed close together is . . . consonance:

> The moan of doves in *imm*em*o*rial el*m*s,
> And mur*m*uring of innu*m*erable bees.
>
> Tennyson, *The Princess*

And there is cacophony, a combination of discordant sounds:

> The ice was here, the ice was there,
> The ice was all around:
> It *cracked* and *growled*, and roared and howled,
> Like noises in a swound!
>
> Coleridge, *The Rime of the Ancient Mariner*

I have said that meter alone cannot convey meaning. Nor can onomatopoeia, the forming of words in imitation of sounds. In the lines from Tennyson's *The Princess*, we may think that we hear, in the alliterative and consonant *m* sounds, and the assonant *o* and *u* sounds, the moaning of doves and humming of bees. But without the nouns "doves" and "bees," these sounds would not conjure up doves and bees. We might be thinking of the ocean, or wind in the grass. In the "cracked" and "growled" of Coleridge's description we may think that we hear ice grinding and splitting, but without the word "ice" it might as well be breaking timber. Like meter, sound can reinforce meaning, but sounds alone are nonsense.

FREE VERSE

Free verse—verse with an irregular metrical pattern—is an old form. The Hebrew psalms were written in lines that are more or less free; in the last century Whitman wrote free verse, and nowadays many poets write in this form. Free verse is not just prose broken into irregular lines. As Eliot said, no verse is free for the man who wants to do a good job—and free verse, to be written well, requires as much art as writing in regular meters. However, this has not been apparent to some people. Robert Frost said he would as soon play tennis without a net as try to write free verse. Even if we think that poetry is a game, there are games—jai alai, for example—that do not use a net, though they are not played in New England.

Poetry used to be chanted or sung, and patterned on music. The Tudor poet Wyatt composed his poems as songs for the lute. At the end of the eighteenth century when Burns wrote he imitated the popular songs of Scotland. But poetry and music have drifted apart; most poets no longer think of their art as singing and do not follow a beat of music. Instead, they follow the cadence of a speaking voice.

D. H. Lawrence has this to say about free verse:

> Perfected bygone moments, perfected moments in the glimmering futurity, these are the treasured gemlike lyrics of Shelley and Keats. . . . But there is another kind of poetry: the poetry of that which is at hand: the immediate present. . . . Whitman's is the best poetry of this kind. . . . The clue to all his utterance lies in the sheer appreciation of the instant moment . . . Whitman pruned away his clichés—perhaps his clichés of rhythm as well as phrase. And this is about all we can do, deliberately, with free verse. . . . We can break the stiff neck of habit. We can be in ourselves spontaneous and flexible as flame, we can see that utterance rushes out without artificial foam or artificial smoothness. But we cannot positively prescribe any motion, any rhythm. All the laws we invent or discover—it amounts to pretty much the same—will fail to apply to free verse. They will only apply to some form of restricted, limited unfree verse . . . in free verse we look for the insurgent naked throb of the instant moment. . . . The law must come new each time from within.
>
> *"Poetry of the Present,"* 1918

"The law from within" is a hard prescription. For the writer of free verse every poem is a new experience and he must find a new form to express it. He cannot use orthodox forms. In practice, free-verse poets have found it difficult to sustain the cadence of a speaking voice—indeed, to sustain it would destroy the spontaneity Lawrence speaks of—so they have concentrated on making images.

Many free-verse poems depend on images and patterns of images, rather than on patterns of rhythm and sound.

There has been as much dull writing in free verse as there has been in sonnets. The poem breaks down into phrases, fragments of rhythm. It is static. Then the images are only a collection of snapshots, objects that do not move, a mosaic.

Therefore, in recent years, in order to restore the movement of the line, poets have been looking for new meters. The American poet William Carlos Williams experimented with lines measured not in iambs or syllables, but units of speech. As he would read them, each of the following lines is a single stress:

    (1) The smell of the heat is boxwood
      (2) when rousing us
        (3) a movement of the air
   (4) stirs our thoughts
     (5) that had no life in them
       (6) to a life, a life in which . . .

Experiments like this are producing new orthodoxies. Lawrence would have called them "shackles and death," but the freedom he asked for is hard to bear.

Reading the Poem

IN DISCUSSING the following poems I have used technical terms and references that may be unfamiliar to the reader. These words are explained in the Glossary.

Sir Patrick Spens

The king sits in Dumferling toune,
   Drinking the blude-reid wine:
"O whar will I get guid sailor,
   To sail this schip of mine?"

Up and spak an eldern knicht,
   Sat at the kings richt kne:
"Sir Patrick Spens is the best sailor
   That sails upon the se."

The king has written a braid° letter,   *broad*
   And signd it wi his hand,
And sent it to Sir Patrick Spens,
   Was walking on the sand.

The first line that Sir Patrick red,
   A loud lauch lauched he;
The next line that Sir Patrick red,
   The teir blinded his ee.°   *eye*

"O wha° is this has don this deid,   *who*
   This ill deid don to me,
To send me out this time o' the yeir,
   To sail upon the se!

"Mak haste, mak haste, my mirry men all,
   Our guid° schip sails the morne."   *good*
"O say na sae,° my master deir,   *so*
   For I feir a deadlie storme.

"Late late yestreen I saw the new moone,
 Wi the auld moone in hir arme,
And I feir, I feir, my deir master,
 That we will cum to harme."

O our Scots nobles wer richt laith°   *loath*
 To weet their cork-heild schoone;°   *cork-heeled shoes*
Bot lang owre° a' the play wer playd,   *before*
 Thair hats they swam aboone.°   *above*

O lang, lang may their ladies sit,
 Wi thair fans into their hand,
Or eir° they se Sir Patrick Spens   *before*
 Cum sailing to the land.

O lang, lang may the ladies stand
 Wi thair gold kems° in their hair,   *combs*
Waiting for thair ain deir lords,
 For they'll se thame na mair.

Haf owre,° haf owre to Abedour,   *half over*
 It's fiftie fadom deip,
And thair lies guid Sir Patrick Spens,
 Wi the Scots lords at his feit.

"Sir Patrick Spens" is a ballad—a narrative song. It was composed in the fifteenth or sixteenth century and passed on from one ballad-singer to another. Ballads are community property, yet I suspect that the best were created by one man or woman. Committees do not write poetry, though they may be able to make improvements, once the thing has been done.

This ballad is written in the quick-moving quatrain of tetrameters and trimeters, rhyming *a b c b*, that is so common that it is called *the* ballad stanza. However, this is not the only stanza in which ballads are composed, and within a ballad there may be several variations of rhyme and meter. In the fourth stanza of "Sir Patrick Spens," the word "red" is repeated at the end of line three; in stanza six, instead of the usual perfect rhyme, there is an approximate or slant rhyme: "morn," "storme."

The language is Scots-English, a mixture of Scottish and English words and phrases; both the English and Scots would have been recited with a Scottish accent. Though the ballad is old, there are few archaisms—words that have gone out of use. "Eldern" and "schoone" are close to their modern equivalents. As ballads are meant to be sung, the "makar" sticks close to the vernacular—familiar, simple words that will not interrupt the music by calling attention to themselves. Words such as these do not change in a hurry.

The narrative has speed and compression; the scenes shift quickly; the action is related in striking, visual details. When the king asks his question, an old knight praises Sir Patrick's seamanship. Nothing, coming at this time, could be more harmful. From what Sir Patrick will say later on, we are probably right if we think he has been the victim of a plot, some rankling malice. We see the king writing the letter. Then the poet moves us from the court to the shore where Sir Patrick is walking, by a device that is simple yet ingenious and "modern." The camera focuses on the letter. We see the king signing the letter, then we see Sir Patrick reading it. Also, we learn about the contents of the letter through another visual trick—watching the changes on Sir Patrick's face. The king's letter must have begun with flattery or a joke, followed immediately by the request that Sir Patrick take out the ship. And with kings, to request is to command.

Sir Patrick complains, then hastens to obey, calling on his men to ready the ship for sailing. One of them protests, citing the sailor's belief that when the new moon has "the auld moone in hir arme," a storm is brewing. But the ship sails, and Sir Patrick Spens and his men are drowned.

The effect of the poem is in the way it is told, a mixture of mystery and realism. The personification of the new and old moons is eerie. On the other hand, our attention is drawn to particular, concrete objects; the high heels of the Scottish noblemen, their hats floating on the water. The pride and beauty of the ladies is seen in the fans they hold and the golden combs they wear. These particulars rivet our gaze and compel us to imagine the rest; there are real hearts under this finery. Though we may look upon high heels and golden combs with dour Scottish disapproval, yet the ladies have waited for their men for a long time, and deep grief is coming on.

30

Last, as we visualize Sir Patrick and his men fifty fathoms under the sea, there is something else we feel. As Sir Patrick obeyed his king, so Sir Patrick's men have obeyed him. There is a hierarchy of which the final position of the dead men, at Sir Patrick's feet, is symbolic. These men are obedient and loyal even in death.

Some of the students on whom I tried this poem thought that the ballad-maker was complaining about the death of Sir Patrick and his crew. They thought it was a poem of social protest. Down with the feudal system! Away with kings and courts! However, though the ballad-maker shows the pathos of Sir Patrick's death, and suggests the intrigue and malice that are found at courts, I think that to protest against the "system" was not in his mind. He would not have been able to imagine another world than that of kings, nobles, and commoners, each man in his place—even if that place were the bottom of the sea.

The students who read this as social protest were good citizens but limited readers. They lacked a sense of history. Of course we must stand by our opinions, if they are good, but in order to understand a poem we must be willing to suspend our prejudices for a while and enter into the mind of the poet. There are three main questions in criticism: What is the poet saying? How does he say it? Are his assumptions right or wrong? If we begin with the third question, and stay there, unable to enjoy poetry that does not agree with our opinions—if we are at the mercy of stock responses—then we shall lose most of the pleasure of reading.

The Sun Rising

Busy old fool, unruly sun,
    Why dost thou thus
Through windows and through curtains call on us?
Must to thy motions lovers' seasons run?
    Saucy, pedantic wretch, go chide
    Late schoolboys and sour 'prentices,
Go tell court huntsmen that the king will ride,
Call country ants to harvest offices.

Love, all alike, no season knows nor clime,
Nor hours, days, months, which are the rags of time.

     Thy beams, so reverend and strong
       Why shouldst thou think?
I could eclipse and cloud them with a wink,
But that I would not lose her sight so long.
     If her eyes have not blinded thine,
      Look, and tomorrow late tell me
    Whether both th' Indias of spice and mine
    Be where thou left'st them, or lie here with me;
Ask for those kings whom thou saw'st yesterday,
And thou shalt hear: All here in one bed lay.

     She's all states, and all princes I;
      Nothing else is.
Princes do but play us; compared to this,
All honor's mimic, all wealth alchemy.
     Thou, sun, art half as happy's we,
     In that the world's contracted thus;
    Thine age asks ease, and since thy duties be
    To warm the world, that's done in warming us.
Shine here to us, and thou art everywhere;
This bed thy center is, these walls thy sphere.

John Donne, 1633

In the twentieth century much has been written about Donne
and the metaphysical poets. T. S. Eliot discovered in Donne's
verse the "unified sensibility" that he was aiming at in his own
lines. Donne was able to make sense of a variety of experiences
at the same time; sense perception and reflection took place at
once. Eliot, himself working out images that could render simul-
taneously thought, the smell of cabbage, and the clatter of type-
writing, found Donne usable in a way that Milton and Dryden
were not. Between their thoughts and feelings there were gaps.

Several critics—including, it seems, the later Eliot—have found
fault with his first enthusiastic validation of Donne. In *The
Monarch of Wit*, J. B. Leishman argues that Donne's main quality

is not metaphysical thinking, nor does he have "unified sensibility." To the contrary, he is, like Hamlet, subject to fits and starts. He wants to be witty at any price, and is never happier than when developing an outrageous paradox. Donne's most striking characteristics, says Leishman, are wit, self-dramatization, and the use of the colloquial.

Certainly, the actor in Donne strikes us forcibly. He is always throwing himself into one role or another. He is John Donne pretending to be a cynic, or a Platonic lover, or a man terrified at the thought of death. He thinks best in dialogue. Even when he is not addressing another person or God, he carries on a dialogue with himself. The poems are a little theater, with curtain raisers:

> Busy old fool, unruly sun . . .
> For Godsake hold your tongue, and let me love . . .
> Batter my heart, three personed God . . .

The poems have the scenery and furniture of stage sets: a bedroom into which the sun is shining, a sick room, an open grave, a panorama of the Last Judgment. A poem to his mistress suddenly lets in a view of Alps where a traveler, attacked by brigands, is stabbed and falling. This is the Donne of whom Sir Richard Baker said that after leaving Oxford he "lived at the *Inns of Court*, not dissolute, but very neat, a great visiter of ladies, a great frequenter of Plays, a great writer of conceited verses," and of whom it is reported that when he was dying he had his portrait painted in grave clothes and kept it beside his bed. This also is the man who ruined his chances of preferment by running off with Sir George More's daughter: "John Donne, Anne Donne, Un-done."

How serious is the drama? Donne seems in dead earnest, and then he is off on the scent of a pun or some wild comparison. In this he deserves the criticism Johnson makes of Shakespeare—he would throw away everything for a quibble. Does this mean Donne was not serious? I do not think so. Men of the Elizabethan age were serious in humorous ways. Hamlet was in earnest when he ran his sword through the arras and Polonious fell out, but at the same time Hamlet jested. This was barbarous to the age of Johnson, and must have seemed sheer fantasy to the Victorians. But in our century, which has seen violent extremes, peace and war, juxtaposed, and like the age of Donne sees new gulfs of science opening, Donne's taste for shock does not invalidate his seriousness.

To emphasize Donne's playfulness, J. B. Leishman says that he did not care what happened to his poems, once he wrote them. However, though Donne may have given the impression of tossing off his poems—a manner of acting that can be observed at any gathering of poets today—they are too well written to be jokes, and besides he knew there were copies in circulation and people were keeping them.

The sign of metaphysical poetry, as Johnson said, is a use of wild conceits, ransacking all fields of knowledge for comparisons. The technique has often been described: images are taken from science as well as nature, and the poet goes ranging over heaven and earth. But I do not think the purpose of the technique has been sufficiently underscored, and it is serious. The aim is not merely to astonish by showing how seemingly contradictory things can be yoked together. True, when Donne compares a flea to a marriage bed, something odd is happening for the sake of oddness. But when, as in "The Sun Rising," he brings into the bedroom of two lovers a vision of "both th' Indias of spice and mine," the leap does more than astonish, it joins two disparate areas of experience.

This is the real function of the metaphysical conceit: to join again the parts of a fractured world. In Donne's time, because of the new discoveries in astronomy, the earth is no longer at the center of the universe, no longer at the center of God's attention. Man is suddenly diminished. As Donne says, this new philosophy "calls all in doubt." On the earth itself, things are sliding off, east and west, as the explorers circumnavigate the globe. But the metaphysical conceit pulls the fractions together again; it draws the disordered parts back into order, the order of the poem and the mind. The man who controls the poem controls the world. Then, if the man is religious, God still orders the universe.

"The Sun Rising" is one of Donne's complimentary love poems. Here he is not proving that women are all untrue, nor is he engaged in a Platonic disquisition. The subject is clear: the centering, controlling power of love. A man and woman are in bed, and the sun looks in. The poet tells the sun to go about his business. There is a man-about-town's contemptuous reference to "country ants," a topical reference to King James' passion for hunting, and a picture of "Late schoolboys and sour 'prentices" which shows that morning scenes have not changed from that time to this. Then the theme of the poem is stated:

> Love, all alike, no season knows nor clime,
> Nor hours, days, months, which are the rags of time.

There follows a solipsism that has occurred to everyone, at one time or another: if you simply shut your eyes, reality goes away. Is reality in the perceiver or in the world perceived? This question, which has occupied some poets greatly—Wordsworth answered "half-and-half"—Donne solves, or rather evades, by tossing off a pretty compliment to the lady. He does not want to stop looking at her for as long as the wink of an eye. Then comes the advice to the sun which brings the Indies into the poem with a glimpse of potentates on their thrones. If the sun comes back tomorrow, he will have to confess that the lady is more beautiful than anything else in the world.

"She is all states." And by possessing her, the persona—Donne in one of his speaking roles—is "all princes." Everything but love is play-acting; honor and riches are poor imitations of the reality, love. Then, to polish off the poem, Donne has a happy conceit. The sun should be pleased to have them stay in bed, for the sun is old and tired, and here he can do his job all at once—warm the world by warming them. In the lovers' astronomy:

> This bed thy center is, these walls thy sphere.

(Donne is perfectly aware of the theory that the sun does not go round the world, but it appears to do so, and that is enough for a poem.)

Donne wrote "strong lines." Leishman speaks of the "colloquial vigor of the language, together with the absence of classical allusions, traditional ornaments, and, generally speaking, of anything obviously 'poetical'." However, I do not agree with his opinion that Donne was the first to introduce into lyrical verse "those natural speech-rhythms . . . that colloquial diction" which Shakespeare and his fellows introduced into dramatic verse. Wyatt had already done this, when he tuned his speech to the lute.

If we take Spenser as one extreme, with smoothness and softness:

Sweete *Themmes* run softlie, till I end my Song.

then Donne is the other. Spenser is all for *mollitia* (smoothness), *suavitas* (winsomeness) and *puritas*. He uses classical allusions, ornaments, and Petrarchan conceits. He attaches his feelings to ideal things and so climbs the Platonic ladder. Donne, on the other hand, uses plain speech; he is full of *incitatio* (rapidity of thought) and *acre* (incisiveness). It is tempting to divide the poets of the early seventeenth century into two camps, those who followed Spenser and those who followed Donne. But this is too simple; poets do not fit neatly into categories. Also, among the poets—Donne, Vaughan, Crashaw, Herbert, and others—who are grouped together as metaphysicals, there is so much temperamental variety that perhaps their only resemblance is in the use of metaphysical conceits.

FROM *Absalom and Achitophel*

Of these the false Achitophel was first;
A name to all succeeding ages curst:
For close designs and crooked counsels fit;
Sagacious, bold, and turbulent of wit;
Restless, unfixed in principles and place;
In power unpleased, impatient of disgrace:
A fiery soul, which, working out its way,
Fretted the pigmy body to decay,
And o'er-informed the tenement of clay.
A daring pilot in extremity;
Pleased with the danger, when the waves went high,
He sought the storms; but, for a calm unfit,
Would steer too nigh the sands, to boast his wit.
Great wits are sure to madness near allied,
And thin partitions do their bounds divide;
Else why should he, with wealth and honor blest,
Refuse his age the needful hours of rest?
Punish a body which he could not please;
Bankrupt of life, yet prodigal of ease?

And all to leave what with his toil he won,
To that unfeathered two-legged thing, a son;
Got, while his soul did huddled notions try;
And born a shapeless lump, like anarchy.
In friendship false, implacable in hate;
Resolved to ruin or to rule the State.
To compass this the triple bond he broke;
The pillars of the public safety shook;
And fitted Israel for a foreign yoke:
Then seized with fear, yet still affecting fame,
Usurped a patriot's all-atoning name.
So easy still it proves in factious times,
With public zeal to cancel private crimes.

John Dryden, 1681

Absalom and Achitophel is political satire in the form of an allegory. The satire is strong and biting. Dryden exhibits the despicable traits of his characters and holds them up to ridicule.

The poet pretends to be retelling the Biblical story of the revolt of Absalom and Achitophel against King David (2 Samuel, 14-18), but actually it is the story of the treason of the Duke of Monmouth and the Earl of Shaftesbury against King Charles II. They had plotted to secure the succession for Monmouth, Charles' illegitimate son, though rightfully it belonged to the Duke of York, the king's brother.

In Dryden's allegory Israel represents England; David is King Charles; Absalom is his son Monmouth; Achitophel is Shaftesbury. In the Bible story the illegitimate Absalom was the apple of his father's eye, and Charles dotes on Monmouth. Prudently Dryden avoids harsh criticism of Monmouth and throws all the blame on Shaftesbury, Lord Chancellor and leader of the Whig faction that plotted to cut out the Catholic Duke of York.

The poem is written in heroic couplets—iambic pentameter rhymed couplets, the lines end-stopped, the thought completed at the end of the second line. The meter is fairly regular, except for an occasional trochaic opening to a line. The thought is organized by the regular meter and by rhyme, but it is especially the syntax that creates the special sense of the line.

In the portrait of Achitophel, the first two lines are very even iambic, with no caesuras. Moving relentlessly, they declare Dryden's point of view. In line 3 the cramped parallel structure of "close designs" and "crooked counsels" emphasizes Achitophel's secretive character; the inversion of the syntactical order suggests his crooked and inverted ways. The repetition of *p* in lines 5 and 6 ("*p*ower un*p*leased, im*p*atient of disgrace"), with its explosive quality, creates a tone of contempt. The zeugma in this sentence, "principles" and "place" both depending on the word "unfixed," produces an ironic effect—Achitophel is as unsure of his footing as he is confused in his mind. The chiasmus in line 6 makes a cross structure:

$$\text{power} \diagdown \diagup \text{unpleased}$$
$$\text{impatient} \diagup \diagdown \text{disgrace}$$

As these nouns and adjectives cross over, so does Achitophel; perversely he hastens from honor to dishonor.

The lines linked by the triple rhyme "way," "decay," "clay," may be read in different ways. Achitophel's body was puny; his soul "fretted" it like the teeth of an animal; his soul "over-informed," over-filled his little body. Or Dryden may be using "fret" not in the sense of "gnaw," but to mean "fermentation" or "working" (heating and agitating), for it is a "fiery" soul that is "working out its way." In "o'er-inform'd" Dryden is playing on the scholastic notion of the soul as the "form" of the body. All these meanings are valid; they do not exclude each other; to the contrary, from different directions they reinforce the central argument.

Another image dominates the following lines. Achitophel is a pilot steering a ship, an eccentric pilot who welcomes storms but is incompetent in calm seas. In the line, "Would steer too nigh the sands, to boast his wit," the syntactical inversion creates an anticlimax—just as Achitophel's grandiose, dangerous actions reveal small motives.

For Dryden, Achitophel's wit is close to madness; otherwise why should he "Refuse his age the needful hours of rest"? The word "age" has a double meaning. It means not only his "many years" but also his "times." The present age would like Achitophel to retire so that the body politic may rest. Instead, he is working himself to death, punishing both himself and the state, so that his son may inherit the fruits of his toil.

The son is an "unfeathered two-legged thing," an allusion to Plato's definition of man. The comparison becomes more ludicrous when we recall that Diogenes plucked the feathers of a cock and presented it as Plato's man. The heavy stress on the monosyllable "Got" and the caesura after the first syllable of the line, an unusual position, ironically emphasizes the word. It means not only "begot" but also "acquired," and his son is reduced to a thing acquired, like his other possessions, by hard work. The son is born a "shapeless lump," an image of formlessness and insignificance. He is further compared, in a simile, to anarchy, an abstract term. He is thus reduced from a thing to an abstraction, to nothingness.

Anticipating Dr. Johnson's remark that patriotism is the last refuge of scoundrels, Dryden goes on to knock this prop from under the figure he is demolishing. And this is not all, but perhaps it is enough to show what could be done by Dryden, and by Pope some years later, in the heroic couplet as a vehicle for satire. The couplet bites off a statement neatly in two lines; it has a logical movement, and with syntactical devices such as I have shown, lends itself to strokes of wit.

About forty years ago, Dryden was "rediscovered" by critics. T. S. Eliot said, "The effect of the portraits of Dryden is to transform the object into something greater." Quoting the lines:

> A fiery soul, which working out its way,
> Fretted the pigmy body to decay:
> And o'er informed the tenement of clay,

he commented: "These lines are not merely a magnificent tribute. They create the object which they contemplate." Dryden, he said, had great comic talent.

I think this is true. Dryden's portrait of Achitophel is entertaining; I am not sure that it improved anyone's morals. Writers of satire, men such as Dryden, Swift, and Pope, claimed that their purpose in writing was to improve morals and make the world a better place to live in. However, the world goes on much as it has, and satirists are remembered only because they are amusing.

Ode to a Nightingale

1

My heart aches, and a drowsy numbness pains
  My sense, as though of hemlock I had drunk
Or emptied some dull opiate to the drains
  One minute past, and Lethe-wards[1] had sunk:
'Tis not through envy of thy happy lot,
  But being too happy in thine happiness,—
    That thou, light-winged Dryad[2] of the trees,
      In some melodious plot
Of beechen green, and shadows numberless,
  Singest of summer in full-throated ease.

2

O, for a draught of vintage! that hath been
  Cooled a long age in the deep-delved earth,
Tasting of Flora[3] and the country green,
  Dance, and Provençal song, and sunburnt mirth!
O for a beaker full of the warm South,
  Full of the true, the blushful Hippocrene,[4]
    With beaded bubbles winking at the brim,
      And purple-stained mouth;
That I might drink, and leave the world unseen,
  And with thee fade away into the forest dim:

3

Fade far away, dissolve, and quite forget
  What thou among the leaves hast never known,
The weariness, the fever, and the fret
  Here, where men sit and hear each other groan;
Where palsy shakes a few, sad, last gray hairs,
  Where youth grows pale, and specter-thin, and dies;
    Where but to think is to be full of sorrow
      And leaden-eyed despairs,
    Where Beauty cannot keep her lustrous eyes,
      Or new Love pine at them beyond tomorrow.

[1] Lethe is the river of forgetfulness.
[2] wood nymph.
[3] goddess of flowers.
[4] a spring sacred to the Muses.

4

Away! away! for I will fly to thee,
　Not charioted by Bacchus[5] and his pards,
But on the viewless wings of Poesy,
　Though the dull brain perplexes and retards:
Already with thee! tender is the night,
　And haply the Queen-Moon is on her throne,
　　Clustered around by all her starry Fays;[6]
　　　But here there is no light,
　Save what from heaven is with the breezes blown
　　Through verdurous glooms and winding mossy ways.

5

I cannot see what flowers are at my feet,
　Nor what soft incense hangs upon the boughs,
But, in embalmed darkness, guess each sweet
　Wherewith the seasonable month endows
The grass, the thicket, and the fruit-tree wild;
　White hawthorn, and the pastoral eglantine;
　　Fast fading violets covered up in leaves;
　　　And mid-May's eldest child,
　The coming musk-rose, full of dewy wine,
　　The murmurous haunt of flies on summer eves.

6

Darkling I listen; and, for many a time
　I have been half in love with easeful Death,
Called him soft names in many a musèd rhyme,
　To take into the air my quiet breath;
Now more than ever seems it rich to die,
　To cease upon the midnight with no pain,
　　While thou art pouring forth thy soul abroad
　　　In such an ecstasy!
　Still wouldst thou sing, and I have ears in vain—
　　To thy high requiem become a sod.

7

Thou wast not born for death, immortal Bird!
　No hungry generations tread thee down;

[5] god of wine.
[6] fairies.

The voice I hear this passing night was heard
  In ancient days by emperor and clown:
Perhaps the self-same song that found a path
  Through the sad heart of Ruth,[7] when, sick for home,
    She stood in tears amid the alien corn;
      The same that oft-times hath
Charmed magic casements, opening on the foam
  Of perilous seas, in faery lands forlorn.

8

Forlorn! the very word is like a bell
  To toll me back from thee to my sole self!
Adieu! the fancy cannot cheat so well
  As she is famed to do, deceiving elf.
Adieu! adieu! thy plaintive anthem fades
  Past the near meadows, over the still stream,
    Up the hill-side; and now 'tis buried deep
      In the next valley-glades:
Was it a vision, or a waking dream?
  Fled is that music:— Do I wake or sleep?

John Keats, 1819

Most poems are a mixture of elements. In a song there may be a dramatic situation; in narrative poems there are lyrical passages and discursive stretches. Keats' odes are mixtures of lyrical and descriptive writing, and reflection. The ode is a large form; a poet can do almost anything he likes in it. There are classic forms of the ode, notably the Pindaric and Horatian, but the poet may invent his own and range, as Keats does, away from his subject. For his odes, Keats invented stanzas that have the fullness and complex music of the sonnet:

> Sandals more interwoven and complete
> To fit the naked foot of Poesy . . .

His stanzas are suited to the progress of an argument, eddyings of thought, descriptions.

[7] after her husband's death, Ruth left her native land and lived in Palestine with her mother-in-law Naomi. See the Book of Ruth in the Old Testament.

From his beginnings as a writer, Keats speculated upon the nature of art and its relationship to experience. If, he thought, the joy of poetry is in representing the sensory world as fully as possible, does this not imply that art is less important than sensation? Why should a man bother to make copies of nature when he might be enjoying the original, lying in the grass, making love, daydreaming? Poets are ambitious; they wish to be famous. But fame is an illusion. Keats declares that he does not wish to be a "pet lamb in a sentimental farce." But poetry is more than daydreaming, more than mere fancy—it is "soul-making." Poetry is action; the real poet, unlike the dreamer, "pours out a balm upon the world." A poet, he thinks, could be a philosopher. Yet on the other hand the pleasures of the senses are so acute that perhaps, after all, these are reality.

So his thoughts eddied, and he resolved nothing. The odes are a record of his thoughts. He picks up a theme, plays with it, and gives the poem an aesthetic ending. But as a philosopher he has settled nothing. In the next ode he will take up these threads again, weaving a different pattern. The odes are not logically conclusive. And yet they are works of art. For art differs from philosophy; the first aim of art is to give pleasure; the aim of philosophy is to discover truth.

When the "Ode to a Nightingale" begins, the poet is in a state of lassitude; he has just heard a nightingale singing—a pleasure so keen that it has left him exhausted. The bird has vanished. He wishes to follow, to exhaust the pleasure of listening to the end. One way to do this might be to heighten his senses with wine. He will follow the nightingale to its nest.

Then, in an abrupt contrast, Keats shows the actuality from which he is longing to escape:

> The weariness, the fever, and the fret
> Here, where men sit and hear each other groan...

In the everyday world, youth, beauty, and love are ephemeral. On the other hand, in moments of acute pleasure we feel a sufficiency that is a glimpse of what it must be like to be immortal. Therefore, the poet will follow the nightingale's song to its source—however, not with wine, but through poetry.

Already, even as he thinks of it (and, we might add, only because he is imagining it), he is in the world of the nightingale. It is night, in a leafy wood. The moon and stars are shining; flowers and leaves overwhelm him with their odors. This is like death. It may be that poetry leads to death. He has often called on death to take him away from actuality. Now, at this moment, as the nightingale sings again, he could almost be willing to die.

The argument suddenly turns upon itself. If he were to die, then he could not hear the nightingale's song at all. The song would continue, but he would be only a lump of earth. To give oneself wholly over to pleasure is to die and lose the capacity for feeling any pleasure at all.

Here Keats might have made a point and ended his poem neatly, saying that, after all, a man must not carry things to extremes. Such a conclusion would have been reasonable, but it would not have been true to his feelings. For, in fact, though Keats knows that he cannot live entirely in his senses, and in the kind of poetry that is purely sensual, yet he still wants to do so.

Keats confesses his frustration, like an honest man, and this is the triumph of his art. Instead of concluding the poem as a philosopher, he continues it as a man, expressing his hunger for a life that remains beyond him. Instead of denying the perfection he cannot have, he expresses his hunger for perfection. He tries to express his sense of wonder at the nightingale. In a series of striking images he shows us the bird singing through the ages: in a palace; a field where Ruth stands listening; and windows overlooking a sea, "in faery lands forlorn," a place midway between the world we have and a world we long for.

Then Keats returns to himself and the place where he is. His imagination, it seems, has solved nothing; he cannot stay in poetry, where the nightingale lives. The nightingale vanishes as it sings, and the ode ends with a question: Is this self, this world around me, reality? Or is life a sleep, a kind of death, while reality is the song I heard and the places I glimpsed through poetry.

Beside the thoughts of the poem, there are images and phrases that strike us as having poetic force. When we begin to examine them, we are faced with a difficulty. The "Ode to a Nightingale" does not seem capable of improvement. At least we could not improve upon it. Then are we simply to praise the poet? The better a poem, the less it seems we are able to criticize it.

Nonetheless, criticism can show how an artist arrives at certain effects. The critic points. We are able to point to Keats' use of musical devices, which help to make striking phrases. There is alliteration:

> With beaded bubbles winking at the brim . . .

and assonance:

> In some melodious plot
> Of beechen green, and shadows numberless,
> Singest of summer in full-throated ease . . .

The correspondence of vowels imitates the music that is being described.

In the following lines there is synesthesia. Words belonging to one sense perception are used to describe another. The effect is to bring both senses into play at the same time.

> I cannot see what flowers are at my feet,
> Nor what soft incense hangs upon the boughs . . .

To suggest the thickness of the smell of flowers, Keats says that it is visible and tangible. It "hangs" from the boughs.

At moments, the ode opens on an infinite view—night, where the moon and stars are supernatural beings; Palestine, Ruth's story, and a depth of sorrow; casements that merge with a fairy ocean. These views enlarge our imagination, and though the poem returns us to the clear, hard world of everyday, we cannot entirely return. In a part of our mind we continue to live in these scenes. When we are reading the ode, and as we continue to think about it, the poem itself becomes the song of the nightingale. Keats has created a version of the ideal world that, according to common sense and his own honest statement, should lie beyond human reach. As he has said, the poet is not able to live at the pitch of receptivity and creation. Yet the poem continues to live.

The Magi

Now as at all times I can see in the mind's eye,
In their stiff, painted clothes, the pale unsatisfied ones
Appear and disappear in the blue depth of the sky
With all their ancient faces like rain-beaten stones,
And all their helms of silver hovering side by side,
And all their eyes still fixed, hoping to find once more,
Being by Calvary's turbulence unsatisfied,
The uncontrollable mystery on the bestial floor.

William Butler Yeats, 1914

A symbol is a thing that stands for something else. The cross is used to evoke Christianity, the rose to mean love, the sword to mean war. These are common symbols; their meanings have been fixed for centuries. But some symbols do not have easily recognizable meanings. The meaning of the symbol can be determined only from its context. In Yeats' poems "To the Rose upon the Rood of Time" and "The Rose of the World," a rose is not simply love, or idealized woman, but an Irish peasant woman and the love of things of this world as well as spiritual love.

In the writings of the Symbolist school, which influenced Yeats strongly, symbols do not have explicit meanings. The Symbolists often seem to be hiding, rather than revealing, their meaning in symbols. This is not a perverse unwillingness to be understood; rather, it is an attempt to create a mystery, to make the poem infinitely suggestive. A mystery cannot be explained; it can only be suggested. To attach symbols to specific meanings would destroy the magic of poetry. "Evocation, allusion, suggestion," said Mallarmé, are the essence of poetry. The Symbolist "shuns the materials in nature, avoids any thought that might tend to arrange them too directly or precisely, and retains only the suggestiveness of things." The Symbolist poet "must establish a careful relationship between two images, from which a third element, clear and fusible, will be distilled and caught by our imagination." The poetry is in the spaces between the images, in the "shudder of the forest" rather than in the palpable wood of trees. The poetry is felt in silence after the words have stopped.

From his researches in the occult, his study of Blake's symbolism, and exposure to the symbolist movement in France, Yeats derived symbols and arranged them in a system. He found correspondences among seasons, the ages of man, the elements, the points of the compass, and certain objects—sword, stone, spear, and cauldron. For example, the word "wave" or "dew" evokes the element of water. This is connected with autumn, evening, manhood, and the west. The west, as in the phrase "stepping westward," is the place of death. In later poems Yeats perfected symbols of his own. To know what he meant by sun, moon, tower, mask, tree, well, sphere, gyre, or dance, we must go to his poems and see what the words mean there.

Much modern writing is symbolist in method and writers invent their own symbolic systems, each different from the rest. There is really no such thing as modern poetry—there are only modern poets. To travel from Yeats to Pound we have to get a new visa. Each poet creates his own world, makes his own meanings, and rules in his own way.

> "When I use a word," Humpty Dumpty said, in rather a scornful tone, "it means just what I choose it to mean—neither more nor less."
>
> "The question is," said Alice, "whether you *can* make words mean so many different things."
>
> "The question is," said Humpty Dumpty, "which is to be master—that's all."

"The Magi" is not a long poem—but some great poems have only a few lines, and some epics are unreadable. Within its small space "The Magi" accomplishes much. Yeats takes a familiar symbol, the nursery picture of the Wise Men following the star to Bethlehem, where Jesus was born. In Yeats's hands, the kindly figures turn into something quite different—faces hovering with obsessive, fanatical appetite. The faces are as remote from tenderness as stones, inhuman, filled with supernatural desire.

Also, the peaceful crib at Bethlehem and the cud-chewing oxen are changed. They are "bestial." The Christ child is remembered not as a harbinger of peace, but a cause of turbulence, the mob swarming around Calvary. It is not peace that these strange, unChristian Magi desire, but the disorder and bloodshed of the world. The crucifixion has not satisfied them. They want an even more

passionate event. The conventional symbols of Christianity have
been charged by Yeats and altered so that they symbolize urgent
spiritual unrest, a hunger that will not be satisfied. This is not at
all a Christian solution.

The poem has great intensity. The Magi have a wonderful lightness, appearing and disappearing in the sky. They share the imper-
sonality of objects. They are moved by a rhythm from beyond nature. Their silver helmets are like gleams in a painting. Their
clothes are painted. Everything is fixed in a design that shows the
permanence of desire.

The River-Merchant's Wife: a Letter
(After Rihaku)

While my hair was still cut straight across my forehead
I played about the front gate, pulling flowers.
You came by on bamboo stilts, playing horse,
You walked about my seat, playing with blue plums.
And we went on living in the village of Chokan:
Two small people, without dislike or suspicion.

At fourteen I married My Lord you.
I never laughed, being bashful.
Lowering my head, I looked at the wall.
Called to, a thousand times, I never looked back.

At fifteen I stopped scowling,
I desired my dust to be mingled with yours
Forever and forever and forever.
Why should I climb the look out?

At sixteen you departed,
You went into far Ku-to-yen, by the river of swirling eddies,
And you have been gone five months.
The monkeys make sorrowful noise overhead.

You dragged your feet when you went out.
By the gate now, the moss is grown, the different mosses,
Too deep to clear them away!

The leaves fall early this autumn, in wind.
The paired butterflies are already yellow with August
Over the grass in the West garden;
They hurt me. I grow older.
If you are coming down through the narrows of the river Kiang,
Please let me know beforehand,
And I will come out to meet you
    As far as Cho-fu-Sa.

Ezra Pound, 1915

This poem is a complaint, and if it had been written by a sentimental poet, say one of the worse imitators of Tennyson in the
nineteenth century, it might be very sad indeed—a three-handker-
chief movie, brimming with bathos. The poet would play on our
heartstrings, the Hammond organ would moan, there would be a
flitting of purple, violet, and pink, and we would walk out into the
hard light of afternoon with a headache. Fortunately, neither Li Po
nor Pound is sentimental. In his imitation of a poem by Li Po, the
eighth-century Chinese poet whose name in Japanese—from which
Pound was translating—is Rihaku, Pound keeps the delicate tone of
the original.

A poem is many things moving together, and what holds them
together is tone, the poet's attitude toward the subject. The personality of the poet is the essential force in the poem. It is his humor
or seriousness, his tenderness or callousness, that is being expressed.
Or, more exactly, it is the mood that he has put on, that we feel—
for, of course, when he is not writing the poem, he may have quite
different feelings that have nothing to do with poetry.

The persona, the speaker of this dramatic monologue, does not
utter her complaint directly; she implies and understates her feelings. Instead of talking about herself she tells us what she has experienced. Her world has been altered. She points to this and that, and
we see how the appearances of things have changed. As we see
through her eyes we become aware of her intelligence; we begin to
wonder about the woman who is seeing all this. She begins to matter to us; the feelings of such a person are important.

Pound had learned from Ford Madox Ford how to write in easy,
conversational phrases. From the French critic Rémy de Gourmont

he learned how to "make it new" by writing in images. This is the characteristic technique of some Chinese poetry and the Japanese poems of seventeen syllables called haiku. In haiku, sadness may be represented by a fallen leaf, joy by a butterfly, and there are moments of experience that cannot be translated into abstract words such as sadness or joy—for instance, the sound of a frog jumping into a pond. The poem is a moment of perception conveyed to the reader through images.

In an imagist poem, Pound said, "one is trying to record the precise instant when a thing outward and objective transforms itself, or darts into a thing inward and subjective."

Writing in images is not photography, not a mere listing of concrete details. There have been many "modern" poems of this kind, and they are tedious as bad eighteenth-century didactic verse or Victorian effusions. The new poetry that Pound called for would give the reader, through a selection of significant details and appropriate movement of the line, an experience similar to that which the poet originally had. Writing a hundred years before Pound, Wordsworth formulated much the same theory of poetic composition in the preface to *Lyrical Ballads*.

It is not always clear what writers mean by image or symbol. But there is a difference. An image, as I have said, is the means by which a particular emotion is conveyed. The meaning of an image is determined by its context; in a sense, an image is the poem itself. A symbol, on the other hand, has connotations that range beyond the particular context, and these are more or less constant. Symbols may be carried from one place to another and still retain their value. But an image has only a moment of life.

An image may be symbolic, for the moment. In "The River-Merchant's Wife" the monkeys symbolize grief; the mosses that have grown next to the gate symbolize an accumulation of time. However, removed from these contexts, monkeys and mosses would not mean what they do here. In another poem they might have quite different connotations.

"The River-Merchant's Wife" is written in free verse; there is no regular meter. Most of the sentences are simple declaratives—subject, verb, object:

> The leaves fall early in autumn, in wind.

With the exception of the ending, no sentence is longer than one or two lines. This gives the poem an insistent, forward motion, as compelling as the motion imparted to metrical verse by a recurring foot. In another short line:

> They hurt me. I grow older.

there are two complete sentences balancing against each other, an antiphonal structure frequently used in the Hebrew psalms and the *Song of Solomon*. Repetition of sentence structure, or parallelism, used by Pound throughout this poem, is one of the main resources of free verse, giving the poem cohesion and a kind of rhythm. Instead of recurrence of feet and use of rhyme, there is the rhythm of a syntactical pattern.

After the imagists came the surrealists. Surrealism, said André Breton, is "thought's dictation in the absence of control exercised by the reason and outside of all aesthetic or moral preoccupations." Breton's kind of surrealism amounted to automatic writing; the poet seemed to be putting down anything that came into his head, with no connections. But the mind cannot be divided into rational and irrational compartments, and there is no such thing as a purely irrational poem. If surrealist poems are effective, it is because they too are a form of composition.

Though surrealism has not been perfect in theory, it has been stimulating in practice. The surrealist poets have broken with convention, especially the labored, rationalistic poetry into which poetry in English degenerates. They have restored gaiety and felt free to imagine anything. Surrealist images have the appearance of things that have not been seen before. The Poundian image took its origin from the world perceived by the senses; the surrealist image seems to rise from depths of the psyche and to represent nothing but itself. It is new.

> . . . Let my word be
> The thing itself,
> Created by my soul anew.

Let all who do not know them
Go to the things, through me . . .

—Juan Ramón Jiménez, translated from the Spanish
by Carlos de Francisco Zea.

The following poem by Dylan Thomas contains surrealist images, but it would not have met with Breton's approval, for, as Thomas explains, a good deal of thought has gone into making logical connections. Thomas sent the poem to Vernon Watkins, probably in May 1939 (the letter is undated). Watkins comments:

In the poem which came with the next letter, I did, as he anticipated, object to the last line. I thought it let the poem down.

[May 1939]
Sea View, Laugharne

Dear Vernon,
   Here's my new poem. I hope you'll think it's good; I'm extremely pleased with it at the moment—it was written in a very enjoyable mood, (or any other better word) of surly but optimistic passion— though it is, as you'll see, in places a little awkward. I am not sure of the word "animal" in the last line but one of the first stanza; it says more or less what I mean, that the rails, the frame if you like, of the bed of the grave is living, sensual, serpentine, but it's a word I've used perhaps too often.
   "Crotch"—last line, third stanza—I've also used, once fairly startlingly, but I'm afraid the word is quite essential here. Or so, at the moment, I think. The last two lines I can see you disliking, especially the crude last lump. But that sudden crudeness is (again) essential to the argument, to, if you don't mind, the philosophy. Perhaps I should, or could, have found a stronger & nobler adjective for the light, to be in greater opposition to the very real crudity of the lump of the earth. And is the internal rhyme in the last line but one effective? I think so. Do let me know what you think of the poem, & soon, if you can.

Love,
Dylan

   Don't bother too much about other details in it; apart from what I've mentioned, it's the spirit of this poem that matters.

[Watkins comments] *A comparison between this early version which appeared, with two adjectival changes, in Life and Letters Today (October 1939) and the poem printed in Deaths and Entrances and finally in Collected Poems shows that all the changes made in its re-writing were movements away from ironical, and towards religious, statement.*

Poem

TO CAITLIN

Unluckily for a death
Waiting with phoenix under a stone
And long fidelity grown gray in her lop-briared
And thigh-describing wreath
Intact among the passionate dead and gone
In the burial holes of enticement
Though the brawl of the kiss has not occurred,
On the wanting mouth,
On the split, exhibiting forehead,
That binds her constant,
Nor the naked, original, lyrical
Aggression of love in a bridal broth
Or a continent-sheeted bed with animal rails
And a tucked crust of fossils,

Loving on a sea-banged shelf
My lucky burly body
Holy happy and greedy under the managed storm,
Luckily my sore ghost
In this collapsing day, the dark our pity,
Cut in this mustard moment, soothed of fever
By your kind health that keeps the west wrongs calm,
Fireworks at your breast,
And weeps on the inflammable gulf,
Myself will never
Arch that turkey's neck of a far-gone woman
To sing underground like a married thrush
Or shoo up the light that extinct, sparkling bird to heaven:

The dust-drenched two must wait my wish.

I see the tigron in tears
In the androgynous dark
To escape from the hot, brown caves and ramming columns
Of his half families
That stripe the forests with want, and the duck-
Billed platypus broody in the sexless bush.
There from a red and white clot of women
Juan runs like the waters.
In an imagining of tumbled mantime
Suddenly cold as fish,
I see through briar and stone, the black our business,
That patient love below and almost mistress,
Through masterless ground all loaded events of her flesh,
Great crotch, and giant continence.

Love, my fate got luckily,
May teach me now with no telling
That every drop of water is both kind and cruel,
With articulate eyes
Tell me the money-colored sun sees poorly,
Teach that the child who sucks on innocence
Is spinning fast and loose on a fiery wheel,
All that we do, cruelly, kindly,
Will kiss in a huddle:
In the teeth of that black-and-white wedding
I chuck my armed happiness.
Though the puffed phoenix stir in the rocks
And lucklessly fair or sycorax the widow wait,
We abide with our pride, the unalterable light,
On this turning lump of mistakes.

[May or June 1939]
Sea View, Laugharne

Dear Vernon,

I don't find your way of criticizing at all irritating; you know that. It's the most helpful there is for me, and I want it to go on. About many suggestions of yours we'll always, of course, disagree, especially when they seem completely to misunderstand my meaning; but, as nobody else has done—though this is a late and wrong place for a recommendation of your complete intellectual honesty, a thing we needn't talk about—without rancor, affectation, or the felt need to surprise. I think you are liable, in your criticisms of me, to under-rate the value—or, rather, the integrity, the wholeness—of what I am saying or trying to make clear that I am saying, and often to suggest alterations or amendments for purely musical motives. For instance, "Caught in a somersault of tumbled mantime" may (and I doubt it) sound more agreeable—we'll leave out any suggestion of it sounding inevitable because it is, however good the implied criticism, a group of words *outside* the poem—to the "prophesying ear" than "In an imagining of tumbled mantime," a line I worked out *for* its sounds & not in spite of them. My criticism of your critical suggestion in this case is that your "ear" is deaf to the logic of my poem;

> "Caught in a somersault etc etc
> Suddenly cold as fish"

is an ambiguous tangle, very like nonsense. (I know your suggestion was not meant to be the last substitutive word for my first words, but was meant mainly to suggest further things, allway pointers, to me myself; but the suggestion still does, I believe, show the way your criticism often works: towards the aural betterment (ugh) of de-tails, without regard for their significance in a worked-out, if not a premeditated-*in-detail*, whole). This is certainly one critical way, but when it suggests "withered" for "sheeted" in the last line but one of the first stanza, *I* suggest it cuts across the poem and does not come out of it. It is a poet saying "This is what I would have done"; not a critic saying, "This, I think, is what the poet should have done." I suppose, argumentatively, not randomly speaking, that all criticism which is not an analysis of reasons for praise must primarily be sus-picion; and that's stimulating. Nothing but the inevitable can be taken for granted, and it always excites me to find you dealing sus-piciously with a word, a line, that I had, in a naturally blind or arti-ficially blinkered moment, taken, myself, with too much trust, trust-ing too much the fallible creative rush of verse—small or large rushes of verse—that comes, in many cases, between the mechanical prepara-tions for that (in a way) accidental rush. (Wooly writing, I'm afraid; I hope the meaning comes clearly.) With your annoyance at the word "chuck" I agree; and my use of it is sentimental. I have tried "cast", but that is too static a word; I'll find what I really want. And, yes the poem did appear to tire of itself at the end—: (by the way, I resent that "tire of itself" idea, which arrogantly supposes the self-contained *identity* of the poem even in its forming phases; the poem is not, of course, itself until the poet has left it). The jingle of "abide with our pride" I'm retaining; I wanted the idea of an almost jolly jingle there, a certain carelessness to lead up to the flat, hard, ugly last line of truth, a suggestion of "Well, that's over, O atta boy we live with our joy"; a purposeful intolerance—no, I meant an intolerance on purpose—of the arguments I had been setting against my own instinctive delight in the muddled world. Whether that intolerance, carelessness, etc. is *poetically* effective is another kettle of wishes. . . .

Dylan

There is no progress in poetry. Scientists agree on certain laws, and their discoveries are made in common. But poets are independent and resolutely go their own way. Ezra Pound was continuously experimenting, but Robert Frost was untouched by the new theories and movements of his time. These are both modern poets—living in the twentieth century—but it would be impossible to arrive at a clear idea of modern poetry from reading the works of two men who are so unlike each other.

However, though poetry does not progress, it changes. A new theory about poetry causes a shift of emphasis and fills poets with enthusiasm. The poems that, in my opinion, are most interesting are being written by poets who have adapted the ideas of the imagists and surrealists. They have escaped the deadening influence of teachers who can think of nothing better to do with poetry than to turn it into prose, and critics who treat a poem as though it were a machine designed to produce criticism. They are not writing light verse for magazines, or confessions for an audience that is emotionally bankrupt. These poets have an inner life which they express in original images.

Rip

It can't be the passing of time that casts
That white shadow across the waters
Just offshore.

I shiver a little, with the evening.
I turn down the steep path to find
What's left of the river gold.
I whistle a dog lazily, and lazily
A bird whistles me.
Close by a big river, I am alive in my own country,
I am home again.
Yes: I lived here, and here, and my name,
That I carved young, with a girl's, is healed over, now,
And lies sleeping beneath the inward sky
Of a tree's skin, close to the quick.
It's best to keep still.
But:
There goes that bird that whistled me down here
To the river a moment ago.
Who is he? A little white barn owl from Hudson's Bay,
Flown out of his range here, and lost?
Oh, let him be home here, and, if he wants to,
He can be the body that casts
That white shadow across the waters
Just offshore.

James Wright, 1966

At the center of the poem stands a tree with names carved under the bark. The tree is like the man; in fact, it encloses his name in its secret growth. The carving in the trunk is a wound, but it is also a memory of love.

The man has come home. He is relaxed, open to whatever happens. The lines of the poem have a lapping, indolent motion. The man is accepted into the lazy life of the river. He whistles to a dog, and a bird whistles to him. He imagines that an owl has flown here, from a far way off. The bird, too, is like the man. The bird, "if he wants to,"

> ... can be the body that casts
> That white shadow across the waters
> Just offshore.

The bird can be anything it wants to be; the poet gives it leave to inhabit everything. There was a white shadow on the water at the beginning—the shadow of time, perhaps the shadow of death. Now, as the poem ends, the shadow is no longer ominous, for the poet has imagined the bird and made it cast the shadow. His imagination is the landscape, and he is free to come and go as he chooses.

An Anthology of Poems

GEOFFREY CHAUCER [1340?–1400]

FROM *The Canterbury Tales*

Whan that Aprill with his shoures° soote° — *showers / sweet*
The droghte of March hath perced to the roote,
And bathed every veyne in swich licour° — *such liquid*
Of which vertu° engendred is the flour; — *by power of which*
Whan Zephirus eek° with his sweete breeth — *also*
Inspired hath in every holt° and heeth — *wood*
The tendre croppes, and the yonge sonne
Hath in the Ram his halve cours yronne,° — *run*
And smale foweles° maken melodye, — *birds*
That slepen al the nyght with open ye° — *eye*
(So priketh hem° nature in hir corages°), — *inspires them / their hearts*
Thanne longen° folk to goon on pilgrimages, — *long*
And palmeres° for to seken straunge strondes,° — *pilgrims / shores*
To ferne halwes,° kowthe° in sondry londes; — *distant shrines / known*
And specially from every shires ende
Of Engelond to Caunterbury they wende,
The hooly blisful martir[1] for to seke,
That hem hath holpen° whan that they were
    seeke.° — *helped / sick*
Bifil° that in that seson on a day, — *It befell*
In Southwerk at the Tabard as I lay
Redy to wenden° on my pilgrymage, — *go*
To Caunterbury with ful devout corage,° — *heart*
At nyght was come into that hostelrye° — *inn*
Wel nyne and twenty in a compaignye,
On sondry folk, by aventure yfalle° — *by chance fallen*
In felaweshipe, and pilgrimes were they alle,
That toward Caunterbury wolden° ryde. — *wanted to*
The chambres and the stables weren wyde,
And wel we weren esed° atte beste. — *entertained*
And shortly, whan the sonne was to reste,
So hadde I spoken with hem everichon° — *every one*
That I was of hir felaweshipe anon,
And made forward° erly for to ryse, — *agreement*
To take oure wey ther as I yow devyse.° — *impart*

[1] Thomas à Beckett, Archbishop of Canterbury, murdered in 1170.

♦

With hym[2] ther was his sone, a yong Squier,
A lovyere° and a lusty bacheler,   *lover*
With lokkes crulle° as they were leyd in presse.   *curled*
Of twenty yeer of age he was, I gesse.
Of his stature he was of evene lengthe,°   *medium height*
And wonderly delyvere,° and of greet strengthe.   *agile*
And he hadde been somtyme in chyvachie°   *on a raid*
In Flaundres, in Artoys, and Pycardie,
And born° hym weel, as of so litel space,°   *conducted / time*
In hope to stonden in his lady grace.
Embrouded° was he, as it were a meede°   *embroidered / meadow*
Al ful of fresshe floures, whyte and reede.
Syngynge he was, or floytynge,° al the day;   *playing the flute*
He was a fressh as is the monthe of May.
Short was his gowne, with sleves longe and wyde.
Wel koude he sitte on hors and faire ryde.
He koude songes make and wel endite,°   *write lyrics*
Juste° and eek° daunce, and weel purtreye°   *Joust / also / draw*
    and write.
So hoote he lovede that by nyghtertale°   *night*
He slepte namoore° than dooth a nyghtyngale.   *no more*
Curteis he was, lowely, and servysable,°   *willing to serve*
And carf° biforn his fader at the table.   *carved*

♦

A Monk ther was, a fair for the maistrie,°   *better than all others*
An outridere,° that lovede venerie,°   *overseer / hunting*
A manly man, to been° an abbot able.   *become*
Ful many a deyntee hors hadde he in stable,
And whan he rood, men myghte his brydel heere
Gynglen° in a whistlynge wynd as cleere   *jingling*
And eek as loude as dooth the chapel belle
Ther as this lord was kepere of the celle.°   *smaller monastery*
The reule° of seint Maure or of seint Beneit,[3]   *rule*
By cause that it was old and somdel° streit°   *somewhat / strict*
This ilke° Monke leet olde thynges pace,°   *same / pass by*

[2] the Knight.
[3] St. Benedict, founder of Benedictine Order; St. Maur, his follower.

62

And heeld after the newe world the space.°   *meanwhile*
He yaf° nat of that text a pulled hen°   *gave / plucked hen*
That seith that hunters been nat hooly men,
Ne that a monk, whan he is recchelees,°   *careless*
Is likned til° a fissh that is waterlees,—   *to*
This is to seyn,° a monk out of his cloystre.   *say*
But thilke° text heeld he nat worth an oystre;   *that*
And I seyde his opinioun was good.
What° sholde he studie and make hymselven wood,°   *why / mad*
Upon a book in cloystre alwey to poure,
Or swynken° with his handes, and laboure,   *work*
As Austyn° bit?° How shal the world be   *St. Augustine / bid*
    served?
Lat Austyn have his swynk° to hym reserved!   *work*
Therfore he was a prikasour° aright;   *hunter on horseback*
Grehoundes he hadde as swift as fowel in flight.
Of prikyng° and of huntyng for the hare   *tracking*
Was al his lust;° for no cost wolde he spare.   *desire*
I seigh his sleves ypurfiled at the hond°   *trimmed at the borders*
With grys,° and that the fyneste of a lond;   *expensive fur*
And, for to festne° his hood under his chyn,   *fasten*
He hadde of gold ywroght° a ful curious pyn;   *contrived*
A love-knotte in the gretter ende ther was.
His heed was balled, that shoon as any glas,
And eek° his face as he hadde been enoynt.°   *also / anointed*
He was a lord ful fat and in good poynt;°   *condition*
His eyen stepe,° and rollynge in his heed,   *protruding*
That stemed° as a forneys° of a leed;°   *shone / furnace / boiler*
His bootes souple, his hors in greet estaat.
Now certeinly he was a fair prelaat;
He was nat pale as a forpyned° goost.   *suffering*
A fat swan loved he best of any roost.
His palfrey was as broun as is a berye.

◆

A good Wif was ther of biside° Bathe,   *near*
But she was somdel° deef, and that was scathe.°   *somewhat / a pity*
Of clooth-makyng she hadde swich an haunt,°   *skill*
She passed° hem of Ypres and of Gaunt.⁴   *surpassed*

⁴ Flemish towns famous for cloth-making.

In al the parisshe wif ne was ther noon
That to the offrynge° bifore hire sholde goon;   *offering of alms*
And if ther° dide, certeyn so wrooth was she,   *they*
That she was out of alle charitee.
Hir coverchiefs° ful fyne weren of ground;°   *kerchiefs / texture*
I dorste° swere they weyeden° ten pound   *dare / weighed*
That on a Sonday weren upon hir heed.
Hir hosen weren of fyn scarlet reed,
Ful streite yteyd,° and shoes ful moyste and newe.   *tied*
Boold was hir face, and fair, and reed of hewe.
She was a worthy womman al hir lyve:
Housbondes at chirche dore she hadde fyve,
Withouten° oother compaignye in youthe,—   *apart from*
But therof nedeth° nat to speke as nowthe.°   *need / now*
And thries hadde she been at Jerusalem;
She hadde passed many a straunge strem;
At Rome she hadde been, and at Boloigne,
In Galice at Seint-Jame, and at Coloigne.
She koude° muchel of wandrynge by the weye.   *knew*
Gat-tothed° was she, soothly for to seye.   *teeth wide apart*
Upon an amblere° esily she sat,   *slow horse*
Ywympled° wel, and on hir heed an hat   *veiled*
As brood as is a bokeler° or a targe;°   *buckler / shield*
A foot-mantel° aboute hir hipes large,   *skirt*
And on hir feet a paire of spores° sharpe.   *spurs*
In felaweshipe wel koude she laughe and carpe.°   *talk*
Of remedies of love she knew per chaunce,
For she koude° of that art the olde daunce.°   *knew / dance*

ANONYMOUS

I Sing of a Maiden

I sing of a maiden
    That is makeles;°   *matchless*
King of all kings
    To° her son she ches.°   *for / chose*

He came al so still
    There his mother was,

As dew in April
    That falleth on the grass.

He came al so still
    To his mother's bour,
As dew in April
    That falleth on the flour.

He came al so still
    There his mother lay,
As dew in April
    That falleth on the spray.

Mother and maiden
    Was never none but she;
Well may such a lady
    Goddes mother be.

Sumer Is Icumen In

Sumer is icumen in,
    Lhudé° sing cuccu;   *loud*
Groweth sed and bloweth° med°   *blossoms / meadow*
    And springth the wudé nu.°   *wood now*
    Sing cuccu!
Awé° bleteth after lomb,   *ewe*
    Lhouth° after calvé cu;°   *lows / cow*
Bulluc sterteth, bucké verteth;°   *breaks wind*
    Murie sing cuccu.
    Cuccu, cuccu,
    Wel singés thu, cuccu,
    Ne swik° thu naver nu.°   *stop / now*
Sing cuccu nu! Sing cuccu!
Sing cuccu! Sing cuccu nu!

Westron Winde, When Will Thou Blow

    Westron winde, when will thou blow
    The small rain down can rain?
    Christ, if my love were in my arms,
    And I in my bed again.

Thomas the Rhymer

True Thomas lay on Huntlie bank;
   A ferlie° he spied wi' his e'e; *marvel*
And there he saw a ladye bright
   Come riding doun by Eildon Tree.

Her skirt was o' the grass-green silk,
   Her mantle o' the velvet fyne;
At ilka° tett° o' her horse's mane *each / lock*
   Hung fifty siller bells and nine.

True Thomas he pu'd aff his cap,
   And louted° low doun on his knee: *bowed*
"Hail to thee, Mary, Queen of Heaven! 11
   For thy peer on earth could never be."

"O no, O no, Thomas," she said,
   "That name does not belang to me;
I'm but the Queen o' fair Elfland,
   That am hither come to visit thee.

"Harp and carp,° Thomas," she said; *sing*
   "Harp and carp along wi' me;
And if ye dare to kiss my lips,
   Sure of your bodie I will be." 20

"Betide me weal, betide me woe,
   That weird° shall never daunten me." *fate*
Syne he has kissed her rosy lips,
   All underneath the Eildon Tree.

"Now ye maun° go wi' me," she said, *must*
   "True Thomas, ye maun go wi' me;
And ye maun serve me seven years,
   Thro' weal or woe as may chance to be."

She's mounted on her milk-white steed,
   She's ta'en true Thomas up behind;
And aye, whene'er her bridle rang, 30
   The steed gaed° swifter than the wind. *went*

O they rade on, and farther on,
   The steed gaed swifter than the wind;
Until they reached a desert wide,
   And living land was left behind.

"Light down, light down now, true Thomas,
    And lean your head upon my knee;
Abide ye here a little space,
    And I will show you ferlies three.   **40**

"O see ye not yon narrow road,
    So thick beset wi' thorns and briars?
That is the Path of Righteousness,
    Though after it but few inquires.

"And see ye not yon braid,° braid road,   *broad*
    That lies across the lily leven?°   *white light*
That is the Path of Wickedness,
    Though some call it the Road to Heaven.

"And see ye not yon bonny road
    That winds about the fernie brae°?   *hill*
That is the road to fair Elfland,   **51**
    Where thou and I this night maun gae.

"But, Thomas, ye sall haud° your tongue,   *hold*
    Whatever ye may hear or see;
For speak ye word in Elfyn-land,
    Ye'll ne'er win back to your ain countrie."

O they rade on, and farther on,
    And they waded rivers abune° the knee;   *above*
And they saw neither sun nor moon,
    But they heard the roaring of the sea.   **60**

It was mirk,° mirk night, there was nae starlight,   *dark*
    They waded thro' red blude to the knee;
For a' the blude that's shed on the earth
    Rins° through the springs o' that countrie.   *runs*

Syne° they came to a garden green,   *soon*
    And she pu'd an apple frae a tree:
"Take this for thy wages, true Thomas;
    It will give thee the tongue that can never lee."°   *lie*

"My tongue is my ain,°" true Thomas he said;   *own*
    "A gudely gift ye wad gie° to me!   *would give*
I neither dought° to buy or sell   *am able*
    At fair or tryst° where I might be.   *appointed place*

67

"I dought neither speak to prince or peer,
    Nor ask of grace from fair ladye!"
"Now haud° thy peace, Thomas," she said,   *hold*
    "For as I say, so must it be."

He has gotten a coat of the even cloth,
    And a pair o' shoon° of the velvet green;   *shoes*
And till seven years were gane and past,
    True Thomas on earth was never seen.   80

Edward, Edward

"Why does your brand° sae drop wi' blude,   *sword*
    Edward, Edward?
Why does your brand sae drop wi' blude,
    And why sae sad gang ye, O?"—
"O I hae kill'd my hawk sae gude,
    Mither, mither;
O I hae kill'd my hawk sae gude,
    And I had nae mair but he, O."

"Your hawk's blude was never sae red,
    Edward, Edward;   10
Your hawk's blude was never sae red,
    My dear son, I tell thee, O."—
"O I hae kill'd my red-roan° steed,   *reddish-brown*
    Mither, mither;
O I hae kill'd my red-roan steed,
    That earst° was sae fair and free, O."   *previously*

"Your steed was auld, and ye hae got mair,°   *more*
    Edward, Edward;
Your steed was auld, and ye hae got mair;
    Some other dule° ye dree,° O."   *grief / suffer*
"O I hae kill'd my father dear,   21
    Mither, mither;
O I hae kill'd my father dear,
    Alas, and wae is me, O!"

"And whatten penance will ye dree° for that,   *undergo*
    Edward, Edward?
Whatten penance will ye dree for that?
    My dear son, now tell me, O."—

68

"I'll set my feet in yonder boat,
   Mither, mither;
I'll set my feet in yonder boat,
   And I'll fare over the sea, O."   30

"And what will ye do wi' your tow'rs and your ha',°   *hall*
   Edward, Edward?
And what will ye do wi' your tow'rs and your ha',
   That were sae fair to see, O?"
"I'll let them stand till they doun fa',°   *fall*
   Mither, mither;
I'll let them stand till they doun fa',
   For here never mair maun° I be, O."   *must*

"And what will ye leave to your bairns° and your wife,   *children*
   Edward, Edward?
And what will ye leave to your bairns and your wife,
   When ye gang owre the sea, O?"—
"The warld's room: let them beg through life,
   Mither, mither;
The warld's room: let them beg through life;
   For them never mair will I see, O."

"And what will ye leave to your ain mither dear,
   Edward, Edward?
And what will ye leave to your ain mither dear,   50
   My dear son, now tell me, O?"—
"The curse of hell frae me sall ye bear,
   Mither, mither;
The curse of hell frae me sall ye bear:
   Sic° counsels ye gave to me, O!"   *such*

SIR THOMAS WYATT [1503?–1542]

What Should I Say

What should I say
   Since faith is dead,
And truth away
   From you is fled?
Should I be led

With doubleness?
Nay, nay, mistress!

I promised you
    And you promised me
To be as true
    As I would be;
    But since I see
Your double heart,
Farewell my part!

Though for to take
    It is not my mind
But to forsake—
    I am not blind—
    And as I find
So will I trust.
Farewell, unjust!

Can ye say nay?
    But you said
That I alway
    Should be obeyed;
    And thus betrayed
Or that I wist—
Fare well, unkissed!

The Lover Showeth How He Is Forsaken
of Such as He Sometime Enjoyed

They flee from me that sometime did me seek,
    With naked foot stalking in my chamber.
I have seen them gentle, tame and meek,
    That now are wild and do not remember
    That sometime they put themselves in danger
        To take bread at my hand; and now they range
        Busily seeking with a continual change.

Thanked be fortune, it hath been otherwise
    Twenty times better; but once, in special,
In thin array, after a pleasant guise,

When her loose gown from her shoulders did fall,
And she me caught in her arms long and small,
　　Therewith all sweetly did me kiss,
　　And softly said: "Dear heart, how like you this?"

It was no dream; I lay broad waking:
　　But all is turned thorough my gentleness
Into a strange fashion of forsaking;
　　And I have leave to go of her goodness;
　　And she also to use new-fangleness.
　　　　But since that I so kindly[1] am served,
　　　　I fain would know what she hath deserved.

BARNABE GOOGE [1540–1594]

Out of Sight, Out of Mind

　　The oftener seen, the most I lust,
　　　　The more I lust, the more I smart,
　　The more I smart, the more I trust,
　　　　The more I trust, the heavier heart;
　　The heavy heart breeds mine unrest,
　　Thy absence, therefore, like I best.

　　The rarer seen, the less in mind,
　　　　The less in mind, the lesser pain,
　　The lesser pain, less grief I find,
　　　　The lesser grief, the greater gain,
　　The greater gain, the merrier I,
　　Therefore I wish thy sight to fly.

　　The further off, the more I joy,
　　　　The more I joy, the happier life,
　　The happier life, less hurts annoy,
　　　　The lesser hurts, pleasure most rife:
　　Such pleasures rife shall I obtain
　　When distance doth depart us twain.

[1] naturally.

SIR WALTER RALEGH [1552?–1618]

To His Son

Three things there be that prosper all apace
And flourish, while they are asunder far;
But on a day they meet all in a place,
And when they meet, they one another mar.
And they be these: the wood, the weed, the wag.
The wood is that that makes the gallows tree;
The weed is that that strings the hangman's bag;
The wag, my pretty knave, betokens thee.
Now mark, dear boy: while these assemble not,
Green springs the tree, hemp grows, the wag is wild;
But when they meet, it makes the timber rot,
It frets the halter, and it chokes the child.
God bless the child!

EDMUND SPENSER [1552?–1599]

Epithalamion[1]

Ye learned sisters[2] which have oftentimes
Beene to me ayding, others to adorne:
Whom ye thought worthy of your gracefull rymes,
That even the greatest did not greatly scorne
To heare theyr names sung in your simple layes,
But joyéd in theyr prayse.
And when ye list your owne mishaps to mourne,
Which death, or love, or fortunes wreck did rayse,
Your string could soone to sadder tenor turne,
And teach the woods and waters to lament   10
Your dolefull dreriment.

[1] a wedding song, celebrating Spenser's marriage to Elizabeth Boyle in 1594.
[2] the Muses.

Now lay those sorrowfull complaints aside,
And having all your heads with girland crownd,
Helpe me mine owne loves prayses to resound,
Ne let the same of any be envide:
So Orpheus did for his owne bride,[3]
So I unto my selfe alone will sing,
The woods shall to me answer and my Eccho ring.

Early before the worlds light giving lampe,
His golden beame upon the hils doth spred,   20
Having disperst the nights unchearefull dampe,
Doe ye awake, and with fresh lustyhed
Go to the bowre of my belovéd love,
My truest turtle dove,
Bid her awake; for Hymen[4] is awake,
And long since ready forth his maske to move,
With his bright Tead[5] that flames with many a flake,
And many a bachelor to waite on him,
In theyr fresh garments trim.
Bid her awake therefore and soone her dight,[6]   30
For lo the wishéd day is come at last,
That shall for al the paynes and sorrowes past,
Pay to her usury of long delight:
And whylest she doth her dight,
Doe ye to her of joy and solace sing,
That all the woods may answer and your eccho ring.

Bring with you all the Nymphes that you can heare
Both of the rivers and the forrests greene:
And of the sea that neighbours to her neare,
Al with gay girlands goodly wel beseene.   40
And let them also with them bring in hand,
Another gay girland
For my fayre love of lillyes and of roses,
Bound truelove wize with a blew silke riband.
And let them make great store of bridale poses,
And let them eeke bring store of other flowers
To deck the bridale bowers.

[3] Orpheus, on the death of his wife, Eurydice, descended to Hades and charmed the god of the underworld with his song so that she was released.
[4] god of marriage.
[5] a torch used in Roman wedding ceremonies.
[6] dress.

And let the ground whereas her foot shall tread,
For feare the stones her tender foot should wrong
Be strewed with fragrant flowers all along,   50
And diapred lyke the discolored mead.[7]
Which done, doe at her chamber dore awayt,
For she will waken strayt,
The whiles doe ye this song unto her sing,
The woods shall to you answer and your Eccho ring.

Ye Nymphes of Mulla[8] which with carefull heed,
The silver scaly trouts doe tend full well,
And greedy pikes which use therein to feed,
(Those trouts and pikes all others doo excell)
And ye likewise which keepe the rushy lake,   60
Where none doo fishes take,
Bynd up the locks the which hang scatterd light,
And in his waters which your mirror make,
Behold your faces as the christall bright,
That when you come whereas my love doth lie,
No blemish she may spie.
And eke ye lightfoot mayds which keepe the deere,
That on the hoary mountayne use to towre,
And the wylde wolves which seeke them to devoure,
With your steele darts doo chace from comming neer   70
Be also present heere,
To helpe to decke her and to help to sing,
That all the woods may answer and your eccho ring.

Wake, now my love, awake; for it is time,
The Rosy Morne long since left Tithones bed,[9]
All ready to her silver coche to clyme,
And Phoebus[10] gins to shew his glorious hed.
Hark how the cheerefull birds do chaunt theyr laies
And carroll of loves praise.
The merry Larke hir mattins sings aloft,   80
The thrush replyes, the Mavis descant playes,
The Ouzell shrills, the Ruddock warbles soft,[11]

[7] diversified like the many-colored meadow.
[8] a river near Spenser's home in Ireland.
[9] Tithonius, whose wife, the dawn goddess Aurora ("Rosy Morne"), obtained immortality for him but not eternal youth.
[10] Apollo, the sun god, also god of music and the arts.
[11] Mavis, Ouzell, and Ruddock are birds.

So goodly all agree with sweet consent,
To this dayes merriment.
Ah my deere love why doe ye sleepe thus long,
When meeter were that ye should now awake,
T' awayt the comming of your joyous make,[12]
And hearken to the birds lovelearnéd song,
The deawy leaves among.
For they of joy and pleasance to you sing,   90
That all the woods them answer and theyr eccho ring.

My love is now awake out of her dreame,
And her fayre eyes like stars that dimméd were
With darksome cloud, now shew theyr goodly beams
More bright then Hesperus[13] his head doth rere.
Come now ye damzels, daughters of delight,
Helpe quickly her to dight,
But first come ye fayre houres which were begot
In Joves sweet paradice, of Day and Night,
Which doe the seasons of the yeare allot,   100
And al that ever in this world is fayre
Doe make and still repayre.
And ye three handmayds of the Cyprian Queene,[14]
The which doe still adorne her beauties pride,
Helpe to addorne my beautifullest bride:
And as ye her array, still throw betweene
Some graces to be seene,
And as ye use to Venus, to her sing,
The whiles the woods shal answer and your eccho ring.

Now is my love all ready forth to come,   110
Let all the virgins therefore well awayt,
And ye fresh boyes that tend upon her groome
Prepare your selves; for he is comming strayt.
Set all your things in seemely good aray
Fit for so joyfull day,
The joyfulst day that ever sunne did see.
Faire Sun, shew forth thy favourable ray,
And let thy lifull[15] heat not fervent be

[12] mate.
[13] evening star.
[14] Venus, to whom a temple on Cyprus was dedicated.
[15] vital.

For feare of burning her sunshyny face,
Her beauty to disgrace. 120
O fayrest Phoebus, father of the Muse,
If ever I did honour thee aright,
Or sing the thing, that mote thy mind delight,
Doe not thy servants simple boone refuse,
But let this day let this one day be myne,
Let all the rest be thine.
Then I thy soverayne prayses loud wil sing,
That all the woods shal answer and theyr eccho ring.

Harke how the Minstrels gin to shrill aloud
Their merry Musick that resounds from far, 130
The pipe, the tabor, and the trembling Croud,[16]
That well agree withouten breach or jar.
But most of all the Damzels doe delite,
When they their tymbrels smyte,
And thereunto doe daunce and carrol sweet,
That all the sences they doe ravish quite,
The whyles the boyes run up and down the street,
Crying aloud with strong confuséd noyce,
As if it were one voyce.
Hymen iô Hymen, Hymen they do shout, 140
That even to the heavens theyr shouting shrill
Doth reach, and all the firmament doth fill,
To which the people standing all about,
As in approvance doe thereto applaud
And loud advaunce her laud,
And evermore they *Hymen Hymen* sing,
That al the woods them answer and theyr eccho ring.

Loe where she comes along with portly pace
Lyke Phoebe[17] from her chamber of the East,
Arysing forth to run her mighty race, 150
Clad all in white, that seemes a virgin best.
So well it her beseemes that ye would weene
Some angell she had beene.
Her long loose yellow locks lyke golden wyre,
Sprinckled with perle, and perling flowres a tweene,
Doe lyke a golden mantle her attyre,

---

[16] violin.
[17] Diana, goddess of the moon; also called Cinthia (*l.* 374).

76

And being crownéd with a girland greene,
Seeme lyke some mayden Queene.
Her modest eyes abashéd to behold
So many gazers, as on her do stare,   160
Upon the lowly ground affixéd are.
Ne dare lift up her countenance too bold,
But blush to heare her prayses sung so loud,
So farre from being proud.
Nathlesse doe ye still loud her prayses sing.
That all the woods may answer and your eccho ring.

Tell me ye merchants daughters did ye see
So fayre a creature in your towne before,
So sweet, so lovely, and so mild as she,
Adornd with beautyes grace and vertues store,   170
Her goodly eyes lyke Saphyres shining bright,
Her forehead yvory white,
Her cheekes lyke apples which the sun hath rudded,
Her lips lyke cherryes charming men to byte,
Her brest lyke to a bowle of creame uncrudded,
Her paps lyke lyllies budded,
Her snowie necke lyke to a marble towre,
And all her body like a pallace fayre,
Ascending uppe with many a stately stayre,
To honors seat and chastities sweet bowre.   180
Why stand ye still ye virgins in amaze,
Upon her so to gaze,
Whiles ye forget your former lay to sing,
To which the woods did answer and your eccho ring.

But if ye saw that which no eyes can see,
The inward beauty of her lively spright,[18]
Garnisht with heavenly guifts of high degree,
Much more then would ye wonder at that sight,
And stand astonisht lyke to those which red
Medusaes mazeful hed.[19]   190
There dwels sweet love and constant chastity,
Unspotted fayth and comely womanhood,
Regard of honour and mild modesty,

[18] soul.
[19] Medusa had serpents instead of hair, and those who saw her ("red")
were turned to stone.

There vertue raynes as Queene in royal throne,
And giveth lawes alone.
The which the base affections doe obay,
And yeeld theyr services unto her will,
Ne thought of thing uncomely ever may
Thereto approch to tempt her mind to ill.
Had ye once seene these her celestial threasures,   200
And unrevealéd pleasures,
Then would ye wonder and her prayses sing,
That al the woods should answer and your eccho ring.

Open the temple gates unto my love,
Open them wide that she may enter in,
And all the postes adorne as doth behove,
And all the pillours deck with girlands trim,
For to recyve this Saynt with honour dew,
That commeth in to you.
With trembling steps and humble reverence,   210
She commeth in, before th' almighties vew,
Of her ye virgins learne obedience,
When so ye come into those holy places,
To humble your proud faces:
Bring her up to th' high altar, that she may
The sacred ceremonies there partake,
The which do endlesse matrimony make,
And let the roring Organs loudly play
The praises of the Lord in lively notes,
The whiles with hollow throates,   220
The Choristers the joyous Antheme sing,
That al the woods may answere and their eccho ring.

Behold whiles she before the altar stands
Hearing the holy priest that to her speakes
And blesseth her with his two happy hands,
How the red roses flush up in her cheekes,
And the pure snow with goodly vermill stayne,
Like crimsin dyde in grayne,
That even th' Angels which continually,
About the sacred Altare doe remaine,   230
Forget their service and about her fly,
Ofte peeping in her face that seemes more fayre,
The more they on it stare.

78

But her sad eyes still fastened on the ground,
Are governéd with goodly modesty,
That suffers not one looke to glaunce awry,
Which may let in a little thought unsownd.
Why blush ye love to give to me your hand,
The pledge of all our band?
Sing ye sweet Angels, Alleluya sing,   240
That all the woods may answere and your eccho ring.

Now al is done; bring home the bride againe,
Bring home the triumph of our victory,
Bring home with you the glory of her gaine,
With joyance bring her and with jollity.
Never had man more joyfull day then this,
Whom heaven would heape with blis.
Make feast therefore now all this live long day,
This day for ever to me holy is,
Poure out the wine without restraint or stay,   250
Poure not by cups, but by the belly full,
Poure out to all that wull,
And sprinkle all the postes and wals with wine,
That they may sweat, and drunken be withall.
Crowne ye God Bacchus[20] with a coronall,
And Hymen also crowne with wreathes of vine,
And let the Graces daunce unto the rest;
For they can doo it best:
The whiles the maydens doe theyr carroll sing,
To which the woods shal answer and theyr eccho ring.   260

Ring ye the bels, ye yong men of the towne,
And leave your wonted labors for this day:
This day is holy; doe ye write it downe,
That ye for ever it remember may.
This day the sunne is in his chiefest hight,
With Barnaby[21] the bright,
From whence declining daily by degrees,
He somewhat loseth of his heat and light,
When once the Crab[22] behind his back he sees.
But for this time it ill ordainéd was,   270

[20] god of wine and festivity.
[21] the wedding took place on June 11, St. Barnabas' day.
[22] a sign of the zodiac, which the sun enters in June.

To chose the longest day in all the yeare,
And shortest night, when longest fitter weare:
Yet never day so long, but late would passe.
Ring ye the bels, to make it weare away,
And bonefiers make all day,
And daunce about them, and about them sing:
That all the woods may answer, and your eccho ring.

Ah when will this long weary day have end,
And lende me leave to come unto my love?
How slowly do the houres theyr numbers spend?   280
How slowly does sad Time his feathers move?
Hast thee O fayrest Planet to thy home
Within the Westerne fome:
Thy tyred steedes long since have need of rest.
Long though it be, at last I see it gloome,
And the bright evening star with golden creast
Appeare out of the East.
Fayre childe of beauty, glorious lampe of love
That all the host of heaven in rankes doost lead,
And guydest lovers through the nightés dread,   290
How chearefully thou lookest from above,
And seems to laugh atweene thy twinkling light
As joying in the sight
Of these glad many which for joy doe sing,
That all the woods them answer and their echo ring.

Now ceasse ye damsels your delights forepast;
Enough is it, that all the day was youres:
Now day is doen, and night is nighing fast:
Now bring the Bryde into the brydall boures.
Now night is come, now soone her disaray,   300
And in her bed her lay;
Lay her in lillies and in violets,
And silken courteins over her display,
And odourd sheetes, and Arras coverlets.
Behold how goodly my faire love does ly
In proud humility;
Like unto Maia;[23] when as Jove her tooke,
In Tempe, lying on the flowry gras,
Twixt sleepe and wake, after she weary was,

[23] mother of Mercury by Jove.

With bathing in the Acidalian brooke.
Now it is night, ye damsels may be gon,
And leave my love alone,
And leave likewise your former lay to sing:
The woods no more shal answere, nor your echo ring.

Now welcome night, thou night so long expected,
That long daies labour doest at last defray,
And all my cares, which cruell love collected,
Hast sumd in one, and cancelléd for aye:
Spread thy broad wing over my love and me,
That no man may us see,
And in thy sable mantle us enwrap,
From feare of perrill and foule horror free.
Let no false treason seeke us to entrap,
Nor any dread disquiet once annoy
The safety of our joy:
But let the night be calme and quietsome,
Without tempestuous storms or sad afray:
Lyke as when Jove with fayre Alcmena[24] lay,
When he begot the great Tirynthian groome:
Or lyke as when he with thy selfe did lie,
And begot Majesty.
And let the mayds and yongmen cease to sing:
Ne let the woods them answer, nor theyr eccho ring.

Let no lamenting cryes, nor dolefull teares,
Be heard all night within nor yet without:
Ne let false whispers, breeding hidden feares,
Breake gentle sleepe with misconceivéd dout.
Let no deluding dreames, nor dreadful sights
Make sudden sad affrights;
Ne let housefyres, nor lightnings helpelesse harmes,
Ne let the Pouke, nor other evill sprights,
Ne let mischivous witches with theyr charmes,
Ne let hob Goblins, names whose sence we see not,
Fray us with things that be not.
Let not the shriech Oule, nor the Storke be heard:
Nor the night Raven that still deadly yels,
Nor damnéd ghosts cald up with mighty spels,
Nor griesly vultures make us once affeard:

[24] mother, by Jove, of Hercules, the "great Tirynthian groome."

Ne let th' unpleasant Quyre of Frogs still croking
Make us to wish theyr choking.   350
Let none of these theyr drery accents sing;
Ne let the woods them answer, nor theyr eccho ring.

But let stil Silence trew night watches keepe,
That sacred peace may in assurance rayne,
And tymely sleep, when it is tyme to sleepe,
May poure his limbs forth on your pleasant playne,
The whiles an hundred little wingéd loves,
Like divers fethered doves,
Shall fly and flutter round about your bed,
And in the secret darke, that none reproves,   360
Their prety stealthes shal worke, and snares shal spread
To filch away sweet snatches of delight,
Conceald through covert night.
Ye sonnes of Venus, play your sports at will,
For greedy pleasure, carelesse of your toyes,
Thinks more upon her paradise of joyes,
Then what ye do, albe it good or ill.
All night therefore attend your merry play,
For it will soone be day:
Now none doth hinder you, that say or sing,   370
Ne will the woods now answer, nor your Eccho ring.

Who is the same, which at my window peepes?
Or whose is that faire face, that shines so bright,
Is it not Cinthia, she that never sleepes,
But walkes about high heaven al the night?
O fayrest goddesse, do thou not envy
My love with me to spy:
For thou likewise didst love, though now unthought.
And for a fleece of woll, which privily,
The Latmian shephard[25] once unto thee brought,   380
His pleasures with thee wrought.
Therefore to us be favorable now;
And sith of wemens labours thou hast charge,
And generation goodly dost enlarge,
Encline thy will t' effect our wishfull vow,
And the chast wombe informe with timely seed,

[25] the goddess of the moon fell in love with the shepherd Endymion while
he was sleeping on Mt. Latmus.

That may our comfort breed:
Till which we cease our hopefull hap to sing,
Ne let the woods us answere, nor our Eccho ring.

And thou great Juno, which with awful might   390
The lawes of wedlock still dost patronize,
And the religion of the faith first plight
With sacred rites hast taught to solemnize:
And eeke for comfort often calléd art
Of women in their smart,
Eternally bind thou this lovely band,
And all thy blessings unto us impart.
And thou glad Genius,[26] in whose gentle hand,
The bridale bowre and geniall bed remaine,
Without blemish or staine,   400
And the sweet pleasures of theyr loves delight
With secret ayde doest succour and supply,
Till they bring forth the fruitfull progeny,
Send us the timely fruit of this same night.
And thou fayre Hebe,[27] and thou Hymen free,
Grant that it may so be.
Til which we cease your further prayse to sing,
Ne any woods shal answer, nor your Eccho ring.

And ye high heavens, the temple of the gods,
In which a thousand torches flaming bright   410
Doe burne, that to us wretched earthly clods,
In dreadful darknesse lend desired light;
And all ye powers which in the same remayne,
More then we men can fayne,
Poure out your blessing on us plentiously,
And happy influence upon us raine,
That we may raise a large posterity,
Which from the earth, which they may long possesse,
With lasting happinesse,
Up to your haughty pallaces may mount,   420
And for the guerdon of theyr glorious merit
May heavenly tabernacles there inherit,
Of blessed Saints for to increase the count.

[26] god of reproduction.
[27] the goddess of youth and cupbearer to Jove. She became the wife of
Hercules after he was deified.

So let us rest, sweet love, in hope of this,
And cease till then our tymely joyes to sing,
The woods no more us answer, nor our eccho ring.

Song made in lieu of many ornaments,
With which my love should duly have bene dect,
Which cutting off through hasty accidents,
Ye would not stay your dew time to expect,   430
But promist both to recompens,
Be unto her a goodly ornament,
And for short time an endlesse moniment.

SIR PHILIP SIDNEY [1554–1586]

31   *With How Sad Steps*

With how sad steps, Oh Moon, thou clim'st the skies!
How silently, and with how wan a face!
What, may it be that even in heavenly place
That busy archer his sharp arrows tries?
Sure, if that long-with-love-acquainted eyes
Can judge of love, thou feel'st a lover's case,
I read it in thy looks; thy languished grace,
To me, that feel the like, thy state descries.
Then, even of fellowship, Oh Moon, tell me,
Is constant love deemed there but want of wit?
Are beauties there as proud as here they be?
Do they above love to be loved, and yet
Those lovers scorn whom that love doth possess?
Do they call virtue there ungratefulness?

GEORGE PEELE [1559–1596]

Gently Dip

Gently dip, but not too deep;
For fear you make the golden beard to weep.
Fair maiden white and red,

Comb me smooth, and stroke my head:
And thou shalt have some cockle bread.
Gently dip, but not too deep,
For fear thou make the golden beard to weep.
Fair maiden white and red,
Comb me smooth, and stroke my head;
And every hair, a sheaf shall be,
And every sheaf a golden tree.

A Sonnet

His golden locks time hath to silver turned;
O time too swift, O swiftness never ceasing!
His youth gainst time and age hath ever spurned,
But spurned in vain; youth waneth by increasing.
　　Beauty, strength, youth, are flowers but fading seen,
　　Duty, faith, love are roots, and ever green.

His helmet now shall make a hive for bees,
And, lovers' sonnets turned to holy psalms,
A man at arms must now serve on his knees,
And feed on prayers, which are age his alms.
　　But though from court to cottage he depart,
　　His saint is sure of his unspotted heart.

And when he saddest sits in homely cell,
He'll teach his swains this carol for a song,
Blessed be the hearts that wish my sovereign well,
Cursed be the souls that think her any wrong.
　　Goddess, allow this agéd man his right,
　　To be your bedesman now, that was your knight.

CHIDIOCK TICHBORNE [1558–1586]

Tichborne's Elegy

WRITTEN WITH HIS OWN HAND IN THE TOWER BEFORE HIS EXECUTION

My prime of youth is but a frost of cares,
My feast of joy is but a dish of pain,
My crop of corn is but a field of tares,

85

And all my good is but vain hope of gain;
The day is past, and yet I saw no sun,
And now I live, and now my life is done.

My tale was heard and yet it was not told,
My fruit is fallen and yet my leaves are green,
My youth is spent and yet I am not old,
I saw the world and yet I was not seen;
My thread is cut and yet it is not spun,
And now I live, and now my life is done.

I sought my death and found it in my womb,
I looked for life and saw it was a shade,
I trod the earth and knew it was my tomb,
And now I die, and now I was but made;
My glass is full, and now my glass is run,
And now I live, and now my life is done.

ROBERT SOUTHWELL [1561–1595]

The Burning Babe

As I in hoary winter's night stood shivering in the snow,
Surprised I was with sudden heat, which made my heart to glow;
And lifting up a fearful eye to view what fire was near,
A pretty babe all burning bright, did in the air appear,
Who scorched with excessive heat, such floods of tears did shed,
As though his floods should quench his flames which with his tears
          were fed;
"Alas!" quoth he, "but newly born, in fiery heats I fry,
Yet none approach to warm their hearts or feel my fire but I!
My faultless breast the furnace is, the fuel wounding thorns,
Love is the fire, and sighs the smoke, the ashes shame and scorns;
The fuel justice layeth on, and mercy blows the coals,
The metal in this furnace wrought are men's defiled souls,
For which, as now on fire I am to work them to their good,
So will I melt into a bath to wash them in my blood."
With this he vanished out of sight, and swiftly shrank away,
And straight I called unto mind that it was Christmas day.

SAMUEL DANIEL [1562–1619]

45 *Care-Charmer Sleep*

Care-charmer sleep, son of the sable night,
Brother to death, in silent darkness born,
Relieve my languish and restore the light;
With dark forgetting of my cares, return.
And let the day be time enough to mourn
The shipwreck of my ill-adventured youth;
Let waking eyes suffice to wail their scorn
Without the torment of the night's untruth.
Cease, dreams, th' imagery of our day desires,
To model forth the passions of the morrow;
Never let rising sun approve you liars,
To add more grief to aggravate my sorrow.
Still let me sleep, embracing clouds in vain,
And never wake to feel the day's disdain.

MICHAEL DRAYTON [1563–1631]

61 *Since There's No Help*

Since there's no help, come let us kiss and part;
Nay, I have done, you get no more of me;
And I am glad, yea, glad with all my heart,
That thus so cleanly I myself can free.
Shake hands for ever, cancel all our vows,
And when we meet at any time again,
Be it not seen in either of our brows
That we one jot of former love retain.
Now at the last gasp of love's latest breath,
When, his pulse failing, passion speechless lies,
When faith is kneeling by his bed of death,
And innocence is closing up his eyes,
Now if thou wouldst, when all have given him over,
From death to life thou might'st him yet recover.

CHRISTOPHER MARLOWE [1564–1593]

The Passionate Shepherd to His Love

Come live with me, and be my love,
And we will all the pleasures prove,
That valleys, groves, hills and fields,
Woods, or steepy mountains yields.

And we will sit upon the rocks,
Seeing the shepherds feed their flocks,
By shallow rivers, to whose falls,
Melodious birds sing madrigals.

And I will make thee beds of roses,
And a thousand fragrant posies,
A cap of flowers, and a kirtle[1]
Embroidered all with leaves of myrtle;

A gown made of the finest wool,
Which from our pretty lambs we pull,
Fair-linéd slippers for the cold,
With buckles of the purest gold;

A belt of straw and ivy buds
With coral clasps and amber studs:
And if these pleasures may thee move,
Come live with me, and be my love.

The shepherd swains shall dance and sing,
For thy delight each May morning:
If these delights thy mind may move,
Then live with me, and be my love.

FROM *Doctor Faustus*

SCENE I

Faustus discovered in his study

Faust. Settle thy studies, Faustus, and begin
To sound the depth of that thou wilt profess;
Having commenced, be a divine in show,

[1] skirt.

Yet level at the end of every art,
And live and die in Aristotle's works.
Sweet Analytics, 'tis thou hast ravished me,   [*Reads*]
Bene disserere est finis logices.
Is to dispute well logic's chiefest end?
Affords this art no greater miracle?
Then read no more, thou hast attained the end;   10
A greater subject fitteth Faustus' wit:
Bid ὸν χαὶ μὴ ὸν[1] farewell; Galen[2] come,
Seeing *Ubi desinit Philosophus ibi incipit Medicus*;[3]
Be a physician, Faustus, heap up gold,
And be eternized for some wondrous cure.   [*Reads*]
Summum bonum medicinæ sanitas,
The end of physic is our body's health.
Why, Faustus, hast thou not attained that end?
Is not thy common talk found aphorisms?
Are not thy bills hung up as monuments,   20
Whereby whole cities have escaped the plague,
And thousand desperate maladies been eased?
Yet art thou still but Faustus and a man.
Couldst thou make men to live eternally,
Or, being dead, raise them to life again,
Then this profession were to be esteemed.
Physic, farewell.—Where is Justinian?[4]   [*Reads*]
Si una eademque res legatur duobus, alter rem, alter valorem rei, etc.[5]
A pretty case of paltry legacies!   [*Reads*]
Exhæreditare filium non potest pater nisi, etc.[6]   30
Such is the subject of the Institute
And universal Body of the Law.
This study fits a mercenary drudge,
Who aims at nothing but external trash;
Too servile and illiberal for me.
When all is done divinity is best;
Jerome's Bible, Faustus, view it well.   [*Reads*]

[1] Aristotle's "being and not being."
[2] Greek physician famous throughout the Middle Ages and Renaissance.
[3] "Where the philosopher stops, the doctor begins."
[4] the Byzantine emperor Justinian codified Roman law in the *Institutes* (*l.* 31).
[5] "If the same thing is bequeathed to two persons, let one have it, the other its value in other property" is cited in his *Digest*.
[6] "A father cannot disinherit his son unless, etc."

Stipendium peccati mors est.[7] Ha! *Stipendium, etc.*
The reward of sin is death. That's hard.   *[Reads]*
Si peccasse negamus fallimur et nulla est in nobis veritas.[8]   40
If we say that we have no sin we deceive ourselves, and
there's no truth in us. Why then, belike we must sin,
and so consequently die.
Ay, we must die an everlasting death.
What doctrine call you this, *Che sera sera,*
What will be, shall be? Divinity, adieu!
These metaphysics of magicians
And necromantic books are heavenly:
Lines, circles, scenes, letters, and characters: 50
Ay, these are those that Faustus most desires.
Oh, what a world of profit and delight,
Of power, of honor, of omnipotence
Is promised to the studious artisan!
All things that move between the quiet poles
Shall be at my command: emperors and kings
Are but obeyed in their several provinces,
Nor can they raise the wind or rend the clouds;
But his dominion that exceeds in this
Stretcheth as far as doth the mind of man,   60
A sound magician is a mighty god:
Here, Faustus, tire thy brains to gain a deity.
Wagner!

Enter *Wagner*

                   Commend me to my dearest friends,
The German Valdes and Cornelius;
Request them earnestly to visit me.
    Wag. I will, sir.   *[Exit]*
    Faust. Their conference will be a greater help to me
than all my labors, plod I ne'er so fast.

Enter *Good Angel* and *Evil Angel*

    G. Ang. O Faustus! lay that damnèd book aside,   70
And gaze not on it lest it tempt thy soul,
And heap God's heavy wrath upon thy head.
Read, read the Scriptures: that is blasphemy.

    [7] "the wages of sin is death" (Romans, vi. 23).
    [8] "If we say we have no sin, we deceive ourselves, and the truth is not in us"
(I Epistle of St. John, i. 8).

E. Ang. Go forward, Faustus, in that famous art,
Wherein all Nature's treasure is contained:
Be thou on earth as Jove is in the sky,
Lord and commander of these elements.   [*Exeunt* Angels]
  Faust. How am I glutted with conceit of this!
Shall I make spirits fetch me what I please,
Resolve me of all ambiguities,   80
Perform what desperate enterprise I will?
I'll have them fly to India for gold,
Ransack the ocean for orient pearl,
And search all corners of the new-found world
For pleasant fruits and princely delicates;
I'll have them read me strange philosophy
And tell the secrets of all foreign kings;
I'll have them wall all Germany with brass,
And make swift Rhine circle fair Wertenberg,
I'll have them fill the public schools with silk   90
Wherewith the students shall be bravely clad;
I'll levy soldiers with the coin they bring,
And chase the Prince of Parma from our land,
And reign sole king of all the provinces;
Yea, stranger engines for the brunt of war
Than was the fiery keel[9] at Antwerp's bridge,
I'll make my servile spirits to invent.

Enter Valdes and Cornelius

Come, German Valdes and Cornelius,
And make me blest with your sage conference.
Valdes, sweet Valdes, and Cornelius,   100
Know that your words have won me at the last
To practice magic and concealed arts:
Yet not your words only, but mine own fantasy
That will receive no object; for my head
But ruminates on necromantic skill.
Philosophy is odious and obscure,
Both law and physic are for petty wits;
Divinity is basest of the three,
Unpleasant, harsh, contemptible, and vile:
'Tis magic, magic that hath ravished me.   110

[9] the fire-ship used by the defenders of Antwerp in 1585 to destroy the
bridge Parma, the Governor of the Netherlands, had built across the Scheldt
river.

Faustus discovered in his study

Faust. Now, Faustus, must
Thou needs be damned, and canst thou not be saved:
What boots it then to think of God or Heaven?
Away with such vain fancies, and despair:
Despair in God, and trust in Belzebub;
Now go not backward: no, Faustus, be resolute:
Why waver'st thou? Oh, something soundeth in mine ears
"Abjure this magic, turn to God again!"
Ay, and Faustus will turn to God again.
To God?—He loves thee not—   10
The God thou serv'st is thine own appetite,
Wherein is fixed the love of Belzebub;
To him I'll build an altar and a church,
And offer lukewarm blood of new-born babes.

Enter *Good Angel* and *Evil Angel*

G. Ang. Sweet Faustus, leave that execrable art.
Faust. Contrition, prayer, repentance! What of them?
G. Ang. Oh, they are means to bring thee unto Heaven.
E. Ang. Rather, illusions—fruits of lunacy,
That makes men foolish that do trust them most.
G. Ang. Sweet Faustus, think of Heaven, and heavenly things.   20
E. Ang. No, Faustus, think of honor and of wealth.

                                            [*Exeunt* Angels]
Faust. Of wealth!
Why the signiory of Embden[10] shall be mine.
When Mephistophiles shall stand by me,
What God can hurt thee? Faustus, thou art safe:
Cast no more doubts. Come, Mephistophiles,
And bring glad tidings from great Lucifer;
Is't not midnight? Come, Mephistophiles;
Veni, veni, Mephistophile!

Enter *Mephistophiles*

Now tell me, what says Lucifer, thy lord?   30

    [10] capital of East Friesland, on friendly terms with England during the
reign of Elizabeth.

Meph. That I shall wait on Faustus whilst he lives,
So he will buy my service with his soul.

Faust. Already Faustus hath hazarded that for thee.

Meph. But, Faustus, thou must bequeath it solemnly,
And write a deed of gift with thine own blood,
For that security craves great Lucifer.
If thou deny it, I will back to hell.

Faust. Stay, Mephistophiles! and tell me what good
Will my soul do thy lord.

Meph. Enlarge his kingdom.   40

Faust. Is that the reason why he tempts us thus?

Meph. Solamen miseris socios habuisse doloris.[11]

Faust. Why, have you any pain that tortures others?

Meph. As great as have the human souls of men.
But tell me, Faustus, shall I have thy soul?
And I will be thy slave, and wait on thee,
And give thee more than thou hast wit to ask.

Faust. Ay, Mephistophiles, I give it thee.

Meph. Then, Faustus, stab thine arm courageously,
And bind thy soul that at some certain day   50
Great Lucifer may claim it as his own;
And then be thou as great as Lucifer.

Faust. [*stabbing his arm.*] Lo, Mephistophiles, for love of thee,
I cut mine arm, and with my proper blood
Assure my soul to be great Lucifer's,
Chief lord and regent of perpetual night!
View here the blood that trickles from mine arm,
And let it be propitious for my wish.

Meph. But, Faustus, thou must
Write it in manner of a deed of gift.   60

Faust. Ay, so I will. [*Writes*] But, Mephistophiles,
My blood congeals, and I can write no more.

Meph. I'll fetch thee fire to dissolve it straight.   [*Exit*]

Faust. What might the staying of my blood portend?
Is it unwilling I should write this bill?
Why streams it not that I may write afresh?
Faustus gives to thee his soul. Ah, there it stayed.
Why should'st thou not? Is not thy soul thine own?
Then write again, *Fautus gives to thee his soul.*

11 "misery loves company."

93

Meph. Here's fire. Come, Faustus, set it on.   70
  Faust. So now the blood begins to clear again;
Now will I make an end immediately.   [*Writes*]
  Meph. Oh, what will not I do to obtain his soul.   [*Aside*]
  Faust. Consummatum est:[12] this bill is ended,
And Faustus hath bequeathed his soul to Lucifer.
But what is this inscription on mine arm?
Homo, fuge![13] Whither should I fly?
If unto God, he'll throw me down to hell.
My senses are deceived; here's nothing writ—
I see it plain; here in this place is writ   80
Homo, fuge! Yet shall not Faustus fly.
  Meph. I'll fetch him somewhat to delight his mind.   [*Exit*]

SCENE VI

Enter *Faustus* and *Mephistophiles*

Faust. When I behold the heavens, then I repent,
And curse thee, wicked Mephistophiles,
Because thou hast deprived me of those joys.
  Meph. Why, Faustus,
Thinkest thou Heaven is such a glorious thing?
I tell thee 'tis not half so fair as thou,
Or any man that breathes on earth.
  Faust. How prov'st thou that?
  Meph. 'Twas made for man, therefore is man more excellent.
  Faust. If it were made for man, 'twas made for me;   10
I will renounce this magic and repent.

Enter *Good Angel* and *Evil Angel*

G. Ang. Faustus, repent; yet God will pity thee.
E. Ang. Thou art a spirit; God cannot pity thee.
Faust. Who buzzeth in mine ears I am a spirit?
Be I a devil, yet God may pity me;
Ay, God will pity me if I repent.
  E. Ang. Ay, but Faustus never shall repent.   [*Exeunt* Angels]

[12] "It is finished" (St. John, xix. 30).
[13] "Man, flee."

Faust. My heart's so hardened I cannot repent.
Scarce can I name salvation, faith, or Heaven,
But fearful echoes thunder in mine ears   20
"Faustus, thou art damned!" Then swords and knives,
Poison, gun, halters, and envenomed steel
Are laid before me to dispatch myself,
And long ere this I should have slain myself,
Had not sweet pleasure conquered deep despair.
Have not I made blind Homer sing to me
Of Alexander's[14] love and Oenon's death?
And hath not he that built the walls of Thebes
With ravishing sound of his melodious harp,
Made music with my Mephistophiles?   30
Why should I die then, or basely despair?
I am resolved: Faustus shall ne'er repent—
Come, Mephistophiles, let us dispute again,
And argue of divine astrology.

SCENE XIII

Faust. One thing, good servant, let me crave of thee,
To glut the longing of my heart's desire—
That I might have unto my paramour
That heavenly Helen, which I saw of late,
Whose sweet embracings may extinguish clean
These thoughts that do dissuade me from my vow,
And keep mine oath I made to Lucifer.
Meph. Faustus, this or what else thou shalt desire
Shall be performed in twinkling of an eye.   90

Re-enter *Helen*

Faust. Was this the face that launched a thousand ships
And burnt the topless towers of Ilium?
Sweet Helen, make me immortal with a kiss.   [*Kisses her*]
Her lips suck forth my soul; see where it flies!—
Come, Helen, come, give me my soul again.
Here will I dwell, for Heaven is in these lips,
And all is dross that is not Helena.

[14] Paris, lover of Oenone and Helen of Troy.

I will be Paris, and for love of thee,
Instead of Troy, shall Wertenberg be sacked:
And I will combat with weak Menelaus,[15]   100
And wear thy colors on my plumed crest:
Yea, I will wound Achilles in the heel,
And then return to Helen for a kiss.
Oh, thou art fairer than the evening air
Clad in the beauty of a thousand stars;
Brighter art thou than flaming Jupiter
When he appeared to hapless Semele:[16]
More lovely than the monarch of the sky
In wanton Arethusa's[17] azured arms:
And none but thou shalt be my paramour!   [*Exeunt*]   110

SCENE XIV

Faust. Ah, Faustus,
Now hast thou but one bare hour to live,
And then thou must be damned perpetually!
Stand still, you ever-moving spheres of Heaven,
That time may cease, and midnight never come;
Fair Nature's eye, rise, rise again and make   70
Perpetual day; or let this hour be but
A year, a month, a week, a natural day,
That Faustus may repent and save his soul!
O lente, lente, currite noctis equi![18]
The stars move still, time runs, the clock will strike,
The Devil will come, and Faustus must be damned.
Oh, I'll leap up to my God! Who pulls me down?
See, see where Christ's blood streams in the firmament!
One drop would save my soul—half a drop: ah, my Christ!
Ah, rend not my heart for naming of my Christ!   80
Yet will I call on him: Oh, spare me, Lucifer!—
Where is it now? 'tis gone; and see where God
Stretcheth out his arm, and bends his ireful brows!
Mountain and hills come, come and fall on me,

[15] husband of Helen of Troy.
[16] a mortal woman whom Jove loved and destroyed by lightning when she asked to see him in the splendor in which he appeared to Juno.
[17] a fountain nymph.
[18] adapted from Ovid, *Amores*, I. xiii. 40: "Run slowly, slowly, horses of of the night!"

And hide me from the heavy wrath of God!
No! no!
Then will I headlong run into the earth;
Earth gape! Oh, no, it will not harbor me!
You stars that reigned at my nativity,
Whose influence hath allotted death and hell,   90
Now draw up Faustus like a foggy mist
Into the entrails of yon laboring clouds,
That when they vomit forth into the air,
My limbs may issue from their smoky mouths,
So that my soul may but ascend to Heaven.
[The clock strikes the half hour]
Ah, half the hour is past! 'twill all be past anon!
O God!
If thou wilt not have mercy on my soul,
Yet for Christ's sake whose blood hath ransomed me,
Impose some end to my incessant pain;   100
Let Faustus live in hell a thousand years—
A hundred thousand, and—at last—be saved!
Oh, no end is limited to damnèd souls!
Why wert thou not a creature wanting soul?
Or why is this immortal that thou hast?
Ah, Pythagoras' metempsychosis![19] were that true,
This soul should fly from me, and I be changed
Unto some brutish beast! all beasts are happy,
For, when they die,
Their souls are soon dissolved in elements;   110
But mine must live, still to be plagued in hell.
Curst be the parents that engendered me!
No, Faustus: curse thyself: curse Lucifer
That hath deprived thee of the joys of Heaven.
[The clock strikes twelve]
Oh, it strikes, it strikes! Now, body, turn to air,
Or Lucifer will bear thee quick to hell.   [Thunder and lightning]
O soul, be changed into little water-drops,
And fall into the ocean—ne'er be found.   [Enter Devils]
My God! my God! look not so fierce on me!
Adders and serpents, let me breathe awhile!   120
Ugly hell, gape not! come not, Lucifer!
I'll burn my books!—Ah Mephistophiles! [Exeunt Devils with Faustus]

[19] Pythagoras' doctrine of the transmigration of souls.

97

Cho. Cut is the branch that might have grown full straight,
And burnèd is Apollo's laurel bough,
That sometime grew within this learnèd man.
Faustus is gone; regard his hellish fall,
Whose fiendful fortune may exhort the wise
Only to wonder at unlawful things,
Whose deepness doth entice such forward wits
To practise more than heavenly power permits.   [*Exit*]

Terminat hora diem; terminat auctor opus.[20]

ANONYMOUS

As You Came from the Holy Land
of Walsingham

As you came from the holy land
　　Of Walsingham,
Met you not with my true love,
　　By the way as you came?

"How should I know your true love
　　That have met many a one
As I came from the holy land,
　　That have come, that have gone?"

She is neither white nor brown,
　　But as the heavens fair;
There is none hath her form so divine,   10
　　On the earth, in the air.

"Such a one did I meet, good sir,
　　With angel-like face,
Who like a nymph, like a queen did appear
　　In her gait, in her grace."

[20] "The hour ends the day; the author ends his work."

She hath left me here alone,
   All alone unknown,
Who sometime loved me as her life,
   And called me her own.   20

"What is the cause she hath left thee alone,
   And a new way doth take,
That sometime did thee love as herself,
   And her joy did thee make?"

I have loved her all my youth,
   But now am old as you see;
Love liketh not the falling fruit,
   Nor the withered tree.

For love is a careless child,
   And forgets promise past;   30
He is blind, he is deaf, when he list,
   And in faith never fast.

His desire is fickle found,
   And a trustless joy;
He is won with a world of despair,
   And is lost with a toy.

Such is the love of womenkind,
   Or the word, love, abused,
Under which many childish desires
   And conceits are excused.   40

But love, it is a durable fire
   In the mind ever burning,
Never sick, never dead, never cold,
   From itself never turning.

Crabbed Age and Youth

Crabbed age and youth cannot live together:
Youth is full of pleasance, age is full of care;
Youth like summer morn, age like winter weather;
Youth like summer brave, age like winter bare.

Youth is full of sport, age's breath is short;
   Youth is nimble, age is lame;
Youth is hot and bold, age is weak and cold;
   Youth is wild, and age is tame.
Age, I do abhor thee, youth, I do adore thee;
   Oh! my love, my love is young:
Age, I do defy thee: Oh! sweet shepherd, hie thee,
   For methinks thou stay'st too long.

WILLIAM SHAKESPEARE [1564–1616]

When Icicles Hang by the Wall

When icicles hang by the wall,
   And Dick the shepherd blows his nail,
And Tom bears logs into the hall,
   And milk comes frozen home in pail,
When blood is nipped, and ways be foul,
Then nightly sings the staring owl,
      To-whit!
To-who!—a merry note,
While greasy Joan doth keel[1] the pot.

When all aloud the wind doth blow,
   And coughing drowns the parson's saw,
And birds sit brooding in the snow,
   And Marian's nose looks red and raw,
When roasted crabs hiss in the bowl,
Then nightly sings the staring owl,
      To-whit!
To-who!—a merry note,
While greasy Joan doth keel the pot.

(*Love's Labour's Lost*)

[1] to prevent boiling over by stirring, skimming, or pouring in something cold.

Under the Greenwood Tree

Under the greenwood tree
Who loves to lie with me,
And turn his merry note
Unto the sweet bird's throat,
Come hither, come hither, come hither:
    Here shall he see
    No enemy
But winter and rough weather.

Who doth ambition shun
And loves to lie i' the sun,
Seeking the food he eats
And pleased with what he gets,
Come hither, come hither, come hither:
    Here shall he see
    No enemy
But winter and rough weather.

(*As You Like It*)

Blow, Blow, Thou Winter Wind!

Blow, blow, thou winter wind!
Thou art not so unkind
As man's ingratitude;
Thy tooth is not so keen
Because thou art not seen,
Although thy breath be rude.
Heigh ho! sing heigh ho! unto the green holly:
Most friendship is feigning, most loving mere folly:
Then, heigh ho! the holly!
This life is most jolly.

Freeze, freeze, thou bitter sky,
Thou dost not bite so nigh
As benefits forgot:
Though thou the waters warp,
Thy sting is not so sharp
As friend remembered not.

Heigh ho! sing heigh ho! unto the green holly:
Most friendship is feigning, most loving mere folly:
    Then, heigh ho! the holly!
    This life is most jolly.

                    (As You Like It)

It Was a Lover

It was a lover and his lass,
    With a hey, and a ho, and a hey nonino!
That o'er the green corn-field did pass,
    In spring time, the only pretty ring time,
When birds do sing, hey ding a ding, ding;
    Sweet lovers love the spring.

Between the acres of the rye,
    With a hey, and a ho, and a hey nonino!
Those pretty country folks would lie,
    In spring time, the only pretty ring time,
When birds do sing, hey ding a ding, ding;
    Sweet lovers love the spring.

This carol they began that hour,
    With a hey, and a ho, and a hey nonino!
How that a life was but a flower
    In spring time, the only pretty ring time,
When birds do sing, hey ding a ding, ding;
    Sweet lovers love the spring.

And therefore take the present time,
    With a hey, and a ho, and a hey nonino!
For love is crownéd with the prime
    In spring time, the only pretty ring time,
When birds do sing, hey ding a ding, ding;
    Sweet lovers love the spring.

                    (As You Like It)

O Mistress Mine

O mistress mine, where are you roaming?
O stay and hear; your true love's coming,
    That can sing both high and low.

Trip no further, pretty sweeting;
Journeys end in lovers' meeting,
  Every wise man's son doth know.

What is love? 'Tis not hereafter;
Present mirth hath present laughter;
  What's to come is still unsure.
In delay there lies no plenty;
Then come kiss me, sweet and twenty;
  Youth's a stuff will not endure.

(Twelfth Night)

Take, O! Take

Take, O! take those lips away,
  That so sweetly were forsworn,
And those eyes, the break of day,
  Lights that do mislead the morn;
But my kisses bring again, bring again,
Seals of love, but sealed in vain, sealed in vain.

(Measure for Measure)

Fear No More

Fear no more the heat o' the sun
  Nor the furious winter's rages;
Thou thy worldly task hast done,
  Home art gone and ta'en thy wages.
Golden lads and girls all must,
As chimney-sweepers, come to dust.

Fear no more the frown o' the great,
  Thou art past the tyrant's stroke;
Care no more to clothe and eat;
  To thee the reed is as the oak.
The scepter, learning, physic, must
All follow this, and come to dust.

Fear no more the lightning-flash,
  Nor the all-dreaded thunder-stone:

Fear not slander, censure rash;
   Thou hast finished joy and moan.
All lovers young, all lovers must
Consign to thee, and come to dust.

(Cymbeline)

Full Fathom Five

Full fathom five thy father lies;
   Of his bones are coral made;
Those are pearls, that were his eyes;
   Nothing of him that doth fade
But doth suffer a sea-change
Into something rich and strange.
Sea-nymphs hourly ring his knell.
   Ding-dong!
Hark, now I hear them
   Ding dong, bell!

(The Tempest)

FROM *Sonnets*

18

Shall I compare thee to a summer's day?
Thou are more lovely and more temperate.
Rough winds do shake the darling buds of May,
And summer's lease hath all too short a date.
Sometime too hot the eye of heaven shines,
And often is his gold complexion dimmed;
And every fair from fair sometime declines,
By chance, or nature's changing course, untrimmed;
But thy eternal summer shall not fade
Nor lose possession of that fair thou ow'st,[1]
Nor shall Death brag thou wand'rest in his shade
When in eternal lines to time thou grow'st.
   So long as men can breathe or eyes can see,
   So long lives this, and this gives life to thee.

---

[1] beauty you possess.

29

When, in disgrace with fortune and men's eyes,
I all alone beweep my outcast state,
And trouble deaf heaven with my bootless cries,
And look upon myself and curse my fate,
Wishing me like to one more rich in hope,
Featured like him, like him with friends possessed,
Desiring this man's art, and that man's scope,
With what I most enjoy contented least;
Yet in these thoughts myself almost despising,
Haply I think on thee, and then my state,
Like to the lark at break of day arising
From sullen earth, sings hymns at heaven's gate;
    For thy sweet love remembered such wealth brings
    That then I scorn to change my state with kings.

30

When to the sessions[1] of sweet silent thought
I summon up remembrance of things past,
I sigh the lack of many a thing I sought
And with old woes new wail my dear time's waste.
Then can I drown an eye (unused to flow)
For precious friends hid in death's dateless night,
And weep afresh love's long since canceled woe,
And moan th' expense[2] of many a vanished sight.
Then can I grieve at grievances foregone,
And heavily from woe to woe tell o'er
The sad account of fore-bemoanéd moan,
Which I new pay as if not paid before.
    But if the while I think on thee, dear friend,
    All losses are restored and sorrows end.

[1] sittings of a court of justice.
[2] loss.

66

Tired with all these, for restful death I cry:
As, to behold desert[1] a beggar born,
And needy nothing trimmed in jollity,[2]
And purest faith unhappily forsworn,

[1] merit.
[2] emptiness clothed in finery.

And gilded honor shamefully misplaced,
And maiden virtue rudely strumpeted,
And right perfection wrongfully disgraced,
And strength by limping sway disabled,
And art made tongue-tied by authority,
And folly (doctor-like) controlling skill,
And simple truth miscalled simplicity,[3]
And captive good attending captain ill.
   Tired with all these, from these would I be gone,
   Save that, to die, I leave my love alone.

[3] ignorance, silliness.

73

That time of year thou mayst in me behold
When yellow leaves, or none, or few, do hang
Upon those boughs which shake against the cold,
Bare ruined choirs where late the sweet birds sang.
In me thou see'st the twilight of such day
As after sunset fadeth in the West,
Which by-and-by black night doth take away,
Death's second self, that seals up all in rest.
In me thou see'st the glowing of such fire
That on the ashes of his youth doth lie,
As the deathbed whereon it must expire,
Consumed with that which it was nourished by.
   This thou perceiv'st, which makes thy love more strong,
   To love that well which thou must leave ere long.

106

When in the chronicle of wasted time
I see descriptions of the fairest wights,[1]
And beauty making beautiful old rhyme
In praise of ladies dead and lovely knights,
Then, in the blazon of sweet beauty's best,
Of hand, of foot, of lip, of eye, of brow,
I see their antique pen would have expressed
Even such a beauty as you master now.
So all their praises are but prophecies
Of this our time, all you prefiguring;

[1] persons.

And, for they looked but with divining eyes,[2]
They had not skill enough your worth to sing;
   For we, which now behold these present days,
   Have eyes to wonder, but lack tongues to praise.

THOMAS NASHE [1567–1601]

Spring, the Sweet Spring

Spring, the sweet spring, is the year's pleasant king,
Then blooms each thing, then maids dance in a ring,
Cold doth not sting, the pretty birds do sing:
   Cuckoo, jug-jug, pu-we, to-witta-woo!

The palm and may make country houses gay,
Lambs frisk and play, the shepherds pipe all day,
And we hear aye birds tune this merry lay:
   Cuckoo, jug-jug, pu-we, to-witta-woo!

The fields breathe sweet, the daisies kiss our feet,
Young lovers meet, old wives a-sunning sit,
In every street these tunes our ears do greet:
   Cuckoo, jug-jug, pu-we, to-witta-woo!
     Spring, the sweet spring!

THOMAS CAMPION [1567–1620]

Rose-Cheeked Laura

Rose-cheeked Laura, come,
Sing thou smoothly with thy beauty's
Silent music, either other
   Sweetly gracing.

[2] because they looked only with eyes that saw into the future.

Lonely forms do flow
From concent divinely framéd;
Heav'n is music, and thy beauty's
    Birth is heavenly.

These dull notes we sing
Discords need for helps to grace them;
Only beauty purely loving
    Knows no discord,

But still moves delight,
Like clear springs renewed by flowing,
Ever perfect, ever in them-
    Selves eternal.

SIR JOHN DAVIES [1569–1626]

FROM *Orchestra*[1]

"If then fire, air, wandering and fixéd lights,   330
In every province of th' imperial sky,
Yield perfect forms of dancing to your sights,
In vain I teach the ear that which the eye
With certain view already doth descry;
But for your eyes perceive not all they see,
In this I will your senses' master be.

"For lo, the sea that fleets about the land
And like a girdle clips her solid waist
Music and measure both doth understand,   340
For his great crystal eye is always cast
Up to the moon and on her fixéd fast,
And as she danceth in her pallid sphere,
So danceth he about the center here.

"Sometimes his proud green waves in order set,
One after other, flow unto the shore;
Which when they have with many kisses wet

[1] Love is persuading men to dance.

They ebb away in order, as before;
And to make known his courtly love the more
He oft doth lay aside his three-forkéd mace   350
And with his arms the timorous earth embrace.

"Only the earth doth stand forever still:
Her rocks remove not, nor her mountains meet,
Although some wits enriched with learning's skill
Say heaven stands firm and that the earth doth fleet
And swiftly turneth underneath their feet;
Yet, though the earth is ever steadfast seen,
On her broad breast hath dancing ever been.

"For those blue veins that through her body spread,
Those sapphire streams which from great hills do spring,   360
The earth's great dugs, for every wight[2] is fed
With sweet fresh moisture from them issuing,
Observe a dance in their wild wandering;
And still their dance begets a murmur sweet,
And still the murmur with the dance doth meet.

"Of all their ways, I love Meander's[3] path,
Which, to the tunes of dying swans, doth dance
Such winding sleights. Such turns and tricks he hath,
Such creeks, such wrenches, and such dalliance,
That, whether it be hap or heedless chance,   370
In his indented course and wriggling play
He seems to dance a perfect cunning hay.

"But wherefore do these streams forever run?
To keep themselves forever sweet and clear.
For, let their everlasting course be done,
They straight corrupt and foul with mud appear.
O ye sweet nymphs, that beauty's loss do fear,
Condemn the drugs that physic doth devise
And learn of Love this dainty exercise.

"See how those flowers, that have sweet beauty too,   380
The only jewels that the earth doth wear
When the young sun in bravery her doth woo,
As oft as they the whistling wind do hear

---

[2] living being.
[3] a winding river in Asia Minor.

109

Do wave their tender bodies here and there;
And though their dance no perfect measure is,
Yet oftentimes their music makes them kiss.

"What makes the vine about the elm to dance
With turnings, windings, and embracements round?
What makes the lodestone to the north advance
His subtle point, as if from thence he found   390
His chief attractive virtue to redound?
Kind nature first doth cause all things to love;
Love makes them dance, and in just order move.

"Hark how the birds do sing, and mark then how,
Jump with the modulation of their lays,
They lightly leap and skip from bough to bough;
Yet do the cranes deserve a greater praise,
Which keep such measure in their airy ways
As when they all in order rankéd are
They make a perfect form triangular.   400

"In the chief angle flies the watchful guide,
And all the followers their heads do lay
On their foregoers' backs, on either side;
But, for the captain hath no rest to stay
His head, forwearied with the windy way,
He back retires, and then the next behind
As his lieutenant leads them through the wind.

"But why relate I every singular,
Since all the world's great fortunes and affairs
Forward and backward rapt and whirléd are,   410
According to the music of the spheres;
And Chance herself her nimble feet upbears
On a round slippery wheel, that rolleth aye,
And turns all states with her impetuous sway?

"Learn then to dance, you that are princes born,
And lawful lords of earthly creatures all;
Imitate them, and thereof take no scorn,
For this new art to them is natural.
And imitate the stars celestial;
For when pale Death your vital twist shall sever,   420
Your better parts must dance with them forever."

Thus Love persuades, and all the crown[4] of men
That stands around doth make a murmuring,
As when the wind, loos'd from his hollow den,
Among the trees a gentle bass doth sing,
Or as a brook through pebbles wandering.
But in their looks they uttered this plain speech:
That they would learn to dance if Love would teach.

[4] ring; in Latin, "corona," crown, may mean a crowd.

JOHN DONNE [1572–1631]

Love's Alchemy: Mummy

Some that have deeper digged love's mine than I,
Say where his centric happiness doth lie.
      I have loved, and got, and told,
But should I love, get, tell, till I were old,
I should not find that hidden mystery.
      O, 'tis imposture all!
And as no chemic yet th' elixir got,
      But glorifies his pregnant pot
      If by the way to him befall
Some odorif'rous thing, or med'cinal,   10
      So lovers dream a rich and long delight,
      But get a winter-seeming summer's night.

Our ease, our thrift, our honor, and our day,
Shall we for this vain bubble's shadow pay?
      Ends love in this, that my man
Can be as happy's I can, if he can
Endure the short scorn of a bridegroom's play?
      That loving wretch that swears
'Tis not the bodies marry, but the minds
      (Which he in her angelic finds),
      Would swear as justly that he hears,
In that day's rude, hoarse minstrelsy, the spheres.
      Hope not for mind in women. At their best
      Sweetness and wit, they're but mummy[1] possessed.

[1] powder from a mummified body used as a drug.

Song

Go and catch a falling star,
 Get with child a mandrake root,
Tell me where all past years are,
 Or who cleft the devil's foot;
Teach me to hear mermaids singing,
Or to keep off envy's stinging,
 And find
 What wind
Serves to advance an honest mind.

If thou be'st born to strange sights,   10
 Things invisible to see,
Ride ten thousand days and and nights
 Till age snow white hairs on thee;
Thou, when thou return'st, wilt tell me
All strange wonders that befell thee,
 And swear
 No where
Lives a woman true, and fair.

If thou find'st one, let me know;
 Such a pilgrimage were sweet.   20
Yet do not; I would not go,
 Though at next door we might meet.
Though she were true when you met her,
And last, till you write your letter,
 Yet she
 Will be
False, ere I come, to two, or three.

A Valediction Forbidding Mourning

As virtuous men pass mildly away,
 And whisper to their souls to go,
Whilst some of their sad friends do say,
 The breath goes now, and some say, No:

So let us melt, and make no noise,
 No tear-floods, nor sigh-tempests move;

'Twere profanation of our joys
  To tell the laity our love.

Moving of th' earth brings harms and fears,
  Men reckon what it did, and meant;   10
But trepidation of the spheres,[1]
  Though greater far, is innocent.

Dull sublunary[2] lovers' love
  (Whose soul is sense) cannot admit
Absence, because it doth remove
  Those things which elemented it.

But we by a love so much refined
  That ourselves know not what it is,
Inter-assuréd of the mind,
  Care less eyes, lips and hands to miss.   20

Our two souls therefore, which are one,
  Though I must go, endure not yet
A breach, but an expansion,
  Like gold to airy thinness beat.

If they be two, they are two so
  As still twin compasses are two;
Thy soul, the fixed foot, makes no show
  To move, but doth, if th' other do.

And though it in the center sit,
  Yet, when the other far doth roam,   30
It leans, and hearkens after it,
  And grows erect, as that comes home.

Such wilt thou be to me, who must,
  Like th' other foot, obliquely run;
Thy firmness makes my circle just,
  And makes me end where I begun.

ELEGIE 9 *The Autumnal*

No spring, nor summer beauty hath such grace,
  As I have seen in one autumnal face.

[1] An attempt to explain oscillation of heavenly bodies while still maintaining the belief in a stationary earth.
[2] under the moon, earthly, and therefore subject to mutability.

113

Young beauties force our love, and that's a rape,
  This doth but counsel, yet you cannot 'scape.
If t'were a shame to love, here t'were no shame,
  Affection here takes reverence's name.
Were her first years the Golden Age; that's true,
  But now she's gold oft tried, and ever new.
That was her torrid and inflaming time,
  This is her tolerable tropic clime.
Fair eyes, who asks more heat than comes from hence,
  He in a fever wishes pestilence.
Call not these wrinkles, graves; if graves they were,
  They were love's graves; for else he is no where.
Yet lies not love dead here, but here doth sit
  Vowed to this trench, like an anchorite.
And here, till hers, which must be his death, come,
  He doth not dig a grave, but build a tomb.
Here dwells he, though he sojourn every where,
  In progress,[1] yet his standing house is here.
Here, where still evening is; not noon, nor night,
  Where no voluptuousness, yet all delight.
In all her words, unto all hearers fit,
  You may at revels, you at counsel, sit.
This is love's timber, youth his under-wood;
  There he, as wine in June, enrages blood,
Which then comes seasonabliest, when our taste
  And appetite to other things, is past.
Xerxes strange Lydian love, the platan tree,[2]
  Was loved for age, none being so large as she,
Or else because, being young, nature did bless
  Her youth with age's glory, barrenness.
If we love things long sought, age is a thing
  Which we are fifty years in compassing.
If transitory things, which soon decay,
  Age must be loveliest at the latest day.
But name not winter faces, whose skin's slack;
  Lank, as an unthrift's purse; but a soul's sack;
Whose eyes seek light within, for all here's shade;
  Whose mouths are holes, rather worn out, than made,

[1] state journey of royalty.
  [2] Xerxes the Great was smitten by the plane-tree's beauty and had it decorated with gold.

Whose every tooth to a several place is gone,
 To vex their souls at resurrection;
Name not these living deaths-heads unto me,
 For these, not ancient, but antique be.
I hate extremes; yet I had rather stay
 With tombs than cradles, to wear out a day.
Since such love's natural lation[3] is, may still
 My love descend, and journey down the hill,
Not panting after growing beauties, so,
 I shall ebb out with them, who homeward go.

FROM *Holy Sonnets*

7

At the round earth's imagined corners, blow
Your trumpets, angels; and arise, arise
From death, you numberless infinities
Of souls, and to your scattered bodies go;
All whom the flood did, and fire shall, o'erthrow,
All whom war, dearth, age, agues, tyrannies,
Despair, law, chance hath slain, and you whose eyes
Shall behold God, and never taste death's woe.
But let them sleep, Lord, and me mourn a space;
For, if above all these, my sins abound,
'Tis late to ask abundance of Thy grace
When we are there. Here on this lowly ground,
Teach me how to repent; for that's as good
As if Thou hadst sealed my pardon with Thy blood.

14

Batter my heart, three-personed God; for You
As yet but knock, breathe, shine, and seek to mend;
That I may rise and stand, o'erthrow me, and bend
Your force to break, blow, burn, and make me new.
I, like an usurped town, to another due,
Labor to admit You, but O, to no end;
Reason, Your viceroy in me, me should defend,
But is captived, and proves weak or untrue.

---

[3] motion (astrology).

Yet dearly I love You, and would be loved fain,
But am bethrothed unto Your enemy.
Divorce me, untie or break that knot again;
Take me to You, imprison me, for I,
Except You enthrall me, never shall be free,
Nor ever chaste, except You ravish me.

BEN JONSON [1572–1637]

Clerimont's Song

Still to be neat, still to be dressed
As you were going to a feast:
Still to be powdered, still perfumed:
Lady, it is to be presumed,
Though art's hid causes are not found,
All is not sweet, all is not sound.

Give me a look, give me a face
That makes simplicity a grace;
Robes loosely flowing, hair as free:
Such sweet neglect more taketh me,
Than all the adulteries of art,
That strike mine eyes, but not my heart.

The Triumph of Charis

See the chariot at hand here of Love,
   Wherein my lady rideth!
Each that draws is a swan or a dove,
   And well the car Love guideth.
As she goes, all hearts do duty
      Unto her beauty;
And enamored do wish, so they might
      But enjoy such a sight,
That they still were to run by her side,
Through swords, through seas, whither she would ride.   10

Do but look on her eyes, they do light
  All that Love's world compriseth!
Do but look on her hair, it is bright
  As Love's star when it riseth!
Do but mark, her forehead's smoother
    Than words that soothe her;
And from her arched brows such a grace
    Sheds itself through the face,
As alone there triumphs to the life
All the gain, all the good of the elements' strife.   20

Have you seen but a bright lily grow
  Before rude hands have touched it?
Have you marked but the fall of the snow
  Before the soil hath smutched it?
Have you felt the wool o' the beaver,
    Or swan's down ever?
Or have smelt o' the bud o' the brier,
    Or the nard¹ i' the fire?
Or have tasted the bag o' the bee?
Oh so white, oh so soft, oh so sweet is she!   30

JOHN WEBSTER [1580?–1638]

Cornelia's Song

Call for the robin-redbreast, and the wren,
Since o'er shady groves they hover.
And with leaves and flowers do cover
The friendless bodies of unburied men.
Call unto his funeral dole
The ant, the field-mouse, and the mole,
To rear him hillocks that shall keep him warm,
And, when gay tombs are robbed, sustain no harm;
But keep the wolf far thence, that's foe to men,
For with his nails he'll dig them up again.

                                          (*The White Devil*)

¹ a sweet-smelling ointment.

Hark, now everything is still;
The screech-owl and the whistler shrill
Call upon our dame aloud,
And bid her quickly don her shroud;
Much you had of land and rent,
Your length in clay's now competent.
A long war disturbed your mind;
Here your perfect peace is signed.
Of what is 't fools make such vain keeping?
Sin their conception, their birth weeping,
Their life a general mist of error,
Their death a hideous storm of terror.
Strew your hair with powders sweet,
Don clean linen, bathe your feet,
And, the foul fiend more to check,
A crucifix let bless your neck;
'Tis now full tide, 'tween night and day,
End your groan and come away.

(The Duchess of Malfi)

ROBERT HERRICK [1591–1674]

To the Virgins, to Make Much of Time

Gather ye rosebuds while ye may:
    Old Time is still a-flying,
And this same flower that smiles to-day
    Tomorrow will be dying.

The glorious lamp of heaven, the sun,
    The higher he's a-getting,
The sooner will his race be run,
    And nearer he's to setting.

That age is best which is the first,
    When youth and blood are warmer;

But, being spent, the worse, and worst
   Times, still succeed the former.

Then be not coy, but use your time,
   And while ye may, go marry:
For having lost but once your prime,
   You may for ever tarry.

To Daffodils

Fair daffodils, we weep to see
   You haste away so soon:
As yet the early rising sun
   Has not attained his noon.
      Stay, stay,
    Until the hasting day
      Has run
    But to the Evensong;
And, having prayed together, we
    Will go with you along.

We have short time to stay, as you,
   We have as short a spring;
As quick a growth to meet decay,
   As you, or any thing.
      We die,
As your hours do, and dry
      Away,
   Like to the summer's rain;
Or as the pearls of morning's dew
    Ne'er to be found again.

Upon Julia's Clothes

Whenas in silks my Julia goes,
Then, then, methinks how sweetly flows
The liquefaction of her clothes.

Next, when I cast mine eyes, and see
That brave vibration, each way free,
O, how that glittering taketh me!

The Collar

I struck the board,[1] and cried, No more.
　　I will abroad.
What? shall I ever sigh and pine?
My lines and life are free; free as the road,
Loose as the wind, as large as store.[2]
　　　　Shall I be still in suit?
Have I no harvest but a thorn
To let me blood, and not restore
What I have lost with cordial fruit?
　　　　Sure there was wine　　　　　　　　　　10
Before my sighs did dry it: there was corn
　　Before my tears did drown it.
Is the year only lost to me?
　　Have I no bays[3] to crown it?
No flowers, no garlands gay? all blasted?
　　　　All wasted?
Not so, my heart: but there is fruit,
　　And thou hast hands.
Recover all thy sigh-blown age
On double pleasures: leave thy cold dispute　　　20
Of what is fit and not; forsake thy cage,
　　　　Thy rope of sands,
Which petty thoughts have made, and made to thee
Good cable, to enforce and draw,
　　　　And be thy law,
While thou didst wink and would not see.
　　　　Away; take heed:
　　　　I will abroad.
Call in thy death's-head there: tie up thy fears.
　　　　He that forbears　　　　　　　　　　30
To suit and serve his need,
　　Deserves his load.

---

[1] table.
[2] abundance.
[3] laurel wreath, symbol of honor.

But as I raved and grew more fierce and wild
      At every word,
Methought I heard one calling, *Child*;
      And I replied, *My Lord*.

The Altar

A broken A L T A R, Lord, thy servant rears,
Made of a heart, and cemented with tears:
  Whose parts are as thy hand did frame;
  No workman's tool hath touched the same.
        A H E A R T alone
        Is such a stone ,
        As nothing but
        Thy power doth cut.
        Wherefore each part
        Of my hard heart
        Meets in this frame,
        To praise thy Name:
  That, if I chance to hold my peace,
  These stones to praise thee may not cease.
O let thy blessed S A C R I F I C E be mine,
And sanctify this A L T A R to be thine.

Redemption

Having been tenant long to a rich Lord,
  Not thriving, I resolved to be bold,
  And make a suit unto him, to afford
A new small-rented lease, and cancel th' old.
In heaven at his manor I him sought:
  They told me there, that he was lately gone
  About some land, which he had dearly bought
Long since on earth, to take possession.
I straight returned, and knowing his great birth,
  Sought him accordingly in great resorts;
  In cities, theaters, gardens, parks, and courts:
At length I heard a ragged noise and mirth
  Of thieves and murderers: there I him espied,
  Who straight, *Your suit is granted*, said, and died.

Prayer (1)

Prayer the Churches banquet, Angels age,
  Gods breath in man returning to his birth,
  The soul in paraphrase, heart in pilgrimage,
The Christian plummet sounding heaven and earth;
Engine against th' Almighty, sinners tower,
  Reversed thunder, Christ-side-piercing spear,
  The six-days' world transposing in an hour,
A kind of tune, which all things hear and fear;
Softness, and peace, and joy, and love, and bliss,
  Exalted Manna, gladness of the best,
  Heaven in ordinary, man well dressed,
The milky way, the bird of Paradise,
  Church-bells beyond the stars heard, the souls blood,
  The land of spices; something understood.

Artillery

As I one evening sat before my cell,
Me thoughts a star did shoot into my lap.
I rose, and shook my clothes, as knowing well,
That from small fires comes oft no small mishap.
  When suddenly I heard one say,
  Do as thou usest, disobey,
  Expel good motions[1] *from thy breast,*
Which have the face of fire, but end in rest.

I, who had heard of music in the spheres,
But not of speech in stars, began to muse: 10
But turning to my God, whose ministers
The stars and all things are; If I refuse,
  Dread Lord, said I, so oft my good;
  Then I refuse not ev'n with blood
  To wash away my stubborn thought:
For I will do or suffer what I ought.

But I have also stars and shooters[2] too,
Born where thy servants both artilleries use.

[1] impulses.
[2] shooting stars.

122

My tears and prayers night and day do woo,
And work up to thee; yet thou dost refuse.   20
   Not but I am (I must say still)
   Much more obliged to do thy will,
    Then thou to grant mine: but because
Thy promise now hath ev'n set thee thy laws.

Then we are shooters both, and thou dost deign
To enter combat with us, and contest
With thine own clay. But I would parley fain:
Shun not my arrows, and behold my breast.
   Yet if thou shunnest, I am thine:
   I must be so, if I am mine.   30
   There is no articling[3] with thee:
I am but finite, yet thine infinitely.

THOMAS CAREW [1594?–1640?]

A Song

   Ask me no more where Jove bestows,
   When June is past, the fading rose;
   For in your beauty's orient deep
   These flowers, as in their causes, sleep.

   Ask me no more whither do stray
   The golden atoms of the day;
   For, in pure love, heaven did prepare
   Those powders to enrich your hair.

   Ask me no more whither doth haste
   The nightingale, when May is past;
   For in your sweet dividing throat
   She winters, and keeps warm her note.

   Ask me no more where those stars light
   That downwards fall in dead of night;
   For in your eyes they sit, and there
   Fixed become, as in their sphere.

[3] bargaining.

Ask me no more if east or west
The phoenix[1] builds her spicy nest;
For unto you at last she flies,
And in your fragrant bosom dies.

[1] a mythical Egyptian bird believed to live for five hundred years, to consume itself in flames, and to rise from its own ashes.

JOHN MILTON [1608–1674]

Lycidas

Yet once more, O ye laurels, and once more,
Ye myrtles brown, with ivy never sere,
I come to pluck your berries harsh and crude,
And with forced fingers rude
Shatter your leaves before the mellowing year.
Bitter constraint and sad occasion dear
Compels me to disturb your season due:
For Lycidas[1] is dead, dead ere his prime,
Young Lycidas, and hath not left his peer.
Who would not sing for Lycidas? he knew   10
Himself to sing, and build the lofty rhyme.
He must not float upon his watery bier
Unwept, and welter[2] to the parching wind,
Without the meed[3] of some melodious tear.
   Begin then, Sisters[4] of the sacred well
That from beneath the seat of Jove doth spring;
Begin, and somewhat loudly sweep the string;
Hence with denial vain and coy excuse:
So may some gentle Muse
With lucky words favor *my* destined urn;   20
And as he passes, turn
And bid fair peace be to my sable shroud.

[1] a pastoral name for Edward King, a fellow student of Milton's at Cambridge, who drowned in the Irish seas in 1637.
[2] toss about.
[3] gift.
[4] the Muses.

For we were nursed upon the self-same hill,
Fed the same flock by fountain, shade, and rill.
Together both, ere the high lawns appeared
Under the opening eye-lids of the Morn,
We drove a-field, and both together heard
What time the gray-fly winds her sultry horn,
Battening our flocks with the fresh dews of night;
Oft till the star, that rose at evening bright,   30
Toward heaven's descent had sloped his westering wheel.
Meanwhile the rural ditties were not mute;
Tempered to the oaten flute,
Rough Satyrs danced, and Fauns with cloven heel
From the glad sound would not be absent long;
And old Damoetas[5] loved to hear our song.

But, O! the heavy change, now thou art gone,
Now thou art gone, and never must return!
Thee, Shepherd, thee the woods and desert caves,
With wild thyme and the gadding vine o'ergrown,   40
And all their echoes, mourn:
The willows and the hazel copses green
Shall now no more be seen
Fanning their joyous leaves to thy soft lays.
As killing as the canker to the rose,
Or taint-worm to the weanling herds that graze,
Or frost to flowers, that their gay wardrobe wear
When first the white-thorn blows;
Such, Lycidas, thy loss to shepherd's ear.

Where were ye, Nymphs, when the remorseless deep   50
Closed o'er the head of your loved Lycidas?
For neither were ye playing on the steep
Where your old bards, the famous Druids, lie,
Nor on the shaggy top of Mona high,
Nor yet where Deva[6] spreads her wizard stream.
Ay me! I fondly dream
"Had ye been there,"—for what could that have done?
What could the Muse herself that Orpheus[7] bore,
The Muse herself, for her enchanting son,

[5] probably a Cambridge tutor.

[6] Deva is a river in Wales; Mona, an island off Wales where the Druids, poets and priests of the ancient Celtic religion, celebrated their rites.

[7] son of Calliope the muse of epic poetry, who was torn to pieces by the Thracian woman.

Whom universal nature did lament, 60
When by the rout that made the hideous roar
His gory visage down the stream was sent,
Down the swift Hebrus to the Lesbian[8] shore?
    Alas! what boots it with uncessant care
To tend the homely, slighted, shepherd's trade
And strictly meditate the thankless Muse?
Were it not better done, as others use,
To sport with Amaryllis in the shade,
Or with the tangles of Neaera's[9] hair?
Fame is the spur that the clear spirit doth raise 70
(That last infirmity of noble mind)
To scorn delights, and live laborious days;
But the fair guerdon when we hope to find,
And think to burst out into sudden blaze,
Comes the blind Fury[10] with the abhorred shears
And slits the thin-spun life. "But not the praise,"
Phoebus[11] replied, and touched my trembling ears:
"Fame is no plant that grows on mortal soil,
Nor in the glistering foil
Set off to the world, nor in broad rumor lies: 80
But lives and spreads aloft by those pure eyes
And perfect witness of all-judging Jove;
As he pronounces lastly on each deed,
Of so much fame in heaven expect thy meed."
    O fountain Arethuse, and thou honored flood,
Smooth-sliding Mincius,[12] crowned with vocal reeds,
That strain I heard was of a higher mood.
But now my oat proceeds,
And listens to the herald of the sea
That came in Neptune's plea; 90
He asked the waves, and asked the felon winds,
What hard mishap hath doomed this gentle swain?
And questioned every gust of rugged wings
That blows from off each beaked promontory:

[8] Orpheus' head was thrown into the Hebrus river, and floated to the island Lesbos.
[9] Amaryllis and Naera are pastoral maidens.
[10] Atropos, one of the three Fates, who cuts the thread of life.
[11] Apollo, god of poetry.
[12] Arethuse and Mincius are a fountain and river associated with pastoral poetry.

They knew not of his story;
And sage Hippotades[13] their answer brings,
That not a blast was from his dungeon strayed;
The air was calm, and on the level brine
Sleek Panope[14] with all her sisters played.
It was that fatal and perfidious bark,   100
Built in the eclipse, and rigged with curses dark,
That sunk so low that sacred head of thine.

    Next Camus,[15] reverend sire, went footing slow,
His mantle hairy, and his bonnet sedge,
Inwrought with figures dim, and on the edge
Like to that sanguine flower[16] inscribed with woe.
"Ah! who hath reft," quoth he, "my dearest pledge?"
Last came, and last did go
The Pilot of the Galilean lake;
Two massy keys[17] he bore of metals twain   110
(The golden opes, the iron shuts amain);
He shook his mitred[18] locks, and stern bespake:
"How well could I have spared for thee, young swain,
Enow of such, as for their bellies' sake
Creep and intrude and climb into the fold!
Of other care they little reckoning make
Than how to scramble at the shearers' feast,
And shove away the worthy bidden guest.
Blind mouths! that scarce themselves know how to hold
A sheep-hook, or have learned aught else the least   120
That to the faithful herdman's art belongs!
What recks it them? What need they? They are sped;
And when they list, their lean and flashy songs
Grate on their scrannel pipes of wretched straw;
The hungry sheep look up, and are not fed,
But, swoll'n with wind and the rank mist they draw,
Rot inwardly, and foul contagion spread:
Besides what the grim wolf with privy paw
Daily devours apace, and nothing said:

[13] Aeolus, god of winds.
[14] a sea nymph.
[15] personification of the River Cam, Cambridge.
[16] the hyacinth, which sprang from the blood of Hyacinthus, a young boy loved and accidentally killed by Apollo.
[17] keys of the kingdom of heaven given to St. Peter (the "Pilot") by Christ.
[18] miter: bishops' headdress.

—But that two-handed engine at the door   130
Stands ready to smite once, and smite no more."
    Return, Alpheus;[19] the dread voice is past
That shrunk thy streams; return, Sicilian Muse,
And call the vales, and bid them hither cast
Their bells and flowerets of a thousand hues.
Ye valleys low, where the mild whispers use
Of shades, and wanton winds, and gushing brooks
On whose fresh lap the swart star[20] sparely looks;
Throw hither all your quaint enameled eyes
That on the green turf suck the honeyed showers,   140
And purple all the ground with vernal flowers.
Bring the rathe primrose that forsaken dies,
The tufted crow-toe, and pale jessamine,
The white pink, and the pansy freaked with jet,
The glowing violet,
The musk-rose, and the well-attired woodbine,
With cowslips wan that hang the pensive head,
And every flower that sad embroidery wears;
Bid amaranthus[21] all his beauty shed,
And daffadillies fill their cups with tears   150
To strew the laureate hearse where Lycid lies.
For so to interpose a little ease,
Let our frail thoughts dally with false surmise.
Ay me! whilst thee the shores and sounding seas
Wash far away, where'er thy bones are hurled;
Whether beyond the stormy Hebrides
Where thou, perhaps, under the whelming tide,
Visit'st the bottom of the monstrous world;
Or whether thou, to our moist vows denied,
Sleep'st by the fable of Bellerus old,   160
Where the great Vision of the guarded mount[22]
Looks toward Namancos and Bayona's hold.[23]
    Look homeward, Angel, now, and melt with ruth:

[19] river god in love with Arethusa.
[20] Sirius, the Dog Star, whose rising in the late summer brings heat which may burn the landscape.
[21] an imaginary flower that never fades.
[22] Bellerus is a legendary hero after whom the Romans named a part of Cornwall, where there is a mountain guarded by the archangel Michael.
[23] a Spanish fortification in Namancos, a mountainous region on the north-west coast of Spain.

128

And, O ye dolphins, waft the hapless youth!
Weep no more, woeful shepherds, weep no more,
For Lycidas, your sorrow, is not dead,
Sunk though he be beneath the watery floor;
So sinks the day-star in the ocean bed,
And yet anon repairs his drooping head,
And tricks his beams, and with new-spangled ore   170
Flames in the forehead of the morning sky:
So Lycidas sunk low, but mounted high
Through the dear might of Him that walked the waves;
Where, other groves and other streams along,
With nectar pure his oozy locks he laves,
And hears the unexpressive nuptial song
In the blest kingdoms meek of joy and love.
There entertain him all the saints above
In solemn troops, and sweet societies,
That sing, and singing in their glory move,   180
And wipe the tears for ever from his eyes.
Now, Lycidas, the shepherds weep no more;
Henceforth thou art the Genius of the shore
In thy large recompense, and shalt be good
To all that wander in that perilous flood.
Thus sang the uncouth swain to the oaks and rills,
While the still morn went out with sandals gray;
He touched the tender stops of various quills,
With eager thought warbling his Doric[24] lay:
And now the sun had stretched out all the hills,   190
And now was dropt into the western bay.
At last he rose, and twitched his mantle blue:
Tomorrow to fresh woods, and pastures new.

FROM *Paradise Lost*, BOOK I

Thus Satan talking to his nearest mate
With head uplift above the wave, and eyes
That sparkling blazed; his other parts besides,
Prone on the flood, extended long and large,
Lay floating many a rood, in bulk as huge
As whom the fables name of monstrous size,

[24] dialect in which Greek pastorals were written.

Titanian or Earth-born, that warred on Jove,
Briareos or Typhon,[1] whom the den
By ancient Tarsus held, or that sea-beast   200
Leviathan, which God of all his works
Created hugest that swim the ocean stream:
Him haply slumbering on the Norway foam,
The pilot of some small night-foundered skiff,
Deeming some island, oft, as seamen tell,
With fixéd anchor in his scaly rind,
Moors by his side under the lee, while night
Invests the sea, and wishéd morn delays:
So stretched out huge in length the Arch-Fiend lay
Chained on the burning lake; nor ever thence   210
Had risen or heaved his head, but that the will
And high permission of all-ruling Heaven
Left him at large to his own dark designs,
That with reiterated crimes he might
Heap on himself damnation, while he sought
Evil to others, and enraged might see
How all his malice served but to bring forth
Infinite goodness, grace and mercy shown
On Man by him seduced, but on himself
Treble confusion, wrath and vengeance poured.   220
    Forthwith upright he rears from off the pool
His mighty stature; on each hand the flames
Driven backward slope their pointing spires, and rolled
In billows, leave in the midst a horrid vale.
Then with expanded wings he steers his flight
Aloft, incumbent on the dusky air
That felt unusual weight till on dry land
He lights, if it were land that ever burned
With solid, as the lake with liquid fire,
And such appeared in hue; as when the force   230
Of subterranean wind transports a hill
Torn from Pelorus,[2] or the shattered side
Of thundering Aetna, whose combustible
And fueled entrails thence conceiving fire,
Sublimed with mineral fury, aid the winds,
And leave a singéd bottom all involved
With stench and smoke: such resting found the sole

[1] giants who warred in heaven.
[2] promontory near Mt. Aetna.

Of unblest feet. Him followed his next mate,
Both glorying to have escaped the Stygian[3] flood
As gods, and by their own recovered strength,   240
Not by the sufferance of supernal power.
    "Is this the region, this the soil, the clime,"
Said then the lost Archangel, "this the seat
That we must change for Heaven, this mournful gloom
For that celestial light? Be it so, since he
Who now is sovereign can dispose and bid
What shall be right. Farthest from him is best,
Whom reason hath equaled, force hath made supreme
Above his equals. Farewell happy fields
Where joy for ever dwells: Hail horrors, hail   250
Infernal world, and thou profoundest Hell
Receive thy new possessor: one who brings
A mind not to be changed by place or time.
The mind is its own place, and in itself
Can make a Heaven of Hell, a Hell of Heaven.
What matter where, if I be still the same,
And what I should be, all but less than he
Whom thunder hath made greater? Here at least
We shall be free; the Almighty hath not built
Here for his envy, will not drive us hence: 260
Here we may reign secure, and in my choice
To reign is worth ambition, though in Hell:
Better to reign in Hell than serve in Heaven...."

FROM BOOK IV

Two of far nobler shape erect and tall,
God-like erect, with native honor clad
In naked majesty seemed lords of all,   290
And worthy seemed, for in their looks divine
The image of their glorious Maker shone,
Truth, wisdom, sanctitude severe and pure,
Severe but in true filial freedom placed;
Whence true authority in men; though both
Not equal, as their sex not equal seemed;
For contemplation he and valor formed,

---

[3] Styx is a river in the underworld.

For softness she and sweet attractive grace;
He for God only, she for God in him.
His fair large front and eye sublime declared   300
Absolute rule; and hyacinthine locks
Round from his parted forelock manly hung
Clustering, but not beneath his shoulders broad:
She as a veil down to the slender waist
Her unadornéd golden tresses wore
Disheveled, but in wanton ringlets waved
As the vine curls her tendrils, which implied
Subjection, but required with gentle sway,
And by her yielded, by him best received,
Yielded with coy submission, modest pride,   310
And sweet reluctant amorous delay.
Nor those mysterious parts were then concealed;
Then was not guilty shame, dishonest shame
Of Nature's works, honor dishonorable,
Sin-bred, how have ye troubled all mankind
With shows instead, mere shows of seeming pure,
And banished from man's life his happiest life,
Simplicity and spotless innocence.
So passed they naked on, nor shunned the sight
Of God or angel, for they thought no ill;   320
So hand in hand they passed, the loveliest pair
That ever since in love's embraces met:
Adam the goodliest man of men since born
His sons, the fairest of her daughters Eve.

On His Blindness

When I consider how my light is spent
Ere half my days in this dark world and wide,
And that one talent[1] which is death to hide
Lodged with me useless, though my soul more bent
To serve therewith my Maker, and present
My true account, lest He returning chide,
"Doth God exact day-labor, light denied?"
I fondly ask. But Patience, to prevent

[1] refers to the parable of the servants to whom various talents (weights of
gold) were entrusted. The man who received only one talent neglected it and
deserved the reproach of his master (Matthew, xxv. 14-30).

That murmur, soon replies, "God doth not need
Either man's work or his own gifts. Who best
Bear His mild yoke, they serve Him best. His state
Is kingly: thousands at His bidding speed,
And post o'er land and ocean without rest;
They also serve who only stand and wait."

SIR JOHN SUCKLING [1609–1642]

Song

Why so pale and wan, fond lover?
    Prithee why so pale?
Will, when looking well can't move her,
    Looking ill prevail?
    Prithee why so pale?

Why so dull and mute, young sinner?
    Prithee why so mute?
Will, when speaking well can't win her,
    Saying nothing do 't?
    Prithee why so mute?

Quit, quit, for shame; this will not move,
    This cannot take her;
If of herself she will not love,
    Nothing can make her:
    The devil take her!

RICHARD LOVELACE [1618–1657]

To Lucasta, Going to the Wars

Tell me not, Sweet, I am unkind
    That from the nunnery
Of thy chaste breast and quiet mind
    To war and arms I fly.

True, a new mistress now I chase,
    The first foe in the field;
And with a stronger faith embrace
    A sword, a horse, a shield.

Yet this inconstancy is such
    As you too shall adore;
I could not love thee, Dear, so much,
    Loved I not Honor more.

ANDREW MARVELL [1621–1678]

To His Coy Mistress

Had we but world enough, and time,
This coyness, lady, were no crime.
We would sit down, and think which way
To walk, and pass our long love's day.
Thou by the Indian Ganges' side
Should'st rubies find: I by the tide
Of Humber[1] would complain. I would
Love you ten years before the Flood,
And you should, if you please, refuse
Till the conversion of the Jews.   10
My vegetable love should grow
Vaster than empires, and more slow.
An hundred years should go to praise
Thine eyes, and on thy forehead gaze:
Two hundred to adore each breast:
But thirty thousand to the rest;
An age at least to every part,
And the last age should show your heart.
For, lady, you deserve this state,
Nor would I love at lower rate.   20
    But at my back I always hear
Time's wingèd chariot hurrying near:
And yonder all before us lie
Deserts of vast eternity.

[1] river flowing by Hull, where Marvell lived.

Thy beauty shall no more be found;
Nor, in thy marble vault, shall sound
My echoing song: then worms shall try
That long-preserved virginity,
And your quaint honor turn to dust,
And into ashes all my lust.   30
The grave's a fine and private place,
But none, I think, do there embrace.
    Now, therefore, while the youthful hue
Sits on thy skin like morning dew,
And while thy willing soul transpires
At every pore with instant fires,
Now let us sport us while we may;
And now, like amorous birds of prey,
Rather at once our Time devour,
Than languish in his slow-chapt[2] power.   40
Let us roll all our strength and all
Our sweetness up into one ball,
And tear our pleasures with rough strife
Thorough the iron gates of life.
Thus, though we cannot make our sun
Stand still, yet we will make him run.

[2] slow-devouring.

The Definition of Love

My love is of a birth as rare
As 'tis for object[1] strange and high;
It was begotten by despair
Upon impossibility.

Magnanimous despair alone
Could show me so divine a thing,
Where feeble hope could ne'er have flown,
But vainly flapped its tinsel wing.

And yet I quickly might arrive
Where my extended soul is fixed,   10
But fate does iron wedges drive,
And always crowds itself betwixt.

[1] in the philosophical sense of *objectum,* a thing thrown before the mind.

For fate with jealous eye does see
Two perfect loves, nor lets them close;[2]
Their union would her ruin be,
And her tyrannic power depose.

And therefore her decrees of steel
Us as the distant poles have placed,
Though love's whole world on us doth wheel,
Not by themselves to be embraced;   20

Unless the giddy heaven fall,
And earth some new convulsion tear,
And, us to join, the world should all
Be cramped into a planisphere.[3]

As lines, so loves, oblique may well
Themselves in every angle greet;
But ours so truly parallel,
Though infinite, can never meet.

Therefore the love which us doth bind,
But fate so enviously debars,   30
Is the conjunction of the mind,
And opposition[4] of the stars.

HENRY VAUGHAN [1622–1695]

Peace

My soul, there is a country
    Far beyond the stars,
Where stands a wingéd sentry
    All skillful in the wars:
There, above noise and danger,
    Sweet Peace sits crowned with smiles,

[2] unite.
[3] a sphere represented on a plane.
[4] "conjunction" is the astronomical term for the apparent proximity of two planets or stars; "opposition" is the relative position of two heavenly bodies when exactly opposite each other as seen from the earth's surface.

And One born in a manger
  Commands the beauteous files.
He is thy gracious Friend,
  And—O my soul awake!—
Did in pure love descend,
  To die here for thy sake.
If thou canst get but thither,
  There grows the flower of Peace,
The Rose that cannot wither,
  Thy fortress, and thy ease.
Leave then thy foolish ranges;[1]
  For none can thee secure,
But One, who never changes,
  Thy God, thy life, thy cure.

[1] wanderings.

The Retreat

Happy those early days! when I
Shined in my angel-infancy.
Before I understood this place
Appointed for my second race,
Or taught my soul to fancy aught
But a white, celestial thought;
When yet I had not walked above
A mile or two from my first love,
And looking back, at that short space
Could see a glimpse of his bright face;   10
When on some gilded cloud or flower
My gazing soul would dwell an hour,
And in those weaker glories spy
Some shadows of eternity;
Before I taught my tongue to wound
My conscience with a sinful sound,
Or had the black art to dispense
A several[1] sin to every sense,
But felt through all this fleshly dress
Bright shoots of everlastingness.   20

[1] different.

Oh, how I long to travel back,
And tread again that ancient track!
That I might once more reach that plain,
Where first I left my glorious train;
From whence the enlightened spirit sees
That shady city of palm trees;[2]
But ah! my soul with too much stay
Is drunk, and staggers in the way.
Some men a forward motion love,
But I by backward steps would move;   30
And when this dust falls to the urn,
In that state I came, return.

JOHN BUNYAN [1628–1688]

The Pilgrim Song

Who would true valor see,
Let him come hither;
One here will constant be,
Come wind, come weather.
There's no discouragement
Shall make him once relent
His first avowed intent,
To be a pilgrim.

Who so beset him round
With dismal stories,
Do but themselves confound;
His strength the more is.
No lion can him fright,
He'll with a giant fight,
But he will have a right
To be a pilgrim.

Hobgoblin, nor foul fiend,
Can daunt his spirit:
He knows, he at the end

---

[2] as Moses was permitted a vision of the Promised Land, "the valley of Jericho, the city of palmtrees" (Deut., xxxiv. 3).

Shall life inherit.
Then fancies fly away,
He'll fear not what men say,
He'll labor night and day
To be a pilgrim.

JOHN DRYDEN [1631–1700]

To the Memory of Mr. Oldham[1]

Fare well, too little and too lately known,
Whom I began to think and call my own:
For sure our souls were near allied, and thine
Cast in the same poetic mold with mine.
One common note on either lyre did strike,
And knaves and fools we both abhorred alike.
To the same goal did both our studies drive:
The last set out the soonest did arrive.
Thus Nisus[2] fell upon the slippery place,
Whilst his young friend performed and won the race.
O early ripe! to thy abundant store
What could advancing age have added more?
It might (what nature never gives the young)
Have taught the numbers of thy native tongue.
But satire needs not those, and wit will shine
Through the harsh cadence of a rugged line.
A noble error, and but seldom made,
When poets are by too much force betrayed.
Thy gen'rous fruits, though gathered ere their prime,
Still showed a quickness; and maturing time
But mellows what we write to the dull sweets of rhyme.
Once more, hail, and farewell! farewell, thou young,
But ah! too short, Marcellus[3] of our tongue!
Thy brows with ivy and with laurels bound;
But fate and gloomy night encompass thee around.

[1] John Oldham, a satiric poet, died at the age of 30.
[2] in Virgil's *Aeneid*, V. 315–39, Nisus slipped in the blood of a slain steer but tripped the runner-up and thus helped his friend Euryalus win the race.
[3] nephew and heir to the emperor Augustus. He died at the age of 20.

A Song for St. Cecilia's Day[1]

1

From harmony, from heavenly harmony
    This universal frame began:
    When Nature underneath a heap
      Of jarring atoms lay,
      And could not heave her head,
The tuneful voice was heard from high:
      "Arise, ye more than dead."
Then cold, and hot, and moist, and dry,
In order to their stations leap,
    And Music's power obey.   10
From harmony, from heavenly harmony
    This universal frame began:
    From harmony to harmony
Through all the compass of the notes it ran,
The diapason closing full in man.

2

What passion cannot Music raise and quell!
    When Jubal[2] struck the corded shell,
    His listening brethren stood around,
    And, wondering, on their faces fell
    To worship that celestial sound   20
Less than a god they thought there could not dwell
    Within the hollow of that shell
    That spoke so sweetly and so well.
What passion cannot Music raise and quell!

3

    The trumpet's loud clangor
      Excites us to arms,
    With shrill notes of anger,
      And mortal alarms.
    The double double double beat
      Of the thundering drum   30

---

[1] St. Cecilia is the patron saint of music.
[2] a descendant of Cain and "father of all those who play the lyre and pipe" (Genesis, iv. 21).

Cries: "Hark! the foes come;
Charge, charge, 'tis too late to retreat."

4

The soft complaining flute
In dying notes discovers
The woes of hopeless lovers,
Whose dirge is whispered by the warbling lute.

5

Sharp violins proclaim
Their jealous pangs, and desperation,
Fury, frantic indignation,
Depth of pains, and height of passion,   40
For the fair, disdainful dame.

6

But O! what art can teach,
What human voice can reach,
The sacred organ's praise?
Notes inspiring holy love,
Notes that wing their heavenly ways
To mend the choirs above.

7

Orpheus could lead the savage race;
And trees unrooted left their place,
Sequacious of the lyre;   50
But bright Cecilia raised the wonder higher:
When to her organ vocal breath was given,
An angel heard, and straight appeared,
Mistaking earth for heaven.

GRAND CHORUS

As from the power of sacred lays
The spheres began to move,
And sung the great Creator's praise
To all the blest above;
So, when the last and dreadful hour
This crumbling pageant shall devour,   60

The trumpet shall be heard on high,
The dead shall live, the living die,
And Music shall untune the sky.

All, All of a Piece

All, all of a piece throughout;
Thy chase had a beast in view,
Thy wars brought nothing about,
Thy lovers were all untrue;
'Tis well an old age is out
And time to begin a new.

JONATHAN SWIFT [1667–1745]

A Description of the Morning

Now hardly here and there an hackney coach
Appearing, showed the ruddy morn's approach.
Now Betty from her master's bed had flown,
And softly stole to discompose her own;
The slipshod 'prentice from his master's door
Had pared the dirt, and sprinkled round the floor.
Now Moll had whirled her mop with dextrous airs,
Prepared to scrub the entry and the stairs.
The youth with broomy stumps began to trace
The kennel's edge,[1] where wheels had worn the place.
The small-coal man was heard with cadence deep,
Till drowned in shriller notes of chimney sweep:
Duns at his lordship's gate began to meet;
And brickdust Moll had screamed through half the street.
The turnkey now his flock returning sees,
Duly let out a-nights to steal for fees:
The watchful bailiffs take their silent stands,
And schoolboys lag with satchels in their hands.

[1] edge of the gutter.

ALEXANDER POPE [1688–1744]

Epistle to Dr. Arbuthnot[1]

ADVERTISEMENT

To the First Publication of this Epistle

This paper is a sort of bill of complaint, begun many years since, and drawn up by snatches, as the several occasions offered. I had no thoughts of publishing it, till it pleased some persons of rank and fortune (the authors of *Verses to the Imitator of Horace*, and of an *Epistle to a Doctor of Divinity from a Nobleman at Hampton Court*) to attack, in a very extraordinary manner, not only my writings (of which, being public, the public is judge) but my person, morals, and family, whereof, to those who know me not, a truer information may be requisite. Being divided between the necessity to say something of myself, and my own laziness to undertake so awkward a task, I thought it the shortest way to put the last hand to this Epistle. If it have anything pleasing, it will be that by which I am most desirous to please, the truth and the sentiment; and if anything offensive, it will be only to those I am least sorry to offend, the vicious or the ungenerous.

Many will know their own pictures in it, there being not a circumstance but what is true; but I have, for the most part, spared their names, and they may escape being laughed at, if they please.

I would have some of them know, it was owing to the request of the learned and candid friend to whom it is inscribed, that I make not as free use of theirs as they have done of mine. However, I shall have this advantage, and honor, on my side, that whereas, by their proceeding, any abuse may be directed at any man, no injury can possibly be done by mine, since a nameless character can never be found out, but by its truth and likeness.

P. Shut, shut the door, good John! (fatigued, I said),
Tie up the knocker, say I'm sick, I'm dead.
The Dog Star[2] rages! nay 'tis past a doubt

---

[1] John Arbuthnot was a close and faithful friend of Pope's, and, like Pope and Swift, a member of the "Scriblerus Club," which produced satiric verse and prose. Arbuthnot was Queen Anne's favorite physician.

[2] Sirius, which is prominent in the heavens in late summer, the customary time for rehearsing poetry in ancient Rome.

All Bedlam, or Parnassus,[3] is let out:
Fire in each eye, and papers in each hand,
They rave, recite, and madden round the land.
    What walls can guard me, or what shades can hide?
They pierce my thickets, through my grot they glide,
By land, by water, they renew the charge,
They stop the chariot, and they board the barge.   10
No place is sacred, not the church is free;
Even Sunday shines no Sabbath day to me:
Then from the Mint[4] walks forth the man of rhyme,
Happy to catch me just at dinner time.
    Is there a parson, much bemused in beer,
A maudlin poetess, a rhyming peer,
A clerk foredoomed his father's soul to cross,
Who pens a stanza when he should engross?
Is there who, locked from ink and paper, scrawls
With desperate charcoal round his darkened walls?   20
All fly to Twit'nam,[5] and in humble strain
Apply to me to keep them mad or vain.
Arthur,[6] whose giddy son neglects the laws,
Imputes to me and my damned works the cause:
Poor Cornus[7] sees his frantic wife elope,
And curses wit, and poetry, and Pope.
    Friend to my life (which did not you prolong,
The world had wanted many an idle song)
What drop or nostrum can this plague remove?
Or which must end me, a fool's wrath or love?   30
A dire dilemma! either way I'm sped,
If foes, they write, if friends, they read me dead.
Seized and tied down to judge, how wretched I!
Who can't be silent, and who will not lie.
To laugh were want of goodness and of grace,
And to be grave exceeds all power of face.

[3] Bedlam is the oldest English insane asylum; Parnassus is a mountain sacred to Apollo and the Muses.
[4] a sanctuary for insolvent debtors.
[5] Pope's home, Twickenham, a suburb of London.
[6] Arthur Moore's son James refused to remove from a play of his some unpublished verses by Pope.
[7] "horn," caricatural name for cuckold.

I sit with sad civility, I read
With honest anguish and an aching head,
And drop at last, but in unwilling ears,
This saving counsel, "Keep your piece nine years."   40
    "Nine years!" cries he, who high in Drury Lane,[8]
Lulled by soft zephyrs through the broken pane,
Rhymes ere he wakes, and prints before term[9] ends
Obliged by hunger and request of friends:
"The piece, you think, is incorrect? why, take it,
I'm all submission, what you'd have it, make it."
    Three things another's modest wishes bound,
My friendship, and a prologue, and ten pound.
    Pitholeon[10] sends to me: "You know his Grace,
I want a patron; ask him for a place."   50
Pitholeon libeled me—"but here's a letter
Informs you, sir, 'twas when he knew no better.
Dare you refuse him? Curll[11] invites to dine,
He'll write a *Journal*, or he'll turn Divine."
Bless me! a packet.—" 'Tis a stranger sues,
A virgin tragedy, an orphan Muse."
If I dislike it, "Furies, death, and rage!"
If I approve, "Commend it to the stage."
There (thank my stars) my whole commission ends,
The players and I are, luckily, no friends.   60
Fired that the house reject him, " 'Sdeath, I'll print it,
And shame the fools—Your interest, sir, with Lintot!"
Lintot, dull rogue, will think your price too much.
"Not, sir, if you revise it, and retouch."
All my demurs but double his attacks;
At last he whispers, "Do; and we go snacks."
Glad of a quarrel, straight I clap the door,
"Sir, let me see your works and you no more."
    'Tis sung, when Midas' ears began to spring
(Midas, a sacred person and a king),   70
His very minister who spied them first,

[8] London street and theater district.
[9] "terms" were judicial sessions, with which the publishing "seasons" were synchronized.
[10] "A foolish poet at Rhodes who pretended much to Greek" (Pope).
[11] Edmund Curll and Bernard Lintot were booksellers.

(Some say his queen) was forced to speak, or burst.[12]
And is not mine, my friend, a sorer case,
When every coxcomb perks them in my face?
   A. Good friend, forbear! you deal in dangerous things.
I'd never name queens, ministers, or kings;
Keep close to ears, and those let asses prick;
'Tis nothing—— P. Nothing? if they bite and kick?
Out with it, *Dunciad!*[13] let the secret pass,
That secret to each fool, that he's an ass: 80
The truth once told (and wherefore should we lie?)
The queen of Midas slept, and so may I.
   You think this cruel? take it for a rule,
No creature smarts so little as a fool.
Let peals of laughter, Codrus[14]! round thee break,
Thou unconcerned canst hear the mighty crack.
Pit, box, and gallery in convulsions hurled,
Thou stand'st unshook amidst a bursting world.
Who shames a scribbler? break one cobweb through,
He spins the slight, self-pleasing thread anew: 90
Destroy his fib or sophistry, in vain;
The creature's at his dirty work again,
Throned in the center of his thin designs,
Proud of a vast extent of flimsy lines.
Whom have I hurt? has poet yet or peer
Lost the arched eyebrow or Parnassian sneer?
And has not Colley still his lord and whore?
His butchers Henley? his freemasons Moore?
Does not one table Bavius still admit?
Still to one bishop Philips seem a wit?   100
Still Sappho[15]—— A. Hold! for God's sake—you'll offend.
No names—be calm—learn prudence of a friend.

---

[12] Midas, king of Phrygia, judged a musical contest between Pan and
Apollo; when Midas favored Pan, Apollo changed Midas' ears into those of an
ass.
[13] Pope's mock heroic poem celebrating the triumph of dullness.
[14] a poet ridiculed by Virgil and Juvenal.
[15] Colley Ciber was a contemporary poet laureate; Henley preached on the
uses of the butcher's calling; Bavius was an enemy of the Roman poet Virgil;
Philips, a rival of Pope's and secretary to an Irish archbishop. Sappho was a
Greek poetess of the seventh century B.C.; the reference is to Lady Mary
Wortley Montagu.

I too could write, and I am twice as tall;
But foes like these!—— P. One flatterer's worse than all.
Of all mad creatures, if the learn'd are right,
It is the slaver kills, and not the bite.
A fool quite angry is quite innocent:
Alas! 'Tis ten times worse when they repent.
   One dedicates in high heroic prose,
And ridicules beyond a hundred foes;   110
One from all Grub Street[16] will my fame defend,
And, more abusive, calls himself my friend.
This prints my letters, that expects a bribe,
And others roar aloud, "Subscribe, subscribe!"
   There are, who to my person pay their court:
I cough like Horace, and, though lean, am short;
Ammon's great son[17] one shoulder had too high,
Such Ovid's nose, and "Sir! you have an eye—"
Go on, obliging creatures, make me see
All that disgraced my betters met in me.   120
Say for my comfort, languishing in bed,
"Just so immortal Maro[18] held his head":
And when I die, be sure you let me know
Great Homer died three thousand years ago.
   Why did I write? what sin to me unknown
Dipped me in ink, my parents', or my own?
As yet a child, nor yet a fool to fame,
I lisped in numbers, for the numbers came.
I left no calling for this idle trade,
No duty broke, no father disobeyed.   130
The Muse but served to ease some friend, not wife,
To help me through this long disease, my life,
To second, Arbuthnot! thy art and care,
And teach the being you preserved, to bear.
   A. But why then publish? P. Granville the polite,
And knowing Walsh, would tell me I could write;
Well-natured Garth inflamed with early praise,
And Congreve loved, and Swift endured my lays;
The courtly Talbot, Somers, Sheffield, read;

---

[16] satiric name for Fleet Street, the publishing center of London.
[17] Alexander the Great.
[18] Virgil.

Even mitered Rochester would nod the head,   140
And St. John's self (great Dryden's friends before)
With open arms received one poet more.[19]
Happy my studies, when by these approved!
Happier their author, when by these beloved!
From these the world will judge of men and books,
Not from the Burnets, Oldmixons, and Cookes.[20]
    Soft were my numbers; who could take offense
While pure description held the place of sense?
Like gentle Fanny's[21] was my flowery theme,
A painted mistress, or a purling stream.   150
Yet then did Gildon draw his venal quill;
I wished the man a dinner, and sat still.
Yet then did Dennis[22] rave in furious fret;
I never answered, I was not in debt.
If want provoked, or madness made them print,
I waged no war with Bedlam or the Mint.
    Did some more sober critic come abroad?
If wrong, I smiled; if right, I kissed the rod.
Pains, reading, study are their just pretense,
And all they want is spirit, taste, and sense.   160
Commas and points they set exactly right,
And 'twere a sin to rob them of their mite.
Yet ne'er one sprig of laurel graced these ribalds,
From slashing Bentley down to piddling Tibbalds.[23]
Each wight who reads not, and but scans and spells,
Each word-catcher that lives on syllables,
Even such small critics some regard may claim,
Preserved in Milton's or in Shakespeare's name.
Pretty! in amber to observe the forms
Of hairs, or straws, or dirt, or grubs, or worms!   170
The things, we know, are neither rich nor rare,
But wonder how the devil they got there.

[19] Granville, Walsh, Garth, poets, and Congreve, the playwright, were contemporary with Pope; and Talbot, Somers, Sheffield, the Bishop of Rochester, and Henry St. John were statesmen and patrons of the arts.

[20] "Authors of secret and scandalous history" (Pope).

[21] reference to a poem by Thomas Parnell.

[22] authors who had censured some of Pope's poetry.

[23] Bentley had meddled with the text of Milton's *Paradise Lost;* Tibbald with Shakespeare's plays.

Were others angry? I excused them too;
Well might they rage; I gave them but their due.
A man's true merit 'tis not hard to find;
But each man's secret standard in his mind,
That casting weight pride adds to emptiness,
This, who can gratify? for who can guess?
The bard whom pilfered pastorals renown,
Who turns a Persian tale for half a crown,   180
Just writes to make his barrenness appear,
And strains from hard-bound brains eight lines a year:
He, who still wanting, though he lives on theft,
Steals much, spends little, yet has nothing left;
And he who now to sense, now nonsense leaning,
Means not, but blunders round about a meaning:
And he whose fustian's so sublimely bad,
It is not poetry, but prose run mad:
All these, my modest satire bade translate,
And owned that nine such poets made a Tate.[24]   190
How did they fume, and stamp, and roar, and chafe!
And swear, not Addison[25] himself was safe.

Peace to all such! but were there one whose fires
True Genius kindles, and fair Fame inspires;
Blessed with each talent and each art to please,
And born to write, converse, and live with ease:
Should such a man, too fond to rule alone,
Bear, like the Turk, no brother near the throne;
View him with scornful, yet with jealous eyes,
And hate for arts that caused himself to rise;   200
Damn with faint praise, assent with civil leer,
And without sneering, teach the rest to sneer;
Willing to wound, and yet afraid to strike,
Just hint a fault, and hesitate dislike;
Alike reserved to blame or to commend,
A timorous foe, and a suspicious friend;
Dreading even fools; by flatterers besieged,
And so obliging that he ne'er obliged;

[24] an inferior British poet who became poet laureate.
[25] Joseph Addison, to whom Pope gives the name Atticus, was the author of a tragedy, *Cato*, but more important, reformed English taste and manners through his articles in *The Tatler* and *The Spectator*.

Like Cato, give his little senate laws,
And sit attentive to his own applause;   210
While wits and Templars every sentence raise,
And wonder with a foolish face of praise—
Who but must laugh, if such a man there be?
Who would not weep, if Atticus were he?
    What though my name stood rubric on the walls
Or plastered posts, with claps, in capitals?
Or smoking forth, a hundred hawkers' load,
On wings of winds came flying all abroad?
I sought no homage from the race that write;
I kept, like Asian monarchs, from their sight: 220
Poems I heeded (now berhymed so long)
No more than thou, great George![26] a birthday song.
I ne'er with wits or witlings passed my days
To spread about the itch of verse and praise;
Nor like a puppy daggled through the town
To fetch and carry sing-song up and down;
Nor at rehearsals sweat, and mouthed, and cried,
With handkerchief and orange at my side;
But sick of fops, and poetry, and prate,
To Bufo left the whole Castalian state.[27]   230
    Proud as Apollo on his forkéd hill,
Sat full-blown Bufo, puffed by every quill;
Fed with soft dedication all day long,
Horace and he went hand in hand in song.
His library (where busts of poets dead
And a true Pindar stood without a head)
Received of wits an undistinguished race,
Who first his judgment asked, and then a place:
Much they extolled his pictures, much his seat,
And flattered every day, and some days eat: 240
Till grown more frugal in his riper days,
He paid some bards with port, and some with praise;
To some a dry rehearsal was assigned,
And others (harder still) he paid in kind.
Dryden alone (what wonder?) came not nigh;
Dryden alone escaped this judging eye:

[26] George II, King of England, 1727–1760.
[27] Bufo, caricatural name for a patron; Castalia, a spring on Mt. Parnassus, sacred to Apollo and the Muses, and hence a source of poetic inspiration.

But still the great have kindness in reserve;
He helped to bury whom he helped to starve.
    May some choice patron bless each gray goose quill!
May every Bavius have his Bufo still!   250
So when a statesman wants a day's defense,
Or Envy holds a whole week's war with Sense,
Or simple Pride for flattery makes demands,
May dunce by dunce be whistled off my hands!
Blessed be the great! for those they take away,
And those they left me—for they left me Gay;[28]
Left me to see neglected genius bloom,
Neglected die, and tell it on his tomb;
Of all thy blameless life the sole return
My verse, and Queensberry weeping o'er thy urn!   260
Oh, let me live my own, and die so too!
("To live and die is all I have to do")
Maintain a poet's dignity and ease,
And see what friends, and read what books I please;
Above a patron, though I condescend
Sometimes to call a minister my friend.
I was not born for courts or great affairs;
I pay my debts, believe, and say my prayers,
Can sleep without a poem in my head,
Nor know if Dennis be alive or dead.   270
    Why am I asked what next shall see the light?
Heavens! was I born for nothing but to write?
Has life no joys for me? or (to be grave)
Have I no friend to serve, no soul to save?
"I found him close with Swift"—"Indeed? no doubt"
Cries prating Balbus, "something will come out."
'Tis all in vain, deny it as I will.
"No, such a genius never can lie still,"
And then for mine obligingly mistakes
The first lampoon Sir Will or Bubo makes.[29]   280
Poor guiltless I! and can I choose but smile,
When every coxcomb knows me by my style?
    Cursed be the verse, how well soe'er it flow,

[28] John Gay, close friend of Pope and author of the *Beggar's Opera,* had a
monument erected to him by the Duke of Queensberry.
[29] Sir William Yonge and Bubb Dodington, Whig politicians and patrons
of the arts.

That tends to make one worthy man my foe,
Give Virtue scandal, Innocence a fear,
Or from the soft-eyed virgin steal a tear!
But he who hurts a harmless neighbor's peace,
Insults fallen worth, or Beauty in distress,
Who loves a lie, lame Slander helps about,
Who writes a libel, or who copies out: 290
That fop whose pride affects a patron's name,
Yet absent, wounds an author's honest fame;
Who can your merit selfishly approve,
And show the sense of it without the love;
Who has the vanity to call you friend,
Yet wants the honor, injured, to defend;
Who tells whate'er you think, whate'er you say,
And, if he lie not, must at least betray:
Who to the dean and silver bell can swear,
And sees at Cannons what was never there: [30]   300
Who reads but with a lust to misapply,
Make satire a lampoon, and fiction, lie:
A lash like mine no honest man shall dread,
But all such babbling blockheads in his stead.
    Let Sporus [31] tremble— A. What? that think of silk,
Sporus, that mere white curd of ass's milk?
Satire or sense, alas! can Sporus feel?
Who breaks a butterfly upon a wheel?
    P. Yet let me flap this bug with gilded wings,
This painted child of dirt, that stinks and stings;   310
Whose buzz the witty and the fair annoys,
Yet wit ne'er tastes, and beauty ne'er enjoys;
So well-bred spaniels civilly delight
In mumbling of the game they dare not bite.
Eternal smiles his emptiness betray,
As shallow streams run dimpling all the way.
Whether in florid impotence he speaks,
And, as the prompter breathes, the puppet squeaks;
Or at the ear of Eve, familiar toad,
Half froth, half venom, spits himself abroad,   320

[30] Pope's enemies unjustly accused him of satirizing the estate of the Duke of
Chandos at Cannons.
[31] name for Lord Hervey, who had collaborated with Lady Mary Wortley
Montagu in attacks on Pope.

In puns, or politics, or tales, or lies,
Or spite, or smut, or rhymes, or blasphemies.
His wit all seesaw between *that* and *this*,
Now high, now low, now master up, now miss,
And he himself one vile antithesis.
Amphibious thing! that acting either part,
The trifling head or the corrupted heart,
Fop at the toilet, flatterer at the board,
Now trips a lady, and now struts a lord.
Eve's tempter thus the rabbins[32] have expressed,   330
A cherub's face, a reptile all the rest;
Beauty that shocks you, parts that none will trust,
Wit that can creep, and pride that licks the dust.

     Not Fortune's worshiper, nor Fashion's fool,
Not Lucre's madman, nor Ambition's tool,
Not proud, nor servile, be one poet's praise,
That if he pleased, he pleased by manly ways:
That flattery, even to kings, he held a shame,
And thought a lie in verse or prose the same:
That not in fancy's maze he wandered long,   340
But stooped to truth, and moralized his song:
That not for fame, but Virtue's better end,
He stood the furious foe, the timid friend,
The damning critic, half approving wit,
The coxcomb hit, or fearing to be hit;
Laughed at the loss of friends he never had,
The dull, the proud, the wicked, and the mad;
The distant threats of vengeance on his head,
The blow unfelt, the tear he never shed;
The tale revived, the lie so oft o'erthrown,   350
The imputed trash, and dullness not his own;
The morals blackened when the writings 'scape,
The libeled person, and the pictured shape;[33]
Abuse on all he loved, or loved him, spread,
A friend in exile, or a father dead;
The whisper, that to greatness still too near,
Perhaps yet vibrates on his Sovereign's ear—
Welcome for thee, Fair Virtue! all the past!

[32] rabbis, Jewish theologians and scholars.
[33] Hervey ridiculed Pope's deformed back by an illustration in a book he published.

For thee, fair Virtue! welcome even the last!
    A. But why insult the poor, affront the great?   360
P. A knave's a knave to me in every state:
Alike my scorn, if he succeed or fail,
Sporus at court, or Japhet[34] in a jail,
A hireling scribbler, or a hireling peer,
Knight of the post corrupt, or of the shire,
If on a pillory, or near a throne,
He gain his prince's ear, or lose his own.

    Yet soft by nature, more a dupe than wit,
Sappho can tell you how this man was bit:
This dreaded satirist Dennis will confess   370
Foe to his pride, but friend to his distress:
So humble, he has knocked at Tibbald's door,
Has drunk with Cibber, nay, has rhymed for Moore.
Full ten years slandered, did he once reply?
Three thousand suns went down on Welsted's lie.[35]
To please a mistress one aspersed his life;
He lashed him not, but let her be his wife.
Let Budgell charge low Grub Street on his quill,
And write whate'er he pleased, except his will,
Let the two Curlls of town and court,[36] abuse   380
His father, mother, body, soul, and muse.
Yet why? that father held it for a rule,
It was a sin to call our neighbor fool;
That harmless mother thought no wife a whore:
Hear this, and spare his family, James Moore!
Unspotted names, and memorable long,
If there be force in virtue, or in song.

    Of gentle blood (part shed in honor's cause,
While yet in Britain honor had applause)
Each parent sprung— A. What fortune, pray?— P. Their own,   390
And better got than Bestia's[37] from the throne.
Born to no pride, inheriting no strife,
Nor marrying discord in a noble wife,

[34] Japhet Crook, a forger.
[35] "This man had the impudence to tell in print that Mr. P. had occasioned
a Lady's death, and to name a person he never heard of" (Pope).
[36] Budgell, poet and miscellaneous writer, was thought to have forged a will
in order to obtain property; the two Curlls are the bookseller and Hervey.
[37] a Roman consul who was bribed to make a dishonorable peace.

Stranger to civil and religious rage,
The good man walked innoxious through his age.
No courts he saw, no suits would ever try,
Nor dared an oath, nor hazarded a lie.
Unlearn'd, he knew no schoolman's subtle art,
No language but the language of the heart.
By nature honest, by experience wise,   400
Healthy by temperance, and by exercise;
His life, though long, to sickness passed unknown,
His death was instant, and without a groan.
Oh, grant me thus to live, and thus to die!
Who sprung from kings shall know less joy than I.
    O friend! may each domestic bliss be thine!
Be no unpleasing melancholy mine:
Me, let the tender office long engage,
To rock the cradle of reposing Age,
With lenient arts extend a mother's breath,   410
Make Languor smile, and smooth the bed of Death,
Explore the thought, explain the asking eye,
And keep a while one parent from the sky!
On cares like these if length of days attend,
May Heaven, to bless those days, preserve my friend,
Preserve him social, cheerful, and serene,
And just as rich as when he served a Queen!
A. Whether that blessing be denied or given,
Thus far was right—the rest belong to Heaven.

SAMUEL JOHNSON [1709–1784]

A Short Song of Congratulation

Long-expected one and twenty,
Lingering year, at last is flown;
Pomp and pleasure, pride and plenty,
Great Sir John,[1] are all your own.

[1] the poem is addressed to the nephew of Henry Thrale, whose wife was a
friend of Johnson's.

Loosen'd from the minor's tether,
Free to mortgage or to sell,
Wild as wind, and light as feather,
Bid the slaves of thrift farewell.

Call the Bettys, Kates, and Jennys,
Every name that laughs at care,
Lavish of your grandsire's guineas,
Show the spirit of an heir.

All that prey on vice and folly
Joy to see their quarry fly,
Here the gamester light and jolly,
There the lender grave and sly.

Wealth, Sir John, was made to wander,
Let it wander as it will:
See the jockey, see the pander,
Bid them come, and take their fill.

When the bonny blade carouses,
Pockets full, and spirits high,
What are acres? What are houses?
Only dirt, or wet or dry.

If the guardian or the mother
Tell the woes of wilful waste,
Scorn their counsel and their pother,
You can hang or drown at last.

THOMAS GRAY [1716–1771]

Elegy

WRITTEN IN A COUNTRY CHURCHYARD

The curfew tolls the knell of parting day,
  The lowing herd wind slowly o'er the lea,
The plowman homeward plods his weary way,
  And leaves the world to darkness and to me.

Now fades the glimmering landscape on the sight,
    And all the air a solemn stillness holds,
Save where the beetle wheels his droning flight,
    And drowsy tinklings lull the distant folds;

Save that from yonder ivy-mantled tower
    The moping owl does to the moon complain   10
Of such, as wandering near her secret bower,
    Molest her ancient solitary reign.

Beneath those rugged elms, that yew-tree's shade,
    Where heaves the turf in many a mouldering heap,
Each in his narrow cell for ever laid,
    The rude forefathers of the hamlet sleep.

The breezy call of incense-breathing Morn,
    The swallow twittering from the straw-built shed,
The cock's shrill clarion, or the echoing horn,
    No more shall rouse them from their lowly bed.   20

For them no more the blazing hearth shall burn,
    Or busy housewife ply her evening care:
No children run to lisp their sire's return,
    Or climb his knees the envied kiss to share.

Oft did the harvest to their sickle yield,
    Their furrow oft the stubborn glebe[1] has broke;
How jocund did they drive their team afield!
    How bowed the woods beneath their sturdy stroke!

Let not Ambition mock their useful toil,
    Their homely joys, and destiny obscure;   30
Nor Grandeur hear with a disdainful smile
    The short and simple annals of the poor.

The boast of heraldry, the pomp of power,
    And all that beauty, all that wealth e'er gave,
Awaits alike the inevitable hour.
    The paths of glory lead but to the grave.

Nor you, ye proud, impute to these the fault,
    If Memory o'er their tomb no trophies raise,
Where through the long-drawn aisle and fretted vault
    The pealing anthem swells the note of praise.   40

[1] soil.

Can storied urn or animated bust
   Back to its mansion call the fleeting breath?
Can honor's voice provoke the silent dust,
   Or flattery sooth the dull cold ear of death?

Perhaps in this neglected spot is laid
   Some heart once pregnant with celestial fire;
Hands, that the rod of empire might have swayed,
   Or waked to ecstasy the living lyre.

But Knowledge to their eyes her ample page
   Rich with the spoils of time did ne'er unroll;   50
Chill Penury repressed their noble rage,
   And froze the genial current of the soul.

Full many a gem of purest ray serene,
   The dark unfathomed caves of ocean bear:
Full many a flower is born to blush unseen,
   And waste its sweetness on the desert air.

Some village Hampden,[2] that with dauntless breast
   The little Tyrant of his fields withstood;
Some mute inglorious Milton here may rest,
   Some Cromwell guiltless of his country's blood.   60

The applause of listening senates to command,
   The threats of pain and ruin to despise,
To scatter plenty o'er a smiling land,
   And read their history in a nation's eyes,

Their lot forbade: nor circumscribed alone
   Their growing virtues, but their crimes confined;
Forbade to wade through slaughter to a throne,
   And shut the gates of mercy on mankind,

The struggling pangs of conscious truth to hide,
   To quench the blushes of ingenuous shame,   70
Or heap the shrine of Luxury and Pride
   With incense kindled at the Muse's flame.

Far from the madding crowd's ignoble strife,
   Their sober wishes never learned to stray;
Along the cool sequestered vale of life
   They kept the noiseless tenor of their way.

    [2] John Hampden opposed Charles I's taxes, which were unconstitutionally imposed.

Yet even these bones from insult to protect,
    Some frail memorial still erected nigh,
With uncouth rhymes and shapeless sculpture decked,
    Implores the passing tribute of a sigh.   80

Their name, their years, spelt by the unlettered muse,
    The place of fame and elegy supply:
And many a holy text around she strews,
    That teach the rustic moralist to die.

For who to dumb Forgetfulness a prey,
    This pleasing anxious being e'er resigned,
Left the warm precincts of the cheerful day,
    Nor cast one longing lingering look behind?

On some fond breast the parting soul relies,
    Some pious drops the closing eye requires;   90
Ev'n from the tomb the voice of Nature cries,
    Ev'n in our ashes live their wonted fires.

For thee, who mindful of the unhonored dead
    Dost in these lines their artless tale relate,
If chance, by lonely contemplation led,
    Some kindred spirit shall inquire thy fate,

Haply some hoary-headed swain may say,
    "Oft have we seen him at the peep of dawn
Brushing with hasty steps the dews away
    To meet the sun upon the upland lawn.   100

"There at the foot of yonder nodding beech
    That wreathes its old fantastic roots so high,
His listless length at noontide would he stretch,
    And pore upon the brook that babbles by.

"Hard by yon wood, now smiling as in scorn,
    Muttering his wayward fancies he would rove,
Now drooping, woeful wan, like one forlorn,
    Or crazed with care, or crossed in hopeless love.

"One morn I missed him on the customed hill,
    Along the heath and near his favorite tree;
Another came; nor yet beside the rill,
    Nor up the lawn, nor at the wood was he;

"The next with dirges due in sad array
   Slow through the church-way path we saw him borne.
Approach and read (for thou can'st read) the lay,
   Graved on the stone beneath yon agéd thorn."

THE EPITAPH

Here rests his head upon the lap of earth
   A youth to fortune and to fame unknown.
Fair Science frowned not on his humble birth,
   And Melancholy marked him for her own.   120

Large was his bounty, and his soul sincere,
   Heaven did a recompense as largely send:
He gave to Misery all he had, a tear,
   He gained from Heaven ('twas all he wished) a friend.

No farther seek his merits to disclose,
   Or draw his frailties from their dread abode,
(There they alike in trembling hope repose)
   The bosom of his Father and his God.

WILLIAM BLAKE [1757–1827]

FROM *Songs of Innocence*

Introduction

Piping down the valleys wild,
Piping songs of pleasant glee,
On a cloud I saw a child,
And he laughing said to me:

"Pipe a song about a Lamb!"
So I piped with merry cheer.
"Piper, pipe that song again";
So I piped: he wept to hear.

"Drop thy pipe, thy happy pipe;
Sing thy songs of happy cheer":
So I sung the same again,
While he wept with joy to hear.

"Piper, sit thee down and write
In a book that all may read."
So he vanished from my sight,
And I plucked a hollow reed,

And I made a rural pen,
And I stained the water clear,
And I wrote my happy songs
Every child may joy to hear.

The Lamb

Little Lamb, who made thee?
Dost thou know who made thee?
Gave thee life, and bid thee feed
By the stream and o'er the mead;
Gave thee clothing of delight,
Softest clothing, woolly, bright;
Gave thee such a tender voice,
Making all the vales rejoice?
   Little Lamb, who made thee?
   Dost thou know who made thee?

   Little Lamb, I'll tell thee,
   Little Lamb, I'll tell thee:
He is calléd by thy name,
For he calls himself a Lamb.
He is meek, and he is mild;
He became a little child.
I a child, and thou a lamb,
We are calléd by his name.
   Little Lamb, God bless thee!
   Little Lamb, God bless thee!

Holy Thursday

'Twas on a Holy Thursday, their innocent faces clean,
The children walking two and two, in red and blue and green,
Gray-headed beadles walked before, with wands as white as snow,
Till into the high dome of Paul's[1] they like Thames' waters flow.

[1] St. Paul's Cathedral in London.

O what a multitude they seemed, these flowers of London town!
Seated in companies they sit with radiance all their own.
The hum of multitudes was there, but multitudes of lambs,
Thousands of little boys and girls raising their innocent hands.

Now like a mighty wind they raise to heaven the voice of song,
Or like harmonious thunderings the seats of Heavens among.
Beneath them sit the aged men, wise guardians of the poor;
Then cherish pity, lest you drive an angel from your door.

FROM *Songs of Experience*

Introduction

Hear the voice of the Bard!
Who Present, Past, and Future sees;
Whose ears have heard
The Holy Word
That walked among the ancient trees,

Calling the lapséd Soul,
And weeping in the evening dew;
That might control
The starry pole,
And fallen, fallen light renew!

"O Earth, O Earth, return!
Arise from out the dewy grass;
Night is worn,
And the morn
Rises from the slumberous mass.

"Turn away no more;
Why wilt thou turn away?
The starry floor,
The watery shore,
Is given thee till the break of day."

Earth's Answer

Earth raised up her head
From the darkness dread and drear.

Her light fled,
Stony dread!
And her locks covered with gray despair.

"Prisoned on watery shore,
Starry Jealousy does keep my den:
Cold and hoar,
Weeping o'er,
I hear the Father of the ancient men.

"Selfish Father of men!
Cruel, jealous, selfish fear!
Can delight,
Chained in night,
The virgins of youth and morning bear?

"Does spring hide its joy
When buds and blossoms grow?
Does the sower
Sow by night,
Or the plowman in darkness plow?

"Break this heavy chain
That does freeze my bones around.
Selfish! vain!
Eternal bane!
That free Love with bondage bound."

The Clod and the Pebble

"Love seeketh not Itself to please,
Nor for itself hath any care,
But for another gives its ease,
And builds a Heaven in Hell's despair."

So sang a little Clod of Clay
Trodden with the cattle's feet,
But a Pebble of the brook
Warbled out these meters meet:

"Love seeketh only Self to please,
To bind another to Its delight,
Joys in another's loss of ease,
And builds a Hell in Heaven's despite."

Holy Thursday

Is this a holy thing to see
In a rich and fruitful land,
Babes reduced to misery,
Fed with cold and usurous hand?

Is that trembling cry a song?
Can it be a song of joy?
And so many children poor?
It is a land of poverty!

And their sun does never shine,
And their fields are bleak and bare,
And their ways are filled with thorns:
It is eternal winter there.

For where'er the sun does shine,
And where'er the rain does fall,
Babe can never hunger there,
Nor poverty the mind appall.

The Sick Rose

O Rose, thou art sick!
The invisible worm
That flies in the night,
In the howling storm,

Has found out thy bed
Of crimson joy:
And his dark secret love
Does thy life destroy.

The Tiger

Tiger! Tiger! burning bright
In the forests of the night,
What immortal hand or eye
Could frame thy fearful symmetry?

In what distant deeps or skies
Burnt the fire of thine eyes?
On what wings dare he aspire?[1]
What the hand dare seize the fire?

And what shoulder, and what art,
Could twist the sinews of thy heart?
And when thy heart began to beat,
What dread hand? and what dread feet?

What the hammer? what the chain?
In what furnace was thy brain?
What the anvil? what dread grasp
Dare its deadly terrors clasp?

When the stars threw down their spears,[2]
And watered heaven with their tears,
Did he smile his work to see?
Did he who made the Lamb make thee?

Tiger! Tiger! burning bright
In the forests of the night,
What immortal hand or eye
Dare frame thy fearful symmetry?

[1] fly upward.
[2] allusion to the fallen angels who rebelled against heaven.

London

I wander through each chartered[1] street,
Near where the chartered Thames does flow,
And mark in every face I meet
Marks of weakness, marks of woe.

In every cry of every Man,
In every Infant's cry of fear,
In every voice, in every ban,
The mind-forged manacles I hear.

[1] to charter: originally, to grant privileges or concede rights; in commercial usage: to let or to hire by contract.

How the Chimney-sweeper's cry
Every blackening Church appalls;
And the hapless Soldier's sigh
Runs in blood down Palace walls.

But most through midnight streets I hear
How the youthful Harlot's curse
Blasts the new born Infant's tear,
And blights with plagues the Marriage hearse.

Infant Sorrow

My mother groaned! my father wept.
Into the dangerous world I leapt:
Helpless, naked, piping loud:
Like a fiend hid in a cloud.

Struggling in my father's hands,
Striving against my swaddling bands,
Bound and weary I thought best
To sulk upon my mother's breast.

FROM *Milton*

And did those feet in ancient time
Walk upon England's mountains green?
And was the holy Lamb of God
On England's pleasant pastures seen?

And did the Countenance Divine
Shine forth upon our clouded hills?
And was Jerusalem builded here
Among these dark Satanic Mills?

Bring me my Bow of burning gold!
Bring me my Arrows of desire!
Bring me my Spear! O clouds unfold!
Bring me my Chariot of fire!

I will not cease from Mental Fight,
Nor shall my Sword sleep in my hand,
Till we have built Jerusalem
In England's green and pleasant Land.

Never Seek to Tell Thy Love

Never seek to tell thy love,
Love that never told can be;
For the gentle wind does move
Silently, invisibly.

I told my love, I told my love,
I told her all my heart;
Trembling, cold, in ghastly fears,
Ah! she doth depart.

Soon as she was gone from me,
A traveler came by,
Silently, invisibly:
He took her with a sigh.

ROBERT BURNS [1759-1796]

Holy Willie's Prayer

And send the godly in a pet to pray—POPE.

ARGUMENT

Holy Willie was a rather oldish bachelor
elder, in the parish of Mauchline, and much and
justly famed for that polemical chattering
which ends in tippling orthodoxy, and for that
spiritualized bawdry which refines to liquorish
devotion. In a sessional process with a gentleman
in Mauchline—a Mr. Gavin Hamilton—Holy
Willie and his priest, Father Auld, after full
hearing in the Presbytery of Ayr, came off but
second best, owing partly to the oratorical

powers of Mr. Robert Aiken, Mr. Hamilton's
counsel; but chiefly to Mr. Hamilton's being one
of the most irreproachable and truly respectable
characters in the country. On losing his process,
the muse overheard him at his devotions as
follows—

O Thou, wha in the Heavens dost dwell,
Wha, as it pleases best Thysel',
Sends ane to heaven and ten to hell,
   A' for Thy glory,
And no for ony guid or ill
   They've done afore Thee!

I bless and praise Thy matchless might,
Whan thousands Thou has left in night,
That I am here afore Thy sight,
   For gifts an' grace   10
A burnin' an' a shinin' light,
   To a' this place.

What was I, or my generation,
That I should get sic° exaltation?   *such*
I, wha deserve most just damnation,
   For broken laws,
Sax° thousand years 'fore my creation,   *six*
   Thro' Adam's cause.

When frae° my mither's womb I fell,   *from*
Thou might hae plunged me in Hell,   20
To gnash my gums, to weep and wail,
   In burnin' lakes,
Where damnéd devils roar and yell,
   Chained to their stakes;

Yet I am here a chosen sample,
To show Thy grace is great and ample;
I'm here a pillar in Thy temple,
   Strong as a rock,
A guide, a buckler, an example
   To a' Thy flock.   30

O Lord, Thou kens° what zeal I bear, *knows*
When drinkers drink, and swearers swear,
And singin' there and dancin' here,
   Wi' great an' sma':
For I am keepit by thy fear
   Free frae them a'.

But yet, O Lord! confess I must
At times I'm fashed° wi' fleshly lust; *plagued*
An' sometimes too, in warldly trust,
   Vile self gets in; 40
But Thou remembers we are dust,
   Defiled in sin.

O Lord! yestreen, Thou kens, wi' Meg—
Thy pardon I sincerely beg—
O! may't ne'er be a livin' plague
   To my dishonor,
An' I'll ne'er lift a lawless leg
   Again upon her.

Besides I farther maun° allow, *must*
Wi' Lizzie's lass, three times I trow°— *believe*
But, Lord, that Friday I was fou,° *drunk*
   When I cam near her,
Or else Thou kens Thy servant true
   Wad never steer° her. *touch*

May be Thou lets this fleshly thorn
Beset Thy servant e'en and morn
Lest he owre high and proud should turn,
   That he's sae gifted;
If sae, Thy hand maun e'en be borne,
   Until Thou lift it. 60

Lord, bless Thy chosen in this place,
For here Thou hast a chosen race;
But God confound their stubborn face,
   An' blast their name,
Wha bring Thy elders to disgrace
   An' public shame.

Lord, mind Gawn Hamilton's deserts,
He drinks, an' swears, an' plays at cartes,
Yet has sae mony takin' arts
        Wi' grit an' sma',
Frae God's ain priest the people's hearts   70
        He steals awa'.

An' when we chastened him therefor,
Thou kens how he bred sic a splore°   *disturbance*
As set the warld in a roar
        O' laughin' at us;
Curse Thou his basket and his store,
        Kail° and potatoes.   *cabbage*

Lord, hear my earnest cry an' pray'r,
Against that Presbyt'ry o' Ayr;   80
Thy strong right hand, Lord, make it bare
        Upo' their heads;
Lord, weigh it down, an' dinna spare,
        For their misdeeds.

O Lord my God, that glib-tongued Aiken,
My very heart and soul are quakin',
To think how we stood sweatin', shakin',
        An' pissed wi' dread,
While he, wi' hingin' lips and snakin',
        Held up his head.   90

Lord, in the day o' vengeance try him;
Lord, visit them wha did employ him,
And pass not in Thy mercy by them,
        Nor hear their prayer:
But, for Thy people's sake, destroy them,
        And dinna spare.

But, Lord, remember me and mine
Wi, mercies temp'ral and divine,
That I for gear an' grace may shine
        Excelled by nane,   100
And a' the glory shall be Thine,
        Amen, Amen!

To a Louse

ON SEEING ONE ON A LADY'S BONNET AT CHURCH

Ha! wh'are ye gaun, ye crowlin' ferlie°!   *wonder*
Your impudence protects you sairly:
I canna say but ye strunt° rarely,   *swagger*
        Owre gauze and lace;
Tho' faith! I fear ye dine but sparely
        On sic° a place.   *such*

Ye ugly, creepin', blastit wonner,°   *wonder*
Detested, shunn'd by saunt an' sinner!
How dare ye set your fit upon her,
        Sae fine a lady?   10
Gae somewhere else, and seek your dinner
        On some poor body.

Swith,° in some beggar's haffet° squattle°;   *get away / temple / squat*
There ye may creep, and sprawl, and sprattle°   *struggle*
Wi' ither kindred jumping cattle,
        In shoals and nations;
Where horn nor bane ne'er dare unsettle
        Your thick plantations.

Now haud ye there, ye're out o' sight,
Below the fatt'rels,° snug an' tight;   *ribbons*
Na, faith ye yet! ye'll no be right   21
        Till ye've got on it,
The very tapmost tow'ring height
        O' Miss's bonnet.

My sooth! right bauld ye set your nose out,
As plump and gray as onie grozet°;   *gooseberry*
O for some rank mercurial rozet,°   *rosin*
        Or fell° red smeddum°!   *deadly / powder*
I'd gie you sic a hearty doze o't,
        Wad dress your droddum°!   *breech*

I wad na been surpris'd to spy   31
You on an auld wife's flannen toy°;   *headdress*
Or aiblins° some bit duddie° boy,   *maybe / tattered*

On's wyliecoat;
But Miss's fine Lunardi!° fie,
How daur ye do't?

balloon-shaped bonnet

O Jenny, dinna toss your head,
An' set your beauties a' abroad!
Ye little ken what curséd speed
The blastie's makin'!
Thae winks and finger-ends, I dread,
Are notice takin'!

40

O wad some Pow'r the giftie gie us
To see oursels as others see us!
It wad frae mony a blunder free us,
And foolish notion:
What airs in dress an' gait wad lea'e us,
And ev'n devotion!

O, My Luve is Like a Red, Red Rose

O, my luve is like a red, red rose,
That's newly sprung in June.
O, my luve is like the melodie,
That's sweetly played in tune.

As fair art thou, my bonnie lass,
So deep in luve am I,
And I will luve thee still, my dear,
Till a' the seas gang dry.

Till a' the seas gang dry, my dear,
And the rocks melt wi' the sun!
And I will luve thee still, my dear,
While the sands o' life shall run.

And fare thee weel, my only luve,
And fare thee weel a while!
And I will come again, my luve,
Though it were ten thousand mile!

O Whistle, and I'll Come to You, My Lad

O whistle, and I'll come to you, my lad;
O whistle, and I'll come to you, my lad:
Tho' father and mither and a' should gae mad,
O whistle, and I'll come to you, my lad.

But warily tent,° when ye come to court me,   *heed*
And come na unless the back-yett° be a-jee°;   *gate / ajar*
Syne up the back-stile, and let naebody see,
And come as ye were na comin' to me.
And come as ye were na comin' to me.

At kirk,° or at market, whene'er ye meet me,   *church*
Gang° by me as tho' that ye car'd na a flee: *go*
But steal me a blink o' your bonnie black ee,
Yet look as ye were na lookin' at me.
Yet look as ye were na lookin' at me.

Aye vow and protest that ye care na for me,
And whiles° ye may lightly my beauty a wee°;   *sometimes / little*
But court na anither, tho' jokin' ye be,
For fear that she wyle your fancy frae me.
For fear that she wyle your fancy frae me.

WILLIAM WORDSWORTH [1770–1850]

Lines Composed a Few Miles Above Tintern Abbey

Five years have passed; five summers, with the length
Of five long winters! and again I hear
These waters, rolling from their mountain-springs
With a soft inland murmur. Once again
Do I behold these steep and lofty cliffs,
That on a wild secluded scene impress
Thoughts of more deep seclusion; and connect
The landscape with the quiet of the sky.
The day is come when I again repose
Here, under this dark sycamore, and view   10

These plots of cottage ground, these orchard tufts,
Which at this season, with their unripe fruits,
Are clad in one green hue, and lose themselves
'Mid groves and copses. Once again I see
These hedgerows, hardly hedgerows, little lines
Of sportive wood run wild; these pastoral farms,
Green to the very door; and wreaths of smoke
Sent up, in silence, from among the trees!
With some uncertain notice, as might seem
Of vagrant dwellers in the houseless woods,   20
Or of some Hermit's cave, whereby his fire
The Hermit sits alone.

                              These beauteous forms,
Through a long absence, have not been to me
As is a landscape to a blind man's eye;
But oft, in lonely rooms, and 'mid the din
Of towns and cities, I have owed to them,
In hours of weariness, sensations sweet,
Felt in the blood, and felt along the heart;
And passing even into my purer mind,
With tranquil restoration—feelings too   30
Of unremembered pleasure; such, perhaps,
As have no slight or trivial influence
On that best portion of a good man's life,
His little, nameless, unremembered, acts
Of kindness and of love. Nor less, I trust,
To them I may have owed another gift,
Of aspect more sublime; that blessed mood,
In which the burthen of the mystery,
In which the heavy and the weary weight
Of all this unintelligible world,   40
Is lightened—that serene and blessed mood,
In which the affections gently lead us on—
Until, the breath of this corporeal frame
And even the motion of our human blood
Almost suspended, we are laid asleep
In body, and become a living soul;
While with an eye made quiet by the power
Of harmony, and the deep power of joy,
We see into the life of things.

Be but a vain belief, yet, oh! how oft—   50
In darkness and amid the many shapes
Of joyless daylight; when the fretful stir
Unprofitable, and the fever of the world,
Have hung upon the beatings of my heart—
How oft, in spirit, have I turned to thee,
O sylvan Wye! thou wanderer through the woods,
How often has my spirit turned to thee!

  And now, with gleams of half-extinguished thought
With many recognitions dim and faint,
And somewhat of a sad perplexity,   60
The picture of the mind revives again;
While here I stand, not only with the sense
Of present pleasure, but with pleasing thoughts
That in this moment there is life and food
For future years. And so I dare to hope,
Though changed, no doubt, from what I was when first
I came among these hills; when like a roe
I bounded o'er the mountains, by the sides
Of the deep rivers, and the lonely streams,
Wherever nature led—more like a man   70
Flying from something that he dreads than one
Who sought the thing he loved. For nature then
(The coarser pleasures of my boyish days,
And their glad animal movements all gone by)
To me was all in all.—I cannot paint
What then I was. The sounding cataract
Haunted me like a passion; the tall rock,
The mountain, and the deep and gloomy wood,
Their colors and their forms, were then to me
An appetite; a feeling and a love,   80
That had no need of a remoter charm,
By thought supplied, nor any interest
Unborrowed from the eye.—That time is past,
And all its aching joys are now no more,
And all its dizzy raptures. Not for this
Faint I, nor mourn nor murmur; other gifts
Have followed; for such loss, I would believe,
Abundant recompense. For I have learned

To look on nature, not as in the hour
Of thoughtless youth; but hearing often times   90
The still, sad music of humanity,
Nor harsh nor grating, though of ample power
To chasten and subdue. And I have felt
A presence that disturbs me with the joy
Of elevated thoughts; a sense sublime
Of something far more deeply interfused,
Whose dwelling is the light of setting suns,
And the round ocean and the living air,
And the blue sky, and in the mind of man:
A motion and a spirit, that impels   100
All thinking things, all objects of all thought,
And rolls through all things. Therefore am I still
A lover of the meadows and the woods,
And mountains; and of all that we behold
From this green earth; of all the mighty world
Of eye, and ear—both what they half create,
And what perceive; well pleased to recognize
In nature and the language of the sense
The anchor of my purest thoughts, the nurse,
The guide, the guardian of my heart, and soul   110
Of all my moral being.

               Nor perchance,
If I were not thus taught, should I the more
Suffer my genial spirits to decay:
For thou art with me here upon the banks
Of this fair river; thou my dearest Friend,[1]
My dear, dear Friend; and in thy voice I catch
The language of my former heart, and read
My former pleasures in the shooting lights
Of thy wild eyes. Oh! yet a little while
May I behold in thee what I was once,   120
My dear, dear Sister! and this prayer I make,
Knowing that Nature never did betray
The heart that loved her; 'tis her privilege,
Through all the years of this our life, to lead
From joy to joy: for she can so inform
The mind that is within us, so impress

[1] his sister Dorothy.

With quietness and beauty, and so feed
With lofty thoughts, that neither evil tongues,
Rash judgments, nor the sneers of selfish men,
Nor greetings where no kindness is, nor all   130
The dreary intercourse of daily life,
Shall e'er prevail against us, or disturb
Our cheerful faith, that all which we behold
Is full of blessings. Therefore let the moon
Shine on thee in thy solitary walk;
And let the misty mountain winds be free
To blow against thee: and, in after years,
When these wild ecstasies shall be matured
Into a sober pleasure; when thy mind
Shall be a mansion for all lovely forms,   140
Thy memory be as a dwelling place
For all sweet sounds and harmonies; oh! then,
If solitude, or fear, or pain, or grief
Should be thy portion, with what healing thoughts
Of tender joy wilt thou remember me,
And these my exhortations! Nor, perchance—
If I should be where I no more can hear
Thy voice, nor catch from thy wild eyes these gleams
Of past existence—wilt thou then forget
That on the banks of this delightful stream   150
We stood together; and that I, so long
A worshiper of Nature, hither came
Unwearied in that service; rather say
With warmer love—oh! with far deeper zeal
Of holier love. Nor wilt thou then forget,
That after many wanderings, many years
Of absence, these steep woods and lofty cliffs,
And this green pastoral landscape, were to me
More dear, both for themselves and for thy sake!

A Slumber Did My Spirit Seal

A slumber did my spirit seal;
   I had no human fears;
She seemed a thing that could not feel
   The touch of earthly years.

No motion has she now, no force;
  She neither hears nor sees;
Rolled round in earth's diurnal course,
  With rocks, and stones, and trees.

Composed Upon Westminster Bridge

Earth has not anything to show more fair:
Dull would he be of soul who could pass by
A sight so touching in its majesty:
This city now doth, like a garment, wear
The beauty of the morning: silent, bare,
Ships, towers, domes, theaters, and temples lie
Open unto the fields, and to the sky;
All bright and glittering in the smokeless air.
Never did sun more beautifully steep
In his first splendor, valley, rock, or hill;
Ne'er saw I, never felt, a calm so deep!
The river glideth at his own sweet will:
Dear God! the very houses seem asleep;
And all that mighty heart is lying still!

The Solitary Reaper

Behold her, single in the field,
Yon solitary Highland lass!
Reaping and singing by herself;
Stop here, or gently pass!
Alone she cuts and binds the grain,
And sings a melancholy strain;
O listen! for the vale profound
Is overflowing with the sound.

No nightingale did ever chaunt
More welcome notes to weary bands   10
Of travelers in some shady haunt,
Among Arabian sands:
A voice so thrilling ne'er was heard
In springtime from the cuckoo-bird,

Breaking the silence of the seas
Among the farthest Hebrides.

Will no one tell me what she sings?—
Perhaps the plaintive numbers flow
For old, unhappy, far-off things,
And battles long ago: 20
Or is it some more humble lay,
Familiar matter of today?
Some natural sorrow, loss, or pain,
That has been, and may be again?

Whate'er the theme, the maiden sang
As if her song could have no ending;
I saw her singing at her work,
And o'er the sickle bending;—
I listened, motionless and still;
And, as I mounted up the hill   30
The music in my heart I bore,
Long after it was heard no more.

FROM *The Prelude*, BOOK VI

When from the Vallais we had turned, and clomb
Along the Simplon's steep and rugged road,[1]
Following a band of muleteers, we reached
A halting place, where all together took
Their noontide meal. Hastily rose our guide,
Leaving us at the board; awhile we lingered,
Then paced the beaten downward way that led
Right to a rough stream's edge, and there broke off;
The only track now visible was one   570
That from the torrent's further brink held forth
Conspicuous invitation to ascend
A lofty mountain. After brief delay
Crossing the unbridged stream, that road we took,
And clomb with eagerness, till anxious fears
Intruded, for we failed to overtake
Our comrades gone before. By fortunate chance,

[1] Vallais is a canton on the Swiss side of the Simplon road, a mountain pass
through the Alps between Italy and Switzerland.

While every moment added doubt to doubt,
A peasant met us, from whose mouth we learned
That to the spot which had perplexed us first   580
We must descend, and there should find the road,
Which in the stony channel of the stream
Lay a few steps, and then along its banks;
And, that our future course, all plain to sight,
Was downwards, with the current of that stream.
Loath to believe what we so grieved to hear,
For still we had hopes that pointed to the clouds,
We questioned him again, and yet again;
But every word that from the peasant's lips
Came in reply, translated by our feelings,   590
Ended in this—*that we had crossed the Alps.*

　　Imagination—here the Power so called
Through sad incompetence of human speech,
That awful Power rose from the mind's abyss
Like an unfathered vapor that enwraps,
At once, some lonely traveler. I was lost;
Halted without an effort to break through;
But to my conscious soul I now can say—
"I recognize thy glory": in such strength
Of usurpation, when the light of sense   600
Goes out, but with a flash that has revealed
The invisible world, doth greatness make abode,
There harbors; whether we be young or old,
Our destiny, our being's heart and home,
Is with infinitude, and only there;
With hope it is, hope that can never die,
Effort, and expectation, and desire,
And something evermore about to be.
Under such banners militant, the soul
Seeks for no trophies, struggles for no spoils   610
That may attest her prowess, blest in thoughts
That are their own perfection and reward,
Strong in herself and in beatitude
That hides her, like the mighty flood of Nile
Poured from his fount of Abyssinian clouds
To fertilize the whole Egyptian plain.

　　The melancholy slackening that ensued
Upon those tidings by the peasant given

Was soon dislodged. Downwards we hurried fast,
And, with the half-shaped road which we had missed,   620
Entered a narrow chasm. The brook and road
Were fellow travelers in this gloomy strait,
And with them did we journey several hours
At a slow pace. The immeasurable height
Of woods decaying, never to be decayed,
The stationary blasts of waterfalls,
And in the narrow rent at every turn
Winds thwarting winds, bewildered and forlorn,
The torrents shooting from the clear blue sky,
The rocks that muttered close upon our ears,   630
Black drizzling crags that spake by the wayside
As if a voice were in them, the sick sight
And giddy prospect of the raving stream,
The unfettered clouds and region of the Heavens,
Tumult and peace, the darkness and the light—
Were all like workings of one mind, the features
Of the same face, blossoms upon one tree;
Characters of the great Apocalypse,[2]
The types and symbols of Eternity,
Of first, and last, and midst, and without end.   640

[2] the book of Revelation.

SAMUEL TAYLOR COLERIDGE [1772–1834]

Kubla Khan

In Xanadu did Kubla Khan[1]
    A stately pleasure dome decree:
Where Alph, the sacred river, ran
Through caverns measureless to man
    Down to a sunless sea.
So twice five miles of fertile ground
With walls and towers were girdled round:

[1] Kubla Khan founded the Mongol empire in the thirteenth century. Xana-du, Alph, and Mount Abora are modifications of exotic geographical names that Coleridge read of in books of travel and exploration.

And here were gardens bright with sinuous rills,
Where blossomed many an incense-bearing tree,
And here were forests ancient as the hills, 10
Enfolding sunny spots of greenery.

But oh! that deep romantic chasm which slanted
Down the green hill athwart a cedarn cover!
A savage place; as holy and enchanted
As e'er beneath a waning moon was haunted
By woman wailing for her demon lover!
And from this chasm, with ceaseless turmoil seething,
As if this earth in fast thick pants were breathing,
A mighty fountain momently was forced,
Amid whose swift half-intermitted burst 20
Huge fragments vaulted like rebounding hail,
Or chaffy grain beneath the thresher's flail:
And 'mid these dancing rocks at once and ever
It flung up momently the sacred river.
Five miles meandering with a mazy motion
Through wood and dale the sacred river ran,
Then reached the caverns measureless to man,
And sank in tumult to a lifeless ocean:
And 'mid this tumult Kubla heard from far
Ancestral voices prophesying war! 30

    The shadow of the dome of pleasure
    Floated midway on the waves;
    Where was heard the mingled measure
    From the fountain and the caves.
It was a miracle of rare device,
A sunny pleasure dome with caves of ice!

    A damsel with a dulcimer
    In a vision once I saw:
    It was an Abyssinian maid,
    And on her dulcimer she played, 40
    Singing of Mount Abora.
    Could I revive within me
    Her symphony and song,
    To such a deep delight 'twould win me,
That with music loud and long,
I would build that dome in air,
That sunny dome! those caves of ice!

And all who heard should see them there,
And all should cry, Beware! Beware!
His flashing eyes, his floating hair! 50
Weave a circle round him thrice,
And close your eyes with holy dread,
For he on honey-dew hath fed,
And drunk the milk of Paradise.

The Rime of the Ancient Mariner

IN SEVEN PARTS

*Facile credo, plures esse Naturas invisibles quam visibiles in rerum
universitate. Sed horum omnium familiam quis nobis enarrabit? et gra-
dus et cognationes et discrimina et singulorum munera? Quid agunt?
quae loca habitant? Harum rerum notitiam semper ambivit ingenium
humanum, nunquam attigit. Juvat, interea, non diffiteor, quandoque in
animo, tanquam in tabula, majoris et melioris mundi imaginem contem-
plari: ne mens assuefacta hodiernae vitae minutiis se contrahat nimis,
et tota subsidat in pusillas cogitationes. Sed veritati interea in vigilandum
est, modusque servandus, ut certa ab incertis, diem a nocte, distinguamus
—T. Burnet, Archæol. Phil. P. 68.*

[I readily believe that there are more invisible than visible beings in
the universe. But who will tell us the family, the ranks, the relationships,
the differences, the respective functions of all these beings? What do
they do? Where do they dwell? The human mind has circled around
this knowledge, but has never reached it. Still, it is pleasant, I have no
doubt, to contemplate sometimes in one's mind, as in a picture, the
image of a bigger and better world; lest the mind, accustomed to the
details of daily life, be too narrowed and settle down entirely on trifling
thoughts. Meanwhile, however, we must be on the lookout for truth
and observe restraint, in order that we may distinguish the certain from
the uncertain, day from night.]

ARGUMENT

How a Ship having passed the Line was driven by storms to the cold
Country towards the South Pole; and how from thence she made her
course to the tropical Latitude of the Great Pacific Ocean; and of the
strange things that befell: and in what manner the Ancyent Marinere
came back to his own Country.

It is an ancient Mariner,
And he stoppeth one of three.
"By thy long gray beard and glittering eye,
Now wherefore stopp'st thou me?

The Bridegroom's doors are opened wide,
And I am next of kin;
The guests are met, the feast is set:
May'st hear the merry din."

He holds him with his skinny hand,
"There was a ship," quoth he.   10
"Hold off! unhand me, graybeard loon!"
Eftsoons[1] his hand dropped he.

He holds him with his glittering eye--
The Wedding Guest stood still,
And listens like a three years' child:
The Mariner hath his will

The Wedding Guest sat on a stone:
He cannot choose but hear;
And thus spake on that ancient man,
The bright-eyed Mariner.   20

"The ship was cheered, the harbor cleared,
Merrily did we drop
Below the kirk, below the hill,
Below the lighthouse top.

The Sun came up upon the left,
Out of the sea came he!
And he shone bright, and on the right
Went down into the sea.

Higher and higher every day,
Till over the mast at noon—"   30
The Wedding Guest here beat his breast,
For he heard the loud bassoon.

[1] at once.
[2] equator.

184

The Wedding
Guest heareth
the bridal
music; but
the Mariner
continueth
his tale.

The bride hath paced into the hall,
Red as a rose is she;
Nodding their heads before her goes
The merry minstrelsy.

The Wedding Guest he beat his breast,
Yet he cannot choose but hear;
And thus spake on that ancient man,
The bright-eyed Mariner.   40

The ship
driven by a
storm towards
the south pole.

"And now the STORM-BLAST came, and he
Was tyrannous and strong:
He struck with his o'ertaking wings,
And chased us south along.

With sloping masts and dipping prow,
As who pursued with yell and blow
Still treads the shadow of his foe,
And forward bends his head,
The ship drove fast, loud roared the blast,
And southward aye we fled.   50

And now there came both mist and snow,
And it grew wondrous cold:
And ice, mast-high, came floating by,
As green as emerald.

The land of
ice, and of
fearful sounds
where no
living thing
was to be seen.

And through the drifts the snowy clifts
Did send a dismal sheen:
Nor shapes of men nor beasts we ken—
The ice was all between.

The ice was here, the ice was there,
The ice was all around: 60
It cracked and growled, and roared and howled,
Like noises in a swound!

Till a great
sea-bird,
called the
Albatross,
came through
the snow-fog,
and was
received with
great joy and
hospitality.

At length did cross an Albatross,
Thorough the fog it came;
As if it had been a Christian soul,
We hailed it in God's name.

It ate the food it ne'er had eat,
And round and round it flew.

The ice did split with a thunder-fit;
The helmsman steered us through!   70

And lo! the
Albatross
proveth a bird
of good omen,
and followeth
the ship as it
returned
northward
through fog
and floating
ice.

And a good south wind sprung up behind;
The Albatross did follow,
And every day, for food or play,
Came to the mariner's hollo!

In mist or cloud, on mast or shroud,[3]
It perched for vespers nine;
Whiles all the night, through fog-smoke white,
Glimmered the white Moon-shine."

The ancient
Mariner
inhospitably
killeth the
pious bird of
good omen.

"God save thee, ancient Mariner!
From the fiends, that plague thee thus!—   80
Why look'st thou so?"—With my cross-bow
I shot the ALBATROSS.

PART II

The Sun now rose upon the right:
Out of the sea came he,
Still hid in mist, and on the left
Went down into the sea.

And the good south wind still blew behind,
But no sweet bird did follow,
Nor any day for food or play
Came to the mariners' hollo!   90

His shipmates
cry out against
the ancient
Mariner, for
killing the
bird of good
luck.

And I had done a hellish thing,
And it would work 'em woe:
For all averred, I had killed the bird
That made the breeze to blow.
Ah wretch! said they, the bird to slay,
That made the breeze to blow!

But when the
fog cleared
off, they
justify the
same, and
thus make
themselves
accomplices
in the crime.

Nor dim nor red, like God's own head,
The glorious Sun uprist:
Then all averred, I had killed the bird
That brought the fog and mist.   100
'Twas right, said they, such birds to slay,
That bring the fog and mist.

[3] rope extending from masthead to the side of the ship.

The fair breeze
continues;
the ship enters
the Pacific
Ocean, and
sails north-
ward, even
till it reaches
the Line.

The fair breeze blew, the white foam flew,
The furrow followed free;
We were the first that ever burst
Into that silent sea.

The ship hath
been suddenly
becalmed.

Down dropped the breeze, the sails dropped down,
'Twas sad as sad could be;
And we did speak only to break
The silence of the sea!   110

All in a hot and copper sky,
The bloody Sun, at noon,
Right up above the mast did stand,
No bigger than the Moon.

Day after day, day after day,
We stuck, nor breath nor motion;
As idle as a painted ship
Upon a painted ocean.

And the Alba-
tross begins to
be avenged.

Water, water, every where
And all the boards did shrink;   120
Water, water, every where,
Nor any drop to drink.

The very deep did rot: O Christ!
That ever this should be!
Yea, slimy things did crawl with legs
Upon the slimy sea.

About, about, in reel and rout
The death-fires[4] danced at night;
The water, like a witch's oils,
Burned green, and blue and white.   130

A Spirit had fol-
lowed them; one
of the invisible
inhabitants of this
planet, neither
departed souls
nor angels; con-
cerning whom
the learned Jew,
Josephus, and the
Platonic Constan-
tinopolitan,
Michael Psellus,
may be consulted.

And some in dreams assuréd were
Of the Spirit that plagued us so;
Nine fathom deep he had followed us
From the land of mist and snow.

And every tongue, through utter drought,
Was withered at the root;
We could not speak, no more than if
We had been choked with soot.

[4] phosphorescent light on the ship's rigging, an omen of disaster to sailors.

They are very
numerous, and
there is no cli-
mate or element
without one or
more.
Ah! well a-day! what evil looks
Had I from old and young!   140
Instead of the cross, the Albatross
About my neck was hung.

PART III

The shipmates,
in their sore
distress, would
fain throw the
whole guilt on
the ancient
Mariner: in sign
whereof they
hang the dead
sea-bird round
his neck.
There passed a weary time. Each throat
Was parched, and glazed each eye.
A weary time! a weary time!
How glazed each weary eye,
When looking westward, I beheld
A something in the sky.

The ancient
Mariner be-
holdeth a sign
in the element
afar off.
At first it seemed a little speck,
And then it seemed a mist;   150
It moved and moved, and took at last
A certain shape, I wist.[5]

A speck, a mist, a shape, I wist!
And still it neared and neared:
As if it dodged a water-sprite,
It plunged and tacked and veered.

At its nearer
approach, it
seemeth him
to be a ship;
and at a dear
ransom he
freeth his
speech from
the bonds of
thirst.
With throats unslaked, with black lips baked,
We could nor laugh nor wail;
Through utter drought all dumb we stood!
I bit my arm, I sucked the blood,   160
And cried, A sail! a sail!

A flash of joy;
With throats unslaked, with black lips baked,
Agape they heard me call:
Gramercy! they for joy did grin,
And all at once their breath drew in,
As they were drinking all.

And horror
follows. for
can it be a
ship that
comes onward
without wind
or tide?
See! see! (I cried) she tacks no more!
Hither to work us weal;
Without a breeze, without a tide,
She steadies with upright keel!   170

The western wave was all aflame.
The day was well nigh done!
Almost upon the western wave

[5] knew.

188

Rested the broad bright Sun;
When that strange shape drove suddenly
Betwixt us and the Sun.

It seemeth
him but the
skeleton of
a ship.

And straight the Sun was flecked with bars,
(Heaven's Mother send us grace!)
As if through a dungeon-grate he peered
With broad and burning face.   180

And its ribs
are seen as
bars on the
face of the
setting Sun.

Alas! (thought I, and my heart beat loud)
How fast she nears and nears!
Are those *her* sails that glance in the Sun,
Like restless gossameres?

The Specter
Woman and
her Deathmate,
and no
other on
board the
skeleton ship.

Are those *her* ribs through which the Sun
Did peer, as through a grate?
And is that Woman all her crew?
Is that a DEATH? and are there two?
Is DEATH that woman's mate?

Like vessel,
like crew!

Her lips were red, *her* looks were free,   190
Her locks were yellow as gold:
Her skin was as white as leprosy,
The Night-mare LIFE-IN-DEATH was she,
Who thicks man's blood with cold.

Death and
Life-in-Death
have diced for
the ship's
crew, and she
(the latter)
winneth the
ancient
Mariner.

The naked hulk alongside came,
And the twain were casting dice;
"The game is done! I've won! I've won!"
Quoth she, and whistles thrice.

No twilight
within the
courts of the
Sun.

The Sun's rim dips; the stars rush out:
At one stride comes the dark;   200
With far-heard whisper, o'er the sea,
Off shot the specter bark.

At the rising
of the Moon,

We listened and looked sideways up!
Fear at my heart, as at a cup,
My life-blood seemed to sip!
The stars were dim, and thick the night,
The steersman's face by his lamp gleamed white;
From the sails the dew did drip—
Till clomb above the eastern bar
The hornéd Moon, with one bright star   210
Within the nether tip.

One after one, by the star-dogged Moon,[6]
Too quick for groan or sigh,
Each turned his face with a ghastly **pang**,
And cursed me with his eye.

His shipmates
drop down
dead.

Four times fifty living men,
(And I heard nor sigh nor groan)
With heavy thump, a lifeless lump,
They dropped down one by one.

But Life-in-
Death begins
her work on
the ancient
Mariner.

The souls did from their bodies fly,—   220
They fled to bliss or woe!
And every soul, it passed me by,
Like the whizz of my cross-bow!

PART IV

The Wedding
Guest feareth
that a Spirit
is talking to
him;

"I fear thee, ancient Mariner!
I fear thy skinny hand!
And thou art long, and lank, and brown,
As is the ribbed sea-sand.

I fear thee and thy glittering eye,
And thy skinny hand, so brown."—

But the
ancient Ma-
riner assureth
him of his
bodily life, and
proceedeth to
relate his hor-
rible penance.

Fear not, fear not, thou Wedding Guest!   230
This body dropped not down.

Alone, alone, all, all alone,
Alone on a wide wide sea!
And never a saint took pity on
My soul in agony.

He despiseth
the creatures
of the calm,

The many men, so beautiful!
And they all dead did lie:
And a thousand thousand slimy things
Lived on; and so did I.

And envi-
eth that *they*
should live,
and so many
be dead.

I looked upon the rotting sea,   240
And drew my eyes away;
I looked upon the rotting deck,
And there the dead men lay.

I looked to heaven, and tried to pray;
But or ever a prayer had gushed,

[6] an omen of evil when a star "dogs the moon."

A wicked whisper came, and made
My heart as dry as dust.

I closed my lids, and kept them close,
And the balls like pulses beat;
For the sky and the sea, and the sea and the sky   250
Lay like a load on my weary eye,
And the dead were at my feet.

But the curse
liveth for him
in the eye of
the dead men.
The cold sweat melted from their limbs,
Nor rot nor reek did they:
The look with which they looked on me
Had never passed away.

An orphan's curse would drag to hell
A spirit from on high;
But oh! more horrible than that
Is the curse in a dead man's eye!   260
Seven days, seven nights, I saw that curse,
And yet I could not die.

In his loneliness
and fixedness he
yearneth towards
the journeying
Moon, and the
stars that still
sojourn, yet still
move onward;
and every where
the blue sky
belongs to them,
and is their
appointed rest,
and their
native country
and their own
natural homes,
which they enter
unannounced,
as lords that
are certainly
expected and
yet there is a
silent joy at
their arrival.
The moving Moon went up the sky,
And no where did abide:
Softly she was going up,
And a star or two beside—

Her beams bemocked the sultry main,
Like April hoar-frost spread;
But where the ship's huge shadow lay,
The charméd water burnt alway   270
A still and awful red.

Beyond the shadow of the ship,
I watched the water-snakes:
They moved in tracks of shining white,
And when they reared, the elfish light
Fell off in hoary flakes.

By the light
of the Moon he
beholdeth
God's crea-
tures of the
great calm.
Within the shadow of the ship
I watched their rich attire:
Blue, glossy green, and velvet black,
They coiled and swam; and every track   280
Was a flash of golden fire.

O happy living things! no tongue
Their beauty might declare:
A spring of love gushed from my heart,
And I blessed them unaware:

Sure my kind saint took pity on me,
And I blessed them unaware.

The self-same moment I could pray;
And from my neck so free
The Albatross fell off, and sank   290
Like lead into the sea.

PART V

Oh sleep! it is a gentle thing,
Beloved from pole to pole!
To Mary Queen the praise be given!
She sent the gentle sleep from Heaven,
That slid into my soul.

The silly[7] buckets on the deck,
That had so long remained,
I dreamt that they were filled with dew;
And when I awoke, it rained.   300

My lips were wet, my throat was cold,
My garments all were dank;
Sure I had drunken in my dreams,
And still my body drank.

I moved, and could not feel my limbs:
I was so light—almost
I thought that I had died in sleep,
And was a blessèd ghost.

And soon I heard a roaring wind:
It did not come anear;   310
But with its sound it shook the sails,
That were so thin and sere.

The upper air burst into life!
And a hundred fire-flags sheen,[8]
To and fro they were hurried about!

---

[7] useless (because empty).
[8] gleaming.

192

And to and fro, and in and out,
The wan stars danced between.

And the coming wind did roar more loud,
And the sails did sigh like sedge;
And the rain poured down from one black cloud;   320
The Moon was at its edge.

The thick black cloud was cleft, and still
The Moon was at its side:
Like waters shot from some high crag,
The lightning fell with never a jag,
A river steep and wide.

The loud wind never reached the ship,
Yet now the ship moved on!
Beneath the lightning and the Moon
The dead men gave a groan.   330

They groaned, they stirred, they all uprose,
Nor spake, nor moved their eyes;
It had been strange, even in a dream,
To have seen those dead men rise.

The helmsman steered, the ship moved on;
Yet never a breeze up-blew;
The mariners all 'gan work the ropes,
Where they were wont to do;
They raised their limbs like lifeless tools—
We were a ghastly crew.   340

The body of my brother's son
Stood by me, knee to knee:
The body and I pulled at one rope,
But he said nought to me.

"I fear thee, ancient Mariner!"
Be calm, thou Wedding Guest!
'Twas not those souls that fled in pain,
Which to their corses came again,
But a troop of spirits blessed:

For when it dawned—they dropped their arms,   350
And clustered round the mast;
Sweet sounds rose slowly through their mouths,
And from their bodies passed.

Around, around, flew each sweet sound,
Then darted to the Sun;
Slowly the sounds came back again,
Now mixed, now one by one.

Sometimes adropping from the sky
I heard the skylark sing;
Sometimes all little birds that are,   360
How they seemed to fill the sea and air
With their sweet jargoning!

And now 'twas like all instruments,
Now like a lonely flute;
And now it is an angel's song,
That makes the heavens be mute.

It ceased; yet still the sails made on
A pleasant noise till noon,
A noise like of a hidden brook
In the leafy month of June,   370
That to the sleeping woods all night
Singeth a quiet tune.

Till noon we quietly sailed on,
Yet never a breeze did breathe:
Slowly and smoothly went the ship,
Moved onward from beneath.

The lonesome Spirit from the south pole carries on the ship as far as the Line, in obedience to the angelic troop, but still requireth vengeance.

Under the keel nine fathom deep,
From the land of mist and snow,
The spirit slid: and it was he
That made the ship to go.   380
The sails at noon left off their tune,
And the ship stood still also.

The Sun, right up above the mast,
Had fixed her to the ocean:
But in a minute she 'gan stir,
With a short uneasy motion—
Backwards and forwards half her length
With a short uneasy motion.

Then like a pawing horse let go,
She made a sudden bound: 390

It flung the blood into my head,
And I fell down in a swound.

How long in that same fit I lay,
I have not to declare;
But ere my living life returned,
I heard and in my soul discerned
Two voices in the air.

"Is it he?" quoth one, "Is this the man?
By him who died on cross,
With his cruel bow he laid full low   400
The harmless Albatross.

The spirit who bideth by himself
In the land of mist and snow,
He loved the bird that loved the man
Who shot him with his bow."

The other was a softer voice,
As soft as honey dew:
Quoth he, "The man hath penance done,
And penance more will do."

PART VI

First Voice

"But tell me, tell me! speak again,   410
Thy soft response renewing—
What makes that ship drive on so fast?
What is the ocean doing?"

Second Voice

"Still as a slave before his lord,
The ocean hath no blast;
His great bright eye most silently
Up to the Moon is cast—

If he may know which way to go;
For she guides him smooth or grim.
See, brother, see! how graciously   420
She looketh down on him."

The Mariner
hath been
cast into a
trance; for the
angelic power
causeth the
vessel to drive
northward
faster than
human life
could endure.

"But why drives on that ship so fast,
Without or wave or wind?"

Second Voice

"The air is cut away before,
And closes from behind.

Fly, brother, fly! more high, more high!
Or we shall be belated:
For slow and slow that ship will go,
When the Mariner's trance is abated."

The super-
natural motion
is retarded;
the Mariner
awakes, and
his penance
begins anew.

I woke, and we were sailing on   430
As in a gentle weather:
'Twas night, calm night, the moon was high;
The dead men stood together.

All stood together on the deck,
For a charnel-dungeon fitter:
All fixed on me their stony eyes,
That in the Moon did glitter.

The pang, the curse, with which they died,
Had never passed away:
I could not draw my eyes from theirs,   440
Nor turn them up to pray.

The curse is
finally
expiated.

And now this spell was snapped: once more
I viewed the ocean green,
And looked far forth, yet little saw
Of what had else been seen—

Like one, that on a lonesome road
Doth walk in fear and dread,
And having once turned round walks on,
And turns no more his head;
Because he knows, a frightful fiend   450
Doth close behind him tread.

But soon there breathed a wind on me,
Nor sound nor motion made:
Its path was not upon the sea,
In ripple or in shade.

It raised my hair, it fanned my cheek
Like a meadow-gale of spring—
It mingled strangely with my fears,
Yet it felt like a welcoming.

Swiftly, swiftly flew the ship,   460
Yet she sailed softly too:
Sweetly, sweetly blew the breeze—
On me alone it blew.

And the
ancient
Mariner be-
holdeth his
native country.
Oh! dream of joy! is this indeed
The lighthouse top I see?
Is this the hill? is this the kirk?
Is this mine own countree?

We drifted o'er the harbor-bar,
And I with sobs did pray—
O let me be awake, my God!   470
Or let me sleep alway.

The harbor-bay was clear as glass,
So smoothly it was strewn!
And on the bay the moonlight lay,
And the shadow of the Moon.

The rock shone bright, the kirk no less,
That stands above the rock:
The moonlight steeped in silentness
The steady weathercock.

The angelic
spirits leave
the dead
bodies,
And the bay was white with silent light,   480
Till rising from the same,
Full many shapes, that shadows were,
In crimson colors came.

And appear in
their own
forms of light.
A little distance from the prow
Those crimson shadows were:
I turned my eyes upon the deck—
Oh, Christ! what saw I there!

Each corse lay flat, lifeless and flat,
And, by the holy rood!
A man all light, a seraph-man,   490
On every corse there stood.

This seraph-band, each waved his hand:
It was a heavenly sight!
They stood as signals to the land,
Each one a lovely light;

This seraph-band, each waved his hand,
No voice did they impart—
No voice; but oh! the silence sank
Like music on my heart.

But soon I heard the dash of oars,   500
I heard the Pilot's cheer;
My head was turned perforce away
And I saw a boat appear.

The Pilot and the Pilot's boy,
I heard them coming fast:
Dear Lord in Heaven! it was a joy
The dead men could not blast.

I saw a third—I heard his voice:
It is the Hermit good!
He singeth loud his godly hymns   510
That he makes in the wood.
He'll shrieve my soul, he'll wash away
The Albatross's blood.

PART VII

The Hermit of
the Wood,

This Hermit good lives in that wood
Which slopes down to the sea.
How loudly his sweet voice he rears!
He loves to talk with marineres
That come from a far countree.

He kneels at morn, and noon, and eve—
He hath a cushion plump: 520
It is the moss that wholly hides
The rotted old oak-stump.

The skiff-boat neared: I heard them talk,
"Why, this is strange, I trow!
Where are those lights so many and fair,
That signal made but now?"

"Strange, by my faith!" the Hermit said—
"And they answered not our cheer!
The planks looked warped! and see those sails,
How thin they are and sere!   530
I never saw aught like to them,
Unless perchance it were

Brown skeletons of leaves that lag
My forest-brook along;
When the ivy-tod[9] is heavy with snow,
And the owlet whoops to the wolf below,
That eats the she-wolf's young."

"Dear Lord! it hath a fiendish look—"
(The Pilot made reply)
"I am a-feared"—"Push on, push on!"   540
Said the Hermit cheerily.

The boat came closer to the ship,
But I nor spake nor stirred;
The boat came close beneath the ship,
And straight a sound was heard.

Under the water it rumbled on,
Still louder and more dread:
It reached the ship, it split the bay;
The ship went down like lead.

The ancient
Mariner is
saved in the
Pilot's boat.

Stunned by that loud and dreadful sound,   550
Which sky and ocean smote,
Like one that hath been seven days drowned
My body lay afloat;
But swift as dreams, myself I found
Within the Pilot's boat.

Upon the whirl, where sank the ship,
The boat spun round and round;
And all was still, save that the hill
Was telling of the sound.

I moved my lips—the Pilot shrieked   560
And fell down in a fit;
The holy Hermit raised his eyes,
And prayed where he did sit.

[9] ivy bush.

I took the oars: the Pilot's boy,
Who now doth crazy go,
Laughed loud and long, and all the while
His eyes went to and fro.
"Ha! ha!" quoth he, "full plain I see,
The Devil knows how to row."

And now, all in my own countree,   570
I stood on the firm land!
The Hermit stepped forth from the boat,
And scarcely he could stand.

"O shrieve me, shrieve[10] me, holy man!"
The Hermit crossed his brow.
"Say quick," quoth he, "I bid thee say—
What manner of man art thou?"

Forthwith this frame of mine was wrenched
With a woeful agony,
Which forced me to begin my tale;   580
And then it left me free.

Since then, at an uncertain hour,
That agony returns:
And till my ghastly tale is told,
This heart within me burns.

I pass, like night, from land to land;
I have strange power of speech;
That moment that his face I see,
I know the man that must hear me:
To him my tale I teach.   590

What loud uproar bursts from that door!
The wedding guests are there:
But in the garden bower the bride
And bride-maids singing are:
And hark the little vesper bell,
Which biddeth me to prayer!

O Wedding Guest! this soul hath been
Alone on a wide wide sea:
So lonely 'twas, that God himself
Scarce seeméd there to be.   600

[10] shrive: hear confession and grant absolution.

O sweeter than the marriage feast,
'Tis sweeter far to me,
To walk together to the kirk
With a goodly company!—

To walk together to the kirk,
And all together pray,
While each to his great Father bends,
Old men, and babes, and loving friends
And youths and maidens gay!

And to teach,
by his own
example, love
and reverence
to all things
that God made
and loveth.

Farewell, farewell! but this I tell   610
To thee, thou Wedding Guest!
He prayeth well, who loveth well
Both man and bird and beast.

He prayeth best, who loveth best
All things both great and small;
For the dear God who loveth us,
He made and loveth all.

The Mariner, whose eye is bright,
Whose beard with age is hoar,
Is gone: and now the Wedding Guest   620
Turned from the bridegroom's door.

He went like one that hath been stunned,
And is of sense forlorn:
A sadder and a wiser man,
He rose the morrow morn.

GEORGE GORDON, LORD BYRON [1788–1824]

FROM *Don Juan*, CANTO THE FIRST

135

'Twas, as the watchmen say, a cloudy night;
   No moon, no stars, the wind was low or loud
By gusts, and many a sparkling hearth was bright
   With the piled wood, round which the family crowd;

There's something cheerful in that sort of light,
    Even as a summer sky's without a cloud:
I'm fond of fire, and crickets, and all that,
A lobster salad, and champagne, and chat.   1080

136

'Twas midnight—Donna Julia was in bed,
    Sleeping, most probably—when at her door
Arose a clatter might awake the dead,
    If they had never been awoke before,
And that they have been so we all have read,
    And are to be so, at the least, once more;
The door was fastened, but with voice and fist
First knocks were heard, then "Madam—Madam—hist!

137

"For God's sake, Madam—Madam—here's my master,
    With more than half the city at his back—   1090
Was ever heard of such a cursed disaster!
    'Tis not my fault—I kept good watch—Alack!
Do, pray, undo the bolt a little faster—
    They're on the stair just now, and in a crack
Will all be here; perhaps he yet may fly—
Surely the window's not so *very* high!"

138

By this time Don Alfonso was arrived,
    With torches, friends, and servants in great number;
The major part of them had long been wived,
    And therefore paused not to disturb the slumber   1100
Of any wicked woman, who contrived
    By stealth her husband's temples to encumber:
Examples of this kind are so contagious,
Were *one* not punished, *all* would be outrageous.

139

I can't tell how, or why, or what suspicion
    Could enter into Don Alfonso's head;
But for a cavalier of his condition
    It surely was exceedingly ill-bred,

Without a word of previous admonition,
　To hold a levee round his lady's bed,　　　　　　1110
And summon lackeys, armed with fire and sword,
To prove himself the thing he most abhorred.

140

Poor Donna Julia! starting as from sleep
　(Mind that I do not say she had not slept),
Began at once to scream, and yawn, and weep;
　Her maid, Antonia, who was an adept,
Contrived to fling the bedclothes in a heap,
　As if she had just now from out them crept:
I can't tell why she should take all this trouble
To prove her mistress had been sleeping double.　　1120

141

But Julia mistress, and Antonia maid,
　Appeared like two poor harmless women, who
Of goblins, but still more of men, afraid,
　Had thought one man might be deterred by two,
And therefore side by side were gently laid,
　Until the hours of absence should run through,
And truant husband should return, and say,
"My dear, I was the first who came away."

142

Now Julia found at length a voice, and cried,
　"In heaven's name, Don Alfonso, what d'ye mean?　1130
Has madness seized you? would that I had died
　Ere such a monster's victim I had been!
What may this midnight violence betide,
　A sudden fit of drunkenness or spleen?
Dare you suspect me, whom the thought would kill?
Search, then, the room!"—Alfonso said, "I will."

143

He searched, *they* searched, and rummaged everywhere,
　Closet and clothes-press, chest and window seat,
And found much linen, lace, and several pair
　Of stockings, slippers, brushes, combs, complete,　1140

With other articles of ladies fair,
　　To keep them beautiful, or leave them neat:
Arras they pricked and curtains with their swords,
And wounded several shutters, and some boards.

144

Under the bed they searched, and there they found—
　　No matter what—it was not that they sought;
They opened windows, gazing if the ground
　　Had signs or footmarks, but the earth said nought;
And then they stared each other's faces round:
　　'Tis odd, not one of all these seekers thought,　　　　1150
And seems to me almost a sort of blunder,
Of looking *in* the bed as well as under.

145

During this inquisition Julia's tongue
　　Was not asleep—"Yes, search and search," she cried,
"Insult on insult heap, and wrong on wrong!
　　It was for this that I became a bride!
For this in silence I have suffered long
　　A husband like Alfonso at my side;
But now I'll bear no more, nor here remain,
If there be law or lawyers in all Spain.　　　　1160

146

"Yes, Don Alfonso! husband now no more,
　　If ever you indeed deserved the name,
Is't worthy of your years?—you have threescore—
　　Fifty, or sixty, it is all the same—
Is't wise or fitting, causeless to explore
　　For facts against a virtuous woman's fame?
Ungrateful, perjured, barbarous Don Alfonso,
How dare you think your lady would go on so?

147

"Is it for this I have disdained to hold
　　The common privileges of my sex?　　　　1170
That I have chosen a confessor so old
　　And deaf, that any other it would vex,

And never once he has had cause to scold,
  But found my very innocence perplex
So much, he always doubted I was married—
How sorry you will be when I've miscarried!

148

"Was it for this that no Cortejo[1] e'er
  I yet have chosen from out the youth of Seville?
Is it for this I scarce went anywhere,
  Except to bull-fights, mass, play, rout, and revel?   1180
Is it for this, whate'er my suitors were,
  I favored none—nay, was almost uncivil?
Is it for this that General Count O'Reilly,
Who took Algiers, declares I used him vilely?

149

"Did not the Italian Musico Cazzani
  Sing at my heart six months at least in vain?
Did not his countryman, Count Corniani,
  Call me the only virtuous wife in Spain?
Were there not also Russians, English, many?
  The Count Strongstroganoff I put in pain,   1190
And Lord Mount Coffeehouse, the Irish peer,
Who killed himself for love (with wine) last year.

150

"Have I not had two bishops at my feet?
  The Duke of Ichar, and Don Fernan Nunez?
And is it thus a faithful wife you treat?
  I wonder in what quarter now the moon is:
I praise your vast forbearance not to beat
  Me also, since the time so opportune is—
Oh, valiant man! with sword drawn and cocked trigger,
Now, tell me, don't you cut a pretty figure?   1200

151

"Was it for this you took your sudden journey,
  Under pretense of business indispensable,
With that sublime of rascals your attorney,
  Whom I see standing there, and looking sensible

[1] publicly acknowledged lover.

Of having played the fool? though both I spurn, he
  Deserves the worst, his conduct's less defensible,
Because, no doubt, 'twas for his dirty fee,
And not from any love to you nor me.

152

"If he comes here to take a deposition,
  By all means let the gentleman proceed;   1210
You've made the apartment in a fit condition:
  There's pen and ink for you, sir, when you need—
Let everything be noted with precision,
  I would not you for nothing should be feed—
But as my maid's undressed, pray turn your spies out."
"Oh!" sobbed Antonia, "I could tear their eyes out."

153

"There is the closet, there the toilet, there
  The antechamber—search them under, over;
There is the sofa, there the great armchair,
  The chimney—which would really hold a lover.   1220
I wish to sleep, and beg you will take care
  And make no further noise, till you discover
The secret cavern of this lurking treasure—
And when 'tis found, let me, too, have that pleasure.

154

"And now, Hidalgo! now that you have thrown
  Doubt upon me, confusion over all,
Pray have the courtesy to make it known
  Who is the man you search for? how d'ye call
Him? what's his lineage? let him but be shown—
  I hope he's young and handsome—is he tall?   1230
Tell me—and be assured, that since you stain
Mine honor thus; it shall not be in vain.

155

"At least, perhaps, he has not sixty years,
  At that age he would be too old for slaughter,
Or for so young a husband's jealous fears—
  (Antonia! let me have a glass of water.)

I am ashamed of having shed these tears,
    They are unworthy of my father's daughter;
My mother dreamed not in my natal hour,
    That I should fall into a monster's power.   1240

156

"Perhaps 'tis of Antonia you are jealous,
    You saw that she was sleeping by my side,
When you broke in upon us with your fellows;
    Look where you please—we've nothing, sir, to hide;
Only another time, I trust, you'll tell us,
    Or for the sake of decency abide
A moment at the door, that we may be
Dressed to receive so much good company.

157

"And now, sir, I have done, and say no more;
    The little I have said may serve to show   1250
The guileless heart in silence may grieve o'er
    The wrongs to whose exposure it is slow:
I leave you to your conscience as before,
    'Twill one day ask you, *why* you used me so?
God grant you feel not then the bitterest grief!
Antonia! where's my pocket handkerchief?"

158

She ceased, and turned upon her pillow; pale
    She lay, her dark eyes flashing through their tears,
Like skies that rain and lighten; as a veil,
    Waved and o'ershading her wan cheek, appears   1260
Her streaming hair; the black curls strive, but fail,
    To hide the glossy shoulder, which uprears
Its snow through all; her soft lips lie apart,
And louder than her breathing beats her heart.

159

The Senhor Don Alfonso stood confused;
    Antonia bustled round the ransacked room,
And, turning up her nose, with looks abused
    Her master, and his myrmidons, of whom

Not one, except the attorney, was amused;
  He, like Achates,[2] faithful to the tomb,   1270
So there were quarrels, cared not for the cause,
Knowing they must be settled by the laws.

160

With prying snub nose, and small eyes, he stood,
  Following Antonia's motions here and there,
With much suspicion in his attitude;
  For reputations he had little care;
So that a suit or action were made good,
  Small pity had he for the young and fair,
And ne'er believed in negatives, till these
Were proved by competent false witnesses.   1280

161

But Don Alfonso stood with downcast looks,
  And, truth to say, he made a foolish figure;
When, after searching in five hundred nooks,
  And treating a young wife with so much rigor,
He gained no point, except some self-rebukes,
  Added to those his lady with such vigor
Had poured upon him for the last half hour,
Quick, thick, and heavy—as a thundershower.

162

At first he tried to hammer an excuse,
  To which the sole reply was tears, and sobs,   1290
And indications of hysterics, whose
  Prologue is always certain throes, and throbs,
Gasps, and whatever else the owners choose—
  Alfonso saw his wife, and thought of Job's;
He saw too, in perspective, her relations,
And then he tried to muster all his patience.

163

He stood in act to speak, or rather stammer,
  But sage Antonia cut him short before

[2] in Virgil's *Aeneid*, Aeneas' faithful friend.

208

The anvil of his speech received the hammer,
  With "Pray, sir, leave the room, and say no more,   1300
Or madam dies."—Alfonso muttered, "D—n her."
  But nothing else, the time of words was o'er;
He cast a rueful look or two, and did,
He knew not wherefore, that which he was bid.

164

With him retired his "*posse comitatus*,"[3]
  The attorney last, who lingered near the door
Reluctantly, still tarrying there as late as
  Antonia let him—not a little sore
At this most strange and unexplained "*hiatus*"
  In Don Alfonso's facts, which just now wore   1310
An awkward look; as he revolved the case,
The door was fastened in his legal face.

165

No sooner was it bolted, than—Oh shame!
  Oh sin! Oh sorrow! and Oh womankind!
How can you do such things and keep your fame,
  Unless this world, and t'other too, be blind?
Nothing so dear as an unfilched good name!
  But to proceed—for there is more behind:
With much heartfelt reluctance be it said,
Young Juan slipped, half-smothered, from the bed.   1320

166

He had been hid—I don't pretend to say
  How, nor can I indeed describe the where—
Young, slender, and packed easily, he lay,
  No doubt, in little compass, round or square;
But pity him I neither must nor may
  His suffocation by that pretty pair;
'Twere better, sure, to die so, than be shut
With maudlin Clarence in his malmsey butt.[4]

---

[3] a group of men assisting an officer.
[4] the Duke of Clarence is said to have drowned in a cask of malmsey wine in the Tower of London.

And, secondly, I pity not, because
   He had no business to commit a sin,   1330
Forbid by heavenly, fined by human laws,
   At least 'twas rather early to begin;
But at sixteen the conscience rarely gnaws
   So much as when we call our old debts in
At sixty years, and draw the accompts of evil,
And find a deuced balance with the devil.

168

Of his position I can give no notion;
   'Tis written in the Hebrew Chronicle,
How the physicians, leaving pill and potion,
   Prescribed, by way of blister, a young belle,   1340
When old King David's blood grew dull in motion,
   And that the medicine answered very well;
Perhaps 'twas in a different way applied,
For David lived, but Juan nearly died.

PERCY BYSSHE SHELLEY [1792–1822]

Ode to the West Wind

I

O wild West Wind, thou breath of Autumn's being,
Thou, from whose unseen presence the leaves dead
Are driven, like ghosts from an enchanter fleeing,

Yellow, and black, and pale, and hectic red,
Pestilence-stricken multitudes: O thou,
Who chariotest to their dark wintry bed

The wingéd seeds, where they lie cold and low,
Each like a corpse within its grave, until
Thine azure sister of the Spring shall blow

Her clarion o'er the dreaming earth, and fill
(Driving sweet buds like flocks to feed in air)
With living hues and odors plain and hill:

Wild Spirit, which art moving everywhere;
Destroyer and preserver; hear, oh, hear!

2

Thou on whose stream, mid the steep sky's commotion,
Loose clouds like earth's decaying leaves are shed,
Shook from the tangled boughs of Heaven and Ocean,

Angels of rain and lightning: there are spread
On the blue surface of thine aery surge,
Like the bright hair uplifted from the head   20

Of some fierce Maenad,[1] even from the dim verge
Of the horizon to the zenith's height,
The locks of the approaching storm. Thou dirge

Of the dying year, to which this closing night
Will be the dome of a vast sepulcher,
Vaulted with all thy congregated might

Of vapors, from whose solid atmosphere
Black rain, and fire, and hail will burst: oh, hear!

3

Thou who didst waken from his summer dreams
The blue Mediterranean, where he lay,   30
Lulled by the coil of his crystálline streams,

Beside a pumice isle in Baiae's bay,[2]
And saw in sleep old palaces and towers
Quivering within the wave's intenser day,

All overgrown with azure moss and flowers
So sweet, the sense faints picturing them! Thou
For whose path the Atlantic's level powers

[1] a female attendant of Bacchus, the god of wine.
[2] near Naples, the site of the palaces of Julius Caesar, Pompey, and Nero.

Cleave themselves into chasms, while far below
The sea-blooms and the oozy woods which wear
The sapless foliage of the ocean, know   40

Thy voice, and suddenly grow gray with fear,
And tremble and despoil themselves: oh, hear!

                              4

If I were a dead leaf thou mightest bear;
If I were a swift cloud to fly with thee;
A wave to pant beneath thy power, and share

The impulse of thy strength, only less free
Than thou, O uncontrollable! If even
I were as in my boyhood, and could be

The comrade of thy wanderings over Heaven
As then, when to outstrip thy skiey speed   50
Scarce seemed a vision; I would ne'er have striven

As thus with thee in prayer in my sore need.
Oh, lift me as a wave, a leaf, a cloud!
I fall upon the thorns of life! I bleed!

A heavy weight of hours has chained and bowed
One too like thee: tameless, and swift, and proud.

                              5

Make me thy lyre, even as the forest is:
What if my leaves are falling like its own!
The tumult of thy mighty harmonies

Will take from both a deep, autumnal tone,   60
Sweet though in sadness. Be thou, Spirit fierce,
My spirit! Be thou me, impetuous one!

Drive my dead thoughts over the universe
Like withered leaves to quicken a new birth!
And, by the incantation of this verse,

Scatter, as from an unextinguished hearth
Ashes and sparks, my words among mankind!
Be through my lips to unawakened earth

The trumpet of a prophecy! O, Wind,
If Winter comes, can Spring be far behind?

Song to the Men of England

Men of England, wherefore plough
For the lords who lay ye low?
Wherefore weave with toil and care
The rich robes your tyrants wear?

Wherefore feed, and clothe, and save,
From the cradle to the grave,
Those ungrateful drones who would
Drain your sweat—nay, drink your blood?

Wherefore, Bees of England, forge
Many a weapon, chain, and scourge,   10
That these stingless drones may spoil
The forced produce of your toil?

Have ye leisure, comfort, calm,
Shelter, food, love's gentle balm?
Or what is it ye buy so dear
With your pain and with your fear?

The seed ye sow, another reaps;
The wealth ye find, another keeps;
The robes ye weave, another wears;
The arms ye forge, another bears.   20

Sow seed—but let no tyrant reap;
Find wealth—let no impostor heap;
Weave robes—let not the idle wear;
Forge arms—in your defense to bear.

Shrink to your cellars, holes, and cells;
In halls ye deck another dwells.
Why shake the chains ye wrought? Ye see
The steel ye tempered glance on ye.

With plough and spade, and hoe and loom,
Trace your grave, and build your tomb,   30
And weave your winding-sheet, till fair
England be your sepulcher.

To a Skylark

Hail to thee, blithe Spirit!
   Bird thou never wert,
That from Heaven, or near it,
   Pourest thy full heart
In profuse strains of unpremeditated art.

Higher still and higher
   From the earth thou springest
Like a cloud of fire;
   The blue deep thou wingest,
And singing still dost soar, and soaring ever singest.   10

In the golden lightning
   Of the sunken sun,
O'er which clouds are bright'ning,
   Thou dost float and run;
Like an unbodied joy whose race is just begun.

The pale purple even
   Melts around thy flight;
Like a star of Heaven,
   In the broad daylight
Thou art unseen, but yet I hear thy shrill delight,   20

Keen as are the arrows
   Of that silver sphere,
Whose intense lamp narrows
   In the white dawn clear
Until we hardly see—we feel that it is there.

All the earth and air
   With thy voice is loud,
As, when night is bare,
   From one lonely cloud
The moon rains out her beams, and Heaven is overflowed.   30

What thou art we know not;
   What is most like thee?
From rainbow clouds there flow not
   Drops so bright to see
As from thy presence showers a rain of melody.

Like a Poet hidden
　　In the light of thought,
Singing hymns unbidden,
　　Till the world is wrought
To sympathy with hopes and fears it heeded not:　　40

Like a high-born maiden
　　In a palace-tower,
Soothing her love-laden
　　Soul in secret hour
With music sweet as love, which overflows her bower:

Like a glow-worm golden
　　In a dell of dew,
Scattering unbeholden
　　Its aereal hue
Among the flowers and grass, which screen it from the view!　　50

Like a rose embowered
　　In its own green leaves,
By warm winds deflowered,
　　Till the scent it gives
Makes faint with too much sweet those heavy-wingéd thieves:

Sound of vernal showers
　　On the twinkling grass,
Rain-awakened flowers,
　　All that ever was
Joyous, and clear, and fresh, thy music doth surpass:　　60

Teach us, Sprite or Bird,
　　What sweet thoughts are thine:
I have never heard
　　Praise of love or wine
That panted forth a flood of rapture so divine.

Chorus Hymeneal,[1]
　　Or triumphal chant,
Matched with thine would be all
　　But an empty vaunt,
A thing wherein we feel there is some hidden want.　　70

[1] marriage song.

What objects are the fountains
    Of thy happy strain?
What fields, or waves, or mountains?
    What shapes of sky or plain?
What love of thine own kind? what ignorance of pain?

With thy clear keen joyance
    Languor cannot be:
Shadow of annoyance
    Never came near thee:
Thou lovest—but ne'er knew love's sad satiety.   80

Waking or asleep,
    Thou of death must deem
Things more true and deep
    Than we mortals dream,
Or how could thy notes flow in such a crystal stream?

We look before and after,
    And pine for what is not:
Our sincerest laughter
    With some pain is fraught;
Our sweetest songs are those that tell of saddest thought.   90

Yet if we could scorn
    Hate, and pride, and fear;
If we were things born
    Not to shed a tear,
I know not how thy joy we ever should come near.

Better than all measures
    Of delightful sound,
Better than all treasures
    That in books are found,
Thy skill to poet were, thou scorner of the ground!   100

Teach me half the gladness
    That thy brain must know,
Such harmonious madness
    From my lips would flow
The world should listen then—as I am listening now.

Bright Star

Bright star, would I were steadfast as thou art—
Not in lone splendor hung aloft the night,
And watching, with eternal lids apart,
Like nature's patient sleepless Eremite,[1]
The moving waters at their priestlike task
Of pure ablution round earth's human shores,
Or gazing on the new soft fallen mask
Of snow upon the mountains and the moors:
No—yet still steadfast, still unchangeable,
Pillowed upon my fair love's ripening breast
To feel for ever its soft fall and swell,
Awake for ever in a sweet unrest;
Still, still to hear her tender-taken breath,
And so live ever—or else swoon to death.

[1] hermit.

La Belle Dame Sans Merci[1]

O what can ail thee, knight at arms,
   Alone and palely loitering?
The sedge has withered from the lake,
   And no birds sing.

O what can ail thee, knight at arms,
   So haggard and so woebegone?
The squirrel's granary is full,
   And the harvest's done.

I see a lily on thy brow
   With anguish moist and fever dew,   10
And on thy cheeks a fading rose
   Fast withereth too.

[1] The Beautiful Lady Without Pity.

I met a lady in the meads,
    Full beautiful, a faery's child:
Her hair was long, her foot was light,
    And her eyes were wild.

I made a garland for her head,
    And bracelets too, and fragrant zone;[2]
She looked at me as she did love,
    And made sweet moan.   20

I set her on my pacing steed,
    And nothing else saw all day long;
For sidelong would she bend and sing
    A faery's song.

She found me roots of relish sweet,
    And honey wild, and manna dew,
And sure in language strange she said,
    "I love thee true!"

She took me to her elfin grot,
    And there she wept and sighed full sore;   30
And there I shut her wild, wild eyes
    With kisses four.

And there she lullèd me asleep,
    And there I dreamed—Ah! woe betide!
The latest dream I ever dreamed
    On the cold hill side.

I saw pale kings, and princes too,
    Pale warriors, death-pale were they all;
Who cried—"La Belle Dame Sans Merci
    Hath thee in thrall!"   40

I saw their starved lips in the gloam,
    With horrid warning gapéd wide,
And I awoke and found me here,
    On the cold hill's side.

And this is why I sojourn here,
    Alone and palely loitering,
Though the sedge is withered from the lake,
    And no birds sing.

[2] belt.

Ode on a Grecian Urn

1

Thou still unravished bride of quietness,
   Thou foster child of silence and slow time,
Sylvan historian, who canst thus express
   A flowery tale more sweetly than our rhyme:
What leaf-fringed legend haunts about thy shape
   Of deities or mortals, or of both,
     In Tempe or the dales of Arcady?[1]
   What men or gods are these? What maidens loth?
What mad pursuit? What struggle to escape?
     What pipes and timbrels? What wild ecstasy?

2

Heard melodies are sweet, but those unheard
   Are sweeter; therefore, ye soft pipes, play on;
Not to the sensual ear, but, more endeared,
   Pipe to the spirit ditties of no tone:
Fair youth, beneath the trees, thou canst not leave
   Thy song, nor ever can those trees be bare;
     Bold Lover, never, never canst thou kiss,
Though winning near the goal—yet, do not grieve;
   She cannot fade, though thou hast not thy bliss,
     For ever wilt thou love, and she be fair!

3

Ah, happy, happy boughs! that cannot shed
   Your leaves, nor ever bid the Spring adieu;
And, happy melodist, unwearied,
   For ever piping songs for ever new;
More happy love! more happy, happy love!
   For ever warm and still to be enjoyed,
     For ever panting, and for ever young;
All breathing human passion far above,
   That leaves a heart high-sorrowful and cloyed,
     A burning forehead, and a parching tongue.

[1] Tempe is a valley sacred to Apollo, god of music and poetry. Arcady is a region in Greece frequently presented as an idyllic pastoral scene.

4

Who are these coming to the sacrifice?
　　To what green altar, O mysterious priest,
Lead'st thou that heifer lowing at the skies,
　　And all her silken flanks with garlands drest?
What little town by river or sea shore,
　　Or mountain-built with peaceful citadel,
　　　　Is emptied of this folk, this pious morn?
And, little town, thy streets for evermore
　　Will silent be; and not a soul to tell
　　　　Why thou art desolate, can e'er return.

5

O Attic² shape! Fair attitude! with brede³
　　Of marble men and maidens overwrought,
With forest branches and the trodden weed;
　　Thou, silent form, dost tease us out of thought
As doth eternity: Cold Pastoral!
　　When old age shall this generation waste,
　　　　Thou shalt remain, in midst of other woe
Than ours, a friend to man, to whom thou say'st,
　　"Beauty is truth, truth beauty,"—that is all
　　　　Ye know on earth, and all ye need to know.

ELIZABETH BARRETT BROWNING [1806–1861]

43　*How Do I Love Thee*

How do I love thee? Let me count the ways.
I love thee to the depth and breadth and height
My soul can reach, when feeling out of sight
For the ends of Being and ideal Grace.

² belonging to Attica, or ancient Athens, and connoting elegance.
³ embroidery.

I love thee to the level of every day's
Most quiet need, by sun and candle light.
I love thee freely, as men strive for right;
I love thee purely, as they turn from praise.
I love thee with the passion put to use
In my old griefs, and with my childhood's faith.
I love thee with a love I seemed to lose
With my lost saints!—I love thee with the breath,
Smiles, tears, of all my life!—and, if God choose,
I shall but love thee better after death.

EDGAR ALLAN POE [1809–1849]

To Helen[1]

Helen, thy beauty is to me
    Like those Nicean[2] barks of yore
That gently, o'er a perfumed sea,
    The weary way-worn wanderer bore
    To his own native shore.

On desperate seas long wont to roam,
    Thy hyacinth hair, thy classic face,
Thy Naiad[3] airs have brought me home
    To the glory that was Greece,
And the grandeur that was Rome.

Lo, in yon brilliant window-niche
    How statue-like I see thee stand,
    The agate lamp within thy hand,
Ah! Psyche,[4] from the regions which
    Are holy land!

[1] Helen of Troy.
[2] pertaining to Nicaea, an ancient city in Asia Minor.
[3] water nymph.
[4] a beautiful princess with whom Cupid fell in love.

ALFRED, LORD TENNYSON [1809–1892]

Ulysses

It little profits that an idle king,
By this still hearth, among these barren crags,
Matched with an aged wife, I mete and dole
Unequal laws unto a savage race,
That hoard, and sleep, and feed, and know not me.
I cannot rest from travel: I will drink
Life to lees: all times I have enjoyed
Greatly, have suffered greatly, both with those
That loved me, and alone; on shore, and when
Through scudding drifts the rainy Hyades[1]   10
Vext the dim sea. I am become a name;
For always roaming with a hungry heart
Much have I seen and known: cities of men
And manners, climates, councils, governments,
Myself not least, but honored of them all,—
And drunk delight of battle with my peers,
Far on the ringing plains of windy Troy.
I am a part of all that I have met;
Yet all experience is an arch wherethrough
Gleams that untraveled world, whose margin fades   20
For ever and for ever when I move.
How dull it is to pause, to make an end,
To rust unburnished, not to shine in use!
As though to breathe were life. Life piled on life
Were all too little, and of one to me
Little remains: but every hour is saved
From that eternal silence, something more,
A bringer of new things; and vile it were
For some three suns to store and hoard myself,
And this gray spirit yearning in desire   30
To follow knowledge, like a sinking star,
Beyond the utmost bound of human thought.
    This is my son, mine own Telemachus,
To whom I leave the scepter and the isle—
Well-loved of me, discerning to fulfill
This labor, by slow prudence to make mild

[1] a group of stars believed to bring rain.

A rugged people, and through soft degrees
Subdue them to the useful and the good.
Most blameless is he, centered in the sphere
Of common duties, decent not to fail
In offices of tenderness, and pay
Meet adoration to my household gods,
When I am gone. He works his work, I mine.

   There lies the port: the vessel puffs her sail:
There gloom the dark broad seas. My mariners,
Souls that have toiled, and wrought, and thought with me—
That ever with a frolic welcome took
The thunder and the sunshine, and opposed
Free hearts, free foreheads—you and I are old;
Old age hath yet his honor and his toil;
Death closes all: but something ere the end,
Some work of noble note, may yet be done,
Not unbecoming men that strove with Gods.
The lights begin to twinkle from the rocks:
The long day wanes: the slow moon climbs: the deep
Moans round with many voices. Come, my friends,
'Tis not too late to seek a newer world.
Push off, and sitting well in order smite
The sounding furrows; for my purpose holds
To sail beyond the sunset, and the baths
Of all the western stars, until I die.
It may be that the gulfs will wash us down:
It may be we shall touch the Happy Isles,[2]
And see the great Achilles, whom we knew.
Though much is taken, much abides; and though
We are not now that strength which in old days
Moved earth and heaven, that which we are, we are,—
One equal temper of heroic hearts,
Made weak by time and fate, but strong in will
To strive, to seek, to find, and not to yield.

Tears, Idle Tears

    Tears, idle tears, I know not what they mean,
    Tears from the depth of some divine despair
    Rise in the heart, and gather to the eyes,

[2] the home of the blessed after death.

In looking on the happy autumn-fields,
And thinking of the days that are no more.

Fresh as the first beam glittering on a sail,
That brings our friends up from the underworld,
Sad as the last which redden over one
That sinks with all we love below the verge;
So sad, so fresh, the days that are no more.

Ah, sad and strange as in dark summer dawns
The earliest pipe of half-awakened birds
To dying ears, when unto dying eyes
The casement slowly grows a glimmering square;
So sad, so strange, the days that are no more.

Dear as remembered kisses after death,
And sweet as those by hopeless fancy feigned
On lips that are for others; deep as love,
Deep as first love, and wild with all regret;
O Death in Life, the days that are no more!

"Frater Ave atque Vale"[1]

Row us out from Desenzano, to your Sirmione[2] row!
So they rowed, and there we landed—"O venusta Sirmio!"[3]
There to me through all the groves of olive in the summer glow,
There beneath the Roman ruin where the purple flowers grow,
Came that "Ave atque Vale" of the poet's hopeless woe,
Tenderest of Roman poets nineteen hundred years ago,
"Frater Ave atque Vale"—as we wandered to and fro
Gazing at the Lydian[4] laughter of the Garda Lake below
Sweet Catullus's all-but-island, olive-silvery Sirmio!

[1] "Brother, Hail and Farewell," a quotation from Catullus, a Latin poet of the first century B.C. Catullus' poem is a last farewell to his brother.
[2] Desenzano is a town on Lake Garda in northern Italy. Sirmione, known as Sirmio in antiquity, is the peninsula on Lake Garda where the villa of Catullus once stood.
[3] "O beautiful Sirmio," a quotation from Catullus.
[4] the Etruscans, who lived near Lake Garda, were believed to have come from Lydia in Asia Minor.

ROBERT BROWNING [1812–1889]

My Last Duchess

FERRARA

That's my last Duchess painted on the wall,
Looking as if she were alive. I call
That piece a wonder, now: Frà Pandolf's hands
Worked busily a day, and there she stands.
Will't please you sit and look at her? I said
"Frà Pandolf" by design, for never read
Strangers like you that pictured countenance,
The depth and passion of its earnest glance,
But to myself they turned (since none puts by
The curtain I have drawn for you, but I)   10
And seemed as they would ask me, if they durst,
How such a glance came there; so, not the first
Are you to turn and ask thus. Sir, 'twas not
Her husband's presence only, called that spot
Of joy into the Duchess' cheek; perhaps
Frà Pandolf chanced to say, "Her mantle laps
Over my lady's wrist too much," or "Paint
Must never hope to reproduce the faint
Half-flush that dies along her throat": such stuff
Was courtesy, she thought, and cause enough   20
For calling up that spot of joy. She had
A heart—how shall I say?—too soon made glad,
Too easily impressed: she liked whate'er
She looked on, and her looks went everywhere.
Sir, 'twas all one! My favor at her breast,
The dropping of the daylight in the West,
The bough of cherries some officious fool
Broke in the orchard for her, the white mule
She rode with round the terrace—all and each
Would draw from her alike the approving speech,   30
Or blush, at least. She thanked men,—good! but thanked
Somehow—I know not how—as if she ranked
My gift of a nine-hundred-years-old name
With anybody's gift. Who'd stoop to blame
This sort of trifling? Even had you skill

In speech—(which I have not)—to make your will
Quite clear to such an one, and say, "Just this
Or that in you disgusts me; here you miss,
Or there exceed the mark"—and if she let
Herself be lessoned so, nor plainly set   40
Her wits to yours, forsooth, and made excuse,
—E'en then would be some stooping; and I choose
Never to stoop. Oh sir, she smiled, no doubt,
Whene'er I passed her; but who passed without
Much the same smile? This grew; I gave commands;
Then all smiles stopped together. There she stands
As if alive. Will't please you rise? We'll meet
The company below, then. I repeat,
The Count your master's known munificence
Is ample warrant that no just pretence   50
Of mine for dowry will be disallowed;
Though his fair daughter's self, as I avowed
At starting, is my object. Nay, we'll go
Together down, sir. Notice Neptune, though,
Taming a sea-horse, thought a rarity,
Which Claus of Innsbruck cast in bronze for me!

Meeting at Night

The gray sea and the long black land;
And the yellow half-moon large and low;
And the startled little waves that leap
In fiery ringlets from their sleep,
As I gain the cove with pushing prow,
And quench its speed i' the slushy sand.

Then a mile of warm sea-scented beach;
Three fields to cross till a farm appears;
A tap at the pane, the quick sharp scratch
And blue spurt of a lighted match,
And a voice less loud, through its joys and fears,
Than the two hearts beating each to each!

Home-Thoughts, from Abroad

Oh, to be in England
Now that April's there,
And whoever wakes in England
Sees some morning, unaware,
That the lowest boughs and the brushwood sheaf
Round the elm-tree bole are in tiny leaf,
While the chaffinch sings on the orchard bough
In England—now!

And after April, when May follows,
And the whitethroat builds, and all the swallows!
Hark, where my blossomed pear-tree in the hedge
Leans to the field and scatters on the clover
Blossoms and dewdrops—at the bent spray's edge—
That's the wise thrush; he sings each song twice over,
Lest you should think he never could recapture
The first fine careless rapture!
And though the fields look rough with hoary dew,
All will be gay when noontide wakes anew
The buttercups, the little children's dower,
—Far brighter than this gaudy melon-flower!

A Likeness

Some people hang portraits up
In a room where they dine or sup:
And the wife clinks tea things under,
And her cousin, he stirs his cup,
Asks, "Who was the lady, I wonder?"
" 'Tis a daub John bought at a sale,"
Quoth the wife—looks black as thunder:
"What a shade beneath her nose!
Snuff-taking, I suppose—"
Adds the cousin, while John's corns ail.   10

Or else, there's no wife in the case,
But the portrait's queen of the place,
Alone mid the other spoils
Of youth—masks, gloves and foils,
And pipe sticks, rose, cherry tree, jasmine,
And the long whip, the tandem-lasher,
And the cast from a fist ("not, alas! mine,
But my master's, the Tipton Slasher")
And the cards where pistol balls mark ace,
And a satin shoe used for cigar case,   20
And the chamois horns ("shot in the Chablais")
And prints—Rarey drumming on Cruiser,
And Sayers, our champion, the bruiser,
And the little edition of Rabelais:
Where a friend, with both hands in his pockets,
May saunter up close to examine it,
And remark a good deal of Jane Lamb in it,
"But the eyes are half out of their sockets;
That hair's not so bad, where the gloss is,
But they've made the girl's nose a proboscis: 30
Jane Lamb, that we danced with at Vichy!
What, is not she Jane? Then, who is she?"

All that I own is a print,
An etching, a mezzotint;
'Tis a study, a fancy, a fiction,
Yet a fact (take my conviction)
Because it has more than a hint
Of a certain face, I never
Saw elsewhere touch or trace of
In women I've seen the face of: 40
Just an etching, and, so far, clever.

I keep my prints, an imbroglio,
Fifty in one portfolio.
When somebody tries my claret,
We turn round chairs to the fire,
Chirp over days in a garret,
Chuckle o'er increase of salary,
Taste the good fruits of our leisure,
Talk about pencil and lyre,
And the National Portrait Gallery: 50

Then I exhibit my treasure.
After we've turned over twenty,
And the debt of wonder my crony owes
Is paid to my Marc Antonios,
He stops me—"*Festina lentè!*[1]
What's that sweet thing there, the etching?"
How my waistcoat-strings want stretching,
How my cheeks grow red as tomatoes,
How my heart leaps! But hearts, after leaps, ache.

"By the by, you must take, for a keepsake,   60
That other, you praised, of Volpato's."

The fool! would he try a flight further and say
He never saw, never before to-day,
What was able to take his breath away,
A face to lose youth for, to occupy age
With the dream of, meet death with—why, I'll not engage
But that, half in a rapture and half in a rage,
I should toss him the thing's self—" 'Tis only a duplicate,
A thing of no value! Take it, I supplicate!"

WALT WHITMAN [1819–1892]

FROM *Starting from Paumanok*

Dead poets, philosophs, priests,
Martyrs, artists, inventors, governments long since,
Language-shapers, on other shores,
Nations once powerful, now reduced, withdrawn, or desolate,
I dare not proceed till I respectfully credit what you have left, wafted
     hither:
I have perused it—own it is admirable, (moving awhile among it;)
Think nothing can ever be greater—nothing can ever deserve more than
     it deserves;
Regarding it all intently a long while—then dismissing it,
I stand in my place, with my own day, here.

[1] "Make haste slowly."

FROM *Song of Myself*

Trippers and askers surround me;
People I meet—the effect upon me of my early life, or the ward and city
     I live in, or the nation,
The latest dates, discoveries, inventions, societies, authors old and new,
My dinner, dress, associates, looks, compliments, dues,   61
The real or fancied indifference of some man or woman I love,
The sickness of one of my folks, or of myself, or ill-doing, or loss or lack
     of money, or depressions or exaltations;
Battles, the horrors of fratricidal war, the fever of doubtful news, the
     fitful events;
These come to me days and nights, and go from me again,
But they are not the Me myself.

Apart from the pulling and hauling stands what I am;
Stands amused, complacent, compassionating, idle, unitary;
Looks down, is erect, or bends an arm on an impalpable certain rest,
Looking with side-curved head, curious what will come next;   70
Both in and out of the game, and watching and wondering at it.

♦

I believe a leaf of grass is no less than the journey-work of the stars,   660
And the pismire[1] is equally perfect, and a grain of sand, and the egg of
     the wren,
And the tree-toad is a chef-d'œuvre for the highest,
And the running blackberry would adorn the parlors of heaven,
And the narrowest hinge in my hand puts to scorn all machinery,
And the cow crunching with depress'd head surpasses any statue,
And a mouse is miracle enough to stagger sextillions of infidels,
And I could come every afternoon of my life to look at the farmer's girl
     boiling her iron tea-kettle and baking shortcake.

I find I incorporate gneiss,[2] coal, long-threaded moss, fruits, grains,
     esculent[3] roots,
And am stucco'd with quadrupeds and birds all over,
And have distanced what is behind me for good reasons,   670
And call anything close again, when I desire it.

  [1] an ant.
  [2] granite-like rock.
  [3] edible.

230

I understand the large hearts of heroes,

The courage of present times and all times;

How the skipper saw the crowded and rudderless wreck of the steamship, and Death chasing it up and down the storm;

How he knuckled tight, and gave not back one inch, and was faithful of
days and faithful of nights,

And chalk'd in large letters, on a board, *Be of good cheer, we will not
desert you:*

How he follow'd with them, and tack'd with them—and would not give
it up;

How he saved the drifting company at last:

How the lank loose-gown'd women look'd when boated from the side
of their prepared graves;

How the silent old-faced infants, and the lifted sick, and the sharp-lipp'd
unshaved men:

All this I swallow—it tastes good—I like it well—it becomes mine;   830

I am the man—I suffer'd—I was there.

The disdain and calmness of olden martyrs;

The mother, condemn'd for a witch, burnt with dry wood, her children
gazing on;

The hounded slave that flags in the race, leans by the fence, blowing,
cover'd with sweat;

The twinges that sting like needles his legs and neck—the murderous
buckshot and the bullets;

All these I feel, or am.

I am the hounded slave, I wince at the bite of the dogs,

Hell and despair are upon me, crack and again crack the marksmen;

I clutch the rails of the fence, my gore dribs, thinn'd with the ooze of my
skin;

I fall on the weeds and stones;   840

The riders spur their unwilling horses, haul close,

Taunt my dizzy ears, and beat me violently over the head with whip-
stocks.

Agonies are one of my changes of garments;

I do not ask the wounded person how he feels—I myself become the
wounded person;

My hurts turn livid upon me as I lean on a cane and observe.

This Compost

1

Something startles me where I thought I was safest;
I withdraw from the still woods I loved;
I will not go now on the pastures to walk;
I will not strip the clothes from my body to meet my lover the sea;
I will not touch my flesh to the earth, as to other flesh, to renew me.

O how can it be that the ground does not sicken?
How can you be alive, you growths of spring?
How can you furnish health, you blood of herbs, roots, orchards, grain?
Are they not continually putting distemper'd corpses within you?
Is not every continent work'd over and over with sour dead?   10

Where have you disposed of their carcasses?
Those drunkards and gluttons of so many generations;
Where have you drawn off all the foul liquid and meat?
I do not see any of it upon you to-day—or perhaps I am deceiv'd;
I will run a furrow with my plough—I will press my spade through the
     sod, and turn it up underneath;
I am sure I shall expose some of the foul meat.

Behold this compost! behold it well!
Perhaps every mite has once form'd part of a sick person—Yet behold!
The grass of spring covers the prairies,
The bean bursts noiselessly through the mould in the garden,   20
The delicate spear of the onion pierces upward,
The apple-buds cluster together on the apple-branches,
The resurrection of the wheat appears with pale visage out of its graves,
The tinge awakes over the willow-tree and the mulberry-tree,
The he-birds carol mornings and evenings, while the she-birds sit on
     their nests,
The young of poultry break through the hatch'd eggs,
The new-born of animals appear—the calf is dropt from the cow, the
     colt from the mare,
Out of its little hill faithfully rise the potato's dark green leaves,
Out of its hill rises the yellow maize-stalk—the lilacs bloom in the door-
     yards;
The summer growth is innocent and disdainful above all those strata of
     sour dead.   30

What chemistry!
That the winds are really not infectious,
That this is no cheat, this transparent green-wash of the sea, which is so
    amorous after me,
That it is safe to allow it to lick my naked body all over with its tongues,
That it will not endanger me with the fevers that have deposited them-
    selves in it,
That all is clean forever and forever.
That the cool drink from the well tastes so good,
That blackberries are so flavorous and juicy,
That the fruits of the apple-orchard, and of the orange-orchard—that
    melons, grapes, peaches, plums, will none of them poison me,
That when I recline on the grass I do not catch any disease,   40
Though probably every spear of grass rises out of what was once a
    catching disease.

3

Now I am terrified at the Earth! it is that calm and patient,
It grows such sweet things out of such corruptions,
It turns harmless and stainless on its axis, with such endless successions of
    diseas'd corpses,
It distils such exquisite winds out of such infused fetor,
It renews with such unwitting looks, its prodigal, annual, sumptuous
    crops,
It gives such divine materials to men, and accepts such leavings from
    them at last.

A Farm Picture

Through the ample open door of the peaceful country barn,
A sun-lit pasture field, with cattle and horses feeding;
And haze, and vista, and the far horizon, fading away.

Beat! Beat! Drums!

I

Beat! beat! drums!—Blow! bugles! blow!
Through the windows—through doors—burst like a ruthless force,
Into the solemn church, and scatter the congregation;

Into the school where the scholar is studying;
Leave not the bridegroom quiet—no happiness must he have now with
his bride;
Nor the peaceful farmer any peace, plowing his field or gathering his
grain;
So fierce you whirr and pound, you drums—so shrill you bugles blow.

2

Beat! beat! drums!—Blow! bugles! blow!
Over the traffic of cities—over the rumble of wheels in the streets:
Are beds prepared for sleepers at night in the houses? No sleepers must
sleep in those beds;   10
No bargainers' bargains by day—no brokers or speculators—Would they
continue?
Would the talkers be talking? would the singer attempt to sing?
Would the lawyer rise in the court to state his case before the judge?
Then rattle quicker, heavier drums—you bugles wilder blow.

3

Beat! beat! drums!—Blow! bugles! blow!
Make no parley—stop for no expostulation;
Mind not the timid—mind not the weeper or prayer;
Mind not the old man beseeching the young man;
Let not the child's voice be heard, nor the mother's entreaties;
Make even the trestles to shake the dead, where they lie awaiting the
hearses,   20
So strong you thump, O terrible drums—so loud you bugles blow.

Cavalry Crossing a Ford

A line in long array, where they wind betwixt green islands;
They take a serpentine course—their arms flash in the sun—Hark to the
musical clank;
Behold the silvery river—in it the splashing horses, loitering, stop to
drink;
Behold the brown-faced men—each group, each person, a picture—the
negligent rest on the saddles;
Some emerge on the opposite bank—others are just entering the ford—
while,
Scarlet, and blue, and snowy white,
The guidon flags flutter gaily in the wind.

An Army Corps on the March

With its cloud of skirmishers in advance,
With now the sound of a single shot snapping like a whip, and now an
    irregular volley,
The swarming ranks press on and on, the dense brigades press on;
Glittering dimly, toiling under the sun—the dust-cover'd men,
In columns rise and fall to the undulations of the ground,
With artillery interspers'd—the wheels rumble, the horses sweat,
As the army corps advances.

FROM *Marches Now the War is Over*

Rhymes and rhymers pass away—poems distill'd from foreign poems
    pass away,
The swarms of reflectors and the polite pass, and leave ashes;
Admirers, importers, obedient persons, make but the soil of literature;
America justifies itself, give it time—no disguise can deceive it, or con-
    ceal from it—it is impassive enough,
Only toward the likes of itself will it advance to meet them,   222
If its poets appear, it will in due time advance to meet them—there is no
    fear of mistake,
(The proof of a poet shall be sternly deferr'd, till his country absorbs
    him as affectionately as he has absorb'd it.)

                   ◆

I swear I begin to see the meaning of these things!
It is not the earth, it is not America, who is so great,
It is I who am great, or to be great—it is you up there, or any one;
It is to walk rapidly through civilizations, governments, theories,
Through poems, pageants, shows, to form great individuals.

                   ◆

I will confront these shows of the day and night!
I will know if I am to be less than they!
I will see if I am not as majestic as they!
I will see if I am not as subtle and real as they!
I will see if I am to be less generous than they!   310
I will see if I have no meaning, while the houses and ships have meaning!
I will see if the fishes and birds are to be enough for themselves, and I
    am not to be enough for myself.

The Runner

On a flat road runs the well-train'd runner;
He is lean and sinewy, with muscular legs;
He is thinly clothed—he leans forward as he runs,
With lightly closed fists, and arms partially rais'd.

The World Below the Brine

The world below the brine;
Forests at the bottom of the sea—the branches and leaves,
Sea-lettuce, vast lichens, strange flowers and seeds—the thick tangle, the openings, and the pink turf,
Different colors, pale gray and green, purple, white, and gold—the play of light through the water,
Dumb swimmers there among the rocks—coral, gluten, grass, rushes—and the aliment of the swimmers,
Sluggish existences grazing there, suspended, or slowly crawling close to the bottom,
The sperm-whale at the surface, blowing air and spray, or disporting with his flukes,
The leaden-eyed shark, the walrus, the turtle, the hairy sea-leopard, and the sting-ray;
Passions there—wars, pursuits, tribes—sight in those ocean-depths—breathing that thick-breathing air, as so many do;
The change thence to the sight here, and to the subtle air breathed by beings like us, who walk this sphere;
The change onward from ours, to that of beings who walk other spheres.

On the Beach, at Night

I

On the beach, at night,
Stands a child, with her father,
Watching the east, the autumn sky.

236

Up through the darkness,
While ravening clouds, the burial clouds, in black masses spreading,
Lower, sullen and fast, athwart and down the sky,
Amid a transparent clear belt of ether yet left in the east,
Ascends, large and calm, the lord-star Jupiter;
And nigh at hand, only a very little above,
Swim the delicate brothers, the Pleiades.[1]   10

2

From the beach, the child, holding the hand of her father,
Those burial-clouds that lower, victorious, soon to devour all,
Watching, silently weeps.

Weep not, child,
Weep not, my darling,
With these kisses let me remove your tears;
The ravening clouds shall not long be victorious,
They shall not long possess the sky—shall devour the stars only in
    apparition:
Jupiter shall emerge—be patient—watch again another night—the
    Pleiades shall emerge,
They are immortal—all those stars, both silvery and golden, shall shine
    out again,   20
The great stars and the little ones shall shine out again—they endure;
The vast immortal suns, and the long-enduring pensive moons, shall
    again shine.

3

Then, dearest child, mournest thou only for Jupiter?
Considerest thou alone the burial of the stars?

Something there is,
(With my lips soothing thee, adding, I whisper,
I give thee the first suggestion, the problem and indirection,)
Something there is more immortal even than the stars,
(Many the burials, many the days and nights, passing away,)
Something that shall endure longer even than lustrous Jupiter,   30
Longer than sun, or any revolving satellite,
Or the radiant brothers, the Pleiades.

[1] a constellation of seven stars.

MATTHEW ARNOLD [1822–1888]

Dover Beach

The sea is calm tonight,
The tide is full, the moon lies fair
Upon the straits;—on the French coast the light
Gleams and is gone; the cliffs of England stand,
Glimmering and vast out in the tranquil bay.
Come to the window, sweet is the night-air!

Only, from the long line of spray
Where the sea meets the moon-blanched land,
Listen! you hear the grating roar
Of pebbles which the waves draw back, and fling,   10
At their return, up the high strand,
Begin, and cease, and then again begin,
With tremulous cadence slow, and bring
The eternal note of sadness in.

Sophocles long ago
Heard it on the Aegean, and it brought
Into his mind the turbid ebb and flow
Of human misery; we
Find also in the sound a thought,
Hearing it by this distant northern sea.   20

The Sea of Faith
Was once, too, at the full, and round earth's shore
Lay like the folds of a bright girdle furled.
But now I only hear
Its melancholy, long, withdrawing roar,
Retreating, to the breath
Of the night-wind, down the vast edges drear
And naked shingles of the world.

Ah, love, let us be true
To one another! for the world, which seems   30
To lie before us like a land of dreams,
So various, so beautiful, so new,
Hath really neither joy, nor love, nor light,
Nor certitude, nor peace, nor help for pain;

And we are here as on a darkling plain
Swept with confused alarms of struggle and flight,
Where ignorant armies clash by night.

EMILY DICKINSON [1830–1884]

Success is Counted Sweetest

Success is counted sweetest
By those who ne'er succeed.
To comprehend a nectar
Requires sorest need.

Not one of all the purple Host
Who took the Flag today
Can tell the definition
So clear of Victory

As he defeated—dying—
On whose forbidden ear
The distant strains of triumph
Burst agonized and clear!

The Soul Selects

The Soul selects her own Society—
Then—shuts the Door—
To her divine Majority—
Present no more—

Unmoved—she notes the Chariots—pausing—
At her low Gate—
Unmoved—an Emperor be kneeling
Upon her Mat—

I've known her—from an ample nation—
Choose One—
Then—close the Valves of her attention—
Like Stone—

After Great Pain

After great pain, a formal feeling comes—
The Nerves sit ceremonious, like Tombs—
The stiff Heart questions was it He, that bore,
And Yesterday, or Centuries before?

The Feet, mechanical, go round—
Of Ground, or Air, or Ought—
A Wooden way
Regardless grown,
A Quartz contentment, like a stone—

This is the Hour of Lead—
Remembered, if outlived,
As Freezing persons, recollect the Snow—
First—Chill—then Stupor—then the letting go—

ALGERNON CHARLES SWINBURNE [1837–1909]

FROM *Atalanta in Calydon*[1]

CHORUS

When the hounds of spring are on winter's traces,
   The mother of months[2] in meadow or plain
Fills the shadows and windy places
   With lisp of leaves and ripple of rain;
And the brown bright nightingale amorous
Is half assuaged for Itylus,[3]   70
For the Thracian ships and the foreign faces,
   The tongueless vigil, and all the pain.

[1] Atalanta, the fastest runner among mortals, challenged her suitors to a race. To trick her, Milanion dropped three golden apples on the course. Atalanta stopped to pick them up, lost the race, and she married Milanion.

[2] Artemis, called mother of months because she was goddess of the moon.

[3] Itylus' mother killed him to revenge his father's rape of her sister. For this she was changed into a nightingale.

Come with bows bent and with emptying of quivers,
    Maiden most perfect, lady of light,
With a noise of winds and many rivers,
    With a clamor of waters, and with might;
Bind on thy sandals, O thou most fleet,
Over the splendor and speed of thy feet;
For the faint east quickens, the wan west shivers,
    Round the feet of the day and the feet of the night.   80

Where shall we find her, how shall we sing to her,
    Fold our hands round her knees, and cling?
Oh, that man's heart were as fire and could spring to her,
    Fire, or the strength of the streams that spring!
For the stars and the winds are unto her
As raiment, as songs of the harp-player;
For the risen stars and the fallen cling to her,
    And the southwest wind and the west wind sing.

For winter's rains and ruins are over,
    And all the season of snows and sins;   90
The days dividing lover and lover,
    The light that loses, the night that wins;
And time remembered is grief forgotten,
And frosts are slain and flowers begotten,
And in green underwood and cover
    Blossom by blossom the spring begins.

The full streams feed on flower of rushes,
    Ripe grasses trammel a traveling foot,
The faint, fresh flame of the young year flushes
    From leaf to flower and flower to fruit;   100
And fruit and leaf are as gold and fire,
And the oat is heard above the lyre,
And the hooféd heel of a satyr crushes
    The chestnut-husk at the chestnut-root.

And Pan[4] by noon and Bacchus[4] by night,
    Fleeter of foot than the fleet-foot kid,
Follows with dancing and fills with delight
    The Maenad[4] and the Bassarid;[4]

[4] Pan and Bacchus are pagan gods. Maenads, Bassarids, and Bacchanals are
female attendants of Bacchus.

And soft as lips that laugh and hide,
The laughing leaves of the trees divide,
And screen from seeing and leave in sight
    The god pursuing, the maiden hid.

The ivy falls with the Bacchanal's[4] hair
    Over her eyebrows hiding her eyes;
The wild vine slipping down leaves bare
    Her bright breast shortening into sighs;
The wild vine slips with the weight of its leaves,
But the berried ivy catches and cleaves
To the limbs that glitter, the feet that scare
    The wolf that follows, the fawn that flies.

THOMAS HARDY [1840–1928]

Her Immortality

Upon a noon I pilgrimed through
    A pasture, mile by mile,
Unto the place where last I saw
    My dead Love's living smile.

And sorrowing I lay me down
    Upon the heated sod:
It seemed as if my body pressed
    The very ground she trod.

I lay, and thought; and in a trance
    She came and stood thereby—
The same, even to the marvelous ray
    That used to light her eye.

"You draw me, and I come to you,
    My faithful one," she said,
In voice that had the moving tone
    It bore ere she was wed.

"Seven years have circled since I died:
    Few now remember me;
My husband clasps another bride:
    My children's love has she.

"My brethren, sisters, and my friends
    Care not to meet my sprite:
Who prized me most I did not know
    Till I passed down from sight."

I said: "My days are lonely here;
    I need thy smile alway:
I'll use this night my ball or blade,
    And join thee ere the day."

A tremor stirred her tender lips,
    Which parted to dissuade:
"That cannot be, O friend," she cried;
    "Think, I am but a Shade!

"A Shade but in its mindful ones
    Has immortality;
By living, me you keep alive,
    By dying you slay me.

"In you resides my single power
    Of sweet continuance here;
On your fidelity I count
    Through many a coming year."

—I started through me at her plight,
    So suddenly confessed:
Dismissing late distaste for life,
    I craved its bleak unrest.

"I will not die, my One of all!—
    To lengthen out thy days
I'll guard me from minutest harms
    That may invest my ways!"

She smiled and went. Since then she comes
    Oft when her birth-moon climbs,
Or at the seasons' ingresses,
    Or anniversary times;

20

30

40

50

But grows my grief. When I surcease,
  Through whom alone lives she,
Her spirit ends its living lease,
  Never again to be!

The Darkling Thrush

I leant upon a coppice gate
  When Frost was specter-gray,
And Winter's dregs made desolate
  The weakening eye of day.
The tangled bine-stems scored the sky
  Like strings of broken lyres,
And all mankind that haunted nigh
  Had sought their household fires.

The land's sharp features seemed to be
  The Century's corpse outleant,   10
His crypt the cloudy canopy,
  The wind his death-lament.
The ancient pulse of germ and birth
  Was shrunken hard and dry,
And every spirit upon earth
  Seemed fervorless as I.

At once a voice arose among
  The bleak twigs overhead
In a full-hearted evensong
  Of joy illimited;   20
An aged thrush, frail, gaunt, and small,
  In blast-beruffled plume,
Had chosen thus to fling his soul
  Upon the growing gloom.

So little cause for carolings
  Of such ecstatic sound
Was written on terrestrial things
  Afar or nigh around,
That I could think there trembled through
  His happy good-night air   30
Some blessed Hope, whereof he knew
  And I was unaware.

Drummer Hodge

1

They throw in Drummer Hodge, to rest
    Uncoffined—just as found:
His landmark is a kopje-crest[1]
    That breaks the veldt around;
And foreign constellations west
    Each night above his mound.

2

Young Hodge the Drummer never knew—
    Fresh from his Wessex home—
The meaning of the broad Karoo,
    The Bush,[2] the dusty loam,
And why uprose to nightly view
    Strange stars amid the gloam.

3

Yet portion of that unknown plain
    Will Hodge for ever be;
His homely Northern breast and brain
    Grow to some Southern tree,
And strange-eyed constellations reign
    His stars eternally.

The Homecoming

Gruffly growled the wind on Toller downland broad and bare,
And lonesome was the house, and dark; and few came there.

"Now don't ye rub your eyes so red; we're home and have no cares;
Here's a skimmer-cake for supper, peckled onions, and some pears;
I've got a little keg o' summat strong, too, under stairs:
—What, slight your husband's victuals? Other brides can tackle theirs!"

The wind of winter mooed and mouthed their chimney like a horn,
And round the house and past the house 'twas leafless and lorn.

[1] a kopje is a hillock in South African dialect; veldt is grassland.
[2] Karoo is a region of dry flatland in South Africa; bush is uncleared land.

"But my dear and tender poppet, then, how came ye to agree
In Ivel church this morning? Sure, there-right you married me!"   10
—"Hoo-hoo!—I don't know—I forgot how strange and far 'twould be,
An' I wish I was at home again with dear daddee!"

Gruffly growled the wind on Toller downland broad and bare,
And lonesome was the house and dark; and few came there.

"I didn't think such furniture as this was all you'd own,
And great black beams for ceiling, and a floor o' wretched stone,
And nasty pewter platters, horrid forks of steel and bone,
And a monstrous crock in chimney. 'Twas to me quite unbeknown!"

Rattle rattle went the door; down flapped a cloud of smoke,
As shifting north the wicked wind assayed a smarter stroke.   20

"Now sit ye by the fire, poppet; put yourself at ease:
And keep your little thumb out of your mouth, dear, please!
And I'll sing to 'ee a pretty song of lovely flowers and bees,
And happy lovers taking walks within a grove o' trees."

Gruffly growled the wind on Toller Down, so bleak and bare,
And lonesome was the house, and dark; and few came there.

"Now, don't ye gnaw your handkercher; 'twill hurt your little tongue,
And if you do feel spitish, 'tis because ye are over young;
But you'll be getting older, like us all, ere very long,
And you'll see me as I am—a man who never did 'ee wrong."   30

Straight from Whit'sheet Hill to Benvill Lane the blusters pass,
Hitting hedges, milestones, handposts, trees, and tufts of grass.

"Well, had I only known, my dear, that this was how you'd be,
I'd have married her of riper years that was so fond of me.
But since I can't, I've half a mind to run away to sea,
And leave 'ee to go barefoot to your d—d daddee!"

Up one wall and down the other—past each window-pane—
Prance the gusts, and then away down Crimmercrock's long lane.

"I—I—don't know what to say to't, since your wife I've vowed to be;
And as 'tis done, I s'pose here I must bide—poor me!   40
Aye—as you are ki-ki-kind, I'll try to live along with 'ee,
Although I'd fain have stayed at home with dear daddee!"

Gruffly growled the wind on Toller Down, so bleak and bare,
And lonesome was the house and dark; and few came there.

246

"That's right, my Heart! And though on haunted Toller Down we be,
And the wind swears things in chimley, we'll to supper merrily!
So don't ye tap your shoe so pettish-like; but smile at me,
And ye'll soon forget to sock and sigh for dear daddee!"

Afterwards

When the Present has latched its postern behind my tremulous stay,
  And the May month flaps its glad green leaves like wings,
Delicate-filmed as new-spun silk, will the neighbors say,
  "He was a man who used to notice such things"?

If it be in the dusk when, like an eyelid's soundless blink,
  The dewfall-hawk comes crossing the shades to alight
Upon the wind-warped upland thorn, a gazer may think,
  "To him this must have been a familiar sight."

If I pass during some nocturnal blackness, mothy and warm,
  When the hedgehog travels furtively over the lawn,
One may say, "He strove that such innocent creatures should come to
    no harm,
  But he could do little for them; and now he is gone."

If, when hearing that I have been stilled at last, they stand at the door,
  Watching the full-starred heavens that winter sees,
Will this thought rise on those who will meet my face no more,
  "He was one who had an eye for such mysteries"?

And will any say when my bell of quittance is heard in the gloom,
  And a crossing breeze cuts a pause in its outrollings,
Till they rise again, as they were a new bell's boom,
  "He hears it not now, but used to notice such things"?

GERARD MANLEY HOPKINS [1844–1889]

Pied Beauty

    Glory be to God for dappled things—
      For skies of couple-color as a brinded[1] cow;
        For rose-moles all in stipple[2] upon trout that swim;

[1] archaic form of "brindled."
[2] painted in small touches of color.

Fresh-firecoal chestnut-falls[3]; finches' wings;
　　Landscapes plotted and pieced—fold, fallow, and plow;
　　　And all trades, their gear and tackle and trim.
All things counter,[4] original, spare,[5] strange;
　　Whatever is fickle, freckled (who knows how?)
　　　With swift, slow; sweet, sour; adazzle, dim;
He fathers-forth whose beauty is past change:
　　Praise Him.

[3] chestnuts without their husks.
[4] opposite, contrary.
[5] rare.

The Windhover[1]

TO CHRIST OUR LORD

I caught this morning morning's minion,[2] king-
　　dom of daylight's dauphin,[3] dapple-dawn-drawn Falcon, in
　　　his riding
Of the rolling level underneath him steady air, and striding
High there, how he rung[4] upon the rein of a wimpling[5] wing
In his ecstasy! then off, off forth on swing,
　　As a skate's heel sweeps smooth on a bow-bend: the hurl
　　　and gliding
　　Rebuffed the big wind. My heart in hiding
Stirred for a bird,—the achieve of, the mastery of the thing!

Brute beauty and valor and act, oh, air, pride, plume, here
　　Buckle![6] And the fire that breaks from thee then, a billion
Times told lovelier, more dangerous, O my chevalier![7]

No wonder of it: sheer plod makes plough down sillion[8]
Shine, and blue-bleak embers, ah my dear,
　　Fall, gall themselves, and gash gold-vermilion.

[1] European falcon.
[2] darling.
[3] heir to the throne.
[4] in faconry "to ring" is to rise in the air spirally; "to ring a horse" is to guide it in a circle on a long rein.
[5] rippling; turning.
[6] gather together (and dive).
[7] knight.
[8] the ridge between plowed furrows.

Binsey Poplars

My aspens dear, whose airy cages quelled,
Quelled or quenched in leaves the leaping sun,
All felled, felled, are all felled;
    Of a fresh and following folded rank
        Not spared, not one
        That dandled a sandalled
      Shadow that swam or sank
On meadow and river and wind-wandering weed-winding bank.

O if we but knew what we do
      When we delve or hew—   10
    Hack and rack the growing green!
      Since country is so tender
    To touch, her being so slender,
    That, like this sleek and seeing ball
    But a prick will make no eye at all,
    Where we, even where we mean
        To mend her we end her,
      When we hew or delve:
After-comers cannot guess the beauty been.
  Ten or twelve, only ten or twelve   20
    Strokes of havoc unselve
      The sweet especial scene,
    Rural scene, a rural scene,
    Sweet especial rural scene.

Spring and Fall: To a Young Child

    Márgarét, are you gríeving
    Over Goldengrove unleaving?
    Leáves, líke the things of man, you
    With your fresh thoughts care for, can you?
    Ah! ás the heart grows older
    It will come to such sights colder
    By and by, nor spare a sigh
    Though worlds of wanwood leafmeal lie;
    And yet you wíll weep and know why.
    Now no matter, child, the name:
    Sórrow's spríngs áre the same.

Nor mouth had, no nor mind, expressed
What heart heard of, ghost guessed:
It ís the blight man was born for,
It is Margaret you mourn for.

No Worst, There Is None

No worst, there is none. Pitched past pitch of grief,
More pangs will, schooled at forepangs, wilder wring.
Comforter, where, where is your comforting?
Mary, mother of us, where is your relief?
My cries heave, herds-long; huddle in a main, a chief
Woe, world-sorrow; on an age-old anvil wince and sing—
Then lull, then leave off. Fury had shrieked "No lingering! Let me be
    fell: force I must be brief."

  O the mind, mind has mountains; cliffs of fall
Frightful, sheer, no-man fathomed. Hold them cheap
May who ne'er hung there. Nor does long our small
Durance deal with that steep or deep. Here! creep,
Wretch, under a comfort serves in a whirlwind: all
Life death does end and each day dies with sleep.

A. E. HOUSMAN [1859–1936]

On Forelands High in Heaven

On forelands high in heaven,
  'Tis many a year gone by,
Amidst the fall of even
  Would stand my friends and I.
Before our foolish faces
  Lay lands we did not see;
Our eyes were in the places
  Where we should never be.

Oh, the pearl seas are yonder,
  The amber-sanded shore;

Shires where the girls are fonder,
 Towns where the pots hold more.
And here fret we and moulder
 By grange and rick and shed
And every moon are older,
 And soon we shall be dead.

Heigho, 'twas true and pity;
 But there we lads must stay.
Troy was a steepled city,
 But Troy was far away.
And round we turned lamenting
 To homes we longed to leave,
And silent hills indenting
 The orange band of eve.

I see the air benighted
 And all the dusking dales,
And lamps in England lighted,
 And evening wrecked in Wales;
And starry darkness paces
 The road from sea to sea,
And blots the foolish faces
 Of my poor friends and me.

WILLIAM BUTLER YEATS [1865–1939]

The Lake Isle of Innisfree

I will arise and go now, and go to Innisfree,
And a small cabin build there, of clay and wattles made;
Nine bean rows will I have there, a hive for the honey bee,
And live alone in the bee-loud glade.

And I shall have some peace there, for peace comes dropping slow,
Dropping from the veils of the morning to where the cricket sings;
There midnight's all a glimmer, and noon a purple glow,
And evening full of the linnet's wings.

I will arise and go now, for always night and day
I hear lake water lapping with low sounds by the shore;
While I stand on the roadway, or on the pavements grey,
I hear it in the deep heart's core.

Paudeen[1]

Indignant at the fumbling wits, the obscure spite
Of our old Paudeen in his shop, I stumbled blind
Among the stones and thorn-trees, under morning light;
Until a curlew cried and in the luminous wind
A curlew answered; and suddenly thereupon I thought
That on the lonely height where all are in God's eye,
There cannot be, confusion of our sound forgot,
A single soul that lacks a sweet crystalline cry.

[1] the Irish name for Paddy.

Sailing to Byzantium[1]

1

That is no country for old men. The young
In one another's arms, birds in the trees
—Those dying generations—at their song,
The salmon-falls, the mackerel-crowded seas,
Fish, flesh, or fowl, commend all summer long
Whatever is begotten, born, and dies.
Caught in that sensual music all neglect
Monuments of unageing intellect.

2

An aged man is but a paltry thing,
A tattered coat upon a stick, unless   10
Soul clap its hands and sing, and louder sing
For every tatter in its mortal dress,
Nor is there singing school but studying

[1] ancient Greek city, renamed Constantinople by the Roman emperor
Constantine I, which became the capital of the Eastern Roman or Byzantine
Empire after the fall of Rome in 476 A.D. The city is famous for its mosaics and
other works of art.

Monuments of its own magnificence;
And therefore I have sailed the seas and come
To the holy city of Byzantium.

3

O sages standing in God's holy fire
As in the gold mosaic of a wall,
Come from the holy fire, perne in a gyre,[2]
And be the singing-masters of my soul.   20
Consume my heart away; sick with desire
And fastened to a dying animal
It knows not what it is; and gather me
Into the artifice of eternity.

4

Once out of nature I shall never take
My bodily form from any natural thing,
But such a form as Grecian goldsmiths make
Of hammered gold and gold enameling
To keep a drowsy Emperor awake;
Or set upon a golden bough to sing   30
To lords and ladies of Byzantium
Of what is past, or passing, or to come.

Byzantium

The unpurged images of day recede;
The Emperor's drunken soldiery are abed;
Night resonance recedes, night-walkers' song
After great cathedral gong;
A starlit or a moonlit dome disdains
All that man is,
All mere complexities,
The fury and the mire of human veins.

Before me floats an image, man or shade,
Shade more than man, more image than a shade;   10

[2] "to perne" is a verb invented by Yeats. He had been told that the noun
"pern" was an Irish name for a spool on which thread is wound; hence, to
turn, spin; "gyre" is a pattern formed by a circling or spiraling motion, pronounced with a hard g.

For Hades' bobbin bound in mummy-cloth
May unwind the winding path;
A mouth that has no moisture and no breath
Breathless mouths may summon;
I hail the superhuman;
I call it death-in-life and life-in-death.

Miracle, bird or golden handiwork,
More miracle than bird or handiwork,
Planted on the star-lit golden bough,
Can like the cocks of Hades crow,   20
Or, by the moon embittered, scorn aloud
In glory of changeless metal
Common bird or petal
And all complexities of mire or blood.

At midnight on the Emperor's pavement flit
Flames that no fagot feeds, nor steel has lit,
Nor storm disturbs, flames begotten of flame,
Where blood-begotten spirits come
And all complexities of fury leave,
Dying into a dance,   30
An agony of trance,
An agony of flame that cannot singe a sleeve.

Astraddle on the dolphin's mire and blood,
Spirit after spirit! The smithies break the flood,
The golden smithies of the Emperor!
Marbles of the dancing floor
Break bitter furies of complexity,
Those images that yet
Fresh images beget,
That dolphin-torn, that gong-tormented sea.   40

Lapis Lazuli[1]

FOR HARRY CLIFTON[2]

I have heard that hysterical women say
They are sick of the palette and fiddle-bow,
Of poets that are always gay,

[1] a deep-blue stone used chiefly for ornament.
[2] friend of Yeats, who had given him a lapis lazuli medallion, on which were
carved the figures of an old man and a servant.

For everybody knows or else should know
That if nothing drastic is done
Aeroplane and Zeppelin will come out,
Pitch like King Billy bomb-balls[3] in
Until the town lie beaten flat.

All perform their tragic play,
There struts Hamlet, there is Lear,   10
That's Ophelia, that Cordelia;
Yet they, should the last scene be there,
The great stage curtain about to drop,
If worthy their prominent part in the play,
Do not break up their lines to weep.
They know that Hamlet and Lear are gay;
Gaiety transfiguring all that dread.
All men have aimed at, found and lost;
Black out; Heaven blazing into the head:
Tragedy wrought to its uttermost.   20
Though Hamlet rambles and Lear rages,
And all the drop-scenes drop at once
Upon a hundred thousand stages,
It cannot grow by an inch or an ounce.

On their own feet they came, or on shipboard,
Camel-back, horse-back, ass-back, mule-back,
Old civilizations put to the sword.
Then they and their wisdom went to rack:
No handiwork of Callimachus,[4]
Who handled marble as if it were bronze,   30
Made draperies that seemed to rise
When sea-wind swept the corner, stands;
His long lamp-chimney shaped like the stem
Of a slender palm, stood but a day;
All things fall and are built again,
And those that build them again are gay.

Two Chinamen, behind them a third,
Are carved in lapis lazuli,
Over them flies a long-legged bird,
A symbol of longevity;   40

[3] William III, King of England from 1689 to 1702. He made war with cannon balls that exploded on impact. "King Billy" also refers to Kaiser Wilhelm II, whose zeppelins and airplanes harried the English in World War I.

[4] Greek sculptor of the fifth century B.C.

The third, doubtless a serving-man,
Carries a musical instrument.

Every discoloration of the stone,
Every accidental crack or dent,
Seems a water-course or an avalanche,
Or lofty slope where it still snows
Though doubtless plum or cherry-branch
Sweetens the little half-way house
Those Chinamen climb towards, and I
Delight to imagine them seated there;   50
There, on the mountain and the sky,
On all the tragic scene they stare.
One asks for mournful melodies;
Accomplished fingers begin to play.
Their eyes mid many wrinkles, their eyes,
Their ancient, glittering eyes, are gay.

A Crazed Girl

That crazed girl improvising her music,
Her poetry, dancing upon the shore,
Her soul in division from itself
Climbing, falling she knew not where,
Hiding amid the cargo of a steamship,
Her knee-cap broken, that girl I declare
A beautiful lofty thing, or a thing
Heroically lost, heroically found.

No matter what disaster occurred
She stood in desperate music wound,
Wound, wound, and she made in her triumph
Where the bales and the baskets lay
No common intelligible sound
But sang, "O sea-starved, hungry sea."

Long-Legged Fly

That civilization may not sink,
Its great battle lost,
Quiet the dog, tether the pony

To a distant post;
Our master Caesar is in the tent
Where the maps are spread,
His eyes fixed upon nothing,
A hand under his head.
Like a long-legged fly upon the stream
His mind moves upon silence.   10

That the topless towers be burnt
And men recall that face,
Move most gently if move you must
In this lonely place.
She thinks, part woman, three parts a child,
That nobody looks; her feet
Practise a tinker shuffle
Picked up on a street.
Like a long-legged fly upon the stream
Her mind moves upon silence.   20

That girls at puberty may find
The first Adam in their thought,
Shut the door of the Pope's chapel,
Keep those children out.
There on that scaffolding reclines
Michael Angelo.
With no more sound than the mice make
His hand moves to and fro.
Like a long-legged fly upon the stream
His mind moves upon silence.   30

ROBERT FROST [1875–1963]

Mending Wall

Something there is that doesn't love a wall,
That sends the frozen-ground-swell under it,
And spills the upper boulders in the sun;
And makes gaps even two can pass abreast.

The work of hunters is another thing:
I have come after them and made repair
Where they have left not one stone on a stone,
But they would have the rabbit out of hiding,
To please the yelping dogs. The gaps I mean,
No one has seen them made or heard them made, 10
But at spring mending-time we find them there.
I let my neighbor know beyond the hill;
And on a day we meet to walk the line
And set the wall between us once again.
We keep the wall between us as we go.
To each the boulders that have fallen to each.
And some are loaves and some so nearly balls
We have to use a spell to make them balance:
"Stay where you are until our backs are turned!"
We wear our fingers rough with handling them. 20
Oh, just another kind of out-door game,
One on a side. It comes to little more:
There where it is we do not need the wall:
He is all pine and I am apple orchard.
My apple trees will never get across
And eat the cones under his pines, I tell him.
He only says, "Good fences make good neighbors."
Spring is the mischief in me, and I wonder
If I could put a notion in his head:
"Why do they make good neighbors? Isn't it 30
Where there are cows? But here there are no cows.
Before I built a wall I'd ask to know
What I was walling in or walling out,
And to whom I was like to give offense.
Something there is that doesn't love a wall,
That wants it down." I could say "Elves" to him,
But it's not elves exactly, and I'd rather
He said it for himself. I see him there
Bringing a stone grasped firmly by the top
In each hand, like an old-stone savage armed. 40
He moves in darkness as it seems to me,
Not of woods only and the shade of trees.
He will not go behind his father's saying,
And he likes having thought of it so well
He says again, "Good fences make good neighbors."

Stopping by Woods on a Snowy Evening

Whose woods these are I think I know.
His house is in the village though;
He will not see me stopping here
To watch his woods fill up with snow.

My little horse must think it queer
To stop without a farmhouse near
Between the woods and frozen lake
The darkest evening of the year.

He gives his harness bells a shake
To ask if there is some mistake.
The only other sound's the sweep
Of easy wind and downy flake.

The woods are lovely, dark and deep,
But I have promises to keep,
And miles to go before I sleep,
And miles to go before I sleep.

Design

I found a dimpled spider, fat and white,
On a white heal-all,[1] holding up a moth
Like a white piece of rigid satin cloth—
Assorted characters of death and blight
Mixed ready to begin the morning right,
Like the ingredients of a witch's broth—
A snow-drop spider, a flower like froth,
And dead wings carried like a paper kite.

What had that flower to do with being white,
The wayside blue and innocent heal-all?
What brought the kindred spider to that height,
Then steered the white moth thither in the night?
What but design of darkness to appall?—
If design govern in a thing so small.

[1] a blue flower.

WALLACE STEVENS [1879–1955]

Disillusionment of Ten O'Clock

The houses are haunted
By white night-gowns.
None are green,
Or purple with green rings,
Or green with yellow rings,
Or yellow with blue rings.
None of them are strange,
With socks of lace
And beaded ceintures.
People are not going
To dream of baboons and periwinkles.
Only, here and there, an old sailor,
Drunk and asleep in his boots,
Catches tigers
In red weather.

Peter Quince[1] at the Clavier

I

Just as my fingers on these keys
Make music, so the selfsame sounds
On my spirit make a music, too.

Music is feeling, then, not sound;
And thus it is that what I feel,
Here in this room, desiring you,

Thinking of your blue-shadowed silk,
Is music. It is like the strain
Waked in the elders by Susanna.[2]

[1] the carpenter who directed the play before the Duke of Athens in Shakespeare's *Midsummer Night's Dream*.

[2] in the apocryphal Old Testament story, Susanna, the faithful wife, was spied on by two elders while her husband was away. When she rejected their advances, they accused her of adultery, but she was saved from death by the prophet Daniel.

Of a green evening, clear and warm,
She bathed in her still garden, while
The red-eyed elders watching, felt

The basses of their beings throb
In witching chords, and their thin blood
Pulse pizzicati of Hosanna.[3]

2

In the green water, clear and warm,
Susanna lay.
She searched
The touch of springs,
And found
Concealed imaginings.
She sighed,
For so much melody.

Upon the bank, she stood
In the cool
Of spent emotions.
She felt, among the leaves,
The dew
Of old devotions.

She walked upon the grass,
Still quavering.
The winds were like her maids,
On timid feet,
Fetching her woven scarves,
Yet wavering.

A breath upon her hand
Muted the night.
She turned—
A cymbal crashed,
And roaring horns.

3

Soon, with a noise like tambourines,
Came her attendant Byzantines.

[3] "pizzicati" are plucking of strings instead of bowing; a Hosanna is a song of praise to God.

They wondered why Susanna cried
Against the elders by her side;

And as they whispered, the refrain
Was like a willow swept by rain.

Anon, their lamps' uplifted flame
Revealed Susanna and her shame.

And then, the simpering Byzantines
Fled, with a noise like tambourines.   50

4

Beauty is momentary in the mind—
The fitful tracing of a portal;
But in the flesh it is immortal.

The body dies; the body's beauty lives.
So evenings die, in their green going,
A wave, interminably flowing.
So gardens die, their meek breath scenting
The cowl of winter, done repenting.
So maidens die, to the auroral
Celebration of a maiden's choral.   60
Susanna's music touched the bawdy strings
Of those white elders; but, escaping,
Left only Death's ironic scraping.
Now, in its immortality, it plays
On the clear viol of her memory,
And makes a constant sacrament of praise.

Study of Two Pears

I

Opusculum pædagogum.[1]
The pears are not viols,
Nudes or bottles.
They resemble nothing else.

[1] "a little pedagogical work."

2

They are yellow forms
Composed of curves
Bulging toward the base.
They are touched red.

3

They are not flat surfaces
Having curved outlines.   10
They are round
Tapering toward the top.

4

In the way they are modeled
There are bits of blue.
A hard dry leaf hangs
From the stem.

5

The yellow glistens.
It glistens with various yellows,
Citrons, oranges and greens
Flowering over the skin.   20

6

The shadows of the pears
Are blobs on the green cloth.
The pears are not seen
As the observer wills.

The Glass of Water

That the glass would melt in heat,
That the water would freeze in cold,
Shows that this object is merely a state,
One of many, between two poles. So,
In the metaphysical, there are these poles.

Here in the center stands the glass. Light
Is the lion that comes down to drink. There
And in that state, the glass is a pool.
Ruddy are his eyes and ruddy are his claws
When light comes down to wet his frothy jaws

And in the water winding weeds move round.
And there and in another state—the refractions,
The *metaphysica*, the plastic parts of poems
Crash in the mind—But, fat Jocundus,[1] worrying
About what stands here in the center, not the glass,

But in the center of our lives, this time, this day,
It is a state, this spring among the politicians
Playing cards. In a village of the indigenes,
One would have still to discover. Among the dogs
    and dung,
One would continue to contend with one's ideas.

WILLIAM CARLOS WILLIAMS [1883–1963]

Danse Russe

If I when my wife is sleeping
and the baby and Kathleen
are sleeping
and the sun is a flame-white disc
in silken mists
above shining trees,—
if I in my north room
dance naked, grotesquely
before my mirror
waving my shirt round my head
and singing softly to myself:
"I am lonely, lonely.
I was born to be lonely,
I am best so!"

[1] a merry-maker.

If I admire my arms, my face
my shoulders, flanks, buttocks
against the yellow drawn shades,—

Who shall say I am not
the happy genius of my household?

This Is Just to Say

I have eaten
the plums
that were in
the icebox

and which
you were probably
saving
for breakfast

Forgive me
they were delicious
so sweet
and so cold

To Elsie

The pure products of America
go crazy—
mountain folk from Kentucky

or the ribbed north end of
Jersey
with its isolate lakes and

valleys, its deaf-mutes, thieves
old names
and promiscuity between

devil-may-care men who have taken
to railroading
out of sheer lust of adventure—

10

and young slatterns, bathed
in filth
from Monday to Saturday

to be tricked out that night
with gauds
from imaginations which have no

peasant traditions to give them
character   20
but flutter and flaunt

sheer rags—succumbing without
emotion
save numbed terror

under some hedge of choke-cherry
or viburnum—
which they cannot express—

Unless it be that marriage
perhaps
with a dash of Indian blood   30

will throw up a girl so desolate
so hemmed round
with disease or murder

that she'll be rescued by an
agent—
reared by the state and

sent out at fifteen to work in
some hard pressed
house in the suburbs—

some doctor's family, some Elsie—   40
voluptuous water
expressing with broken

brain the truth about us—
her great
ungainly hips and flopping breasts

addressed to cheap
jewelry
and rich young men with fine eyes

as if the earth under our feet
were   50
an excrement of some sky

and we degraded prisoners
destined
to hunger until we eat filth

while the imagination strains
after deer
going by fields of goldenrod in

the stifling heat of September
Somehow
it seems to destroy us   60

It is only in isolate flecks that
something
is given off

No one
to witness
and adjust, no one to drive the car

The Sparrow

TO MY FATHER

This sparrow
            who comes to sit at my window
                        is a poetic truth
more than a natural one.
            His voice,
                        his movements,
his habits—
            how he loves to
                        flutter his wings
in the dust—   10
            all attest it;
                        granted he does it
to rid himself of lice
            but the relief he feels
                        makes him

cry out lustily—
　　　　which is a trait
　　　　　　　more related to music
than otherwise.
　　　　Wherever he finds himself 　　　　　　20
　　　　　　　in early spring,
on back streets
　　　　or beside palaces,
　　　　　　　he carries on
unaffectedly
　　　　his amours.
　　　　　　　It begins in the egg,
his sex genders it:
　　　　What is more pretentiously
　　　　　　　useless 　　　　　　　　　30
or about which
　　　　we more pride ourselves?
　　　　　　　It leads as often as not
to our undoing.
　　　　The cockerel, the crow
　　　　　　　with their challenging voices
cannot surpass
　　　　the insistence
　　　　　　　of his cheep!

Once 　　　　　　　　　　　　　　　40
　　　　at El Paso
　　　　　　　toward evening,
I saw—and heard!—
　　　　ten thousand sparrows
　　　　　　　who had come in from
the desert
　　　　to roost. They filled the trees
　　　　　　　of a small park. Men fled
(with ears ringing!)
　　　　from their droppings, 　　　　　50
　　　　　　　leaving the premises
to the alligators
　　　　who inhabit
　　　　　　　the fountain. His image
is familiar
　　　　as that of the aristocratic
　　　　　　　Unicorn, a pity

there are not more oats eaten
          now-a-days
               to make living easier   60
for him.
      At that,
            his small size,
keen eyes,
         serviceable beak
            and general truculence
assure his survival—
        to say nothing
           of his innumerable
brood.   70
      Even the Japanese
        know him
and have painted him
      sympathetically,
         with profound insight
into his minor
      characteristics.
           Nothing even remotely
subtle
      about his lovemaking.   80
        He crouches
before the female,
      drags his wings,
        waltzing,
throws back his head
      and simply—
        yells! The din
is terrific.
      The way he swipes his bill
        across a plank   90
to clean it,
      is decisive.
        So with everything
he does. His coppery
      eyebrows
        give him the air
of being always
      a winner—and yet
        I saw once,

the female of his species
        clinging determinedly
                to the edge of
a waterpipe,
        catch him
                by his crown-feathers
to hold him
        silent,
                subdued,
hanging above the city streets
        until
                she was through with him.
What was the use
        of that?
                She hung there
herself,
        puzzled at her success.
                I laughed heartily.
Practical to the end,
        it is the poem
                of his existence
that triumphed
        finally;
                a wisp of feathers
flattened to the pavement,
        wings spread symmetrically
                as if in flight,
the head gone,
        the black escutcheon
                undecipherable,
an effigy of a sparrow,
        a dried wafer only,
                left to say
and it says it
        without offense,
                beautifully;
This was I,
        a sparrow.
                I did my best;
farewell.

D. H. LAWRENCE [1885–1930]

The Song of a Man Who Has Come Through

Not I, not I, but the wind that blows through me!
A fine wind is blowing the new direction of Time.
If only I let it bear me, carry me, if only it carry me!
If only I am sensitive, subtle, oh, delicate, a winged gift!
If only, most lovely of all, I yield myself and am borrowed
By the fine, fine wind that takes its course through the chaos of the
    world
Like a fine, an exquisite chisel, a wedge-blade inserted;
If only I am keen and hard like the sheer tip of a wedge
Driven by invisible blows,
The rock will split, we shall come at the wonder, we shall find the
    Hesperides.[1]

Oh, for the wonder that bubbles into my soul,
I would be a good fountain, a good well-head,
Would blur no whisper, spoil no expression.

What is the knocking?
What is the knocking at the door in the night?
It is somebody wants to do us harm.

No, no, it is the three strange angels.
Admit them, admit them.

Humming-bird

I can imagine, in some otherworld
Primeval-dumb, far back
In that most awful stillness, that only gasped and hummed,
Humming-birds raced down the avenues.

Before anything had a soul,
While life was a heave of Matter, half inanimate,
This little bit chipped off in brilliance
And went whizzing through the slow, vast, succulent stems.

[1] in Greek mythology, a garden producing golden apples.

I believe there were no flowers then,
In the world where the humming-bird flashed ahead of creation.
I believe he pierced the slow vegetable veins with his long beak.

Probably he was big
As mosses, and little lizards, they say, were once big.
Probably he was a jabbing, terrifying monster.

We look at him through the wrong end of the long telescope of Time,
Luckily for us.

Kangaroo

In the northern hemisphere
Life seems to leap at the air, or skim under the wind
Like stags on rocky ground, or pawing horses, or springy scut-tailed
    rabbits.

Or else rush horizontal to charge at the sky's horizon,
Like bulls or bisons or wild pigs.

Or slip like water slippery towards its ends,
As foxes, stoats, and wolves, and prairie dogs.

Only mice, and moles, and rats, and badgers, and beavers, and perhaps
    bears
Seem belly-plumbed to the earth's mid-navel.
Or frogs that when they leap come flop, and flop to the center of the
    earth.   10

But the yellow antipodal Kangaroo, when she sits up,
Who can unseat her, like a liquid drop that is heavy, and just touches
    earth.
The downward drip
The down-urge.
So much denser than cold-blooded frogs.

Delicate mother Kangaroo
Sitting up there rabbit-wise, but huge, plumb-weighted,
And lifting her beautiful slender face, oh! so much more gently and
    finely lined than a rabbit's, or than a hare's,

Lifting her face to nibble at a round white peppermint drop which she
    loves, sensitive mother Kangaroo.

Her sensitive, long, pure-bred face.   20
Her full antipodal eyes, so dark,
So big and quiet and remote, having watched so many empty dawns in
    silent Australia.

Her little loose hands, and drooping Victorian shoulders.
And then her great weight below the waist, her vast pale belly
With a thin young yellow little paw hanging out, and straggle of a long
    thin ear, like ribbon,
Like a funny trimming to the middle of her belly, thin little dangle of
    an immature paw, and one thin ear.

Her belly, her big haunches
And, in addition, the great muscular python-stretch of her tail.

There, she shan't have any more peppermint drops.
So she wistfully, sensitively sniffs the air, and then turns, goes off in
    slow sad leaps   30

On the long flat skis of her legs,
Steered and propelled by that steel-strong snake of a tail.

Stops again, half turns, inquisitive to look back.
While something stirs quickly in her belly, and a lean little face comes
    out, as from a window,

Peaked and a bit dismayed,
Only to disappear again quickly away from the sight of the world, to
    snuggle down in the warmth,
Leaving the trail of a different paw hanging out.

Still she watches with eternal, cocked wistfulness!
How full her eyes are, like the full, fathomless, shining eyes of an
    Australian black-boy
Who has been lost so many centuries on the margins of existence!   40

She watches with insatiable wistfulness.
Untold centuries of watching for something to come,
For a new signal from life, in that silent lost land of the South.

Where nothing bites but insects and snakes and the sun, small life.
Where no bull roared, no cow ever lowed, no stag cried, no leopard
    screeched, no lion coughed, no dog barked,
But all was silent save for parrots occasionally, in the haunted blue bush.

Wistfully watching, with wonderful liquid eyes.
And all her weight, all her blood, dripping sack-wise down towards the
    earth's center,
And the live little-one taking in its paw at the door of her belly.

Leap then, and come down on the line that draws to the earth's deep,
    heavy center.   50

To Women, As Far As I'm Concerned

The feelings I don't have I don't have.
The feeling I don't have, I won't say I have.
The feelings you say you have, you don't have.
The feelings you would like us both to have, we neither of us have.
The feelings people ought to have, they never have.
If people say they've got feelings, you may be pretty sure they haven't
    got them.
So if you want either of us to feel anything at all
You'd better abandon all idea of feelings altogether.

Bavarian Gentians

Not every man has gentians in his house
in Soft September, at slow, sad Michaelmas.[1]
Bavarian gentians, big and dark, only dark
darkening the day-time, torch-like with the smoking blueness of Pluto's[2]
    gloom,
ribbed and torch-like, with their blaze of darkness spread blue

[1] feast of the archangel Michael, September 29.
[2] Pluto (Dis) was god of the underworld. He came upon Persephone—daughter of Zeus and Demeter, the corn goddess—as she was gathering flowers and carried her off. Demeter searched for her daughter in vain; in her grief she caused a famine, and men would have died had Zeus not persuaded Pluto to let Persephone return to earth for a part of the year.

down flattening into points, flattened under the sweep of white day
torch-flower of the blue-smoking darkness, Pluto's dark-blue daze,
black lamps from the halls of Dis, burning dark blue,
giving off darkness, blue darkness, as Demeter's pale lamps give off light,
lead me then, lead the way.

Reach me a gentian, give me a torch!
let me guide myself with the blue, forked torch of this flower
down the darker and darker stairs, where blue is darkened on blueness
even where Persephone goes, just now, from the frosted September
to the sightless realm where darkness is awake upon the dark
and Persephone herself is but a voice
or a darkness invisible enfolded in the deeper dark
of the arms Plutonic, and pierced with the passion of dense gloom,
among the splendor of torches of darkness, shedding darkness on the
　　　lost bride and her groom.

EZRA POUND [1885–　　]

The Study in Aesthetics

The very small children in patched clothing,
Being smitten with an unusual wisdom,
Stopped in their play as she passed them
And cried up from their cobbles:

　　　　　Guarda! Ahi, guarda! ch'è be'a![1]

But three years after this
I heard the young Dante, whose last name I do not know—
For there are, in Sirmione,[2] twenty-eight young Dantes and thirty-four
　　　Catulli;[3]
And there had been a great catch of sardines,
And his elders
Were packing them in the great wooden boxes

[1] "Look, oh look, how beautiful!"
[2] a peninsula on Lake Garda in northern Italy.
[3] Latin plural of Catullus, Roman lyric poet.

275

For the market in Brescia,[4] and he
Leapt about, snatching at the bright fish
And getting in both of their ways;
And in vain they commanded him to *sta fermo!*[5]
And when they would not let him arrange
The fish in the boxes
He stroked those which were already arranged,
Murmuring for his own satisfaction
This identical phrase:

> *Ch'è be'a.*

And at this I was mildly abashed.

[4] town in northern Italy.
[5] remain still.

FROM *Hugh Selwyn Mauberley*

(LIFE AND CONTACTS)

"Vocat Aestus in Umbram," Nemesianus[1]

I

E. P. ODE POUR L'ELECTION DE SON
SEPULCHRE[1]

For three years, out of key with his time,
He strove to resuscitate the dead art
Of poetry; to maintain "the sublime"
In the old sense. Wrong from the start—

No, hardly, but seeing he had been born
In a half savage country, out of date;
Bent resolutely on wringing lilies from the acorn;
Capaneus,[2] trout for factitious bait;

[1] *"Vocat Aestus . . .":* "the heat calls us into the shade." *"E. P. Ode . . .":* "Ezra Pound: ode for the election of his sepulcher," adapted from Pierre Ronsard's, "Ode de l'élection de son sépulchre" (1550).
[2] one of the seven heroes who marched against Thebes. He defied Zeus and was struck down by a thunderbolt as he was climbing the Theban walls.

Ἴδμεν γάρ τοι πάνθ᾽ ὅσ᾽ ἐνὶ Τροίῃ[3]
Caught in the unstopped ear;   10
Giving the rocks small lee-way
The chopped seas held him, therefore, that year.

His true Penelope was Flaubert,
He fished by obstinate isles;
Observed the elegance of Circe's[4] hair
Rather than the mottoes on sun-dials.

Unaffected by "the march of events,"
He passed from men's memory in *l'an trentiesme
De son eage;*[5] the case presents
No adjunct to the Muses' diadem.   20

I I

The age demanded an image
Of its accelerated grimace,
Something for the modern stage,
Not, at any rate, an Attic grace;

Not, not certainly, the obscure reveries
Of the inward gaze;
Better mendacities
Than the classics in paraphrase!

The "age demanded" chiefly a mould in plaster,
Made with no loss of time,   30
A prose kinema,[6] not, not assuredly, alabaster
Or the "sculpture" of rhyme.

I I I

The tea-rose tea-gown, etc.
Supplants the mousseline of Cos,

[3] "For we know all the things that in Troy [the Greeks and Trojans endured by the will of the gods]," *Odyssey*, XII. 189.
[4] Penelope was Odysseus' faithful wife, and a symbol of devotion; Flaubert was a nineteenth century French novelist who aimed at perfection of form and precision of words; Circe is the goddess who bewitched the followers of Odysseus.
[5] "the thirtieth year of his age"; paraphrased from François Villon's *Grand Testament*.
[6] movement.

The pianola "replaces"
Sappho's barbitos.[7]

Christ follows Dionysus,[8]
Phallic and ambrosial
Made way for macerations;[9]
Caliban casts out Ariel.[10]   40

All things are a flowing,
Sage Heracleitus[11] says;
But a tawdry cheapness
Shall outlast our days.

Even the Christian beauty
Defects—after Samothrace;
We see τὸ καλὸν[12]
Decreed in the market place.

Faun's flesh is not to us,
Nor the saint's vision.   50
We have the press for wafer;
Franchise for circumcision.

All men, in law, are equals.
Free of Pisistratus,[13]
We choose a knave or an eunuch
To rule over us.

O bright Apollo,
τίν' ἀνδρα, τίν ἤρωα, τινα θεὸν,[14]
What god, man, or hero
Shall I place a tin wreath upon!   60

---

[7] Sappho was a Greek poetess of Lesbos, and the barbitos was her lyre; Cos is a Greek island famous for its silks.

[8] the wine god.

[9] macerate: to soften, waste away.

[10] Caliban, the bestial, and Ariel, the ethereal man in Shakespeare's *The Tempest*.

[11] Pre-Socratic philosopher who emphasized the doctrine that all is in flux.

[12] "the beautiful"; Samothrace is the Greek island where the statue of the Winged Victory was found.

[13] Athenian tyrant.

[14] "what man, what hero, what god [shall we praise]?"—Pindar, "Second Olympian Ode."

I V

These fought in any case,
and some believing,

             pro domo,[15] in any case . . .

Some quick to arm,
some for adventure,
some from fear of weakness,
some from fear of censure,
some for love of slaughter, in imagination,
learning later . . .
some in fear, learning love of slaughter;   70

Died some, pro patria,

             non "dulce" non "et decor"[16]. . . .
walked eye-deep in hell
believing in old men's lies, then unbelieving
came home, home to a lie,
home to many deceits,
home to old lies and new infamy;
usury age-old and age-thick
and liars in public places.

Daring as never before, wastage as never before.   80
Young blood and high blood,
fair cheeks, and fine bodies;

fortitude as never before

frankness as never before,
disillusions as never told in the old days,
hysterias, trench confessions,
laughter out of dead bellies.

V

    There died a myriad,
    And of the best, among them,
    For an old bitch gone in the teeth,   90
    For a botched civilization,

[15] "for home."
[16] referring to Horace's line *Dulce et decorum est pro patria mori*, "It is sweet and proper to die for one's country."

Charm, smiling at the good mouth,
Quick eyes gone under earth's lid,

For two gross of broken statues,
For a few thousand battered books.

YEUX GLAUQUES[17]

Gladstone was still respected,
When John Ruskin produced
"King's Treasuries";[18] Swinburne
And Rossetti still abused.

Fœtid Buchanan lifted up his voice   100
When that faun's head of hers[19]
Became a pastime for
Painters and adulterers.

The Burne-Jones cartons
Have preserved her eyes;
Still, at the Tate, they teach
Cophetua[20] to rhapsodize;

Thin like brook-water,
With a vacant gaze.
The English Rubaiyat was still-born   110
In those days.

The thin, clear gaze, the same
Still darts out faunlike from the half-ruin'd face,
Questing and passive. . . .
"Ah, poor Jenny's[21] case" . . .

[17] sea-green eyes. Pound's French translation of the title of a poem by Théophile Gautier, *Caerulei Oculi*.

[18] Ruskin's "Of Kings' Treasuries," the opening lecture in *Sesame and Lilies*.

[19] Buchanan attacked Rossetti and Swinburne in an article titled "The Fleshly School of Poetry"; "faun's head of hers" refers to Elizabeth Siddal, a painter's model whom Rossetti married. Two years later she killed herself.

[20] "Cophetua and the Beggar Maid" is a painting by Burne-Jones now at the Tate Gallery.

[21] the prostitute in a poem by Rossetti. Also, in Shakespeare's *Merry Wives of Windsor*, Mistress Quickly says, "Vengeance of Jinny's case. Fie on her! Never name her, child, if she be a whore."

Bewildered that a world
Shows no surprise
At her last maquero's[22]
Adulteries.

"SIENA MI FE'; DISFECEMI MAREMMA"[23]

Among the pickled fetuses and bottled bones,   120
Engaged in perfecting the catalogue,
I found the last scion of the
Senatorial families of Strasbourg, Monsieur Verog.[24]

For two hours he talked of Gallifet;
Of Dowson; of the Rhymers' Club;[25]
Told me how Johnson (Lionel) died
By falling from a high stool in a pub . . .

But showed no trace of alcohol
At the autopsy, privately performed—
Tissue preserved—the pure mind   130
Arose toward Newman[26] as the whiskey warmed.

Dowson found harlots cheaper than hotels;
Headlam for uplift; Image impartially imbued
With raptures for Bacchus, Terpsichore and the Church.
So spoke the author of "The Dorian Mood,"[27]

M. Verog, out of step with the decade,
Detached from his contemporaries,

[22] pimp's.
[23] "Siena made me; Maremma undid me." Dante, *Purgatorio*, V. 135. Dante's line is spoken by Pia de' Tolomei of Siena, whose husband, in order to marry another woman, murdered her at his castle in the Tuscan Maremma.
[24] Dr. Victor Gustave Plarr was born in Strasbourg but lived in England, where he was a friend of Dowson and Lionel Johnson, and was librarian to the Royal College of Surgeons.
[25] a literary club, whose members included Ernest Dowson, Lionel Johnson, and W. B. Yeats. Galliffet was a French general.
[26] Cardinal John Henry Newman, English theologian and writer.
[27] The Reverend Steward Headlam was an associate of the Rhymers' Club and gave parties where churchmen and theater people mixed. Professor Selwyn Image was a friend of Lionel Johnson's and Plarr's; Plarr wrote a book of verse called *In the Dorian Mood*.

Neglected by the young,
Because of these reveries.

BRENNBAUM[28]

The skylike limpid eyes,   140
The circular infant's face,
The stiffness from spats to collar
Never relaxing into grace;

The heavy memories of Horeb, Sinai and the forty years,
Showed only when the daylight fell
Level across the face
Of Brennbaum "The Impeccable."

MR. NIXON[29]

In the cream gilded cabin of his steam yacht
Mr. Nixon advised me kindly, to advance with fewer
Dangers of delay. "Consider   150
        Carefully the reviewer.

"I was as poor as you are;
When I began I got, of course,
Advance on royalties, fifty at first," said Mr. Nixon,
"Follow me, and take a column,
Even if you have to work free.

"Butter reviewers. From fifty to three hundred
I rose in eighteen months;
The hardest nut I had to crack
Was Dr. Dundas.   160

"I never mentioned a man but with the view
Of selling my own works.
The tip's a good one, as for literature
It gives no man a sinecure.

[28] the English writer and caricaturist, Max Beerbohm.
[29] Arnold Bennett, to whom Pound refers in his letters as an author who
frankly declared that his real interest in literature was financial.

"And no one knows, at sight, a masterpiece.
And give up verse, my boy,
There's nothing in it."

.   .   .   .   .

Likewise a friend of Bloughram's[30] once advised me:
Don't kick against the pricks,
Accept opinion. The "Nineties" tried your game   170
And died, there's nothing in it.

X

Beneath the sagging roof
The stylist[31] has taken shelter,
Unpaid, uncelebrated,
At last from the world's welter

Nature receives him;
With a placid and uneducated mistress
He exercises his talents
And the soil meets his distress.

The haven from sophistications and contentions   180
Leaks through its thatch;
He offers succulent cooking;
The door has a creaking latch.

X I

"Conservatrix of Milésien"[32]
Habits of mind and feeling,
Possibly. But in Ealing
With the most bank-clerkly of Englishmen?

No, "Milesian" is an exaggeration.
No instinct has survived in her

[30] Blougram is a bishop in a poem by Robert Browning.
[31] Ford Madox Ford, novelist.
[32] Pound's adaptation of a phrase from a story by Rémy de Goncourt: *Femmes, conservatrices des traditions milésiennes,* "Women, conservators of Milesian traditions." The *Milesian Tales* were a collection of short stories of love and adventure, by Aristides of Miletus (second century B.C.).

Older than those her grandmother   190
Told her would fit her station.

XII

"Daphne[33] with her thighs in bark
Stretches toward me her leafy hands,"—
Subjectively. In the stuffed-satin drawing-room
I await The Lady Valentine's commands,

Knowing my coat has never been
Of precisely the fashion
To stimulate, in her,
A durable passion;

Doubtful, somewhat, of the value   200
Of well-gowned approbation
Of literary effort,
But never of The Lady Valentine's vocation:

Poetry, her border of ideas,
The edge, uncertain, but a means of blending
With other strata
Where the lower and higher have ending;

A hook to catch the Lady Jane's attention,
A modulation toward the theater,
Also, in the case of revolution,   210
A possible friend and comforter.

                .   .   .   .   .

Conduct, on the other hand, the soul
"Which the highest cultures have nourished"
To Fleet St.[34] where
Dr. Johnson flourished;

[33] Daphne was loved by Apollo, from whom she escaped by being transformed into a laurel tree. The two lines quoted are a translation from a poem by Théophile Gautier, *Le Château du Souvenir*.
[34] a street in London of printers and publishers, now taken over by haberdashers.

Beside this thoroughfare
The sale of half-hose has
Long since superseded the cultivation
Of Pierien roses.[35]

ENVOI (1919)

Go, dumb-born book,[36]   220
Tell her that sang me once that song of Lawes:
Hadst thou but song
As thou hast subjects known,
Then were there cause in thee that should condone
Even my faults that heavy upon me lie,
And build her glories their longevity.

Tell her that sheds
Such treasure in the air,
Recking naught else but that her graces give
Life to the moment,   230
I would bid them live
As roses might, in magic amber laid,
Red overwrought with orange and all made
One substance and one color
Braving time.

Tell her that goes
With song upon her lips
But sings not out the song, nor knows
The maker of it, some other mouth,
May be as fair as hers,   240
Might, in new ages, gain her worshippers,
When our two dusts with Waller's shall be laid,
Siftings on siftings in oblivion,
Till change hath broken down
All things save Beauty alone.

[35] one of Sappho's poems addresses a woman of no culture who will "have
no share in the roses from Pieria." Pieria was a part of ancient Macedonia
where the Muses were worshipped.

[36] based on Edmund Waller's "Go, Lovely Rose," which was set to music
by Henry Lawes, a seventeenth century composer.

What thou lovest well remains,
           the rest is dross
What thou lov'st well shall not be reft from thee
What thou lov'st well is thy true heritage
Whose world, or mine or theirs
           or is it of none?
First came the seen, then thus the palpable
    Elysium, though it were in the halls of hell,
What thou lovest well is thy true heritage

The ant's a centaur in his dragon world.   10
Pull down thy vanity, it is not man
Made courage, or made order, or made grace,
    Pull down thy vanity, I say pull down.
Learn of the green world what can be thy place
In scaled invention or true artistry,
Pull down thy vanity,
              Paquin[1] pull down!
The green casque has outdone your elegance.

"Master thyself, then others shall thee beare"
    Pull down thy vanity   20
Thou art a beaten dog beneath the hail,
A swollen magpie in a fitful sun,
Half black half white
Nor knowst'ou wing from tail
Pull down thy vanity
        How mean thy hates
Fostered in falsity,
        Pull down thy vanity,
Rathe to destroy, niggard in charity,
Pull down thy vanity,   30
        I say pull down.

But to have done instead of not doing
        this is not vanity
To have, with decency, knocked
That a Blunt[2] should open

---

[1] Parisian dress designer.
[2] English scholar, poet, and traveler (1840–1922).

To have gathered from the air a live tradition
or from a fine old eye the unconquered flame
This is not vanity.
        Here error is all in the not done,
all in the diffidence that faltered.

T. S. ELIOT [1888–1965]

The Love Song of J. Alfred Prufrock

*S'io credesse che mia riposta fosse
A persona che mai tornasse al mondo,
Questa fiamma staria senza piu scosse.
Ma perciocche giammai di questo fondo
Non torno vivo alcun, s'i'odo il vero,
Senza tema d'infamia ti rispondo.*[1]

Let us go then, you and I,
When the evening is spread out against the sky
Like a patient etherized upon a table;
Let us go, through certain half-deserted streets,
The muttering retreats
Of restless nights in one-night cheap hotels
And sawdust restaurants with oyster-shells:
Streets that follow like a tedious argument
Of insidious intent
To lead you to an overwhelming question ...   10
Oh, do not ask, "What is it?"
Let us go and make our visit.

In the room the women come and go
Talking of Michelangelo.

The yellow fog that rubs its back upon the window-panes,
The yellow smoke that rubs its muzzle on the window-panes

[1] "If I believed that my answer would be to one who would ever return to
the world, this flame would shake no more; but since no one ever returns alive
from this depth, if what I hear is true, I answer you without fear of infamy."
This is Guido da Montefeltro's answer to Dante when asked why he was being
punished in hell. (Dante's *Inferno*, XXVII, 61–66).

Licked its tongue into the corners of the evening,
Lingered upon the pools that stand in drains,
Let fall upon its back the soot that falls from chimneys,
Slipped by the terrace, made a sudden leap,   20
And seeing that it was a soft October night,
Curled once about the house, and fell asleep.

And indeed there will be time
For the yellow smoke that slides along the street,
Rubbing its back upon the window-panes;
There will be time, there will be time
To prepare a face to meet the faces that you meet;
There will be time to murder and create,
And time for all the works and days² of hands
That lift and drop a question on your plate;   30
Time for you and time for me,
And time yet for a hundred indecisions,
And for a hundred visions and revisions,
Before the taking of a toast and tea.

In the room the women come and go
Talking of Michelangelo.

And indeed there will be time
To wonder, "Do I dare?" and, "Do I dare?"
Time to turn back and descend the stair,
With a bald spot in the middle of my hair—   40
[They will say: "How his hair is growing thin!"]
My morning coat, my collar mounting firmly to the chin,
My necktie rich and modest, but asserted by a simple pin—
[They will say: "But how his arms and legs are thin!"]
Do I dare
Disturb the universe?
In a minute there is time
For decisions and revisions which a minute will reverse.

For I have known them all already, known them all:—
Have known the evenings, mornings, afternoons,   50
I have measured out my life with coffee spoons;
I know the voices dying with a dying fall

² an allusion to Hesiod's *Works and Days*, a poem praising hard work in the fields.

Beneath the music from a farther room.
  So how should I presume?

And I have known the eyes already, known them all—
The eyes that fix you in a formulated phrase,
And when I am formulated, sprawling on a pin,
When I am pinned and wriggling on the wall,
Then how should I begin
To spit out all the butt-ends of my days and ways?   60
  And how should I presume?

And I have known the arms already, known them all—
Arms that are braceleted and white and bare
[But in the lamplight, downed with light brown hair!]
Is it perfume from a dress
That makes me so digress?
Arms that lie along a table, or wrap about a shawl.
  And should I then presume?
  And how should I begin?

              .   .   .   .   .

Shall I say, I have gone at dusk through narrow streets   70
And watched the smoke that rises from the pipes
Of lonely men in shirt-sleeves, leaning out of windows? . . .

I should have been a pair of ragged claws
Scuttling across the floors of silent seas.

              .   .   .   .   .

And the afternoon, the evening, sleeps so peacefully!
Smoothed by long fingers,
Asleep . . . tired . . . or it malingers,
Stretched on the floor, here beside you and me.
Should I, after tea and cakes and ices,
Have the strength to force the moment to its crisis?   80
But though I have wept and fasted, wept and prayed,
Though I have seen my head [grown slightly bald] brought in upon a
      platter,[3]
I am no prophet—and here's no great matter;
I have seen the moment of my greatness flicker,

[3] like the head of John the Baptist. At the request of Salome he was executed,
and his head was brought in to Herod on a platter (Matthew, xiv. 1-11).

And I have seen the eternal Footman hold my coat, and snicker,
And in short, I was afraid.

And would it have been worth it, after all,
After the cups, the marmalade, the tea,
Among the porcelain, among some talk of you and me,
Would it have been worth while,   90
To have bitten off the matter with a smile,
To have squeezed the universe into a ball
To roll it toward some overwhelming question,
To say: "I am Lazarus, come from the dead,[4]
Come back to tell you all, I shall tell you all"—
If one, settling a pillow by her head,
    Should say: "That is not what I meant at all.
    That is not it, at all."

And would it have been worth it, after all,
Would it have been worth while,   100
After the sunsets and the dooryards and the sprinkled streets,
After the novels, after the teacups, after the skirts that trail along the
        floor—
And this, and so much more?—
It is impossible to say just what I mean!
But as if a magic lantern threw the nerves in patterns on a screen:
Would it have been worth while
If one, settling a pillow or throwing off a shawl,
And turning toward the window, should say:
    "That is not it at all,
    That is not what I meant, at all."   110

                    .   .   .   .   .

No! I am not Prince Hamlet, nor was meant to be;
Am an attendant lord, one that will do
To swell a progress, start a scene or two,
Advise the prince; no doubt, an easy tool,
Deferential, glad to be of use,
Politic, cautious, and meticulous;
Full of high sentence, but a bit obtuse;
At times, indeed, almost ridiculous—
Almost, at times, the Fool.

    [4] the brother of Mary and Martha, who was raised from death by Christ
(John, xi. 1–44).

I grow old ... I grow old ...
I shall wear the bottoms of my trousers rolled.[5]   120

Shall I part my hair behind? Do I dare to eat a peach?
I shall wear white flannel trousers, and walk upon the beach.
I have heard the mermaids singing, each to each.

I do not think that they will sing to me.

I have seen them riding seaward on the waves
Combing the white hair of the waves blown back
When the wind blows the water white and black.

We have lingered in the chambers of the sea
By sea-girls wreathed with seaweed red and brown   130
Till human voices wake us, and we drown.

[5] trousers with cuffs, a new fashion then.

The Hollow Men

Mistah Kurtz—he dead.

A penny for the old Guy[1]

I

We are the hollow men
We are the stuffed men
Leaning together
Headpiece filled with straw. Alas!
Our dried voices, when
We whisper together
Are quiet and meaningless
As wind in dry grass
Or rats' feet over broken glass
In our dry cellar

Shape without form, shade without color,
Paralyzed force, gesture without motion;

[1] the first epigraph is the cabin boy announcing Kurtz's death in Joseph Conrad's story, *Heart of Darkness*. The second is the cry of children collecting on Guy Fawkes Day, celebrating the discovery of a plot to blow up the House of Parliament.

Those who have crossed
With direct eyes, to death's other Kingdom
Remember us—if at all—not as lost
Violent souls, but only
As the hollow men
The stuffed men.

II

Eyes I dare not meet in dreams
In death's dream kingdom
These do not appear:
There, the eyes are
Sunlight on a broken column
There, is a tree swinging
And voices are
In the wind's singing
More distant and more solemn
Than a fading star.

Let me be no nearer
In death's dream kingdom
Let me also wear
Such deliberate disguises
Rat's coat, crowskin, crossed staves
In a field
Behaving as the wind behaves
No nearer—

Not that final meeting
In the twilight kingdom

III

This is the dead land
This is cactus land
Here the stone images
Are raised, here they receive
The supplication of a dead man's hand
Under the twinkle of a fading star.

Is it like this
In death's other kingdom

Waking alone
At the hour when we are
Trembling with tenderness
Lips that would kiss
Form prayers to broken stone.

I V

The eyes are not here
There are no eyes here
In this valley of dying stars
In this hollow valley
This broken jaw of our lost kingdoms

In this last of meeting places
We grope together
And avoid speech
Gathered on this beach of the tumid river[2]

Sightless, unless
The eyes reappear
As the perpetual star
Multifoliate rose[3]
Of death's twilight kingdom
The hope only
Of empty men.

V

*Here we go round the prickly pear
Prickly pear prickly pear
Here we go round the prickly pear
At five o'clock in the morning.*

Between the idea
And the reality
Between the motion
And the act
Falls the Shadow
                    For Thine is the Kingdom

[2] the river Acheron in the underworld.
[3] an emblem of Christ and the Virgin.

Between the conception
And the creation
Between the emotion
And the response
Falls the Shadow

           Life is very long

Between the desire
And the spasm
Between the potency
And the existence
Between the essence
And the descent
Falls the Shadow

      For Thine is the Kingdom

For Thine is
Life is
For Thine is the

This is the way the world ends
This is the way the world ends
This is the way the world ends
Not with a bang but a whimper.

JOHN CROWE RANSOM [1888–   ]

Bells for John Whiteside's Daughter

There was such speed in her little body
And such lightness in her footfall,
It is no wonder her brown study
Astonishes us all.

Her wars were bruited in our high window.
We looked among orchard trees and beyond,
Where she took arms against her shadow,
Or harried unto the pond

The lazy geese, like a snow cloud
Dripping their snow on the green grass,

Tricking and stopping, sleepy and proud,
Who cried in goose, Alas,

For the tireless heart within the little
Lady with rod that made them rise
From their noon apple-dreams and scuttle
Goose-fashion under the skies!

But now go the bells and we are ready,
In one house we are sternly stopped
To say we are vexed at her brown study,
Lying so primly propped.

HUGH MACDIARMID [1892–   ]

The Bonnie Broukit° Bairn°   dirty / child

Mars is braw° in crammasy,°   gaily dressed / crimson
Venus in a green silk goun,
The auld mune shak's her gowden° feathers,   golden
Their starry talk's a wheen° o' blethers,°   a good deal / nonsense
Nane for thee a thochtie° sparin',   a little thought
Earth, thou bonnie broukit bairn!
—But greet,° an' in your tears ye'll drown   cry
The haill° clanjamfrie!°   whole / worthless bunch

Crowdieknowe

Oh to be at Crowdieknowe
When the last trumpet blaws,
An' see the deid° come loupin' owre   dead
The auld grey wa's.°   walls

Muckle° men wi' tousled beards.   large
I grat° as a bairn°   wept / child
'll scramble frae the croodit° clay   thickened
Wi' feck° o' swearin'.   plenty

An' glower° at God an' a' his gang　　　　　　　　　stare
O' angels i' the lift°　　　　　　　　　　　　　　　　sky
—Thae trashy bleezin° French-like folk　　　　　　　drunk
Wha gar'd° them shift!　　　　　　　　　　　　　　forced

Fain° the weemun-folk'll seek　　　　　　　　　　　eagerly
To mak' them haud° their row　　　　　　　　　　　hold
—Fegs,° God's no blate° gin he stirs up　　　　Truly / not shy
The men o' Crowdieknowe!

FROM *The Kind of Poetry I Want*

The poetry of one the Russians call "a broad nature"
And the Japanese call "flower heart,"
And we, in Scottish Gaeldom, "*ionraic*."[1]
The poetry of one who practices his art
Not like a man who works that he may live
But as one who is bent on doing nothing but work
Confident that he who lives does not work,
That one must die to life in order to be
Utterly a creator—refusing to sanction　　　　　　130
The irresponsible lyricism in which sense impressions
Are employed to substitute ecstasy for information,
Knowing that feeling, warm heart-felt feeling,
Is always banal and futile.
Only the irrations and icy ecstasies
Of the artist's corrupted nervous system
Are artistic—the very gift of style, of form and expression,
Is nothing else than this cool and fastidious attitude
Towards humanity. The artist is happiest
With an idea which can become
All emotion, and an emotion all idea.

·　　·　　·　　·　　·

And, constantly, I seek　　　　　　　　　　　　　190
A poetry of facts. Even as
The profound kinship of all living substance
Is made clear by the chemical route.

[1] Gaelic.

Without some chemistry one is bound to remain
Forever a dumbfounded savage
In the face of vital reactions.
The beautiful relations
Shown only by biochemistry
Replace a stupefied sense of wonder
With something more wonderful   200
Because natural and understandable.
Nature is more wonderful
When it is at least partly understood.
Such an understanding dawns
On the lay reader when he becomes
Acquainted with the biochemistry of the glands
In their relation to diseases such as goiter
And in their effects on growth, sex, and reproduction.
He will begin to comprehend a little
The subtlety and beauty of the action   210
Of enzymes, viruses, and bacteriophages,
Those substances which are on the borderland
Between the living and the non-living.
He will understand why the biochemist
Can speculate on the possibility
Of the synthesis of life without feeling
That thereby he is shallow or blasphemous.
He will understand that, on the contrary,
He finds all the more
Because he seeks for the endless   220
—"Even our deepest emotions
May be conditioned by traces
Of a derivative of phenanthrene!"

Crystals Like Blood

I remember how, long ago, I found
Crystals like blood in a broken stone.

I picked up a broken chunk of bed-rock
And turned it this way and that,
It was heavier than one would have expected
From its size. One face was caked

With brown limestone. But the rest
Was a hard greenish-gray quartz-like stone
Faintly dappled with darker shadows,
And in this quartz ran veins and beads   10
Of bright magenta.

And I remember how later on I saw
How mercury is extracted from cinnebar
—The double ring of iron piledrivers
Like the multiple legs of a fantastically symmetrical spider
Rising and falling with monotonous precision,
Marching round in an endless circle
And pounding up and down with a tireless, thunderous force,
While, beyond, another conveyor drew the crumbled ore
From the bottom and raised it to an opening high   20
In the side of a gigantic gray-white kiln.

So I remember how mercury is got
When I contrast my living memory of you
And your dear body rotting here in the clay
—And feel once again released in me
The bright torrents of felicity, naturalness, and faith
My treadmill memory draws from you yet.

WILFRED OWEN [1893–1918]

Exposure

Our brains ache, in the merciless iced east winds that knive us ...
Wearied we keep awake because the night is silent ...
Low, drooping flares confuse our memory of the salient ...
Worried by silence, sentries whisper, curious, nervous,
            But nothing happens.

Watching, we hear the mad gusts tugging on the wire,
Like twitching agonies of men among its brambles.
Northward, incessantly, the flickering gunnery rumbles,
Far off, like a dull rumor of some other war.
            What are we doing here?   10

The poignant misery of dawn begins to grow ...
We only know war lasts, rain soaks, and clouds sag stormy.
Dawn massing in the east her melancholy army
Attacks once more in ranks on shivering ranks of gray,
        But nothing happens.

Sudden successive flights of bullets streak the silence.
Less deadly than the air that shudders black with snow,
With sidelong flowing flakes that flock, pause, and renew,
We watch them wandering up and down the wind's nonchalance,
        But nothing happens.   20

Pale flakes with fingering stealth come feeling for our faces—
We cringe in holes, back on forgotten dreams, and stare, snow-dazed,
Deep into grassier ditches. So we drowse, sun-dozed,
Littered with blossoms trickling where the blackbird fusses.
        Is it that we are dying?

Slowly our ghosts drag home: glimpsing the sunk fires, glozed
With crusted dark-red jewels; crickets jingle there;
For hours the innocent mice rejoice: the house is theirs;
Shutters and doors, all closed: on us the doors are closed—
        We turn back to our dying.   30

Since we believe not otherwise can kind fires burn;
Nor ever suns smile true on child, or field, or fruit.
For God's invincible spring our love is made afraid;
Therefore, not loath, we lie out here; therefore were born,
        For love of God seems dying.

To-night, His frost will fasten on this mud and us,
Shriveling many hands, puckering foreheads crisp.
The burying-party, picks and shovels in their shaking grasp,
Pause over half-known faces. All their eyes are ice,
        But nothing happens.   40

Insensibility

I

    Happy are men who yet before they are killed
    Can let their veins run cold.
    Whom no compassion fleers[1]

[1] scoffs at.

Or makes their feet
Sore on the alleys cobbled with their brothers.
The front line withers,
But they are troops who fade, not flowers
For poets' tearful fooling:
Men, gaps for filling:
Losses who might have fought   10
Longer; but no one bothers.

I I

And some cease feeling
Even themselves or for themselves.
Dullness best solves
The tease and doubt of shelling,
And Chance's strange arithmetic
Comes simpler than the reckoning of their shilling.
They keep no check on armies' decimation.

I I I

Happy are these who lose imagination:
They have enough to carry with ammunition.   20
Their spirit drags no pack,
Their old wounds save with cold can not more ache.
Having seen all things red,
Their eyes are rid
Of the hurt of the color of blood for ever.
And terror's first constriction over,
Their hearts remain small-drawn.
Their senses in some scorching cautery of battle
Now long since ironed,
Can laugh among the dying, unconcerned.   30

I V

Happy the soldier home, with not a notion
How somewhere, every dawn, some men attack,
And many sighs are drained.
Happy the lad whose mind was never trained:
His days are worth forgetting more than not.
He sings along the march
Which we march taciturn, because of dusk,

The long, forlorn, relentless trend
From larger day to huger night.

V

We wise, who with a thought besmirch   40
Blood over all our soul,
How should we see our task
But through his blunt and lashless eyes?
Alive, he is not vital overmuch;
Dying, not mortal overmuch;
Nor sad, nor proud,
Nor curious at all.
He cannot tell
Old men's placidity from his.

V I

But cursed are dullards whom no cannon stuns,   50
That they should be as stones;
Wretched are they, and mean
With paucity that never was simplicity.
By choice they made themselves immune
To pity and whatever moans in man
Before the last sea and the hapless stars;
Whatever mourns when many leave these shores;
Whatever shares
The eternal reciprocity of tears.

Disabled

He sat in a wheeled chair, waiting for dark,
And shivered in his ghastly suit of gray,
Legless, sewn short at elbow. Through the park
Voices of boys rang saddening like a hymn,
Voices of play and pleasures after day,
Till gathering sleep had mothered them from him.

About this time Town used to swing so gay
When glow-lamps budded in the light blue trees,
And girls glanced lovelier as the air grew dim,—
In the old times, before he threw away his knees.   10

301

Now he will never feel again how slim
Girls' waists are, or how warm their subtle hands;
All of them touch him like some queer disease.

There was an artist silly for his face,
For it was younger than his youth, last year.
Now, he is old; his back will never brace;
He's lost his color very far from here,
Poured it down shell-holes till the veins ran dry,
And half his lifetime lapsed in the hot race,
And leap of purple spurted from his thigh.   20

One time he liked a blood-smear down his leg,
After the matches, carried shoulder-high.
It was after football, when he'd drunk a peg,
He thought he'd better join.—He wonders why.
Someone had said he'd look a god in kilts,
That's why; and may be, too, to please his Meg;
Aye, that was it, to please the giddy jilts
He asked to join. He didn't have to beg;

Smiling they wrote his lie; aged nineteen years.
Germans he scarcely thought of; all their guilt,   30
And Austria's, did not move him. And no fears
Of Fear came yet. He thought of jeweled hilts
For daggers in plaid socks; of smart salutes;
And care of arms; and leave; and pay arrears;
Esprit de corps, and hints for young recruits.
And soon he was drafted out with drums and cheers.

Some cheered him home, but not as crowds cheer Goal.
Only a solemn man who brought him fruits
Thanked him; and then inquired about his soul.

Now, he will spend a few sick years in Institutes,   40
And do what things the rules consider wise,
And take whatever pity they may dole.
Tonight he noticed how the women's eyes
Passed from him to the strong men that were whole.
How cold and late it is! Why don't they come
And put him into bed? Why don't they come?

E. E. CUMMINGS [1894–1963]

Portrait

Buffalo Bill's
defunct
       who used to
       ride a watersmooth-silver
              stallion
and break onetwothreefourfive pigeonsjustlikethat
                    Jesus

he was a handsome man
             and what i want to know is
how do you like your blueeyed boy
Mister Death

Poem, or Beauty Hurts Mr. Vinal

take it from me kiddo
believe me
my country, 'tis of

you, land of the Cluett
Shirt Boston Garter and Spearmint
Girl With The Wrigley Eyes (of you
land of the Arrow Ide
and Earl &
Wilson
Collars) of you i   10
sing: land of Abraham Lincoln and Lydia E. Pinkham,
land above all of Just Add Hot Water And Serve—
from every B. V. D.

let freedom ring

amen. i do however protest, anent the un
-spontaneous and otherwise scented merde which
greets one (Everywhere Why) as divine poesy per
that and this radically defunct periodical. i would

suggest that certain ideas gestures
rhymes, like Gillette Razor Blades   20
having been used and reused
to the mystical moment of dullness, emphatically are
Not To Be Resharpened. (Case in point

if we are to believe these gently O sweetly
melancholy trillers amid the thrillers
these crepuscular violinists among my and your
skyscrapers— Helen & Cleopatra were Just Too Lovely,
The Snail's On The Thorn enter Morn and God's
In His andsoforth

do you get me?) according   30
to such supposedly indigenous
throstles Art is O World O Life
a formula: example, Turn Your Shirttails Into
Drawers and If It Isn't An Eastman It Isn't A
Kodak therefore my friends let
us now sing each and all fortissimo A-
mer
i

ca, I   40
love,
You. And there're a
hun-dred-mil-lion-oth-ers, like
all of you successfully if
delicately gelded (or spaded)
gentlemen (and ladies)—pretty

littleliverpill-
hearted-Nujolneeding-There's-A-Reason
americans (who tensetendoned and with
upward vacant eyes, painfully
perpetually crouched, quivering, upon the   50
sternly allotted sandpile
—how silently
emit a tiny violetflavored nuisance: Odor?

ono.
comes out like a ribbon lies flat on the brush

HART CRANE [1899–1932]

FROM *The Bridge*

TO BROOKLYN BRIDGE

How many dawns, chill from his rippling rest
The seagull's wings shall dip and pivot him,
Shedding white rings of tumult, building high
Over the chained bay waters Liberty[1]—

Then, with inviolate curve, forsake our eyes
As apparitional as sails that cross
Some page of figures to be filed away;
—Till elevators drop us from our day . . .

I think of cinemas, panoramic sleights
With multitudes bent toward some flashing scene   10
Never disclosed, but hastened to again,
Foretold to other eyes on the same screen;

And Thee, across the harbor, silver-paced
As though the sun took step of thee, yet left
Some motion ever unspent in thy stride,—
Implicitly thy freedom staying thee!

Out of some subway scuttle, cell or loft
A bedlamite speeds to thy parapets,
Tilting there momently, shrill shirt ballooning,
A jest falls from the speechless caravan.   20

Down Wall, from girder into street noon leaks,
A rip-tooth of the sky's acetylene;
All afternoon the cloud-flown derricks turn . . .
Thy cables breathe the North Atlantic still.

And obscure as that heaven of the Jews,
Thy guerdon . . . Accolade thou dost bestow
Of anonymity time cannot raise:
Vibrant reprieve and pardon thou dost show.

[1] Statue of Liberty in New York harbor.

O harp and altar, of the fury fused,
(How could mere toil align thy choiring strings!)   30
Terrific threshold of the prophet's pledge,
Prayer of pariah, and the lover's cry,—

Again the traffic lights that skim thy swift
Unfractioned idiom, immaculate sigh of stars,
Beading thy path—condense eternity:
And we have seen night lifted in thine arms.

Under thy shadow by the piers I waited;
Only in darkness is thy shadow clear.
The City's fiery parcels all undone,
Already snow submerges an iron year . . .   40

O Sleepless as the river under thee,
Vaulting the sea, the prairies' dreaming sod,
Unto us lowliest sometime sweep, descend
And of the curveship lend a myth to God.

National Winter Garden

Outspoken buttocks in pink beads
Invite the necessary cloudy clinch
Of bandy eyes. . . . No extra mufflings here:
The world's one flagrant, sweating cinch.

And while legs waken salads in the brain
You pick your blonde out neatly through the smoke.
Always you wait for someone else though, always—
(Then rush the nearest exit through the smoke).

Always and last, before the final ring
When all the fireworks blare, begins   10
A tom-tom scrimmage with a somewhere violin,
Some cheapest echo of them all—begins.

And shall we call her whiter than the snow?
Sprayed first with ruby, then with emerald sheen—
Least tearful and least glad (who knows her smile?)
A caught slide shows her sandstone gray between.

Her eyes exist in swivelings of her teats,
Pearls whip her hips, a drench of whirling strands.

Her silly snake rings begin to mount, surmount
Each other—turquoise fakes on tinseled hands.

We wait that writhing pool, her pearls collapsed,
—All but her belly buried in the floor;
And the lewd trounce of a final muted beat!
We flee her spasm through a fleshless door. . . .

Yet, to the empty trapeze of your flesh,
O Magdalene,[1] each comes back to die alone.
Then you, the burlesque of our lust—and faith,
Lug us back lifeward—bone by infant bone.

W. H. AUDEN [1907–   ]

Seascape

Look, stranger, on this island now
The leaping light for your delight discovers,
Stand stable here
And silent be,
That through the channels of the ear
May wander like a river
The swaying sound of the sea.

Here at a small field's ending pause
When the chalk wall falls to the foam and its tall ledges
Oppose the pluck
And knock of the tide,
And the shingle scrambles after the suck-
-ing surf,
And a gull lodges
A moment on its sheer side.

Far off like floating seeds the ships
Diverge on urgent voluntary errands,
And this full view
Indeed may enter

[1] Mary Magdalene.

And move in memory as now these clouds do,
That pass the harbor mirror
And all the summer through the water saunter.

Musée des Beaux Arts[1]

About suffering they were never wrong,
The Old Masters: how well they understood
Its human position; how it takes place
While someone else is eating or opening a window or just walking dully
      along;
How, when the aged are reverently, passionately waiting
For the miraculous birth, there always must be
Children who did not specially want it to happen, skating
On a pond at the edge of the wood:
They never forgot
That even the dreadful martyrdom must run its course
Anyhow in a corner, some untidy spot
Where the dogs go on with their doggy life and the torturer's horse
Scratches its innocent behind on a tree.

In Brueghel's *Icarus*,[2] for instance: how everything turns away
Quite leisurely from the disaster; the ploughman may
Have heard the splash, the forsaken cry,
But for him it was not an important failure; the sun shone
As it had to on the white legs disappearing into the green
Water; and the expensive delicate ship that must have seen
Something amazing, a boy falling out of the sky,
Had somewhere to get to and sailed calmly on.

The Fall of Rome

FOR CYRIL CONNOLLY

The piers are pummeled by the waves;
In a lonely field the rain
Lashes an abandoned train;
Outlaws fill the mountain caves.

[1] Museum of Fine Arts.
[2] "The Fall of Icarus," a sixteenth-century painting by Pieter Brueghel. Daedalus constructed wings of wax. His son, Icarus, flew too near the sun, the wax melted, and he fell into the sea and drowned.

Fantastic grow the evening gowns;
Agents of the Fisc[1] pursue
Absconding tax-defaulters through
The sewers of provincial towns.

Prviate rites of magic send
The temple prostitutes to sleep;   10
All the literati keep
An imaginary friend.

Cerebrotonic Catos[2] may
Extol the Ancient Disciplines,
But the muscle-bound Marines
Mutiny for food and pay.

Caesar's double-bed is warm
As an unimportant clerk
Writes I DO NOT LIKE MY WORK
On a pink official form.   20

Unendowed with wealth or pity,
Little birds with scarlet legs,
Sitting on their speckled eggs,
Eye each flu-infected city.

Altogether elsewhere, vast
Herds of reindeer move across
Miles and miles of golden moss,
Silently and very fast.

THEODORE ROETHKE [1908–1963]

Night Journey

Now as the train bears west,
Its rhythm rocks the earth,
And from my Pullman berth

[1] British revenue department.
[2] "cerebrotonic," intellectually invigorating; Cato the Elder was a Roman statesman, Cato the Younger, a Stoic philosopher.

I stare into the night
While others take their rest.
Bridges of iron lace,
A suddenness of trees,
A lap of mountain mist
All cross my line of sight,
Then a bleak wasted place,   10
And a lake below my knees.
Full on my neck I feel
The straining at a curve;
My muscles move with steel,
I wake in every nerve.
I watch a beacon swing
From dark to blazing bright;
We thunder through ravines
And gullies washed with light.
Beyond the mountain pass   20
Mist deepens on the pane;
We rush into a rain
That rattles double glass.
Wheels shake the roadbed stone,
The pistons jerk and shove,
I stay up half the night
To see the land I love.

My Papa's Waltz

The whiskey on your breath
Could make a small boy dizzy;
But I hung on like death:
Such waltzing was not easy.

We romped until the pans
Slid from the kitchen shelf;
My mother's countenance
Could not unfrown itself.

The hand that held my wrist
Was battered on one knuckle;

At every step you missed
My right ear scraped a buckle.

You beat time on my head
With a palm caked hard by dirt,
Then waltzed me off to bed
Still clinging to your shirt.

Dolor

I have known the inexorable sadness of pencils,
Neat in their boxes, dolor of pad and paper-weight,
All the misery of manilla folders and mucilage,
Desolation in immaculate public places,
Lonely reception room, lavatory, switchboard,
The unalterable pathos of basin and pitcher,
Ritual of multigraph, paper-clip, comma,
Endless duplication of lives and objects.
And I have seen dust from the walls of institutions,
Finer than flour, alive, more dangerous than silica,
Sift, almost invisible, through long afternoons of tedium,
Dropping a fine film on nails and delicate eyebrows,
Glazing the pale hair, the duplicate gray standard faces.

Elegy for Jane

MY STUDENT, THROWN BY A HORSE

I remember the neckcurls, limp and damp as tendrils;
And her quick look, a sidelong pickerel smile;
And how, once startled into talk, the light syllables leaped for her,
And she balanced in the delight of her thought,
A wren, happy, tail into the wind,
Her song trembling the twigs and small branches.
The shade sang with her;
The leaves, their whispers turned to kissing;
And the mold sang in the bleached valleys under the rose.

Oh, when she was sad, she cast herself down into such a pure depth,
Even a father could not find her: 11
Scraping her cheek against straw;
Stirring the clearest water.

My sparrow, you are not here,
Waiting like a fern, making a spiny shadow.
The sides of wet stones cannot console me,
Nor the moss, wound with the last light.

If only I could nudge you from this sleep,
My maimed darling, my skittery pigeon.
Over this damp grave I speak the words of my love: 20
I, with no rights in this matter,
Neither father nor lover.

The Waking

I wake to sleep, and take my waking slow.
I feel my fate in what I cannot fear.
I learn by going where I have to go.

We think by feeling. What is there to know?
I hear my being dance from ear to ear.
I wake to sleep, and take my waking slow.

Of those so close beside me, which are you?
God bless the Ground! I shall walk softly there,
And learn by going where I have to go.

Light takes the Tree; but who can tell us how?
The lowly worm climbs up a winding stair;
I wake to sleep, and take my waking slow.

Great Nature has another thing to do
To you and me; so take the lively air,
And, lovely, learn by going where to go.

This shaking keeps me steady. I should know.
What falls away is always. And is near.
I wake to sleep, and take my waking slow.
I learn by going where I have to go.

The Force That Through the Green Fuse Drives the Flower

The force that through the green fuse drives the flower
Drives my green age; that blasts the roots of trees
Is my destroyer.
And I am dumb to tell the crooked rose
My youth is bent by the same wintry fever.

The force that drives the water through the rocks
Drives my red blood; that dries the mouthing streams
Turns mine to wax.
And I am dumb to mouth unto my veins
How at the mountain spring the same mouth sucks.   10

The hand that whirls the water in the pool
Stirs the quicksand; that ropes the blowing wind
Hauls my shroud sail.
And I am dumb to tell the hanging man
How of my clay is made the hangman's lime.

The lips of time leech to the fountain head;
Love drips and gathers, but the fallen blood
Shall calm her sores.
And I am dumb to tell a weather's wind
How time has ticked a heaven round the stars.   20

And I am dumb to tell the lover's tomb
How at my sheet goes the same crooked worm.

Fern Hill

Now as I was young and easy under the apple boughs
About the lilting house and happy as the grass was green,
    The night above the dingle starry,
        Time let me hail and climb
    Golden in the heydays of his eyes,
And honored among wagons I was prince of the apple towns

And once below a time I lordly had the trees and leaves
      Trail with daisies and barley
    Down the rivers of the windfall light.

And as I was green and carefree, famous among the barns   10
About the happy yard and singing as the farm was home,
    In the sun that is young once only,
      Time let me play and be
    Golden in the mercy of his means,
And green and golden I was huntsman and herdsman, the calves
Sang to my horn, the foxes on the hills barked clear and cold,
      And the sabbath rang slowly
    In the pebbles of the holy streams.

All the sun long it was running, it was lovely, the hay
Fields high as the house, the tunes from the chimneys, it was air   20
    And playing, lovely and watery
      And fire green as grass.
    And nightly under the simple stars
As I rode to sleep the owls were bearing the farm away,
All the moon long I heard, blessed among stables, the nightjars
    Flying with the ricks, and the horses
      Flashing into the dark.

And then to awake, and the farm, like a wanderer white
With the dew, come back, the cock on his shoulder: it was all
    Shining, it was Adam and maiden,   30
      The sky gathered again
    And the sun grew round that very day.
So it must have been after the birth of the simple light
In the first, spinning place, the spellbound horses walking warm
    Out of the whinnying green stable
      On to the fields of praise.

And honored among foxes and pheasants by the gay house
Under the new made clouds and happy as the heart was long,
    In the sun born over and over,
      I ran my heedless ways,   40
    My wishes raced through the house high hay
And nothing I cared, at my sky blue trades, that time allows
In all his tuneful turning so few and such morning songs
    Before the children green and golden
      Follow him out of grace,

Nothing I cared, in the lamb white days, that time would take me
Up to the swallow thronged loft by the shadow of my hand,

In the moon that is always rising,
  Nor that riding to sleep
I should hear him fly with the high fields   50
And wake to the farm forever fled from the childless land.
Oh as I was young and easy in the mercy of his means,
  Time held me green and dying
Though I sang in my chains like the sea.

Do Not Go Gentle Into That Good Night

Do not go gentle into that good night,
Old age should burn and rave at close of day;
Rage, rage against the dying of the light.

Though wise men at their end know dark is right,
Because their words had forked no lightning they
Do not go gentle into that good night.

Good men, the last wave by, crying how bright
Their frail deeds might have danced in a green bay,
Rage, rage against the dying of the light.

Wild men who caught and sang the sun in flight,
And learn, too late, they grieved it on its way,
Do not go gentle into that good night.

Grave men, near death, who see with blinding sight
Blind eyes could blaze like meteors and be gay,
Rage, rage against the dying of the light

And you, my father, there on the sad height,
Curse, bless, me now with your fierce tears, I pray.
Do not go gentle into that good night.
Rage, rage against the dying of the light.

HENRY REED [1914–]

Naming of Parts

Today we have naming of parts. Yesterday,
We had daily cleaning. And tomorrow morning,
We shall have what to do after firing. But today,

Today we have naming of parts. Japonica
Glistens like coral in all of the neighboring gardens,
  And today we have naming of parts.

This is the lower sling swivel. And this
Is the upper sling swivel, whose use you will see,
When you are given your slings. And this is the piling swivel,
Which in your case you have not got. The branches   10
Hold in the gardens their silent, eloquent gestures,
  Which in our case we have not got.

This is the safety-catch, which is always released
With an easy flick of the thumb. And please do not let me
See anyone using his finger. You can do it quite easy
If you have any strength in your thumb. The blossoms
Are fragile and motionless, never letting anyone see
  Any of them using their finger.

And this you can see is the bolt. The purpose of this
Is to open the breech, as you see. We can slide it   20
Rapidly backwards and forwards: we call this
Easing the spring. And rapidly backwards and forwards
The early bees are assaulting and fumbling the flowers:
  They call it easing the Spring.

They call it easing the Spring: it is perfectly easy
If you have any strength in your thumb: like the bolt,
And the breech, and the cocking-piece, and the point of balance,
Which in our case we have not got; and the almond-blossom
Silent in all of the gardens and the bees going backwards and forwards,
  For today we have naming of parts.   30

DAVID IGNATOW [1914–   ]

Get the Gasworks

Get the gasworks into a poem,
and you've got the smoke and smokestacks,
the mottled red and yellow tenements,
and grimy kids who curse with the pungency
of the odor of gas. You've got America, boy.

Sketch in the river and barges,
all dirty and slimy.
How do the seagulls stay so white?
And always cawing like little mad geniuses?
You've got the kind of living   10
that makes the kind of thinking we do:
gaswork smokestack whistle tooting wisecracks.
They don't come because we like it that way,
but because we find it outside our window each morning,
in soot on the furniture,
and trucks carrying coal for gas,
the kid hot after the ball under the wheel.
He gets it over the be'ly, all right.
He dies there.

So the kids keep tossing the ball around   20
after the funeral.
So the cops keep chasing them,
so the mamas keep hollering,
and papa flings his newspaper outward,
in disgust with discipline.

ROBERT LOWELL [1917–   ]

At the Altar

I sit at a gold table with my girl
Whose eyelids burn with brandy. What a whirl
Of Easter eggs is colored by the lights,
As the Norwegian dancer's crystalled tights
Flash with her naked leg's high-booted skate,
Like Northern Lights upon my watching plate.
The twinkling steel above me is a star;
I am a fallen Christmas tree. Our car   100
Races through seven red-lights—then the road
Is unpatrolled and empty, and a load
Of ply-wood with a tail-light makes us slow.
I turn and whisper in her ear. You know
I want to leave my mother and my wife,

You wouldn't have me tied to them for life . . .
Time runs, the windshield runs with stars. The past
Is cities from a train, until at last
Its escalating and black-windowed blocks
Recoil against a Gothic church. The clocks   110
Are tolling. I am dying. The shocked stones
Are falling like a ton of bricks and bones
That snap and splinter and descend in glass
Before a priest who mumbles through his Mass
And sprinkles holy water; and the Day
Breaks with its lightning on the man of clay,
Dies amara valde.[1] Here the Lord
Is Lucifer in harness: hand on sword,
He watches me for Mother, and will turn
The bier and baby-carriage where I burn.   120

[1] "a very bitter day."

Mr. Edwards[1] *and the Spider*

I saw the spiders marching through the air,
Swimming from tree to tree that mildewed day
   In latter August when the hay
   Came creaking to the barn. But where
      The wind is westerly,
Where gnarled November makes the spiders fly
Into the apparitions of the sky,
   They purpose nothing but their ease and die
Urgently beating east to sunrise and the sea;

What are we in the hands of the great God?   10
It was in vain you set up thorn and briar
   In battle array against the fire
   And treason crackling in your blood;
      For the wild thorns grow tame
And will do nothing to oppose the flame;
Your lacerations tell the losing game
   You play against a sickness past your cure.
How will the hands be strong? How will the heart endure?

[1] Jonathan Edwards, eighteenth century Calvinist theologian, born in East Windsor, Connecticut.

A very little thing, a little worm,
Or hourglass-blazoned spider, it is said,
    Can kill a tiger. Will the dead
    Hold up his mirror and affirm
        To the four winds the smell
And flash of his authority? It's well
If God who holds you to the pit of hell,
    Much as one holds a spider, will destroy,
Baffle and dissipate your soul. As a small boy

On Windsor Marsh, I saw the spider die
When thrown into the bowels of fierce fire:
    There's no long struggle, no desire
    To get up on its feet and fly—
        It stretches out its feet
And dies. This is the sinner's last retreat;
Yes, and no strength exerted on the heat
    Then sinews the abolished will, when sick
And full of burning, it will whistle on a brick.

But who can plumb the sinking of that soul?
Josiah Hawley,[2] picture yourself cast
    Into a brick-kiln where the blast
    Fans your quick vitals to a coal—
        If measured by a glass,
How long would it seem burning! Let there pass
A minute, ten, ten trillion; but the blaze
    Is infinite, eternal: this is death,
To die and know it. This is the Black Widow, death.

[2] Edwards' cousin, who opposed his revivalist preachings.

20

30

40

Memories of West Street and Lepke

Only teaching on Tuesdays, book-worming
in pajamas fresh from the washer each morning,
I hog a whole house on Boston's
"hardly passionate Marlborough Street,"[1]
where even the man

[1] Henry James said, an example of extreme understatement would be that
Marlborough Street was hardly passionate.

scavenging filth in the back alley trash cans,
has two children, a beach wagon, a helpmate,
and is a "young Republican."
I have a nine months' daughter,
young enough to be my granddaughter.   10
Like the sun she rises in her flame-flamingo infants' wear.

These are the tranquillized *Fifties*,
and I am forty. Ought I to regret my seedtime?
I was a fire-breathing Catholic C.O.,[2]
and made my manic statement,
telling off the state and president, and then
sat waiting sentence in the bull pen
beside a Negro boy with curlicues
of marijuana in his hair.

Given a year,   20
I walked on the roof of the West Street Jail,[3] a short
enclosure like my school soccer court,
and saw the Hudson River once a day
through sooty clothesline entanglements
and bleaching khaki tenements.
Strolling, I yammered metaphysics with Abramowitz,[4]
a jaundice-yellow ("it's really tan")
and fly-weight pacifist,
so vegetarian,
he wore rope shoes and preferred fallen fruit.   30
He tried to convert Bioff and Brown,
the Hollywood pimps, to his diet.
Hairy, muscular, suburban,
wearing chocolate double-breasted suits,
they blew their tops and beat him black and blue.

I was so out of things, I'd never heard
of the Jehovah's Witnesses.
"Are you a C.O.?" I asked a fellow jailbird.

  [2] conscientious objector.
  [3] jail in New York from which prisoners were sent elsewhere. Lowell says
that "all sorts of people were there, including German bundists and Jehovah's
Witnesses."
  [4] Robert Lowell recounts that "Abramowitz didn't eat meat—or fruit, unless fallen from the tree; his clothes were made of fallen vegetables. Bioff and
Brown attacked him."

"No," he answered, "I'm a J.W."
He taught me the "hospital tuck,"   40
and pointed out the T shirted back
of *Murder Incorporated's* Czar Lepke,[5]
there piling towels on a rack,
or dawdling off to his little segregated cell full
of things forbidden the common man:
a portable radio, a dresser, two toy American
flags tied together with a ribbon of Easter palm.
Flabby, bald, lobotomized,
he drifted in a sheepish calm,
where no agonizing reappraisal   50
jarred his concentration on the electric chair—
hanging like an oasis in his air
of lost connections. . . .

[5] Lou (Lepke) Buchalter, one of the leaders of New York's labor and industrial rackets, and a member of the ruling board of Murder, Inc. He went to the electric chair in 1944. Lowell says, "He was a mild soul—looked like an art critic I knew but less dangerous. Lepke was evil as a negative reality."

KEITH DOUGLAS [1920–1944]

Vergissmeinicht

Three weeks gone and the combatants gone,
returning over the nightmare ground
we found the place again, and found
the soldier sprawling in the sun.

The frowning barrel of his gun
overshadowing. As we came on
that day, he hit my tank with one
like the entry of a demon.

Look. Here in the gunpit spoil
the dishonored picture of his girl   10
who has put: *Steffi. Vergissmeinicht*[1]
in a copybook gothic script.

[1] "forget me not."

We see him almost with content
abased, and seeming to have paid
and mocked at by his own equipment
that's hard and good when he's decayed.

But she would weep to see today
how on his skin the swart flies move;
the dust upon the paper eye
and the burst stomach like a cave.   20

For here the lover and killer are mingled
who had one body and one heart.
And death who had the soldier singled
has done the lover mortal hurt.

RICHARD WILBUR [1921–   ]

Love Calls Us to the Things of This World

The eyes open to a cry of pulleys,
And spirited from sleep, the astounded soul
Hangs for a moment bodiless and simple
As false dawn.
                    Outside the open window
The morning air is all awash with angels.

Some are in bed-sheets, some are in blouses,
Some are in smocks: but truly there they are.
Now they are rising together in calm swells
Of halcyon feeling, filling whatever they wear   10
With the deep joy of their impersonal breathing;

Now they are flying in place, conveying
The terrible speed of their omnipresence, moving
And staying like white water; and now of a sudden

322

They swoon down into so rapt a quiet
That nobody seems to be there.
                    The soul shrinks

     From all that it is about to remember,
From the punctual rape of every bléssed day,
And cries,
          "Oh, let there be nothing on earth but laundry,   20
Nothing but rosy hands in the rising steam
And clear dances done in the sight of heaven."

     Yet, as the sun acknowledges
With a warm look the world's hunks and colors,
The soul descends once more in bitter love
To accept the waking body, saying now
In a changed voice as the man yawns and rises,

     "Bring them down from their ruddy gallows;
Let there be clean linen for the backs of thieves;   30
Let lovers go fresh and sweet to be undone,
And the heaviest nuns walk in a pure floating
Of dark habits,
                    keeping their difficult balance."

JAMES DICKEY [1923–   ]

            Listening to Foxhounds

     When in that gold
     Of fires, quietly sitting
     With the men whose brothers are hounds,

     You hear the first tone
     Of a dog on scent, you look from face
     To face, to see whose will light up.

                                        323

When that light comes
Inside the dark light of the fire,
You know which chosen man has heard

A thing like his own dead   10
Speak out in a marvelous, helpless voice
That he has been straining to hear.

Miles away in the dark,
His enchanted dog can sense
How his features glow like a savior's,

And begins to hunt
In a frenzy of desperate pride.
Among us, no one's eyes give off a light

For the red fox
Playing in and out of his scent,   20
Leaping stones, doubling back over water.

Who runs with the fox
Must sit here like his own image,
Giving nothing of himself

To the sensitive flames,
With no human joy rising up,
Coming out of his face to be seen.

And it is hard,
When the fox leaps into his burrow,
To keep that singing down,   30

To sit with the fire
Drawn into one's secret features,
And all eyes turning around

From the dark wood
Until they come, amazed, upon
A face that does not shine

Back from itself,
That holds its own light and takes more,
Like the face of the dead, sitting still,

Giving no sign,   40
Making no outcry, no matter
Who may be straining to hear.

DENISE LEVERTOV [1923–   ]

February Evening in New York

As the stores close, a winter light
    opens air to iris blue,
    glint of frost through the smoke,
    grains of mica, salt of the sidewalk.
As the buildings close, released autonomous
    feet pattern the streets
    in hurry and stroll; balloon heads
    drift and dive above them; the bodies
    aren't really there.
As the lights brighten, as the sky darkens,
    a woman with crooked heels says to another woman
    while they step along at a fair pace,
    "You know, I'm telling you, what I love best
    is life. I love life! Even if I ever get
    to be old and wheezy—or limp! You know?
    Limping along?—I'd still . . . " Out of hearing.
To the multiple disordered tones
    of gears changing, a dance
    to the compass points, out, four-way river.
    Prospect of sky
    wedged into avenues, left at the ends of streets,
    west sky, east sky: more life tonight! A range
    of open time at winter's outskirts.

LOUIS SIMPSON [1923–   ]

Walt Whitman at Bear Mountain

". . . life which does not give the preference to any other life, of any
previous period, which therefore prefers its own existence . . ."
                                                    —ORTEGA Y GASSET

Neither on horseback nor seated,
But like himself, squarely on two feet,

The poet of death and lilacs
Loafs by the footpath. Even the bronze looks alive
Where it is folded like cloth. And he seems friendly.

"Where is the Mississippi panorama
And the girl who played the piano?
Where are you, Walt?
The Open Road goes to the used-car lot.

"Where is the nation you promised?   10
These houses built of wood sustain
Colossal snows,
And the light above the street is sick to death.

"As for the people—see how they neglect you!
Only a poet pauses to read the inscription."

"I am here," he answered.
"It seems you have found me out.
Yet, did I not warn you that it was Myself
I advertised? Were my words not sufficiently plain?

"I gave no prescriptions,   20
And those who have taken my moods for prophecies
Mistake the matter."
Then, vastly amused—"Why do you reproach me?
I freely confess I am wholly disreputable.
Yet I am happy, because you have found me out."

A crocodile in wrinkled metal loafing . . .

Then all the realtors,
Pickpockets, salesmen, and the actors performing
Official scenarios,
Turned a deaf ear, for they had contracted   30
American dreams.

But the man who keeps a store on a lonely road,
And the housewife who knows she's dumb,
And the earth, are relieved.

All that grave weight of America
Cancelled! Like Greece and Rome.
The future in ruins!

The castles, the prisons, the cathedrals
Unbuilding, and roses
Blossoming from the stones that are not there . . . 40

The clouds are lifting from the high Sierras,
The Bay mists clearing.
And the angel in the gate, the flowering plum,
Dances like Italy, imagining red.

Summer Morning

There are whole blocks in New York
Where no one lives—
A district of small factories.
And there's a hotel; one morning

When I was there with a girl
We saw in the window opposite
Men and women working at their machines.
Now and then one looked up.

Toys, hardware—whatever they made,
It's been worn out.
I'm fifteen years older myself—
Bad years and good.

So I have spoiled my chances.
For what? Sheer laziness,
The thrill of an assignation,
My life that I hold in secret.

American Poetry

Whatever it is, it must have
A stomach that can digest
Rubber, coal, uranium, moons, poems.

Like the shark, it contains a shoe.
It must swim for miles through the desert
Uttering cries that are almost human.

ALLEN GINSBERG [1924–　　　]

FROM *Howl*

FOR CARL SOLOMON

I

I saw the best minds of my generation destroyed by madness, starving
　　hysterical naked,
dragging themselves through the negro streets at dawn looking for an
　　angry fix,
angelheaded hipsters burning for the ancient heavenly connection to
　　the starry dynamo in the machinery of night,
who poverty and tatters and hollow-eyed and high sat up smoking in
　　the supernatural darkness of cold-water flats floating across the
　　tops of cities contemplating jazz,
who bared their brains to Heaven under the El and saw Mohammedan
　　angels staggering on tenement roofs illuminated,
who passed through universities with radiant cool eyes hallucinating
　　Arkansas and Blake-light tragedy among the scholars of war,
who were expelled from the academies for crazy & publishing obscene
　　odes on the windows of the skull,
who cowered in unshaven rooms in underwear, burning their money
　　in wastebaskets and listening to the Terror through the wall,
who got busted in their pubic beards returning through Laredo with
　　a belt of marijuana for New York,
who ate fire in paint hotels or drank turpentine in Paradise Alley, death,
　　or purgatoried their torsos night after night　　　　　　10
with dreams, with drugs, with waking nightmares, alcohol and cock
　　and endless balls,
incomparable blind streets of shuddering cloud and lightning in the
　　mind leaping toward poles of Canada & Paterson, illuminating all
　　the motionless world of Time between,
Peyote solidities of halls, backyard green tree cemetery dawns, wine
　　drunkenness over the rooftops, storefront boroughs of teahead
　　joyride neon blinking traffic light, sun and moon and tree vibra-
　　tions in the roaring winter dusks of Brooklyn, ashcan rantings and
　　kind king light of mind,
who chained themselves to subways for the endless ride from Battery
　　to holy Bronx on benzedrine until the noise of wheels and children

brought them down shuddering mouth-wracked and battered
bleak of brain all drained of brilliance in the drear light of Zoo,
who sank all night in submarine light of Bickford's floated out and sat
through the stale beer afternoon in desolate Fugazzi's, listening to
the crack of doom on the hydrogen jukebox,
who talked continuously seventy hours from park to pad to bar to
Bellevue to museum to the Brooklyn Bridge,
a lost battalion of platonic conversationalists jumping down the stoops
off fire escapes off windowsills off Empire State out of the moon,
yacketayakking screaming vomiting whispering facts and memories and
anecdotes and eyeball kicks and shocks of hospitals and jails and
wars,
whole intellects disgorged in total recall for seven days and nights with
brilliant eyes, meat for the Synagogue cast on the pavement,
who vanished into nowhere Zen New Jersey leaving a trail of ambiguous
picture postcards of Atlantic City Hall,   20
suffering Eastern sweats and Tangerian bone-grindings and migraines
of China under junk-withdrawal in Newark's bleak furnished
room,
who wandered around and around at midnight in the railroad yard
wondering where to go, and went, leaving no broken hearts,
who lit cigarettes in boxcars boxcars boxcars racketing through snow
toward lonesome farms in grandfather night,
who studied Plotinus Poe St. John of the Cross telepathy and bop
kaballa[1] because the cosmos instinctively vibrated at their feet in
Kansas,
who loned it through the streets of Idaho seeking visionary indian angels
who were visionary indian angels,
who thought they were only mad when Baltimore gleamed in supernatural ecstasy,
who jumped in limousines with the Chinaman of Oklahoma on the impulse of winter midnight streetlight smalltown rain,
who lounged hungry and lonesome through Houston seeking jazz or
sex or soup, and followed the brilliant Spaniard to converse about
America and Eternity, a hopeless task, and so took ship to Africa,
who disappeared into the volcanoes of Mexico leaving behind nothing
but the shadow of dungarees and the lava and ash of poetry scattered in fireplace Chicago,
who reappeared on the West Coast investigating the F.B.I. in beards and
shorts with big pacifist eyes sexy in their dark skin passing out in-
comprehensible leaflets . . .   30

[1] mystical interpretations of the Scriptures by certain Jewish rabbis.

Denali Road

By the Denali road, facing
north, a battered chair
in which nothing but the wind
was sitting.
            And farther on
toward evening, an old man
with a vague smile,
his rifle rusting in his arms.

Pickers

All day we were bent over,
lifting handfuls of wind and dust.

Scraps of some human conversation
blew by; a coffin on wheels
rolled slowly backward across
the field, and the skinned
bodies of the harvest were loaded.

A red cloud boiling up out
of the darkness became the evening.
Sentinels of a shattered army,
we drank bitter coffee, and spoke
of the field, the light, and the cold.

If the Owl Calls Again

at dusk
from the island in the river
and it's not too cold,

I'll wait for the moon
to rise,

then take wing and glide
to meet him.

We will not speak,
but hooded against the frost
soar above
the alder flats, searching
with tawny eyes.

And then we'll sit
in the shadowy spruce and
pick the bones
of careless mice,

while the long moon drifts
toward Asia
and the river mutters
in its icy bed.

And when morning climbs
the limbs
we'll part without a sound,

fulfilled, floating
homeward as
the cold world awakens.

ROBERT CREELEY [1926–   ]

After Lorca[1]

FOR M. MARTI

The church is a business, and the rich
are the business men.
                    When they pull on the bells, the
poor come piling in and when a poor man dies, he has a wooden
cross, and they rush through the ceremony.

[1] Federico García Lorca, modern Spanish poet and playwright, supported
the Loyalists in the Spanish civil war, and was killed by persons unknown.

But when a rich man dies, they
drag out the Sacrament
and a golden Cross, and go *doucement, doucement*[2]
to the cemetery.

And the poor love it
and think its crazy.

I Know a Man

As I sd to my
friend, because I am
always talking,—John, I

sd, which was not his
name, the darkness sur-
rounds us, what

can we do against
it, or else, shall we &
why not, buy a goddamn big car,

drive, he sd, for
christ's sake, look
out where yr going.

Kore

As I was walking
    I came upon
chance walking
    the same road upon.

As I sat down
    by chance to move
later
    if and as I might,

light the wood was,
    light and green,
and what I saw
    before I had not seen.

[2] slowly, slowly.

It was a lady
accompanied
by goat men
leading her.

Her hair held earth.
Her eyes were dark.
A double flute
made her move.

"O love,
where are you
leading
me now?"

ROBERT BLY [1926–   ]

Waking from Sleep

Inside the veins there are navies setting forth,
Tiny explosions at the water lines,
And seagulls weaving in the wind of the salty blood.

It is the morning. The country has slept the whole winter.
Window seats were covered with fur skins, the yard was full
Of stiff dogs, and hands that clumsily held heavy books.

Now we wake, and rise from bed, and eat breakfast!—
Shouts rise from the harbor of the blood,
Mist, and masts rising, the knock of wooden tackle in the sunlight.

Now we sing, and do tiny dances on the kitchen floor.
Our whole body is like a harbor at dawn;
We know that our master has left us for the day.

Poem Against the British

I

The wind through the box-elder trees
Is like rides at dusk on a white horse,
Wars for your country, and fighting the British.

I wonder if Washington listened to the trees.
All morning I have been sitting in grass,
Higher than my eyes, beneath trees,
And listening upward, to the wind in leaves.
Suddenly I realize there is one thing more:
There is also the wind through the high grass.

I I I

There are palaces, boats, silence among white buildings,
Iced drinks on marble tops, among cool rooms;
It is good also to be poor, and listen to the wind.

Summer, 1960, Minnesota

I

After a drifting day, visiting the bridge near Louisberg,
With its hot muddy water flowing
Under the excited swallows,
Now, at noon
We plunge through the hot beanfields,
And the sturdy alfalfa fields, the farm groves
Like heavy green smoke close to the ground.

I I

Inside me there is a confusion of swallows,
Birds flying through the smoke,
And horses galloping excitedly on fields of short grass.

I I I

Yet, we are falling,
Falling into the open mouths of darkness,
Into the Congo as if into a river,
Or as wheat into open mills.

Love Poem

When we are in love, we love the grass,
And the barns, and the lightpoles,
And the small mainstreets abandoned all night.

JAMES WRIGHT [1927–   ]

Lying in a Hammock at William Duffy's Farm in Pine Island, Minnesota

Over my head, I see the bronze butterfly,
Asleep on the black trunk,
Blowing like a leaf in green shadow.
Down the ravine behind the empty house,
The cowbells follow one another
Into the distances of the afternoon.
To my right,
In a field of sunlight between two pines,
The droppings of last year's horses
Blaze up into golden stones.
I lean back, as the evening darkens and comes on.
A chicken hawk floats over, looking for home.
I have wasted my life.

Autumn Begins in Martins Ferry, Ohio

In the Shreve High football stadium,
I think of Polacks nursing long beers in Tiltonsville,
And gray faces of Negroes in the blast furnace at Benwood,
And the ruptured night watchman of Wheeling Steel,
Dreaming of heroes.

All the proud fathers are ashamed to go home.
Their women cluck like starved pullets,
Dying for love.

Therefore,
Their sons grow suicidally beautiful
At the beginning of October,
And gallop terribly against each other's bodies.

I Try to Waken and Greet the World Once Again

In a pine tree,
A few yards away from my window sill,
A brilliant blue jay is springing up and down, up and down,
On a branch.
I laugh, as I see him abandon himself
To entire delight, for he knows as well as I do
That the branch will not break.

DONALD HALL [1928–   ]

An Airstrip in Essex, 1960

It is a lost road into the air.
It is a desert
among sugar beets.
The tiny wings
of the Spitfires of nineteen-forty-one
flake in the mud of the Channel.

Near the road a brick pillbox
totters under a load of grass,
where Home Guards waited
in the white fogs of the invasion winter.

Goodnight, old ruined war.

In Poland the wind rides on a jagged wall.
Smoke rises from the stones; no, it is mist.

The Long River

The musk-ox smells
in his long head
my boat coming. When
I feel him there,
intent, heavy,

The oars make wings
in the white night,
and deep woods are close
on either side
where trees darken.

I rowed past towns
in their black sleep
to come here. I passed
the northern grass
and cold mountains.

The musk-ox moves
when the boat stops,
in hard thickets. Now
the wood is dark
with old pleasures.

THOM GUNN [1929–   ]

My Sad Captains

One by one they appear in
the darkness: a few friends, and
a few with historical
names. How late they start to shine!
but before they fade they stand
perfectly embodied, all

the past lapping them like a
cloak of chaos. They were men
who, I thought, lived only to
renew the wasteful force they
spent with each hot convulsion.
They remind me, distant now.

True, they are not at rest yet,
but now that they are indeed
apart, winnowed from failures,
they withdraw to an orbit
and turn with disinterested
hard energy, like the stars.

GARY SNYDER [1930–   ]

Milton by Firelight

Piute Creek, August 1955

"O hell, what do mine eyes
            with grief behold?"[1]
Working with an old
Singlejack miner, who can sense
The vein and cleavage
In the very guts of rock, can
Blast granite, build
Switchbacks that last for years
Under the beat of snow, thaw, mule-hooves.
What use, Milton, a silly story   10
Of our lost general parents,
            eaters of fruit?

[1] Satan's exclamation upon first seeing Adam and Eve in Eden (Milton, *Paradise Lost*, Book IV).

The Indian, the chainsaw boy,
And a string of six mules
Came riding down to camp
Hungry for tomatoes and green apples.
Sleeping in saddle-blankets
Under a bright night-sky
Han River slantwise by morning.
Jays squall   20
Coffee boils

In ten thousand years the Sierras
Will be dry and dead, home of the scorpion.
Ice-scratched slabs and bent trees.
No paradise, no fall,
Only the weathering land
The wheeling sky,
Man, with his Satan
Scouring the chaos of the mind.
Oh Hell!   30

Fire down
Too dark to read, miles from a road
The bell-mare clangs in the meadow
That packed dirt for a fill-in
Scrambling through loose rocks
On an old trail
All of a summer's day.

Water

Pressure of sun on the rockslide
Whirled me in dizzy hop-and-step descent,
Pool of pebbles buzzed in a Juniper shadow,
Tiny tongue of a this-year rattlesnake flicked,
I leaped, laughing for little boulder-color coil—
Pounded by heat raced down the slabs to the creek
Deep tumbling under arching walls and stuck
Whole head and shoulders in the water:
Stretched full on cobble—ears roaring
Eyes open aching from the cold and faced a trout.

Hay for the Horses

He had driven half the night
From far down San Joaquin
Through Mariposa, up the
Dangerous mountain roads,
And pulled in at eight a.m.
With his big truckload of hay
   behind the barn.
With winch and ropes and hooks
We stacked the bales up clean
To splintery redwood rafters
High in the dark, flecks of alfalfa
Whirling through shingle-cracks of light,
Itch of haydust in the
   sweaty shirt and shoes.
At lunchtime under Black oak
Out in the hot corral,
—The old mare nosing lunchpails,
Grasshoppers crackling in the weeds—
"I'm sixty-eight" he said,
"I first bucked hay when I was seventeen.
I thought, that day I started,
I sure would hate to do this all my life.
And dammit, that's just what
I've gone and done."

Kyoto: March

A few light flakes of snow
Fall in the feeble sun;
Birds sing in the cold,
A warbler by the wall. The plum
Buds tight and chill soon bloom.
The moon begins first
Fourth, a faint slice west
At nightfall. Jupiter half-way
High at the end of night-
Meditation. The dove cry
Twangs like a bow.

At dawn Mt. Hiei dusted white
On top; in the clear air
Folds of all the gullied green
Hills around the town are sharp,
Breath stings. Beneath the roofs
Of frosty houses
Lovers part, from tangle warm
Of gentle bodies under quilt
And crack the icy water to the face
And wake and feed the children
And grandchildren that they love.

Glossary

A cc e n t—The emphasis given to certain syllables in a line of verse. *Word accent* is the normally spoken pattern of stressed and unstressed syllables. *Rhetorical accent* is the emphasis given to a word because of its importance in a sentence. *Metrical accent* is the stress pattern set up by a regular verse meter. *Wrenched accent*: the meter forces a shift in the normal word accent, as in ballads. *Hovering accent*: it is difficult to decide which of two adjacent syllables should receive greater stress.

A e s t h e t i c i s m (a e s t h e t i c m o v e m e n t)—A literary movement in the nineteenth century whose motto was "art for art's sake." It arose in opposition to the utilitarian doctrine that everything, including art, must be "useful" and contribute to the material progress of society; in practice this ideology had led to cynical materialism and self-righteous middle class morality. Led by Walter Pater and Oscar Wilde, the Aesthetic Movement insisted that art was independent of any didactic end and of any theory of what was morally good or useful. Later, however, the movement deteriorated to interest merely in stylistic polish and unusual subject matter. The term *fin de siècle* ("end of the century"), which had once connoted "Progress," came to connote "decadence." If capitalized, "Decadence" often refers to the Aesthetic Movement itself.

A f f e c t i v e F a l l a c y—In the New Criticism, the alleged error of judging a literary work according to the emotional effect it produces in the reader. "Affect" is the technical term in psychology meaning "feeling or emotion"; it is related to the word "affection."

A l e x a n d r i n e—In English, a line of iambic hexameter. The line conventionally has a *caesura*, or pause, in the middle, dividing it into two symmetrical halves called *hemistiches*:

A needless Alexandrine ends the song
That, like a wounded snake, // drags its slow length along.
Pope, *An Essay on Criticism*

The Alexandrine has been common in French poetry since the twelfth century, and is used in elevated verse such as the tragedies of Racine. In English, the Spenserian stanza (q.v.) ends with an Alexandrine.

A L L E G O R Y—An extended metaphor, with subordinate metaphors depending from the main. In allegorical narrative, the literal action evokes another, parallel action composed of ideas. In simple allegory there is a one-to-one correspondence of literal and abstract meanings.

> Many a green isle needs must be
> In the deep wide sea of Misery,
> Or the mariner, worn and wan,
> Never thus could voyage on—
> Day and night, and night and day,
> Drifting on his weary way . . .
>
> Shelley, "Lines Written Among the Euganean Hills"

Here happiness is a green island, misery is a sea, man is a mariner, and life is a voyage. But allegorical narrative may be a great deal more complicated, with several levels of meaning. In the first book of Spenser's *Faerie Queene*, the Redcross Knight passes through actual adventures. He fights with a real fire-breathing dragon, is seduced by a real woman, suffers actual pain and imprisonment. This is the literal narrative. But at the same time the poem is an allegory of man's spiritual pilgrimage. The Redcross Knight is seeking holiness. In this he is aided by Una (Truth) and misled by Duessa (False Religion) and Archimago (Illusion). Moreover, there is an historical allegory. Redcross is an Englishman; he falls prey to the Church of Rome (the giant Orgoglio); he is rescued by Prince Arthur (the Reformation), and finally weds Una (Anglicanism).

> If the story, literally told, pleases as much as the original, and in the same way, to what purpose was the allegory employed? For the function of allegory is not to hide but to reveal, and it is properly used only for that which cannot be said, or so well said, in literal speech. The inner life, and specially the life of love, religion, and spiritual adventure, has therefore always been the field of true allegory; for here there are intangibles which only allegory can fix and reticences which only allegory can overcome.
>
> C. S. Lewis, *The Allegory of Love*, 1936

A L L I T E R A T I O N (I N I T I A L R H Y M E)—Repetition of sounds at the beginning of words.

Hast thou forgot me then, and do I seem
Now in thine eye so foul, once deemed so fair
                    Milton, *Paradise Lost*

Alliteration unifies these lines and emphasizes the alliterated words
and their relationships of unity and contrast with each other. *Hidden alliteration* is the repetition of sounds within the words, as the
"s" sound above in "Ha*s*t" and "on*c*e."

ALLUSION—A reference, usually brief, to something outside the literary text itself. In the following example, "three-days personage"
refers to Christ:

He does not become a three-days personage,
Imposing his separation,
Calling for pomp.
                    Stevens, "The Death of a Soldier"

Addison says of the use of allusions:

It is this talent of affecting the imagination that gives an embellishment to good sense, and makes one man's compositions more
agreable than another's. It sets off all writings in general, but it is
the very life and highest perfection of poetry. Where it shines in
an eminent degree, it has preserved several poems for many ages,
that have nothing else to recommend them; and where all the
other beauties are present, the work appears dry and insipid, if
this single one be wanting. It has something in it like creation; it
bestows a kind of existence, and draws up to the reader's view
several objects which are not to be found in being. It makes additions to nature, and gives a greater variety to God's works. In a
word, it is able to beautify and adorn the most illustrious scenes in
the universe, or to fill the mind with more glorious shows and apparitions, than can be found in any part of it.
                    Addison, *The Spectator*, 1711-12

AMBIGUITY. MULTIPLE MEANING—The use of language so
that more than one interpretation of a word or passage is relevant to
the meaning. In the following passage from *Paradise Lost*, the army of
devils is facing the army of angels. The devils have artillery concealed
in their ranks and are preparing to use it. Satan, leader of the devils, is
speaking:

"Vanguard, to right and left the front unfold;
That all may see who hate us, how we seek
Peace and composure, and with open breast

Stand ready to receive them, if they like
Our overture, and turn not back perverse;
But that I doubt; however, witness Heaven,
Heaven witness thou anon, while we discharge
Freely our part. Ye who appointed stand,
Do as you have in charge, and briefly touch
What we propound, and loud that all may hear."
    So scoffing in ambiguous words, he scarce
Had ended, when . . .

The words "discharge," "charge," and "touch," are puns, a form of ambiguity. They contain hidden references to the use of artillery: "discharge"—to shoot; "charge"—the load in a gun; "touch"—to set off gunpowder. The lines:

That all may see who hate us, how we seek
Peace and composure . . .

are ambiguous, for the devils seek peace by making war. "Turn not back perverse" hints at what will happen to the angels when the artillery hits them, with a pun on "perverse," meaning both wrong-headed and bowled over. "Propound" is ambiguous; the word sounds like the double thunder of cannon.

In these lines by Dylan Thomas, "grave" is ambiguous, meaning both serious and having to do with death:

I shall not murder
The mankind of her going with a grave truth . . .
                        "A Refusal to Mourn the Death by Fire
                        of a Child in London"

AMPHIBRACH—A metrical foot of three syllables: one weak, one strong, and one weak: $\cup - \cup$, as in the word "arrangement."

ANACREONTIC VERSE—Verse written in the style of Anacreon, a Greek poet of the sixth century B.C., who sang of wine, love, and other pleasures.

ANACRUSIS—The addition of one or more unstressed syllables before the first word of a line whose meter normally begins with a stress, as in the second line of the following:

When the stars threw down their spears,
And watered heaven with their tears,
Did he smile his work to see?
                               Blake, "The Tiger"

ANALOGY—A comparison of two like relationships. *E.g.*, the relationship of man to God is compared to the relationship of a child to his father. For an analogy in verse, see CONCEIT, the lines quoted from Donne's "A Valediction Forbidding Mourning." Loosely, "analogy" may mean any similarity between things.

ANAPEST, ANAPESTIC—A metrical foot of three syllables, with two weak stresses and one strong, thus: ∪ ∪ —. See also METER and RISING METER.

ANTISTROPHE—See ODE.

APOCAPATED RHYME—See RHYME.

APOLLO—The Greek god of poetry—also of medicine, archery, light, youth, prophecy, and music, especially the lyre. *Apollonian* connotes a sense of classical order, moderation, reason, and culture. See DIONYSUS.

APPROXIMATE RHYME—See RHYME.

ARCADIA, ARCADY—A mountainous region of Greece which became, in the conventions of pastoral poetry, the symbol of a retreat from the complexities of the real word to a simple, happy, and uncorrupted world of singing shepherds. See PASTORAL.

ARCHAISM—A word, expression, or spelling that is obsolete.

ARGUMENT OF A POEM—The plot or sequence of ideas that is the poem's intellectual substructure.

ASSOCIATION—A process of thinking in which a given work or image recalls, suggests, or connotes certain other images or emotions.

ASSONANCE—Repetition of vowel sounds preceded and followed by different consonant sounds, as in "time" and "mind." Assonance may be described loosely as a resemblance of vowel sounds.

ATMOSPHERE—The emotional setting in which a fictive world exists—its mood, as perceived by the reader: calm, humorous, mysterious, sinister, oppressive, etc.

AUGUSTAN AGE—In Roman literature, the period of the reign of Caesar Augustus (27 BC–14 AD), which included the classical authors

Ovid, Horace, and Virgil. In English literature, the term is applied to the early eighteenth century, when the authors Pope, Swift, Addison and Steele were writing. Cf. CLASSICAL and NEOCLASSICAL.

BALLAD—A narrative poem, originally intended to be sung. The story is told in compact dramatic scenes, with simple dialogue and concrete imagery, and often a refrain. A folk, or popular ballad, is an anonymous communal creation transmitted orally from one person to another, and therefore may exist in more than one version. A *literary ballad* is a ballad written by a single author in deliberate imitation of the folk ballad. Coleridge's "Rime of the Ancient Mariner" and Keats's "La Belle Dame Sans Merci" are well-known literary ballads.

BALLAD STANZA—A quatrain that alternates tetrameter with trimeter lines, and usually rhymes *a b c b*.

The very deep did rot: O Christ!
That this should ever be!
Yea, slimy things did crawl with legs
Upon the slimy sea.
                        Coleridge, "The Rime of the Ancient Mariner"

BALLADE—A fixed verse form having three identically rhymed 8- or 10-line stanzas and an envoy, whose refrain (R) is the same as that of each stanza. (Rhyme scheme is *a b a b b c b R* in the octaves and *b c b R* in the envoy; or it is *a b a b b c d c R* in the 10-line stanzas and *c c d c R* in the envoy.) A *double ballade* has six regular stanzas but often no envoy. Ballades are more common in French than in English, and in English are usually employed for light verse.

BARD—Originally, a Celtic minstrel-poet who entertained warriors by singing of their feats; later, any poet.

BATHOS (SINKING)—A sudden and unintentional descent from the exalted in style and content to the ridiculous, often because the author is straining for sublimity.

The Eternal heard, and from the heavenly quire
  Chose out the cherub with the flaming sword,
And bad him swiftly drive the approaching fire
  From where our naval magazines were stored.
                        Dryden, "Annus Mirabilis"

Hast thou then survived—
Mild offspring of infirm humanity,
Meek infant! among all forlornest things
The most forlorn—one life of that bright star,
The second glory of the Heavens?—Thou hast.

Wordsworth, "Address to My Infant Daughter"

Bathos may simply mean language that is flat, dismal, or ridiculous.

"Lord Byron" was an Englishman
    A poet I believe,
His first works in old England
    Was poorly received.
Perhaps it was "Lord Byron's" fault
    And perhaps it was not.
His life was full of misfortunes,
    Ah, strange was his lot.

Julia Moore (the Sweet Singer of
Michigan), "Lord Byron's Life"

This last is bathos, but not sinking, for the Sweet Singer was sunk from the start. I would like to add an example of the Great McGonagall, but someone has swiped the book.

BEAST EPIC—A related series of tales (*beast fables*) about animals with human characteristics. The medieval beast epic was often an allegory aimed at social satire, in which Reynard the Fox could be interpreted as the Church, Noble the Lion as the king, and Ysengrim the Wolf as the aristocracy. Chauntecleer the Cock was a favorite character. The genre is as old as Aesop's fables of the sixth century B.C.

BEAT POETRY—A kind of verse first written in the United States in the late 1950's. "Beat" may be derived from "beat up" or "beatific." The most famous of the Beats (Beat poets) is Allen Ginsberg, whose *Howl* epitomized attitudes and techniques of the movement. Beat poetry is usually written in free verse. The language is slangy. The poet writes about his personal habits, friends, experiences of sex, use of hallucinatory drugs. Frequently the beat writer expresses his dislike for middle class ("square") people.

BEAUTY

The sense of beauty is intuitive, and beauty itself is all that inspires pleasure without, and aloof from, and even contrarily to, interest.

Coleridge, *Biographia Literaria*

What the imagination seizes as Beauty must be truth—whether it existed before or not—for I have the same Idea of all our passions as of Love; they are all in their sublime, creative of essential Beauty.

Keats, Letter to Benjamin Bailey

BESTIARY—A medieval collection of descriptions of animals, real and fictitious, which allegorized Christian doctrines. *E.g.*, the phoenix, a legendary bird that rises anew from the ashes of its pyre, represents the immortal soul; the unicorn is a metaphor for Christ.

BLANK VERSE—Unrhymed iambic pentameter. After its introduction by Surrey in the sixteenth century, blank verse was widely used in the drama. Later it was used for nondramatic poetry. The tradition includes the drama of Marlowe and Shakespeare, Milton's *Paradise Lost*, Wordsworth's *Prelude*, and some of Browning's dramatic monologues.

But, soft! What light through yonder window breaks?
It is the east, and Juliet is the sun.

Shakespeare, *Romeo and Juliet*

BOMBAST—Originally, cotton stuffing to make bulges in garments, according to Elizabethan fashion. Bombastic language is pretentious and inflated.

Pistol. I'll see her damned first; to Pluto's damned lake, by this hand, to the infernal deep, with Erebus and tortures vile also.

Shakespeare, *Henry IV*, Part 2

BROKEN RHYME—See RHYME.

BUCOLIC—1. referring to shepherds. 2. a pastoral poem.

BURLESQUE—Any imitation of other literary works, or of people's actions and attitudes, which aims to amuse and to ridicule by distortion or by incongruity of style and subject. *High burlesque* uses a high style and a low subject. Examples of high burlesque are the *parody*, which mocks a specific literary work by applying its style to a trivial subject, and the *mock epic*, or *mock heroic* style, which ridicules a trivial subject by treating it with the high style of the epic, as in Pope's "Rape of the Lock." *Low burlesque*, in contrast, uses a low style with a high subject, as in a *travesty*, which ridicules a specific literary work by treating its dignified subject in a grotesque low style that exaggerates the peculiarities of the original. See also SATIRE.

Byronic—Referring to romantic behavior patterned on the attitudes and opinions of Lord Byron. Symptoms include veiled guilt, proud scorn of society, and rhapsodizing about nature.

Cacophony—A combination of sounds that is harsh, discordant, or hard to articulate, usually because of clusters of consonants. Cacophony can be used to support meaning.

> Blow, winds, and crack your cheeks! rage! blow!
>
> Shakespeare, *King Lear*

Cadence—(Derived from Latin *cadens*, falling). The rising and falling rhythmic flow of spoken language, resulting from the pattern of stressed and unstressed syllables. See FREE VERSE.

Caesura—A pause within a line of verse, dictated by speech rhythm rather than meter. In scanning verse, the caesura may be indicated by vertical bars.

> Know then thyself, // presume not God to scan;
> The proper study of Mankind // is Man.
>
> Pope, *An Essay on Man*

Canon and apocrypha—A canon is a list of an author's works accepted as authentic. *E.g.*, there are thirty-six plays in the canon of Shakespeare. Works doubtfully ascribed to an author are apocrypha.

Carol—Originally, a song for a circle dance, as around the Christmas crib in the Middle Ages; later, traditional Christmas songs or drinking songs.

Caroline—(Derived from Latin *Carolus*, Charles). Of the period of King Charles I of England, 1625–1649. See CAVALIER POETS.

Carpe diem motif—The Latin words mean "Seize the day." A poetic theme as ancient as Greek and Latin lyrics: make the most of the present.

Catalexis—A *catalectic* line omits the final unaccented syllable or syllables of the meter.

> Tiger! / Tiger! / burning / bright [‿]
> In the forests of the night
>
> Blake, "The Tiger"

CAVALIER POETS—Seventeenth-century poets who were sympathetic to King Charles I: Herrick, Carew, Suckling, Lovelace, and Waller. Much of their poetry is in the manner of a song: gallant, witty, devil-may-care.

CELTIC RENAISSANCE (IRISH LITERARY REVIVAL)—The nationalistic Irish literary movement of the late nineteenth and early twentieth centuries, in which Irish intellectuals and writers asserted their cultural independence from Britain. The aim was for art rooted in the Celtic and Gaelic heritage, or in Irish life, as in the writings of Yeats and Synge.

CHANSON—French for "song." CHANSON COURTOIS: "courtly song." CHANSON DE GESTE: "song of noble deeds," a type of Old French (eleventh to fourteenth century) epic tale in verse, centered on a legendary or historical hero, such as Charlemagne. The most famous is the *Chanson de Roland*, or *Song of Roland*. CHANSON POPULAIRE: "song of the people."

CHANT ROYAL—A French fixed verse form having five stanzas of eleven lines each, rhyming *a b a b c c d d e d R*—R being a refrain—and an envoy that rhymes *d d e d R*. Uncommon in English.

CHIASMUS—(Derived from Greek *chiazein*, "to mark crosswise"). A rhetorical figure with two syntactically parallel constructions, one of which has the word order reversed.

They fall successive, and successive rise.

CLASSIC—A work generally recognized as being of enduring significance; a model or a standard of excellence.

CLASSICAL—Referring to Greek and Roman literature.

CLASSICISM—An aesthetic that stresses tradition, convention, form, decorum, balance, restraint, moderation, simplicity, dignity, austerity. See ROMANTICISM.

CLICHÉ—A stale, trite figure of speech. As Pope remarked:

Where'er you find "the cooling western breeze,"
In the next line it "whispers through the trees";
If crystal streams "with pleasing murmurs creep,"
The reader's threatened (not in vain) with "sleep."
An Essay on Criticism

CLOSED COUPLET—An end-stopped, rhymed couplet that contains a complete thought.

> Let such teach others who themselves excel,
> And censure freely who have written well.
>
> *An Essay on Criticism*

COMMONWEALTH (PURITAN INTERREGNUM)—The parliamentary government that controlled England between the execution of Charles I in 1649 and the restoration of Charles II to the throne in 1660.

COMPLAINT—Usually a lyric poem in which the speaker laments the absence or unresponsiveness of his beloved. But poets may complain about anything; for example, Chaucer's "Complaint to his Purse."

COMPLETE RHYME—See RHYME.

CONCEIT—A far-fetched comparison between things seemingly unlike. The *Petrarchan* conceit, as written by the Italian poet Petrarch (1304–74) was a Platonic idealization—usually the poet's idealization of his mistress. He might compare her to precious stones, artifacts, beautiful birds and animals, flowers, plants, and mythical creatures. The conceits in this passage from Spenser's "Epithalamion," in which he celebrates his marriage to Elizabeth Boyle, are in the manner of Petrarch:

> Tell me ye merchants daughters did ye see
> So fayre a creature in your towne before?
> So sweet, so lovely, and so mild as she,
> Adorned with beautyes grace and vertues store,
> Her goodly eyes lyke Saphyres shining bright,
> Her forehead yvory white,
> Her cheekes lyke apples which the sun hath rudded,
> Her lips lyke cherryes charming men to byte,
> Her brest like to a bowle of creame vncrudded,
> Her paps lyke lyllies budded,
> Her snowie necke lyke to a marble towre,
> And all her body like a pallace fayre,
> Ascending uppe with many a stately stayre,
> To honors seat and chastities sweet bowre.
> Why stand ye still ye virgins in amaze,
> Upon her so to gaze,
> Whiles ye forget your former lay to sing,
> To which the woods did answer and your eccho ring.

Conceits such as these were satirized by Shakespeare:

My mistress' eyes are nothing like the sun;
Coral is far more red than her lips' red:
If snows be white, why then her breasts are dun;
If hairs be wires, black wires grow on her head.

Metaphysical conceits, used by John Donne and his followers, exploited all fields of knowledge for comparisons—theology, astronomy, mythology, history, commerce, geography, metallurgy, alchemy, mathematics, etc. In 1693 Dryden said that John Donne's poetry "affects the metaphysics," or resembles the abstruse terms and arguments of the scholastic philosophers. In his "Life of Cowley" (1777) Dr. Johnson finds in the metaphysical poets "a combination of dissimilar images, or discovery of occult resemblances in things apparently unlike. Of wit, thus defined, they have more than enough. The most heterogeneous ideas are yoked by violence together; nature and art are ransacked for illustrations, comparisons, and allusions; their learning instructs, and their subtilty surprises; but the reader commonly thinks his improvement dearly bought, and, though he sometimes admires, is seldom pleased."

In the nineteenth century the metaphysical poets were neglected. Then, the research of scholars and an essay by T. S. Eliot titled "The Metaphysical Poets" (1921) in which he reviewed H. J. C. Grierson's *Metaphysical Lyrics and Poems of the Seventeenth Century* roused new interest in these poets. They have had a strong influence on modern poetry, in the kind of verse in which complex ideas and concrete images are important, as in the poems of Eliot himself.

One of the more famous metaphysical conceits is Donne's comparison of two lovers to the legs of a mathematical compass, in "A Valediction Forbidding Mourning":

If they be two, they are two so
    As stiff twin compasses are two,
Thy soul the fixed foot, makes no show
    To move, but doth, if th' other do.

And though it in the center sit,
    Yet when the other far doth roam,
It leans, and hearkens after it,
    And grows erect, as that comes home.

Such wilt thou be to me, who must
    Like th' other foot, obliquely run;

Thy firmness makes my circle just,
 And makes me end, where I begun.

In these lines, from Crashaw's "Saint Mary Magdalene," metaphysical ingenuity falls into absurdity. The tearful eyes of the repentant Magdalene are described as

> two faithful fountains
> Two walking baths, two weeping motions,
> Portable and compendious oceans.

Here is a modern metaphysical conceit in Eliot's "The Love Song of J. Alfred Prufrock":

> Let us go then, you and I,
> When the evening is spread out against the sky
> Like a patient etherized upon a table.

CONCRETE—A term applied to language that is full of images (words evoking sense perceptions); to be distinguished from language that is abstract.

> Taking the hands of someone you love,
> You see they are delicate cages.
> > Robert Bly, "Taking the Hands"

> Down the ravine behind the empty house,
> The cowbells follow one another
> Into the distances of the afternoon.
> > James Wright, "Lying in a Hammock
> > on William Duffy's Farm in Pine Island,
> > Minnesota"

CONNOTATION—The significance of a word beyond its factual, neutral *denotation*. The associations, attitudes, and emotional meanings the word carries to or evokes from the reader by means of implication or suggestion. In the example below, instead of "boat" and "horses," words with more specific and romantic connotations have been used:

> There is no *frigate* like a book
> To take us lands away,
> Nor any *coursers* like a page
> Of prancing poetry.
> > Emily Dickinson

CONSONANCE—Repetition of consonant sounds in a pattern, as in *"lives* and *loves,"* where the vowel sounds differ. Consonance may be described loosely as a repetition of consonant sounds.

CONSONANTAL RHYME—Synonym for pararhyme. See RHYME.

CONVENTION—Any generally accepted feature of style or subject matter derived from past usage or custom. Conventions in poetry include rhyme, all stanza forms, genres (such as the pastoral elegy, dramatic monologue, and literary ballad), and stock characters (the epic hero, the languishing lover, and his cruel and beautiful mistress).

COUPLET—A pair of successive lines of verse, especially when they rhyme and are of the same length. A two-line stanza. See CLOSED COUPLET and HEROIC COUPLET.

DACTYL, DACTYLIC—A metrical foot of three syllables, with one strong stress and two weak, thus: $- \cup \cup$. See also METER and FALLING METER.

DECADENCE—See AESTHETICISM.

DECORUM—The principle that the style and diction of a literary work should be appropriate to the genre, subject, speaker, audience, and occasion. A high (or grand or elevated) style is required for serious subjects and noble themes and characters in the epic, tragedy, elegy and ode. A low (or plain) style, closer to everyday speech, may be used for comedy, satire, and lyrics.

Aristotle recommended that tragic poets write what is appropriate and avoid incongruities. Horace, in the *Art of Poetry*, said that a speaker's words should be in accord with his station: a slave should speak like a slave, an Assyrian like an Assyrian, and so on. Moreover, comic and tragic themes should never be mingled. These ideas prevailed in the theory of poetry throughout the Renaissance and long after. Neoclassic writers such as Tasso and Mazzoni went further, laying down rules for the epic poem, the dramatic, and the lyric, distinguishing one genre sharply from another and stating what style was appropriate for each. They emphasized propriety, elegance and correct taste, excluding whatever was vulgar or unconventional.

However, medieval poets had not paid much attention to classical theory, and some Renaissance poets, influenced by the Bible and Christian literature, broke with decorum. They wrote tragical comedies, comical tragedies, histories, romances, naive lyrics, vulgar eclogues. These poets appealed to nature, and decorum has often been assaulted by poets who write out of their "feelings" rather than by rules. In 1800, in the Preface to *Lyrical Ballads*, Wordsworth attacked the decorum of the preceding age, arguing that poetry could be written about "humble and rustic" life, in a "selection of language really used by men."

D ENOTATION—The dictionary definition of a word, referring to objects or facts, from which emotion is excluded. See CONNOTATION.

D ICTION—Choice of words, the vocabulary used in a literary text. The appropriateness of a particular word is determined by its context.

D IDACTIC—With intent to teach, especially to instruct in moral virtues or assert a doctrine or thesis as true, as in *Paradise Lost* where Milton's intent is to "justify the ways of God to men." *Didactic* is a neutral and descriptive, rather than a derogatory, critical term, because didactic works can be imaginative. As well as illustrating truths outside the text, they may be interesting and delightful in themselves. Some didactic poems convey practical information. The Greek poet Hesiod's *Works and Days* includes a farmer's almanac, a description of the work to be done at different seasons, advice on navigation, etc.

D IEBRACH—See PYRRHIC.

D IMETER—A line of two metrical feet, as the fourth line of

> Tell me, where is fancy bred,
> Or in the heart, or in the head?
> How begot, how nourished?
> > Reply, reply.
>
> Shakespeare, *The Merchant of Venice*

D IONYSUS—The Greek god of vegetation, vineyards, and wine. *Dionysian* connotes intoxication, ecstasy, frenzy, madness, and the deep irrational source of inspiration for music and poetry. See APOLLO.

D IPODIC VERSE—Verse in which two metrical feet can be considered as one unit for scansion. Not characteristic of English prosody.

DIRGE (THRENODY)—A lyric poem or song commemorating a death and expressing grief. A *monody* is a dirge sung by one person. Cf. ELEGY.

DISSOCIATION OF SENSIBILITY—A term made famous by T. E. Eliot's use of it in his essay "The Metaphysical Poets" (1921). In the metaphysical poets, according to Eliot, there was an immediate correlation between abstract thought and concrete phenomena. However, in later poets, especially Milton, the poet's thinking process was separated from his sense perceptions and, as a result, verse became inflated and its images empty of tangible intellectual application. Metaphors, for example, were merely decorative, instead of embodying thought in images so that the reader could "feel" the thought. "Tennyson and Browning are poets," wrote Eliot, "and they think; but they do not feel their thought as immediately as the odor of a rose. A thought to Donne was an experience . . ."

DISSONANCE—A discord of sounds. Dissonance may be cacophony, harsh and unpleasing, or it may be an interesting variation of sounds.

DISTICH—A couplet.

DITHYRAMB—In ancient Greece, an irregular and wildly passionate choral hymn or chant sung in honor of Dionysus at a sacrificial festival; forerunner of Greek tragedy. A highly emotional or wildly lyrical piece of writing may be termed *dithyrambic.*

DOGGEREL—Rhymed verse that is not poetry because it is too trival or clumsy to be taken seriously. But doggerel can be written intentionally to be comic and humorous, as in Samuel Butler's "Hudibras":

> More peevish, cross, and splenetic
> Than dog distract or monkey sick.

DOUBLE RHYME—See RHYME.

DRAMATIC MONOLOGUE—A poem consisting of words spoken by a fictional character to a silent audience. Sometimes the speaker reveals aspects of his personality of which he himself is unaware. See PERSONA.

DUPLE METERS—Meters with feet consisting of two syllables. Iambic [∪ −] and trochaic [− ∪] are duple meters.

Eclogue—A pastoral poem, especially a pastoral dialogue. In modern usage, any verse dialogue where the setting is important.

Elegaic quatrain—Iambic pentameter rhyming *a b a b*.

> How perfect was the calm! it seemed no sleep;
> No mood, which season takes away, or brings:
> I could have fancied that the mighty Deep
> Was even the gentlest of all gentle Things.
>
> Wordsworth, "Elegaic Stanzas"

Elegy—(Derived from the Greek, *E, E legein!* "To cry woe, woe!"). As early as the time of Mimnermus (ca. 630 b.c.) it was the metrical form for love poetry, in couplets of a long dactylic hexameter and a shorter pentameter line. The elegiac meter was also used for martial verse, dirge and lamentation, and occasional poetry of a descriptive or topical sort. The pastoral elegy has an especially rich tradition.

In England in the sixteenth and early seventeenth century, the word "elegy" is used for Petrarchan love poems, laments, and essays. The elegies of Donne include witty poems on trivial topics; apparently serious defenses of outrageous propositions; dramatic situations, real or imaginary, in which elements of wit or paradox may be incidentally present (J. B. Leishman). Donne's "Anatomy of the World" (1611) applies the elegy to death—he said, "funeral elegy"—and Milton's "Lycidas" (1637) establishes the elegy as a genre, a lament for the dead. However, the word "elegiac" is still applied to meditative verse.

Elevation—Use of a high style or subject; grand or lofty writing.

Elision—The omission of part of a word (o'er, ne'er), or the dropping of an unaccented syllable to make a line conform to a metrical pattern.

> And yet 'tis almost 'gainst my conscience.
>
> Shakespeare, *Hamlet*

Elizabethan—The period of Queen Elizabeth I (1558–1603), which included Spenser, Sidney, Marlowe and Shakespeare. The English Renaissance.

E M O T I V E   L A N G U A G E—Language that expresses or evokes feelings and attitudes:

> And my poor fool is hanged! No, no, no life!
> Why should a dog, a horse, a rat, have life,
> And thou no breath at all?
>
> Shakespeare, King Lear

Emotive language is contrasted to *referential language*, in which neutral statements are made about facts.

E M P A T H Y—(The equivalent word in German is *Einfuhlung*, meaning "feeling into"). A person's mental identification with an object of perception, imagining how it feels to be inside something that is outside himself. "If a Sparrow come before my Window, I take part in its existence and pick about the Gravel."—Keats

E N C O M I A S T I C   V E R S E—A general term for poems which praise or glorify a person, object, or abstract idea, as Wordsworth's "Ode to Duty."

E N D   R H Y M E—See R H Y M E.

E N D - S T O P P E D   L I N E—One in which the end of a syntactical unit (phrase, clause, or sentence) coincides with the end of the line.

> Good nature and good sense must ever join;
> To err is human, to forgive, divine.
>
> Pope, An Essay on Criticism

See R U N - O N   L I N E.

E N J A M B M E N T—See R U N - O N   L I N E.

E N V O Y   (E N V O I)—French for "a sending on the way"; a concluding stanza, dedicating the poem (such as a ballade) to an important person (such as a prince).

> O conquerour of Brutes Albyoun,
> Which that by lyne and free eleccioun
> Been verray kyng, this song to yow I sende;
> And ye, that mowen alle oure harmes amende,
> Have mynde upon my supplicacioun!
>
> Chaucer, "The Complaynt of Chaucer to his Purse"

E P I C—A long narrative poem with an exalted style and a heroic theme. Some epics are modeled on Homer's *Iliad* and *Odyssey*.

> Homer has shown in what meter may best be written the deeds of kings and captains, and the sorrows of war.
>
> Horace, *Art of Poetry*

Homeric conventions include the poet's invocation to his muse for her aid; his asking her an epic question, the answer to which begins the narrative *in medias res*, or in the middle of things; the hero's noble deeds and adventures, such as a descent into the underworld and battles in which the gods (the "machinery") take part; and throughout the poem, a ceremonial high style with epic similes, catalogues, and processions of characters. Virgil's *Aeneid* and Milton's *Paradise Lost* are in the Homeric tradition.

The word "epic" may also be used to describe heroic narrative poems that do not follow the Homeric conventions—e.g., *Beowulf*, Dante's *Divine Comedy*, *La Chanson de Roland*, the *Ramayana* and the *Mahabharata*.

E P I C Q U E S T I O N—Asked by the writer of an epic to the Muse; the answer reveals what started the action.

> Who first seduced them to that foul revolt?
> The infernal Serpent; he it was, whose guile,
> Stirred up with envy and revenge, deceived
> The Mother of Mankind.
>
> Milton, *Paradise Lost*

E P I C S I M I L E—In epics, an extended comparison in which one or both of the subjects compared are described in elaborate detail, and in which the secondary subject (the vehicle) may be developed beyond its specific likeness to the primary subject (the tenor).

> [Satan] stood and called
> His Legions, Angel Forms, who lay entranced
> Thick as Autumnal Leaves that strow the Brooks
> In Vallombrosa, where th' Etrurian shades
> High overarched imbower; or scattered sedge
> Afloat, when with fierce Winds Orion armed
> Hath vexed the Red-Sea Coast, whose waves o'erthrew
> Busiris and his Memphian Chivalry,
> While with perfidious hatred they pursued
> The Sojourners of Goshen, who beheld

From the safe shore thir floating Carcasses
And broken Chariot Wheels; so thick bestrown
Abject and lost lay these, covering the Flood,
Under amazement of thir hideous change.

Milton, *Paradise Lost*

E p i g r a m—A polished, terse, and often witty remark, either in prose or verse. In verse the form is usually a couplet or quatrain, but tone is what distinguishes the epigram, rather than form. In the Renaissance, epigrams were patterned on the satiric examples of Martial and other Roman writers, rather than on Greek epigrams, some of which are delicate lyrics. In England in the seventeenth and eighteenth century, when epigrams were fashionable, there was a variety of types: insults, compliments, and pithy sayings. Epigrams may be parts of a poem. Pope's *Essays* are a series of epigrammatic couplets, each of which is a separate, memorable saying:

> A *little learning* is a dangerous thing;
> Drink deep, or taste not the Pierian spring . . .

An Essay on Criticism

These epigrams by Blake and Landor show the range:

> A petty Sneaking Knave I knew—
> O Mr. Cromek, how do ye do?

> Stand close around, ye Stygian set,
>   With Dirce in one boat conveyed!
> Or Charon, seeing, may forget
>   That he is old and she a shade.

E p i l o g u e—A concluding section, separated from the main body of the literary work.

E p i s t l e—A verse epistle is a poem in the form of a letter addressed to a specific person, *e.g.*, Pope's "Epistle to Dr. Arbuthnot."

E p i t a p h—Writing that could be placed on a grave, though this may not be done or intended. The epitaph sums up a life; some epitaphs are panegyrics, others are ribald. There are epitaphs that satirize a living man or an institution. Milton's poem on Shakespeare is one kind of epitaph:

> What needs my Shakespeare for his honored bones
> The labor of an age in piled stones . . .

361

Ralegh's on Leicester is another:

> Here lies the noble Warrior that never blunted sword;
> Here lies the noble Courtier that never kept his word;
> Here lies his Excellency that governed all the state;
> Here lies the Lord of Leicester that all the world did hate.

E P I T H A L A M I O N—(Greek, "at the bridal chamber"). A lyric poem either solemn or ribald, to be sung outside the bridal chamber on the wedding night.

E P I T H E T—A word or phrase that describes the characteristic quality of a person or thing, as "Ethelred the Unready" or Homer's "wine-faced sea" and "fleet-footed Achilles." A *transferred epithet* is an adjective, word, or phrase that is shifted from the noun it would most obviously modify and applied to an associated but unexpected noun. In Keats' "Ode to a Nightingale," the word "embalmed," which evokes the closeness of an overwhelming perfume of flowers, is applied to the night itself:

> I cannot see what flowers are at my feet,
>   Nor what soft incense hangs upon the boughs,
> But, in embalmed darkness, guess each sweet
>   Wherewith the seasonable month endows
> The grass, the thicket, and the fruit-tree wild.

E P O D E—See O D E.

E U L O G Y—A speech or composition in praise of a person or thing, especially a formal poem praising a dead person.

E U P H O N Y—A combination of sounds that is pleasant, musical, and fluent.

> Full fathom five thy father lies;
>   Of his bones are coral made;
> Those are pearls that were his eyes.

Shakespeare, The Tempest

E X A C T   R H Y M E—See R H Y M E.

E X P L I C A T I O N—An explanation. Originally, a French classroom technique of line-by-line, word-by-word explanation. To explicate a poem is to make it clear by explaining its meaning.

E Y E   R H Y M E—See R H Y M E.

FABLE—A brief tale in prose or verse, intended to illustrate a moral. The characters are often talking animals, as in Aesop's fables.

FABLIAU—(Plural: *fabliaux*). Earthy, comic, medieval tales in verse or prose, which usually satirized the clergy and middle class morality, and were often obscene. Chaucer's "Miller's Tale" is a *fabliau*.

FALLING METER—Meter in which the movement falls away from the stressed syllable of each foot. The trochee. [– ◡] and the dactyl [– ◡ ◡] are falling meters.

FANCY (IMAGINATION)—Fancy is the faculty of arranging ideas and images in pleasant combinations. The creations of fancy are casual, whimsical, and often amusing; they are less profound and exciting than those of *Imagination*, which seems to be discovering new images and ideas. Until the nineteenth century the words Fancy and Imagination were often used to mean the same thing, as in this passage from Edmund Burke's "On Taste," 1757:

> Besides the ideas, with their annexed pains and pleasures, which are presented by the sense, the mind of man possesses a sort of creative power of its own; either in representing at pleasure the images of things in the order and manner in which they were received by the senses, or in combining those images in a new manner, and according to a different order. This power is called imagination; and to this belongs whatever is called wit, fancy, invention, and the like. But it must be observed, that this power of the imagination is incapable of producing anything absolutely new; it can only vary the disposition of those ideas which it has received from the senses.

However some writers had begun to distinguish between Fancy and Imagination. Imagination was originality:

> Original Genius ... above all ... is distinguished by an inventive and plastic Imagination, by which it sketches out a creation of its own, discloses truths that were formerly unknown, and exhibits a succession of scenes and events which were never before contemplated or conceived.
>
> William Duff, *An Essay on Original Genius*, 1767

In 1817 in *Biographia Literaria*, Coleridge differentiated between Fancy and Imagination in these words:

> The imagination, then, I consider either as primary, or secondary. The primary imagination I hold to be the living power and

prime agent of all human perception, and as a repetition in the finite mind of the eternal act of creation in the infinite I AM. The secondary imagination I consider as an echo of the former, co-existing with the conscious will, yet still as identical with the primary in the *kind* of its agency, and differing only in *degree* and in the *mode* of its operation. It dissolves, diffuses, dissipates, in order to recreate; or where this process is rendered impossible, yet still at all events it struggles to idealize and to unify. It is essentially *vital*, even as all objects (*as* objects) are essentially fixed and dead.

Fancy, on the contrary, has no other counters to play with, but fixities and definites. The fancy is indeed no other than a mode of memory emancipated from the order of time and space; while it is blended with, and modified by that empirical phenomenon of the will, which we express by the word *choice*. But equally with the ordinary memory the fancy must receive all its materials ready made from the law of association.

FEMININE RHYME—See RHYME.

FIGURATIVE LANGUAGE—Language which means something more than or other than what it literally says. See TROPE, SIMILE, METAPHOR, METONOMY, SYNECDOCHE, PERSONIFICATION, SYMBOL, ALLEGORY, PARADOX, IRONY, HYPERBOLE and UNDERSTATEMENT.

FIGURES OF SPEECH—Rhetorical devices which depart from the ordinary meaning of words by arranging the words to achieve special effects. In figurative language, on the other hand, the meaning of the words themselves is radically changed. See APOSTROPHE, CHIASMUS, INVOCATION, RHETORICAL QUESTION, and ZEUGMA.

FIN DE SIÈCLE—See AESTHETICISM.

FIXED FORM—Any of the standard, highly structured arrangements of meter and rhyme patterns that define a poem as a sonnet, or ballade, or villanelle, etc. Other forms are: ballad stanza, double ballade, chant royal, closed couplet, elegaic quatrain, heroic quatrain, ottava rima, rime royal (or Chaucerian stanza), rondeau, rondeau redouble, rondel, rondelet, roundel, sapphic, sestina, Spenserian stanza, terza rima, triolet, and virelay.

FLYTING—An impromptu folk contest in which two contenders heap abuse on each other. This is the model for flytings in verse, such as the dispute between Beowulf and Unferth in the Old English epic *Beowulf*, and "The Flyting of Dunbar and Kennedie."

Quod Kennedy to Dumbar

Dathane devillis sone, and dragon dispitous,
 Abironis birth, and bred with Beliall;
 Wod werwolf, worme, and scorpion vennemous . . .

FOLK BALLAD—See BALLAD.

FOOT—A metric unit consisting of one stressed syllable (−) and one or more unstressed syllables ($\smile \smile$). For those feet most commonly used in English, see pp. 19–20.

FORMS—Conventional arrangements of meter and rhyme patterns. See FIXED FORM.

FOURTEENER—Elizabethan term for heptameter (q.v.)

FREE VERSE (VERS LIBRE)—Poetry in which rhythm is based not on strict meter, but on a highly organized pattern of the natural cadences of the spoken language.

The Dream

Someone approaches to say his life is ruined
and to fall down at your feet
and pound his head upon the sidewalk.
Blood spreads in a puddle.
And you, in a weak voice, plead
with those nearby for help;
your life takes on his desperation.
He keeps pounding his head.
It is you who are fated;
and you fall down beside him.
It is then you are awakened,
the body gone, the blood washed from the ground,
the stores lit up with their goods.
      David Ignatow, "The Dream"

See the discussion of free verse, pp. 25–27.

FULL RHYME—See RHYME.

GENRE—A certain type of literature, distinguished rather by the subject and the way the subject is usually treated than by the technical form. Drama, for example, includes the genres of tragedy, comedy, and melodrama. Poetry includes several major genres and many minor ones: folk and literary ballad, beast epic, burlesque, carol, dirge, dramatic monologue, eclogue, elegy, epic, epistle, epithalamion, hymn, idyll, lampoon, lyric, mock epic, paean, parody, pastoral and pastoral elegy, ode, prothalamion, and song.

GEORGIC—A poem about rural life, especially the labor of farming, as in Virgil's *Georgics*; to be distinguished from the pastoral idyll of happy shepherds.

GEORGIAN—Pertaining to the reign of any king named George, but *Georgian poetry* refers to a kind of verse published in England after 1910, early in the reign of George V. The Georgian poets were collected by Sir Edward Marsh in five anthologies. They derived from the romantics, but though they wrote a great deal about nature, there was little pressure of thought. The best known of the Georgians were John Masefield, W. H. Davies, Ralph Hodgson, Rupert Brooke, and a very fine poet indeed—Walter De La Mare. For a while D. H. Lawrence was counted among the Georgians. But Hardy and Yeats were omitted. When Ezra Pound launched the imagist movement, he ridiculed the Georgians for their triteness of thought and technique. They are scarcely read nowadays. The prewar rural English life they described seems unreal and remote.

GLOSS—An explanation or interpretation of a difficult word or passage in a text, often by means of a footnote.

GOTHIC—Characterized by a medieval setting and an atmosphere that is mysterious, frightening, and often supernatural. Gothic influence is apparent in the poetry of the *Graveyard School* (q.v.) and in Romantic poetry such as Coleridge's "The Rime of the Ancient Mariner" and Byron's "Manfred."

GRAVEYARD SCHOOL—A group of mid-eighteenth century poets who wrote mysterious and melancholy poems on death. Unlike their neoclassical contemporaries, they are associated with the Gothic revival, which anticipated the melancholy aspects of the romantic period. Among the poets are Thomas Parnell, Robert Blair, Edward

Young, and Thomas Gray, whose "Elegy Written in a Country Churchyard" is the most famous "Graveyard" poem.

HAIKU (HOKKU)—A Japanese verse form of seventeen syllables divided into sections of five syllables, seven, and five. It is a very old form; the earliest extant examples date from the beginning of the thirteenth century. The haiku may be sad or gay, deep or frivolous, religious, humorous, or satirical. Haikus usually give an image that is a starting point for thought and emotion. The scene is only sketched; the reader infers the rest. In nearly all haiku there is a *kigo*, a word or expression that indicates the time of year.

> Lean frog,
> > don't give up the fight!
> > Issa is here!
> > > *Issa* (1762–1826) (transl. Harold G. Henderson)

HALF RHYME—See RHYME.

HARMONY—The principle by which parts are blended into a unified and pleasing whole.

HEAD RHYME—See RHYME.

HEMISTICH—See ALEXANDRINE.

HEPTAMETER (FOURTEENER, SEPTENARY)—A line of fourteen syllables, usually seven iambic feet, commonly used in England in the sixteenth century, especially for narrative. The line divides into the ballad meter of four stresses followed by three.

> The God now having laide aside his borrowed shape of Bull,
> Had in his likenesse showed himself: And with his pretty trull
> Tane landing in the Isle of Crete. When in that while her Sire
> Not knowing where she was become, sent after to enquire.
> > Ovid, *Metamorphoses*, 1567 (transl. Arthur Golding)

HEROIC COUPLET—Two lines of rhymed iambic pentameter, end-stopped. Especially popular in the eighteenth century.

> His fate was destined to a barren strand,
> A petty fortress, and a dubious hand.
> > Johnson, "The Vanity of Human Wishes"

See END-STOPPED LINE and CLOSED COUPLET.

HEROIC QUATRAIN—Four lines of iambic pentameter, rhymed *a b a b*. Synonymous with *elegaic quatrain*.

HEXAMETER—A line of six feet, as in the final line of

> We look before and after
> And pine for what is not:
> Our sincerest laughter
> With some pain is fraught;
> Our sweetest songs are those that tell of saddest thought.
>
> Shelley, "To a Skylark"

See ALEXANDRINE.

HIDDEN ALLITERATION—See ALLITERATION.

HIGH BURLESQUE—See BURLESQUE.

HISTORICAL RHYME—See RHYME.

HORATIAN ODE—See ODE.

HOVERING STRESS (DISTRIBUTED STRESS)—In metrics, an accent that could be placed equally well on either of two adjacent syllables, so that it seems to hover between them.

> There is sweet music here that softer falls
> Than petals from blown roses on the grass . . .
>
> Tennyson, "The Lotus-Eaters"

HUMOURS—In Medieval and Renaissance psychology, the four fluids of the human body, which released their vapors to the brain and thus influenced physical and psychological health. When the four humours were in balance, the person behaved normally, but if one humour became dominant, it stereotyped his personality. Too much blood made him sanguine: ruddy-faced, cheerful, and amorous. Too much phlegm made him phlegmatic: dull, unresponsive, and cowardly. Too much yellow bile made him choleric: irritable, obstinate, vengeful, and easily aroused to anger. Too much black bile made him melancholic: depressed, brooding, satiric, and gluttonous.

HYMN—From Greek *hymnos*, a song praising heroes or the gods. By extension, a literary hymn is a song of praise, such as Shelley's "Hymn to Intellectual Beauty."

H Y P E R B O L E—Overstatement or exaggeration for the sake of emphasis. Marvell's lines are hyperbolic:

> My vegetable love should grow
> Vaster than empires, and more slow.
> An hundred years should go to praise
> Thine eyes, and on thy forehead gaze . . .
>
> "To His Coy Mistress"

H Y P E R M E T E R—In metrics, the addition of one or more unstressed syllables at the beginning or end of a line.

To bĕ, ŏr nōt tŏ bē; thăt ĭs thĕ quēs/tĭon:

I A M B (U S), I A M B I C—A metrical foot of two syllables, with a weak stress followed by a strong, thus: ‿ —. Iambic is the most common meter in English poetry. See also M E T E R, B L A N K V E R S E, and R I S I N G M E T E R.

I D E N T I C A L R H Y M E—See R H Y M E.

I D Y L L—A short picturesque poem idealizing rural life; the charming pastoral of singing shepherds, as distinguished from the mournful pastoral elegy. See also A R C A D I A.

> Come live with me and be my love,
> And we will all the pleasures prove . . .
> The shepherd swains shall dance and sing
> For thy delight each May morning:
>
> Marlowe, "The Passionate Shepherd to his Love"

I M A G E

> An "image" is that which presents an intellectual and emotional complex in an instant of time.
>
> Ezra Pound, "A Few Don'ts by an Imagiste"

In modern poetry, an image is a word or cluster of words that stimulate sense-perceptions. The words evoke the reader's sense of sight, hearing, smell, taste, or touch, and his imaginary experiences are, to a large extent, the meaning of the poem. In Pound's words, "A poem is an image or a succession of images."

> I am moved by fancies that are curled
> Around these images, and cling . . .
>
> T. S. Eliot, "Preludes"

The hand that whirls the water in the pool
Stirs the quicksand; that ropes the blowing wind
Hauls my shroud sail.
And I am dumb to tell the hanging man
How of my clay is made the hangman's lime.

> Dylan Thomas, "The Force That Through
> the Green Fuse Drives the Flower"

See IMAGISM, SURREALISM.

IMAGERY—Images considered collectively, as the imagery of light in *Oedipus Rex*.

IMAGINATION

The word is predominantly used in cases where, carried away by enthusiasm and passion, you think you see what you describe, and you place it before the eyes of your hearers.

> *On the Sublime*, traditionally ascribed to Longinus,
> first or second century A.D.

The poet's eye, in a fine frenzy rolling,
Doth glance from heaven to earth, from earth to heaven;
And, as imagination bodies forth
The forms of things unknown, the poet's pen
Turns them to shapes, and gives to airy nothing
A local habitation and a name.

> Shakespeare, *A Midsummer-Night's Dream*

The poet . . . brings the whole soul of man into activity. . . . He diffuses a tone and spirit of unity, that blends, and (as it were) *fuses*, each into each, by that synthetic and magical power, to which we have exclusively appropriated the name of imagination. This power . . . reveals itself in the balance or reconciliation of opposite or discordant qualities: of sameness, with difference; of the general, with the concrete; the idea, with the image; the individual with the representative; the sense of novelty and freshness, with old and familiar objects; a more than usual state of emotion, with more than usual order; judgement ever awake and steady self-possession, with enthusiasm and feeling profound or vehement; and while it blends and harmonizes the natural and the artificial, still subordinates art to nature; the manner to the matter; and our admiration of the poet to our sympathy with the poetry.

> Coleridge, *Biographia Literaria*

See FANCY.

IMAGISM—A literary movement that started about 1910, including the critic T. E. Hulme (pronounced Hume), and the poets Ezra Pound, T. S. Eliot, H. D. (Hilda Doolittle), John Gould Fletcher, F. S. Flint and Richard Aldington. Amy Lowell contributed to the movement until she broke with Pound. Pound says, "The tenets of the Imagist faith were published in March 1913 as follows:

1. Direct treatment of the "thing," whether subjective or objective.
2. To use absolutely no word that does not contribute to the presentation.
3. As regarding rhythm: to compose in sequence of the musical phrase, not in sequence of the metronome."

Pound's two-line poem, "In a Station of the Metro," is often quoted as an example of Imagist writing:

The apparition of these faces in the crowd;
Petals on a wet, black bough.

This poem, Pound says, originated in a ride on the metro, when he saw beautiful faces. They obsessed him, till they became

an equation . . . not in speech, but in little splotches of color. It was just that—a "pattern," or hardly a pattern, if by "pattern" you mean something with a "repeat" in it . . . My experience in Paris should have gone into paint . . . In a poem of this sort one is trying to record the precise instant when a thing outward and objective transforms itself, or darts into a thing inward and subjective.

"Vorticism"

The ideas of the imagists have had a powerful influence on writing in the twentieth century, both verse and prose.

See IMAGE, SURREALISM.

IMITATION

The poet being an imitator, like a painter or any other artist, must of necessity imitate one of three objects—things as they were or are, things as they are said or thought to be, or things as they ought to be.

Aristotle, *Poetics*

As Aristotle used it, *mimesis*, or "imitation," meant the artistic process of selecting and arranging material in order to show its true significance. Imitation was not, as S. H. Butcher explains, mere copying; it was creation.

371

"Imitation," in the sense in which Aristotle applies the word to poetry, is equivalent to "producing" or "creating according to a true idea," which forms part of the definition of art in general. The "true idea" for fine art is derived from the εἶδος, the general concept which the intellect spontaneously abstracts from the details of sense. There is an ideal form which is present in each individual phenomenon but imperfectly manifested. This form impresses itself as a sensuous appearance on the mind of the artist; he seeks to give it a more complete expression, to bring to light the ideal which is only half revealed in the world of reality. His distinctive work as an artist consists in stamping the given material with the impress of the form which is universal. . . . "Imitation," so understood, is a creative act.

S. H. Butcher, *Aristotle's Theory of Poetry*

After Aristotle, other critics have said that poetry originates in "imitation." However, for some of them the word seems to mean not bringing forth the ideal or universal form, but a clever representation of things as they are. Such is the effect of the following statement by Vico.

Children excel in imitation; we observe them generally amuse themselves by imitating what they are able to understand. This axiom shows that the world in its infancy was composed of poetic nations, for poetry is nothing but imitation. . . . all the arts of things necessary, useful, convenient, and even in large part those of human pleasure, were invented in the poetic centuries before the philosophers came . . . the arts are nothing but imitations of nature, poems in a certain way made of things.

Vico, *The New Science*

The word "imitation" may be used to mean learning from other men. "The Poet," says Ben Jonson, must be able to "convert the substance, or Riches, of another Poet to his owne use" (*Timber*, 1641). And poets write "imitations"—that is, poems modeled on other poems. Johnson's "Vanity of Human Wishes" is an imitation of Juvenal's "Tenth Satire."

IMPERFECT RHYME—See RHYME.

INITIAL RHYME—See ALLITERATION.

INSPIRATION

A man cannot say, "I will compose poetry." The greatest poet even cannot say it; for the mind in creation is as a fading coal, which some invisible influence, like an inconstant wind, awakens to transitory brightness; this power arises from within, like the colour of a flower which fades and changes as it is developed, and the conscious portions of our natures are unprophetic either of its approach or its departure. Could this influence be durable in its original purity and force, it is impossible to predict the greatness of the results; but when composition begins, inspiration is already on the decline, and the most glorious poetry that has ever been communicated to the world is probably a feeble shadow of the original conceptions of the Poet.

Shelley, A Defense of Poetry

INTENSITY—Concentration of meaning.

Language is a means of communication. To charge language with meaning to the utmost possible degree, we have ... the three chief means:

1. throwing the object (fixed or moving) onto the visual imagination.
2. inducing emotional correlations by the sound and rhythm of the speech.
3. inducing both of the effects by stimulating the associations (intellectual or emotional) that have remained in the receiver's consciousness in relation to the actual words or word groups employed ...

Incompetence will show in the use of too many words.

Pound, ABC of Reading

INTENTIONAL FALLACY—In the "new criticism," according to W. K. Winsatt and M. C. Beardsley, the error of trying to judge a literary work according to the author's statement of his intention in writing it, or according to the known biographical and historical facts surrounding its production.

INTERNAL RHYME—See RHYME.

INTERREGNUM—See COMMONWEALTH.

INVENTION

Invention is nothing other than the natural virtue of an imagination, conceiving the ideas and forms of all things that can be imagined, whether of heaven or of earth, living or inanimate, for the purpose of afterwards representing, describing, imitating: for just as the aim of the orator is to persuade, so that of the poet is to imitate, invent, and represent—things which are, or which may be—in a resemblance to truth.

Ronsard, *A Brief on the Art of French Poetry*, 1565

I N V E R S I O N—The use of a foot opposite from the one required by the meter. An inverted accent, foot, or stress substitutes a dactyl for an anapest or a trochee for an iamb (and vice versa).

I N V O C A T I O N—The poet's appeal to his muse for assistance at the beginning of an epic or other long work.

I R O N Y—A rhetorical device by which a writer implies a discrepancy or an additional meaning that is often contradictory to the literal meaning of his words. In *verbal irony* the meaning is different from, and usually the opposite of, what is said, as in the words "pure" and "religious" in the anonymous sixteenth-century poem "Of Alphus":

> No egg on Friday Alph will eat,
> But drunken will he be
> On Friday still. Oh, what a pure
> Religious man is he!

In *dramatic irony*, there is a discrepancy between what a character says and what the author thinks: when Milton's Satan convinces Eve that she should eat the apple, we know that Milton is against it. Dramatic irony also may refer to the additional significance of a character's speech or action to the audience, when they know certain crucial information that he does not. In *irony of situation*, the outcome of a situation is inappropriate, or different from what was expected. In *romantic irony*, the author creates an illusion and then deliberately destroys it by a change of tone, personal comment, or contradicting statement.

J A C O B E A N—(From the Latin *Jacobus*, James). The period of King James I (1603–1625). At this time Chapman, Bacon, Drayton, Shakespeare, Jonson, Donne, Tourneur, Webster, Beaumont and Fletcher were writing, and the King James version of the Bible was made.

K E N N I N G—A metaphorical compound word or phrase used in Old English and Old Norse poetry. The ocean is the "whale-road" or "the foaming fields"; a lord is "dispenser of rings." A kenning may describe complex emotion:

374

> Sitting day-long
> at an oar's end clenched against clinging sorrow,
> *breast-drought* I have borne, and bitternesses too.
>
>

The Seafarer (transl. from the Anglo-Saxon by Michael Alexander)
>

L A M E N T—A literary work, often a poem, expressing intense grief.

> I am the man that hath seen affliction by the rod of His wrath. . . .
>
> How is the gold become dim! how is the most fine gold changed! the stones of the sanctuary are poured out in the top of every street.
>
> The precious sons of Zion, comparable to fine gold, how are they esteemed as earthen pitchers, the work of the hands of the potter!
>
>

The Lamentations of Jeremiah
>

L A M P O O N—A satirical attack, in verse or prose, upon an individual person, such as Pope's attack on Colley Cibber in *The Dunciad*. Lampoons were common in seventeenth- and eighteenth-century England, until the introduction of libel laws.

L E O N I N E R H Y M E—See R H Y M E.

L I G H T V E R S E—Verse written mainly to entertain or amuse. The category includes nonsense verse, limericks, nursery rhymes, witty epigrams, some lyrics, satire, parodies, occasional verse, and *vers de société*.

L I M E R I C K—A subliterary fixed form, an anapestic jingle, used for making jokes; very popular in English.

> There was a young woman named Bright,
> Whose speed was much faster than light.
> > She set out one day
> > In a relative way
> And returned on the previous night.

L I N E—A row of words. In prose the lines run on; in poetry each line ends or breaks where the rhythm dictates. Prose-writers think in sentences, poets think in lines. A line of poetry may be called a verse. See E N D - S T O P P E D L I N E, R U N - O N L I N E.

LITERALISM—1. Adherence to the letter, the exact words of the original: "a literal translation." 2. Understanding words only in their strict sense, in a matter-of-fact, unimaginative way.

LINKED RHYME—See RHYME.

LITERARY BALLAD—See BALLAD.

LOW BURLESQUE—See BURLESQUE.

LYRE—A musical instrument of ancient Greece, consisting of a sound box (originally a turtle shell), with two curving arms carrying a cross bar (yoke) from which strings were stretched to the body. It was used to accompany the voice in singing and recitation, and became a symbol for music and poetry.

> ... the lyre was invented by the Greek Mercury ... This lyre was given him by Apollo, god of civil light or of the nobility ... and with this lyre Orpheus, Amphion and other theological poets, who professed knowledge of laws, founded and established the humanity of Greece. . . . the lyre was the union of the cords or forces of the fathers, of which the public force was composed which is called civil authority, which finally put an end to all private force and violence. Hence the law was defined with full propriety by the poets as *lyra regnorum*, "the lyre of kingdoms". . . .
> Vico, *The New Science*

LYRIC—In ancient Greece, a poem to be sung or recited accompanied by a lyre. Now, any poem expressing personal emotion rather than describing events. Sonnets, elegies, odes, hymns, etc., are lyric poems.

MADRIGAL—A short lyric poem to be sung in several (as many as eight) parts, often with elaborate counterpoint. The theme may be pastoral, satiric, or concerned with love. Writing madrigals was fashionable in England in the last quarter of the sixteenth century.

MASCULINE RHYME—See RHYME.

MEANING—The meaning of a poem is in the form, images, rhythm, and tone, as well as in those ideas which could equally well be expressed in prose. The meaning of a poem is the poem itself. *Four levels of meaning*: a medieval concept, useful for understanding Dante's *Divine Comedy* and other works. In the *Summa Theologica* Thomas Aquinas stated that works should be read for their allegorical, moral and anagogic meanings as well as their primary, literal meaning.

> So far as the things of the Old Law signify the things of the New Law, there is the allegorical sense; so far as the things done in Christ . . . are signs of what we ought to do, there is the moral sense. But so far as they signify what relates to eternal glory, there is the anagogical sense.

M E T A P H O R—An implied comparison, omitting explicit words of comparison such as "like," "as," "as if," and "than." A metaphor is more compressed than a simile, because it identifies two things with each other or substitutes one for the other: "My love is a rose." A *dead metaphor* is one that is no longer recognized as a comparison: "the arm of a chair." A *submerged metaphor* implies, rather than states, one of the two subjects: "my winged heart" implies that "my heart is a bird." In a *mixed metaphor*, the comparison is strikingly disparate: "to take arms against a sea of troubles." See the discussion of metaphor, pp. 4–7.

M E T A P H Y S I C A L   C O N C E I T—See C O N C E I T.

M E T A P H Y S I C A L   P O E T S—Seventeenth-century poets whose style of writing had a colloquial tone, tightly knit syntax, irony, devices of wit such as puns and paradoxes, and the farfetched original comparisons called metaphysical conceits. The best-known metaphysical poets are John Donne, Andrew Marvell, John Cleveland, Abraham Cowley, George Herbert, Richard Crashaw, and Henry Vaughan. See C O N C E I T, and the discussion of "The Sun Rising," pp. 31–36.

M E T E R—The regular recurrence of patterns of accented and unaccented syllables. The basic metrical unit is the *foot*, which can be iambic, trochaic, anapestic, dactylic, spondaic, or pyrrhic. The number of feet per line is indicated by the terms monometer, dimeter, trimeter, tetrameter, pentameter, hexameter, heptameter, or octameter. (For examples, see individual entries.) A line of poetry is called a verse, and it is described by naming the kind of feet and the number of them in the line: *e.g.*, "iambic pentameter." *Scansion* is the practice of describing the metrical patterns of a poem. See A C C E N T, B L A N K   V E R S E, C A D E N C E, F O O T, F R E E   V E R S E, Q U A N T I T A T I V E   V E R S E, R H Y T H M, S C A N S I O N, S P R U N G   R H Y T H M, V E R S E, and the discussion of meter, pp. 18–22.

METONYMY—A figure of speech in which the thing or idea given to the reader represents some other thing or idea that is closely associated with it. The name of a writer often means "his works," as in the statement, "I have read all of Shakespeare." "The crown" can mean "the monarch." Metonymy may be *synecdoche* (q.v.), using a part for the whole, as when "horse" is used to mean "cavalry."

MIMESIS—See IMITATION.

MOCK EPIC—See BURLESQUE.

MOCK HEROIC STYLE—See BURLESQUE.

MONODY—See DIRGE.

MONOMETER—A line of one metrical foot, as in these lines about fleas:

> Adam
> Had 'em.

MONOSYLLABIC FOOT—A foot of only one syllable:

> *Dīng, / dōng, / bēll;*
>
> Pŭssy's / īn thĕ / wēll.

MOTIF—A recurrent image, word, phrase, theme, character, or situation.

MUSE—In Greek mythology, any of the nine daughters of Zeus and Mnemosyne, goddess of memory, who were the goddesses presiding over the arts. Clio was the muse of history, Calliope of epic poetry, Erato of love poetry, Euterpe of lyric poetry, Melpomene of tragedy, Polyhymnia of songs to the gods, Terpsichore of the dance, Thalia of comedy, and Urania of astronomy. Later "the Muse" came to mean the goddess or power that inspired poets.

MUSICAL DEVICES—A general term for ways of using language that bring out its affinities to music, by the choice and arrangement of accents to form rhythm and meter, or by the choice and arrangement of sounds to form assonance, consonance, alliteration, rhymes, stanza patterns and refrains.

NARRATIVE—A story with characters and a plot.

NATURALISM—1. A kind of art that closely imitates nature. 2. Sometimes used to describe the work of a "nature" poet, such as Wordsworth, who describes country life and scenes. 3. A late nineteenth-century movement in literature, mainly the novel, sometimes described as the extreme form of realism. Its proponents sought to record actual life, documented in scientifically accurate detail, in order to prove that all human actions are determined by heredity and environment. This meant recording dispassionately, even photographically, a "slice of life." However, the slice was usually chosen from the lower class slums, so naturalism had a definite tendency to be sordid as well as deterministic. The major figure of the movement was Emile Zola, who called his technique naturalism to distinguish it from the realism of Balzac and Flaubert. There are naturalistic influences in the poems of Thomas Hardy, E. A. Robinson, and Edgar Lee Masters.

NATURE—"Nature" has been a controlling concept in Western thought since antiquity. In the Middle Ages nature was considered primarily as the entire universe created by God and sustained by Him. Beginning in the Renaissance and culminating in the eighteenth century, "nature" and "nature's laws" were increasingly separated from theological considerations and were emphasized as the universal and necessary foundation of religion, ethics, politics, law and art. Nature was "One clear, unchanged, and universal light" (Pope, *An Essay on Criticism*).

Here are some basic definitions of "nature" as the word occurs in poetry.

1. The creative and regulative physical power which is conceived of as operating in the material world and as the immediate cause of all its phenomena:

Where Nature shall provide Green Grass,
And fat'ning Clover for their Fare.
Dryden, trans. of Virgil's *Georgic III*, 1697

The force that through the green fuse drives the flower
Drives my green age; that blasts the roots of trees
Is my destroyer.
Dylan Thomas, "The Force That Through
the Green Fuse Drives the Flower"

2. The material world, or its collective objects and phenomena, especially those with which man is most directly in contact; fre-

quently the features and products of the earth itself, as contrasted with those of civilization.

> But all her shows did Nature yield,
> To please and win this pilgrim wise.
> He saw the partridge drum in the woods;
> He heard the woodcock's evening hymn;
> He found the tawny thrushes' broods;
> And the shy hawk did wait for him;
>
> Ralph Waldo Emerson, Woodnotes, I, 1840

3. *The* (or *a*) *state of nature*: (*a*) the moral state natural to man, as opposed to a state of grace; (*b*) the condition of man before the foundation of organized society; (*c*) an uncultivated or undomesticated condition.

> Nor think, in NATURE'S STATE they blindly trod;
> The state of Nature was the reign of God:
> Self-love and Social at her birth began,
> Union the bond of all things, and of Man.
> Pride then was not; nor Arts, that Pride to aid;
> Man walked with beast, joint tenant of the shade;
>
> Pope, An Essay on Man

4. The inherent impulse, in men or animals, by which behavior is determined and controlled.

> And smale foweles maken melodye,
> That slepen al the nyght with open ye
> So priketh hem nature in hir corages ...
>
> Chaucer, General Prologue to The Canterbury Tales

> Yet do I fear thy nature;
> It is too full o' the milk of human kindness
> To catch the nearest way.
>
> Shakespeare, Macbeth

NEAR RHYME—See RHYME.

NEGATIVE CAPABILITY

> Several things dove-tailed in my mind, and at once it struck me what quality went to form a Man of Achievement, especially in Literature, and which Shakespeare possessed so enormously—I mean *Negative Capability*, that is, when a man is capable of being in uncertainties, mysteries, doubts, without any irritable reaching

after fact and reason—Coleridge, for instance, would let go by a fine isolated verisimilitude caught from the Penetralium of mystery, from being incapable of remaining content with half-knowledge.

John Keats, Letter to George and Thomas Keats

NEOCLASSICAL—Referring to a revival of classicism during the Augustan Age in England. See AUGUSTAN AGE.

NEW CRITICISM—A term applied to the writings of the literary critics R. P. Blackmur, Cleanth Brooks, John Crowe Ransom, Allen Tate, Robert Penn Warren, and, with less certainty, to those of Kenneth Burke, T. S. Eliot, William Empson, I. A. Richards, and Yvor Winters. In general, New Critics regard a poem as an object for rigorously empirical, objective analysis (textual criticism). The poem is treated "primarily as poetry and not another thing," without reference to the author's life or intention (the intentional fallacy), to the history of the society in which the author lived, to the traditional genre of the work, or to the effect the work has upon either the reader's emotions (the affective fallacy) or later literary history.

NONSENSE VERSE—A kind of light verse with pleasant, orderly, even jingly sounds, absurd statements, and words that are not in the dictionary. The best known writers of nonsense verse are Lewis Carroll and Edward Lear.

OBJECTIVE CORRELATIVE

The only way of expressing emotion in the form of art is by finding an "objective correlative"; in other words, a set of objects, a situation, a chain of events which shall be the formula of that *particular* emotion; such that when the external facts, which must terminate in sensory experience, are given, the emotion is immediately evoked.

T. S. Eliot, "Hamlet and His Problems"

OBJECTIVITY—See SUBJECTIVITY.

OBLIQUE RHYME—See RHYME.

OCCASIONAL POEM—A poem written to commemorate a specific event or occasion, *e.g.*, Yeats's "Easter 1916."

OCTAVE—The first eight lines of a Petrarchan sonnet.

Octet—Synonym for OCTAVE.

Octometer (sometimes OCTAMETER)—A line of eight feet. Because of its awkward length, which often breaks into two tetrameters, the line is rare in English. It is used by Tennyson in *Frater Ave atque Vale*:

> Row us out from Desenzano, to your Sirmione row!
> So they rowed, and there we landed—"O venusta Sirmio!"

Octosyllabic couplet—A stanza in which each of the two lines contains eight syllables.

Ode—In English, a serious and dignified lyric poem, usually fairly long, with an elaborate stanzaic structure for which there is no conventional fixed form. Pindar modeled his odes on the choric songs of the Greek drama, in which the chorus chanted or sang the "strophe" while dancing to the left, the "antristrophe" while retracing the pattern to the right, and the metrically different "epode" while standing still. The Pindaric ode in English is an imitation of this, having the strophe and antistrophe in a stanzaic form different from that of the epode. The Pindaric ode is exalted and enthusiastic. The Horatian ode, modeled on the odes of the Latin poet Horace, is simpler—often one stanzaic pattern throughout—cool and sober.

Off rhyme—See RHYME.

Onomatopoeia—The use of words that imitate sounds: "bang," "buzz," "hiss," "scratch."

Ornament—"Poetic ornament" is a critical term—no longer used—for an image, epithet, or figure of speech.

Orphic—Resembling the music of Orpheus, who is said to have charmed stones and wild beasts with his lyre. Entrancing, mystic, oracular.

Ottava rima—A stanza of eight lines of iambic pentameter rhymed *a b a b a b c c*. It was used by the Italian writers of comic epics, Pulci, Berni, and Ariosto. The stanza was introduced into England in the sixteenth century by Wyatt. Byron adopted it for his "Beppo," "The Vision of Judgment," and *Don Juan*:

> Yes, Don Alfonso! husband now no more,
>   If ever you indeed deserved the name,

Is't worthy of your years?—you have three-score—
  Fifty, or sixty, it is all the same—
Is't wise or fitting, causeless to explore
For facts against a virtuous woman's fame?
Ungrateful, perjured, barbarous Don Alfonso,
How dare you think your lady would go on so?

OVERSTATEMENT—Synonym for HYPERBOLE.

OXYMORON—A figurative use of language in which a paradox contains a direct contradiction. Milton's describes hell as "no light, but rather darkness visible."

PAEAN—A song or hymn of praise, joy, or triumph, originally sung by Greeks in gratitude to Apollo.

PANEGYRIC—A formal speech or piece of writing praising someone.

PARABLE—A short, simple story intended to illustrate a moral lesson. Best known are the parables of Jesus, such as "The Good Samaritan" and "The Prodigal Son."

PARADOX—An apparent contradiction that is nevertheless in some sense true and valid, as in the phrases, "conspicuous by his absence" and "damn by faint praise." An *oxymoron* combines direct contraries, as in "living death."

PARAPHRASE—A restatement of the ideas of a text in words that are different but as close as possible to the meaning of the original. See PROSE PARAPHRASE.

PARARHYME—See RHYME.

PARNASSIANS—The *Parnassiens* were French poets, centering around Leconte de Lisle, who began publishing in the 1860's. The characteristics of their verse are "hardness," precision, clarity:

The best work is made
from hard, strong materials,
  obstinately precise—
the line of the poem, onyx, steel.
                    Théophile Gautier, *L'Art* (transl. Denise Levertov)

They wrote about history, science, nature, philosophy and contemporary life, but some Parnassians were chiefly writers of lyrics. Rebelling against the Romantic subjectivity and social concern of Hugo, Vigny, and Lamartine, they wanted poetry to be impersonal, excluding both the personality of the author and any moral or social usefulness. In the latter they anticipated the aesthetic movement, which adopted their motto, "art for art's sake." They revived the older French fixed verse forms, such as the ballade, rondeau, and villanelle. Baudelaire, Heredia, Sully-Prudhomme, François Coppée, Anatole France, and Mallarmé, were associated with the movement at one time or another. In England in the 1870's, Austin Dobson, Edmund Gosse and Andrew Lang imitated the Parnassians in form and style, though not in thought. The English poets were somewhat inhibited by Victorian conventions.

PARNASSUS—A mountain in central Greece, frequented by Apollo and the Muses. Parnassus is 8068 feet high.

PARODY—A form of *burlesque* (q.v.). Literary or critical parody is an imitation of another man's style or a particular work. Through distortion or exaggeration the parodist points out salient features of the original. Parody may be funny, or malicious, or flattering. Lewis Carroll's parody of Wordsworth's "Resolution and Independence" is funny, and also it is acute literary criticism, emphasizing Wordsworth's earnestness, the circumstantiality of the narrative, and the eccentricity of the character:

> I'll tell thee everything I can;
>   There's little to relate.
> I saw an aged aged man
>   A-sitting on a gate.
> "Who are you, aged man?" I said,
>   "And how is it you live?"
> And his answer trickled through my head,
>   Like water through a sieve . . .

PARTIAL RHYME—See RHYME.

PASTORAL—A genre of poetry, based on classical models, that deals with rustic life, usually with shepherds. The Greek poet Theocritus (third century B.C.) wrote the first pastoral poetry, describing Sicilian shepherds, or "pastors." After he established the conventions, pastoral became a highly artificial genre based on literary imitation, especially of Theocritus and Virgil. The setting was often *Arcadia*, a perpetual summer of meadows, trees, and flowers where shepherds and shepherdesses, who did no work, had love affairs and composed and sang songs of three major kinds: the *eclogue*, or singing match between two shepherds, the *complaint*, in which a shepherd praises his mistress's beauty and laments her cruelty, and the *pastoral elegy*, in which the shepherd bewails the death of a fellow shepherd. The Renaissance developed the pastoral romance—long tales of love and adventure in a pastoral setting—and pastoral drama. Shakespeare's *As You Like It* is derived from these. The pastoral world is often presented as simple and uncorrupted, an escape from the complexities and frustration of urban life into peace and the satisfaction of desires. Pastoral may be called *bucolic* or *idyllic*. Christian literature incorporates some features of the pastoral: the minister is the "shepherd" of his "flock," etc.

P A S T O R A L   E L E G Y—An elegy that incorporates pastoral conventions, such as representing the poet and the person for whom he mourns as shepherds, invoking the muses and making references to classical myths, having all nature join in mourning for the dead shepherd, asking the nymphs where they were when death took their beloved and why they did not save him, questioning divine justice and lamenting the world's corrupt state, having a procession of mourners and a list of appropriate flowers to deck the hearse, and closing with a tone of peaceful assurance that death leads to a better life. Milton's "Lycidas" and Shelley's "Adonais" are the most famous examples of pastoral elegy in English.

P A T H E T I C   F A L L A C Y—The attribution of human characteristics to inanimate objects, in a way less complete and less formal than full personification:

> The one red leaf, the last of its clan,
> That dances as often as dance it can.
>
> Coleridge, "Christabel"

The original use of this term by Ruskin in 1856 was derogatory, but it is now usually considered a standard descriptive term without pejorative connotations.

P A T H O S—The quality in a work of literature which evokes pity, sorrow, or tenderness from the reader. A pathetic situation is often one where the innocent and helpless suffer. Pathos should be distinguished from *bathos* and from *tragedy*.

P A U S E—A moment of hesitation in the rhythm of verse. A pause within a line is called a caesura. A pause at the end of a line or stanza is called a metrical pause. A pause for intensified poetic effect is a rhetorical pause. A pause is often used to compensate for a missing syllable.

P E G A S U S—In classical mythology, a winged horse that sprang from the blood of Medusa when she was slain by Perseus. With his hoof Pegasus caused the spring Hippocrene, the source of poetry, to well forth on Mount Helicon. Thus Pegasus is associated with the Muses and with poetry.

P E N T A M E T E R—A line of five feet:

Rough winds / do shake / the dar/ling buds / of May

Shakespeare, *Sonnet 18*

P E R F E C T R H Y M E—See R H Y M E.

P E R I P H R A S I S—(From the Greek *periphrazein*: to speak around). Circumlocution. Using a longer phrase or indirect, abstract way of stating ideas or naming things, in place of a shorter and plainer expression. Periphrasis may be euphemistic—using mild words instead of strong: "passing away" for "death"—or it may be descriptive, as in Old English *kenning* (q.v.). Periphrasis easily degenerates into verbosity and a habitual avoidance of plain speech:

Up springs the lark...
Amid the dawning clouds, and from their haunts
Calls up the *tuneful nations*...

James Thomson, "Spring," 1728

P E R S O N A—The fictitious narrator imagined by the poet to speak the words of a poem. The persona is a "voice" or "mask" which should not be confused with the author's private personality. In "The Love Song of J. Alfred Prufrock," the speaker is the persona, Prufrock, not T. S. Eliot. In these lines of Browning's *dramatic monologue,* "Soliloquy of the Spanish Cloister," the persona is not Robert Browning but a ridiculous monk:

Gr-r-r—there you go, my heart's abhorrence!
Water your damned flower-pots, do!
If hate killed men, Brother Lawrence,
God's blood, would not mine kill you!

P E R S O N I F I C A T I O N—A figurative use of language in which human qualities or feelings are attributed to nonhuman organisms, inanimate objects, or abstract ideas. Also, personification may be the representation of an abstract quality or idea by a human figure. It is in this sense that Addison uses the word in the following passage:

> . . . when the Author represents any Passion, Appetite, Virtue or Vice, under a visible Shape, and makes it a Person or an Actor in his Poem. Of this Nature are the Descriptions of Hunger and Envy in *Ovid*, of Fame in *Virgil*, and of Sin and Death in *Milton*. We find a whole Creation of the like shadowy Persons in *Spencer* [sic], who had an admirable Talent in Representations of this kind.
>
> Addison, The Spectator, 1711–12

PETRARCHAN CONCEIT—See CONCEIT.

PINDARIC ODE—*See* ODE.

POET—One who writes poetry. The word is derived from the Greek *poiein*, "to make." The poet is traditionally regarded as a "maker" and the poem as *poiema*, "something made."

POETIC LICENSE—The liberty taken by poets to depart from fact and to use the language in unconventional ways in order to achieve special effects.

POETICS—See RHETORIC, POETRY.

POETRY—Many writers have tried to define poetry, describing the aim of poetry, the character of the poet, and how poems are written. Here are a few examples:

> All good poets, epic as well as lyric, compose their beautiful poems not by art, but because they are inspired and possessed. . . . the lyric poets are not in their right mind when they are composing their beautiful strains . . . they are simply inspired to utter that to which the Muse impels them . . . God takes away the mind of poets and uses them as his ministers, as he also uses diviners and holy prophets, in order that we who hear them may know them to be speaking not of themselves who utter these priceless words in a state of unconsciousness, but that God himself is the speaker, and that through them He is conversing with us.
>
> Plato, Ion, c. 390 B.C.

The aim of poets is either to be beneficial or to delight, or in their phrases to combine charm and high applicability to life . . . By at once delighting and teaching the reader, the poet who mixes the sweet with the useful has everybody's approval.

> Horace (65 B.C.–8 B.C.) *Epistle to the Pisos* (*The Art of Poetry*)

Roscommon paraphrases this: "A poet should instruct, or please, or both."

The end [of poetry] is the giving of instruction in pleasurable form, for poetry teaches, and does not simply amuse, as some used to think.

> Scaliger, *Poetics*, 1561

The aim of the poet is to imitate, invent, and represent—things which are, or which may be—in a resemblance to truth.

> Ronsard, *A Brief on the Art of French Poetry*, 1565

[The poet] commeth to you with words sent in delightful proportion, either accompanied with, or prepared for the well inchaunting skill of Music; and with a tale forsooth he commeth unto you: with a tale which holdeth children from play, and old men from the chimney corner. And pretending no more, doth intende the winning of the mind from wickednesse to vertue . . .

> Sidney, *An Apologie for Poetrie*, 1595

He is called a *Poet*, not he which writeth in measure only; but that fayneth and formeth a fable, and writes things like the Truth. For, the Fable and Fiction is (as it were) the form and soul of any poetical work, or poem.

> Ben Jonson, *Timber: or, Discoveries*, 1641

Poetry is the spontaneous overflow of powerful feelings: it takes its origin from emotion recollected in tranquillity: the emotion is contemplated till, by a species of reaction, the tranquillity gradually disappears, and an emotion, kindred to that which was before the subject of contemplation, is gradually produced, and does itself exist in the mind. In this mood successful composition generally begins, and in a mood similar to this is carried on; but the emotion, of whatever kind, and in whatever degree, from various causes, is qualified by various pleasures, so that in describing any passions whatsoever, which are voluntarily described, the mind will, upon the whole, be in a state of enjoyment.

> Wordsworth, Preface to *Lyrical Ballads*, 1800

As to the poetical Character itself (I mean that sort of which, if I am any thing, I am a Member; that sort distinguished from the

Wordsworthian or egotistical sublime; which is a thing per se and stands alone) it is not itself—it has no self—it is everything and nothing—It has no character—it enjoys light and shade; it lives in gusto, be it foul or fair, high or low, rich or poor, mean or elevated—It has as much delight in conceiving an Iago as an Imogen. What shocks the virtuous philosopher, delights the chameleon Poet. It does no harm from its relish of the dark side of things any more than from its taste for the bright one; because they both end in speculation. A Poet is the most unpoetical of anything in existence; because he has no Identity—he is continually informing and filling some other Body—the Sun, the Moon, the Sea and Men and Women who are creatures of impulse are poetical and have about them an unchangeable attribute—the poet has none; no identity—he is certainly the most unpoetical of all God's Creatures.

Keats, Letter to Richard Woodhouse, 1818

A poem is the image of life expressed in its eternal truth. . . . A Poet is a nightingale, who sits in darkness and sings to cheer its own solitude with sweet sounds. . . . Poetry is the record of the best and happiest moments of the happiest and best minds. . . . Poetry turns all things to loveliness; it exalts the beauty of that which is most beautiful, and it adds beauty to that which is most deformed. . . . Poets are the hierophants of an unapprehended inspiration; the mirrors of the gigantic shadows which futurity casts upon the present; the words which express what they understand not; the trumpets which sing to battle and feel not what they inspire; the influence which is moved not, but moves. Poets are the unacknowledged legislators of the world.

Shelley, A Defence of Poetry, 1821

I would define, in brief, the Poetry of words as *The Rhythmical Creation of Beauty*. Its sole arbiter is Taste. With the Intellect or with the Conscience, it has only collateral relations. Unless incidentally, it has no concern whatever either with Duty or with Truth.

Poe, "The Poetic Principle," 1848

Poetry is not magic. In so far as poetry, or any other of the arts, can be said to have an ulterior purpose, it is, by telling the truth, to disenchant and disintoxicate.

Auden, The Dyer's Hand, and Other Essays, 1962

With this idea of poetry, which is about as far removed from Plato's *Ion* as it is possible to get, I'll leave the question.

POPULAR BALLAD—See BALLAD.

PROJECTIVE VERSE—A movement in contemporary American poetry influenced by the work of Ezra Pound and William Carlos Williams. Its practitioners include Charles Olson, Robert Creeley, Robert Duncan, and Denise Levertov. The theories of the school are stated by Charles Olson in an article, "Projective Verse," first published in 1950. Robert Creeley summarizes Olson's ideas as follows.

> He outlines . . . the premise of "composition by field" (the value of which William Carlos Williams was to emphasize by reprinting it in part in his own *Autobiography*); and defines a basis for structure in the poem in term of its '*kinetics*' ("the poem itself must, at all points, be a high energy-construct and, at all points, an energy discharge . . ."), the '*principle*' of its writing (form is never more than an extension of content), and the '*process*' ("One PERCEPTION MUST IMMEDIATELY AND DIRECTLY LEAD TO A FURTHER PERCEPTION . . ."). He equally distinguishes between breathing and hearing, as these relate to the line: "And the line comes (I swear it) from the breath, from the breathing of the man who writes, at that moment that he writes . . ."
>
> *The New American Poetry*, 1960

PROSE PARAPHASE—A restatement in prose of the content of a poem. The use of paraphrase is to help understanding, but the music and images are lost. In fact, the poetry is lost.

PROSODY—The systematic, technical study of versification, including meter, rhyme, sound effects, and stanza patterns. Prosody has nothing to do with prose.

PROTHALAMION—A poem or song heralding a marriage. Edmund Spenser coined the word and used it as the title of one of his poems.

PSEUDO-STATEMENT—In the writings of I. A. Richards (*Science and Poetry*, 1926), pseudo-statement is a statement that is "true" though it is contradicted by fact.

> A pseudo-statement is "true" if it suits and serves some attitude or links together attitudes which on other grounds are desirable . . . A pseudo-statement is a form of words which is justified entirely by its effect in releasing or organizing our impulses and attitudes (due regard being had for the better or worse organizations of these *inter se*); a statement, on the other hand, is justi-

fied by its truth, i.e. its correspondence, in a highly technical sense, with the fact to which it points.

The following are pseudo-statements:

> Machines have made their god. They walk or fly.
> The towers bend like Magi, mountains weep,
> Needles go mad, and metal sheds a tear.
>
> Louis Simpson, "Outward"

P U N—A play on words, use of a word in a context where two or more of its meanings are relevant.

> O Nelly Gray! O, Nelly Gray!
>   Is this your love so warm?
> The love that loves a scarlet coat
>   Should be more uniform!
>
> Thomas Hood, "Faithless Nelly Gray"

P U R E   P O E T R Y—In contrast to didactic poetry, the aim of which is to teach moral or other truth, pure poetry aims only to delight the reader by the beauty of its language, music, and imagery. "Pure poetry," however, is an impossible abstract ideal.

P U R P L E   P A S S A G E—A passage so heightened in style that it stands out from its context.

P Y R R H I C—A metrical foot of two unstressed syllables, thus: ⌣ ⌣. Because the pyrrhic foot has no stress, it is rarely considered a legitimate foot in modern English scansion.

> Nŏr shăll / dēath brāg / thŏu wăn/der'st īn / hĭs shāde

Prosody is not an exact science. The line could just as well be scanned:

> Nōr shăll / dēath brāg / thŏu wăn/der'st ĭn / hĭs shāde

Q U A L I T A T I V E   V E R S E—Also called *accentual verse*. Verse in which the metrical system is based on the language's having stressed (or accented) and unstressed (or unaccented) syllables. English verse is qualitative. See Q U A N T I T A T I V E   V E R S E.

Q U A N T I T A T I V E   V E R S E—Verse in which the metrical system is based on the length of time it takes to pronounce the syllables of the language, as in classical Greek and Latin. A long syllable takes twice as much time to pronounce as a short syllable. One long syllable therefore is considered equal to two short ones; the principle of substitution in classical metrics is based on this relationship. A long syllable contains either a long vowel or diphthong, or a short vowel plus two or more consonants. Stress, or accent, is irrelevant in quantitative verse.

QUATRAIN—A four-line stanza.

REALISM—1. Said to be possessed by a work that closely imitates the details and appearances of real life, especially of commonplace middle or lower class life; often contrasted to "romance," which invents imaginary worlds. 2. "Literary realism" was a nineteenth-century movement of realistic writers, led by Flaubert. At the extreme, literary realism showed the disillusion and determinism of *naturalism* (q.v.).

REFRAIN—A line or lines repeated at regular intervals in a poem, represented by capital "R" in the rhyme scheme. For example, $a\,a\,a\,R, b\,b\,b\,R, c\,c\,c\,R$.

RESTORATION PERIOD—Dating from the end of the Puritan Commonwealth, in 1660, when the monarchy (Charles II) was restored, until about 1700. John Dryden was the major literary figure. Other poets were Marvell, Samuel Butler, and the Earl of Rochester; prose writers, Hobbes, Bunyan, Locke, Newton, Samuel Pepys, and Sir William Temple. The Puritan ban on theater productions was revoked, and playwrights such as Dryden, Etherege, Wycherley, and Congreve wrote comedies and heroic dramas.

RHAPSODY—An unusually intense and irregular poem or piece of prose, ecstatic and enthusiastic. The writer of rhapsodies is called a rhapsodist. However, men who merely recite rhapsodic poems are also called rhapsodists, as in this definition by Scaliger:

> While the poet is the imitator of things, the rhapsodist is he who acts out the imitation, and according as the poet represents, the rhapsodist can reproduce.
>
> *Poetics*

RHETORIC—In the broad sense, the art of persuasion. In the narrow sense, the study of techniques used in public speaking (oratory) and in writing: figures of speech, diction, structure, and rhythm. In the medieval curriculum, grammar, logic and rhetoric constituted the *trivium* or four-year course of undergraduate study. Music, arithmetic, geometry and astronomy made up the *quadrivium* or three-year course from the B.A. to M.A. degree. These were the seven liberal arts.

Critics have often tried to distinguish between rhetoric and *poetics*, the theory of making and judging poetry. Aristotle said that the aim of rhetoric was to persuade, the aim of poetry to imitate. In this stanza Davies says that it is meter that distinguishes poetry from rhetoric; if he had meant rhythm, rather than meter, I would agree:

> For Rhetoric, clothing speech in rich array,
> In looser numbers teacheth her to range
> With twenty tropes, and turnings every way,
> And various figures, and licentious change;
> But poetry, with rule and order strange,
> So curiously doth move each single pace,
> As all is marred if she one foot misplace.
>
> *Orchestra*

Attempts to distinguish between rhetoric and poetry are not conclusive, however, for rhetoric is a part of poetry.

R HETORICAL FIGURES—See FIGURES OF SPEECH.

R HETORICAL QUESTION—A question asked in order to prove a point rather than to find out information.

> O, Wind,
> If Winter comes, can Spring be far behind?
>> Shelley, "Ode to the West Wind"

R H Y M E—The identity or similarity of sound patterns. Rhyme at the end of lines is called *end* or *terminal* rhyme. Rhyme occurring within a line is *internal* rhyme ("I conceive you may use any language you choose to indulge in . . ."). If the word before the caesura rhymes with the concluding words, the rhyme is *leonine* ("Oh! a private buffoon is a light-hearted loon . . ."). The most common rhyme in English is that of the final accented vowels and all following sounds (night–light, heaven–seven, fertility–puerility). This is called *complete, exact, full, perfect, true* rhyme, or *rime suffisante*. A rhyme that is not perfect and has only similarity rather than identity of sound patterns (once–France), can be called *approximate, half, imperfect, near, oblique, off, partial,* or *slant* rhyme. *Assonance* (time–mind) and *consonance* (*lives–loves*, stru*ts–frets*) are sometimes considered variations of rhyme, as is *alliteration*, or *initial* or *head* rhyme (forgot–foul–fair), and *hidden alliteration* (hast–once). *Pararhyme*, or *consonantal rhyme*, has identical consonants with differing vowels (look–luck, fleshes–flashes, braiding–brooding). In *masculine* rhyme, the final syllable is stressed (name–fame, support–retort, roundelay–month of May). In *feminine* rhyme, the stressed syllables are followed by unstressed ones; *double* rhyme rhymes two syllables (double–trouble), and *triple* rhyme—often found in comic verse—rhymes three syllables (intellectual–hen-pecked you all). *Eye* rhyme rhymes only the spellings (cough–bough–though–rough). If an eye rhyme was once pronounced as a true rhyme, it is called a *historical* rhyme. In *identical* rhyme, in contrast, the rhyming words have identical pronunciation but different spelling (to–too–two, their–there), or the same word is used twice with different meanings. This is also called *rime riche*. In *apocapated* rhyme, the final syllable of one of the rhyme words is discounted (mope–ropeless). In *broken* rhyme, one of the rhyming words is completed at the beginning of the next line. In *linked* rhyme, found in early Welsh verse, one of the rhyming words is formed by linking the final syllable of one line to the first sound of the next line:

> Dame, at our *door*
> *D*rowned, and among our shoals,
> Remember us in the roads, the heaven-haven of the Re*ward*
>> Gerard Manley Hopkins, "The Wreck of the Deutschland"

R H Y M E R O Y A L—A seven-line stanza of iambic pentameter, having the rhyme scheme *a b a b b c c*. Rhyme royal took its name from James I of England's writing in this stanza, although he was not the first to use it. It is sometimes called the Chaucerian stanza.

> Flee from the prees, and dwelle with sothfastness,
>> Suffice unto thy good, though it be small;
> For hord hath hate, and climbing tikelnesse,
>> Prees hath envye, and well blent overall;
> Savour no more than thee bihove shall;
>> Reule well thyself, that other folk canst rede;
>> And trouthe thee shall deliver, it is no drede.
>> Geoffrey Chaucer, "Balade de Bon Conseyl"

R H Y M E S C H E M E—The pattern formed by the terminal rhymes of all the lines in a stanza. The rhyming words are assigned letters in the order of their occurrence, and a letter is repeated to show that a later word rhymes with an earlier one. A quatrain, for instance, may have a rhyme scheme of *a b a b, a b c b,* or *a a b a,* etc.

R н ythm—Repetition of stress. Regular rhythm in verse is *meter.* Irregular rhythm is *free verse.*

Rhythm is a form cut into time.

Pound, *ABC of Reading*

Rhythm is the entire movement, the flow, the recurrence of stress and unstress that is related to the rhythms of the blood, the rhythms of nature. It involves certainly stress, time, pitch, the texture of the words, the total meaning of the poem.

Theodore Roethke, "Some Remarks on Rhythm"

R i m e—Alternate spelling for rhyme.

R ising meter—Meter in which the movement rises up to the stressed syllable of each foot. The iamb [∪ ⁻] and the anapest [∪ ∪ ⁻] are rising meters.

R ocking rhythm—A rhythmic effect that occurs when the stressed syllables in a line of verse fall between two unstressed syllables, as with anapestic and dactylic meter.

Believe me, if all those endearing young charms...

R omanticism—An aesthetic that stresses imagination, individualism, the visionary and mysterious, "the spontaneous overflow of powerful feelings." See classicism, neoclassical, romantic period.

R omantic Period—In British literature, the period of the late eighteenth and early nineteenth century when the poets Burns, Blake, Scott, Wordsworth, Coleridge, Byron, Shelley, and Keats were writing. Among prose writers there were Coleridge, Hazlitt, Lamb, De Quincey, Jane Austen, and Scott. The period is sometimes dated from the outbreak of the French Revolution (1789) to the death of Scott (1832).

R ondeau—A French fixed verse form of three stanzas characterized by the use of a refrain and only two rhymes in the pattern *a a b b a, a a b R, a a b b a R.* The refrain is the first half of the opening line. The lines usually contain eight syllables.

Rоundel—A French fixed verse form of three stanzas, having only two rhymes and using the first two lines as a refrain in the seventh and eighth lines and again in the thirteenth and fourteenth, unless the refrain is omitted. The rhyme scheme is *a b b a, a b a b, a b b a a* (*b*).

Run-on line (enjambment)—A line that completes its grammatical unity and meaning by going into the next line without a pause is called a run-on line. Running-on is marked by an absence of punctuation between the lines. It may be called enjambment. The term is also used for carrying-over from one couplet or stanza to the next. See end-stopped line.

> A thing of beauty is a joy for ever:
> Its loveliness increases; it will never
> Pass into nothingness; but still will keep
> A bower quiet for us, and a sleep
> Full of sweet dreams, and health, and quiet breathing.
>
> Keats, *Endymion*

Sapphic—A quatrain written in a meter derived from that of the Greek lyric poet Sappho. Each of the first three lines has eleven syllables, of which the fourth and eleventh may be either long or short: $- \cup / - \underset{\smile}{} / - \cup \cup / - \cup / - \underset{\smile}{}$. The last line has only five syllables: $- \cup \cup / - \cup$.

> All the night sleep came not upon my eyelids,
> Shed not dew, nor shock nor unclosed a feather,
> Yet with lips shut close and with eyes of iron,
>   Stood and beheld me.
>
> Swinburne, "Sapphics"

Satire—Dr. Johnson's definition is probably the best: "a poem in which wickedness or folly is censured." Satire may be Horatian or Juvenalian, after the Roman poet Horace, who was amused at man's foibles and gently mocked them, and Juvenal, who attacked vice with severe ridicule. Donne's "Satire IV" is Horatian; Johnson's "Vanity of Human Wishes" is modeled on Juvenal. Frequently the satiric poet feels called upon to justify his art, as Pope does in "An Epistle to Dr. Arbuthnot." The satirist presents himself as a mild, honest man who is compelled by the evil around him to speak out.

Scansion—The process of analyzing the metrical patterns of a poem. To scan a poem, one goes through it line by line marking the accented and unaccented syllables, then grouping them into metrical feet. One identifies the kind of feet, the number of feet per line, and the stanza pattern, if there is one. The stanza pattern is described by noting the rhyme scheme, with each letter followed by a numerical exponent to indicate the number of feet in the line. A ballad stanza, for instance, which alternates tetrameter and trimeter lines, is notated $a^4\ b^3\ c^4\ b^3$. When the formal pattern of the verse is established it is necessary to see how the rhetorical accents counterpoint with it.

SECONDARY STRESS—An accent on a syllable weaker than the primary stress of a word, but stronger than its unstressed syllables. *E.g.*, the stress on the first syllable of the word "èvocátion."

SENSIBILITY—In the eighteenth century, "sensibility" referred to a person's capacity to respond emotionally, even tearfully, to the joy or distress of others, and to respond to beauty. In the twentieth century, "sensibility" has acquired a meaning closer to "sensitivity," referring to a person's capacity for aesthetic understanding and enjoyment.

SENTENTIA—Aphorisms, pointed statements alleging a truth, such as Aristotle's remark that "Education is learning to take pleasure in the right things." *Sententious verse* aims at instructing rather than giving pleasure. At the worst it is ponderous and trite. Unfortunately, as Northrop Frye says:

> The sententious approach to literature is still the popular one, accounting for the wide appeal of such poems as Kipling's *If* or Longfellow's *Psalm of Life.*
>
> *The Well-Tempered Critic,* 1963

See discussion of sententious verse, pp. 13–17.

SENTIMENTALISM—In the eighteenth century, self-conscious indulgence in emotional tenderness, pity, and sympathy—"the sadly pleasing tear," "the luxury of grief," "dear, delicious pain."

SENTIMENTALITY—Emotion in excess of what the occasion requires.

SEPTENARY—Synonym for *heptameter.*

SESTET (also spelled SEXTET)—A six–line poem or stanza. The term often refers to the final six lines of a Petrarchan sonnet.

SESTINA—A French fixed verse form having six unrhymed six-line stanzas with the same terminal words, in different orders, followed by a tercet using three of them, or all six if two are used per line. In the following diagram, each letter represents the terminal word of a line, and each horizontal line of letters represents one stanza:

```
a b c d e f
f a e b d c
c f d a b e
e c b f a d
d e a c f b
b d f e c a
    e c a
```

SIMILE—An expressed comparison, often using the words "like," "as," "as if," "than":

My luve is *like* a red, red rose.

SINKING—See BATHOS.

SLANT RHYME—See RHYME.

SOLILOQUY—In drama (especially Elizabethan), an extended speech by a solitary character expressing his thoughts aloud to himself and the audience. Hamlet's famous speech beginning "To be or not to be" is a soliloquy.

SONNET—A fixed verse form, having fourteen lines (occasionally twelve or sixteen) of iambic pentameter (in English) with an elaborate rhyme scheme. The *Petrarchan*, or *Italian*, sonnet is divided into an *octave* (or octet) rhyming *a b b a a b b a*, and a *sestet* usually rhyming *c d e c d e* or *c d c d c d*. Between the octet and sestet there is a significant break in meaning, a movement from question to answer, complaint to resolution, cause to effect, etc. The *Miltonic* sonnet has the Petrarchan scheme, but no significant break in meaning between the octave and sestet. The *Shakespearean*, or *English*, sonnet has three quatrains and a final couplet which usually contains an epigrammatic statement of the theme. The rhyme scheme is *a b a b, c d c d, e f e f, g g*, or else *a b b a, c d d c, e f f e, g g*. The *Spenserian*, or *"link"* sonnet rhymes *a b a b, b c b c, c d c d, e e*, and often has no break in meaning between the octave and sestet. See SONNET SEQUENCE.

398

Sᴏɴɴᴇᴛ sᴇǫᴜᴇɴᴄᴇ—A series of sonnets by one author. It may have a single theme.

Sᴘᴇɴsᴇʀɪᴀɴ sᴛᴀɴᴢᴀ—A nine-line stanza rhymed *a b a b b c b c c*. All of the lines are iambic pentameter, except the final one, which is iambic hexameter, an Alexandrine.

> He there does now enjoy eternall rest
> And happie ease, which thou doest want and craue,
> And further from it daily wanderest:
> What if some litle paine the passage haue.
> That makes fraile flesh to feare the bitter waue?
> Is not short paine well borne, that brings long ease,
> And layes the soule to sleepe in quiet graue?
> Sleepe after toyle, port after stormie seas,
> Ease after warre, death after life does greatly please.
>
> Spenser, *The Faerie Queene*

Sᴘᴏɴᴅᴇᴇ, sᴘᴏɴᴅᴀɪᴄ—A metrical foot of two syllables, both of which are stressed, thus: — —. Spondee cannot be the basic meter of a poem. Rather, it is introduced as a variant or substitute foot, especially for an iamb or trochee. Spondee neither rises nor falls. See also ᴍᴇᴛᴇʀ.

Sᴘʀᴜɴɢ ʀʜʏᴛʜᴍ—A term coined by Gerard Manley Hopkins to describe a kind of rhythm between strict meter and free verse. The verse is measured according to the number of stressed syllables, which may stand alone or be followed by any number of unstressed syllables. The stressed syllables are always considered to begin the feet, so the most common feet in Hopkins's verse are the spondee, dactyl, and trochee. Hopkins pointed out that sprung rhythm is characteristic of common speech, written prose, most music, and nursery rhymes: "Little Jack Horner sat in a corner..."

Sᴛᴀɴᴢᴀ—A group of lines considered as a unit, forming a division of a poem, and recurring in the same pattern or variations of the pattern. A stanza pattern is determined by the number of lines, the kind of feet and the number of feet per line, and the rhyme scheme. Many stanzaic forms are conventional and have their own names: see ꜰɪxᴇᴅ ꜰᴏʀᴍ. The common name for a two-line stanza is "couplet," for a three-line stanza, "tercet," and for a four-line stanza, "quatrain." See also sᴄᴀɴsɪᴏɴ.

STOCK CHARACTER—A familiar, conventional character who appears often in certain kinds of literary works. Stock characters include the epic hero, the knight and his lady, the disconsolate lover and his cruel mistress, the villain, the braggart soldier, the clever servant, the cruel stepmother, the clown or fool, the proud tragic hero, the virtuous heroine, the *femme fatale*, etc.

STOCK EPITHET—Frequently repeated lines or phrases, such as occurred in the long, orally recited heroic poems. For example, Homer's "rosy-fingered dawn."

STOCK RESPONSE—An unsophisticated reader's predictable emotional reaction to certain stimuli, such as the word "mother" in a poem. Stock responses are like sentimentality in that they suspend judgment and prevent a deeper understanding and enjoyment of poetry.

STOCK SITUATION—Stock situations are circumstances that appear frequently in literature: mistaken identities, love triangles, separations of twins by shipwreck, etc.

STREAM OF CONSCIOUSNESS—A term coined by William James (*Principles of Psychology*, 1890) to refer to the continuous flow of inner experiences. In literature it refers to a technique of presenting the perceptions, thoughts, and feelings of characters in a narrative. The narrative progresses through psychological association rather than linguistic conventions such as sentences. The term is usually applied to prose fiction—*e.g.*, James Joyce's *Ulysses*—but it might also be applied to the floating consciousness of T. S. Eliot's Prufrock and to parts of *The Waste Land* and Pound's *Cantos*.

STRESS—Synonym for "accent," the emphasis given to certain syllables of words. If a word (usually longer than three syllables) has more than one accented syllable, the heavier accent is called the primary stress, the lighter is the secondary stress, and the other syllables are unstressed.

STROPHE—See ODE.

STRUCTURE—The underlying logic or arrangement and movement in a literary text; its skeleton or paraphrasable content. The term "structure" usually refers to the organization of elements other than words. For the latter the term "style" is used. See ARGUMENT and TEXTURE.

STYLE—The choice and arrangement of words, sentences, and larger units, in a literary text. The term is very broad and includes consideration of the choices a writer must make about diction, figurative and rhetorical devices, tone, and sound patterns of the language (alliteration, rhyme, meter, etc.). Styles may be classified according to authors (Miltonic, Shakespearean), or periods (classical, Renaissance, Romantic), or books (Biblical), or subjects (legal, journalistic). Styles may also be classified as high (or grand), middle, and low (or plain). These divisions used to be finely subdivided, as they are in the "complete and invariable" listing by Scaliger—see text, pp. 7–8.

SUBJECTIVITY—The quality in a literary work which reveals the author's personality, his own feelings and attitudes. Wordsworth's *Prelude* is subjective because it records the growth of the poet's own mind. Shakespeare's plays, in contrast, are impersonal and objective, for they tell us virtually nothing about the poet's personality. The term may be used to refer to the characters in a work, rather than to the author who created them; Browning's dramatic monologues are subjective in that they reveal the personality of the character, or persona, in the poem. In literary criticism, subjectivity means emphasis on the critic's personal taste and response, "impressionistic" criticism.

SUBLIMITY (THE SUBLIME)—

Sublimity is a certain distinction and excellence in expression, and ... it is from no other source than this that the greatest poets and writers have derived their eminence and gained an immortality of renown. The effect of elevated language upon an audience is not persuasion but transport. At every time and in every way imposing speech, with the spell it throws over us, prevails over that which aims at persuasion and gratification. Our persuasions we can usually control, but the influences of the sublime bring power and irresistible might to bear, and reign supreme over every hearer.... Sublimity flashing forth at the right moment scatters everything before it like a thunderbolt.... For, as if instinctively, our soul is uplifted by the true sublime; it takes a proud flight, and is filled with joy and vaunting, as though it had itself produced what it has heard.

On the Sublime, traditionally ascribed to Longinus

SUBSTITUTION—See INVERSION.

SURREALISM—A literary and artistic movement vigorous in the 1920's and 1930's, and still productive. Surrealists want to go "beyond" realism (normal perception of the outer world) deep into the inner world of the unconscious mind. Their work often resembles the stark, strange imagery and nonsyntactical narrative of dreams. In general, surrealists are hostile to, or "go beyond," rationality, bourgeois morality, and artistic conventions. The French poet Guillaume Appollinaire invented the word surrealism; André Breton led the movement. Poets who use surrealist techniques include Aragon and Eluard in French, Lorca and Neruda in Spanish, and Dylan Thomas in English. Max Ernst and Salvador Dali are surrealist painters. A *surrealist image* is not so much "the thing perceived" as "anything as it might be perceived." In practice, most surrealist images are merely juxapositions of objects that have no relationship in the normal world. However, the effective surrealist images are more than this; they seem to be formed by a logic of the subconscious, as things are in dreams.

> When the sun is only a drop of sweat
> the sound of a bell
> the red pearl falling down a vertical needle
>
> > Michel Leiris, "Marécage du sommeil"

Surrealist techniques have always existed in verse. Breton remarks that the eighteenth-century poetry of Edward Young, in *Night Thoughts*, was surrealist. The deliberate, intense application of these techniques in the twentieth century has created a kind of literature that seems, in spite of absurdities, original and stimulating. The following poem by the Chilean Pablo Neruda, here printed in its entirety in translation by Angel Flores, describes the art of a surrealist and uses surrealistic techniques:

Ars Poetica

Between shadow and space, between garrisons and maidens,
endowed with singular heart and doleful dreams,
precipitately pale, the forehead withered,
and with the mourning of an angry widower for each day of life,
alas, for each invisible drop of water which I drink sleepily
and for each sound which I receive, trembling,
I have the same absent thirst and the same cold fever,
an ear that is born, an indirect anguish,
as if thieves or ghosts were approaching,
and in a shell of fixed and deep extent,

like a humiliated waiter, like a bell slightly hoarse,
like an old mirror, like the smell of a lonely house
whose roomers enter by night dead drunk,
and there is a smell of clothing thrown about on the floor, and an
    absence of flowers
possibly in some other way even less melancholy,
but, in truth, suddenly, the wind that strikes my chest
the nights of infinite substance dropped into my bedroom,
the noise of a day that burns with sacrifice,
demand, sadly, whatever there is of prophetic in me,
and there is a knocking of objects which call without being an-
    swered,
and a ceaseless movement, and a confused name.

SYLLABIC VERSE (SYLLABICS)—Verse in which the system of measurement is based on the number of syllables in the line, rather than on stress or quantity.

> They had their men tie
> hippopotami
>   and bring out dapple dog-
>   cats to course antelopes, dikdik, and ibex;
>   or used small eagles. They looked on as theirs,
>   impallas and onigers,
>
> the wild ostrich herd
> with hard feet and bird
>   necks rearing back in the
>   dust like a serpent preparing to strike, cranes,
>   mongooses, storks, anoas, Nile geese;
>   and there were gardens for these—
>
>   Marianne Moore, "The Jerboa"

SYMBOL

Nature is a temple, in which living pillars sometimes utter a babel of words; man traverses it through forests of symbols, that watch him with knowing eyes.
    Charles Baudelaire, *Correspondances* (transl. Francis Scarfe).

A symbol is an image that means not only what it is, but something else as well, and perhaps many things. Part of the meaning of a symbol is emotional and subconscious, in the psychic reality of myth. A symbol is often a means of making concrete and perceptible a meaning that otherwise would remain inexpressible. It is a "loaded" word or image from which meanings ray out; the meanings are determined by the context in which the symbol appears. A symbol may be an object (a rose), a situation (a journey), a character (Coleridge's Ancient Mariner), or the setting of a work (the sea). See SYMBOLISM and the discussion of symbolism, pp. 46–48, 50.

SYMBOLISM (SYMBOLIST MOVEMENT)—A literary movement originating in late nineteenth-century France. Baudelaire was a forerunner of symbolism; Verlaine, Rimbaud, and Mallarmé were the leading Symbolists. Rimbaud said, "The poet makes himself a seer by means of a long, immense and calculated disordering of all the senses." In his *Bateau Ivre*, 1871, he created new rhythms, exotic descriptions of land and sea, and vivid colors, and employed symbols that evoked the creation of the world. Mallarmé evolved a technique of combining verbal music and typographic patterns to suggest his ideas. To Mallarmé, poetry was a mystery; the poet should suggest, not state: "To name a thing is to suppress three quarters of the joy of the poem, which consists in guessing, little by little: suggestion makes the dream." Donald Davie has described symbolist technique as setting the images at a certain distance from one another and letting the meaning flower out of the spaces between. Mallarmé called this forming "constellations." These men also were important in the movement: Jean Moréas, René Ghil, Gustave Khan, Stuart Merrill, Emile Verhaeren, Maurice Maeterlinck, Villiers de l'Isle Adam, Jules Laforgue, and Arthur Symons, who introduced W. B. Yeats to the symbolists.

> All sounds, all colors, all forms, either because of their pre-ordained energies or because of long associations, evoke undefinable and yet precise emotions, or, as I prefer to think, call down among us certain disembodied powers, whose footsteps over our hearts we call emotions; and when sound, and color, and form are in a musical relation, a beautiful relation to one another, they become as it were one sound, one color, one form, and evoke an emotion that is made out of their distinct evocations and yet is one emotion.
>
> Yeats, "The Symbolism of Poetry"

Among British and American poets, T. S. Eliot and Dylan Thomas were influenced by the symbolists, and many other poets have used symbolist techniques. *Axel's Castle* by Edmund Wilson is still a useful introduction to the subject, though it was pioneer work.

SYNECDOCHE—A figurative use of language in which a part of something is substituted for the whole, or the whole for a part. "Roof" is used to mean "house," "sail" to mean "ship," etc. Synecdoche is often regarded as a special type of *metonymy* (q.v.).

SYNESTHESIA—Description of one kind of sense perception in words that usually describe another.

> There are perfumes fresh and cool as the bodies of children, mellow as oboes, green as fields; and others that are perverse, rich, and triumphant.
> Charles Baudelaire, *Correspondances* (transl. by Francis Scarfe)

TENOR (VEHICLE)—Terms used by I. A. Richards to explain the process of metaphor. If we take the sentence "My love is a rose," the principal subject "my love" would be called the *tenor* (because it is what we are "holding on to" or talking about), and the secondary subject, "rose," would be called the *vehicle* (because it carries the weight of the comparison).

TENSION—A technical term in the vocabulary of "new criticism." Allen Tate arrived at it by "lopping the prefixes off the logical terms *ex*tension and *in*tension" and combining their meanings, so that the term "tension" refers to the extent to which the abstract and concrete elements in a poem have an integral relationship or are unified with the idea embodied in images. An additional meaning of the term "tension" involves "conflict-structures," listed by Robert Penn Warren as "tension between the rhythm of the poem and the rhythm of speech . . . between the formality of the rhythm and the informality of language; between the particular and the general, the concrete and the abstract; between the elements of even the simplest metaphor; between the beautiful and the ugly; between ideas; between the elements involved in irony; between prosisms and poeticisms."

TERCET—A three-line stanza. If there is a single rhyme for all three lines, the tercet is a triplet. The term "tercet" may also refer to half the sestet in a Petrarchan sonnet, or to the *terza rima* stanza.

TERMINAL RHYME—See RHYME.

TERZA RIMA—An Italian fixed verse form of tercets with rhymes interlocking in the pattern *a b a*, *b c b*, *c d c*, *d e d*, etc. The form was used by Dante in *The Divine Comedy*.

Tetrameter—A line of four metrical feet:

How the / Chimney-sweeper's / cry
Every black'ning Church appalls;
And the hapless Soldier's sigh
Runs in blood down Palace walls.

Blake, "London"

Tetrastich—A four-line stanza; synonym for quatrain.

Texture—The surface detail of a text, especially the phonetic patterns, the sensory quality of the images, and the additional richness of meaning suggested by the connotations of the words. Texture is contrasted with structure, which is the argument or paraphrasable content of the work. With reference to meter, John Crowe Ransom calls the basic meter the structure and the variations on it the texture.

Theme—A central idea or major point of a literary work; its thesis, as stated in sentence form. Also, loosely used, "theme" can mean the subject of a work, such as time, love, death, beauty, and so on.

Thematic development—The process by which a theme unfolds to the reader or undergoes changes in a work.

Threnody—See dirge.

Tone—The attitude of the writer toward his subject and his audience, as it is implied in the text and inferred by the reader. The tone may be serious or light, formal or intimate, scornful or sympathetic, straightforward or given a double edge by irony.

Total meaning—See meaning.

Tradition—The totality of conventions—of technique, form, subject matter, and point of view or attitude—characteristic of a group of writers in a period. Thus we may speak of the Puritan tradition, the Cavalier tradition, the metaphysical tradition of the seventeenth century, the neoclassical tradition of the eighteenth century, or the romantic tradition of the nineteenth century. The term may also be used to refer to a complex of conventions and themes common to writers of various periods, such as the classical tradition, the Neoplatonic tradition, and the pastoral tradition.

Transferred epithet—See epithet.

Trimeter—A line of three metrical feet.

> My silks / and fine / array,
> My smiles / and lan/guish'd air
> By Love / are driv'n / away; . . .

Blake, "Song"

Triolet—A French fixed form used by late nineteenth-century English poets. It has eight lines, but only two rhymes; the first two lines are repeated as the last two, and the fourth is the same as the first. The rhyme scheme is *a b a a a b a b*.

Triple meters—Meters whose feet consist of three syllables. Dactylic [– ◡ ◡] and anapestic [◡ ◡ –] are triple meters.

Triple rhyme—See rhyme.

Triplet—A three-line stanza with a single rhyme.

Tristich—A three-line stanza; synonym for *tercet*.

Trochee, trochaic—A metrical foot of two syllables, with a strong stress followed by a weak: – ◡. See also meter and falling meter.

Trope—Literally, a "turn," or use of a word with a definite change or extension of its meaning, from literal to figurative. See figurative language.

Troubadour—One of a class of lyric poets who flourished in southern France (and eastern Spain and northern Italy) from the eleventh to the thirteenth centuries. They wrote in the Provençal dialect about courtly love and chivalry. Their interest in metrical technique led to the development of many of the intricate French fixed verse forms. Among the more famous of the troubadours were Bertrans de Born, Arnaut Daniel, and William, Count of Poitiers. See also trouvère.

Trouvère—One of a class of court poets of northern France who flourished at the same time as the Provençal troubadours and were greatly influenced by them. Trouvères, one of whom was Chrétien de Troyes, wrote chivalric romances, love lyrics and *chansons de geste*.

407

TRUE RHYME—See RHYME.

TUMIDITY—Pompous, turgid, bombastic language or literary style.

"UBI SUNT" MOTIF—A common theme in lyric poetry: lamenting the vanished past. The phrase is Latin for "where are," as in Villon's "Where are the snows of yesteryear?"

UNDERSTATEMENT (MEIOSIS)—A figurative use of language in which less is said than is meant. Only a part of the meaning is stated, so that the reader, in order to complete the thought, must enter into the mind and feelings of the author. In doing so, the reader obtains a better understanding than he would from explicit statement. Shakespeare's Othello says: "Keep up your bright swords, for the dew will rust them." He is speaking of a quarrel in the street, between men armed with swords, as though it were a promenade. The effect is to draw the reader into the heroic calm of Othello's mind. He is a man of experience, particularly of battle, to whom a street-fight would be insignificant.

> But now go the bells, and we are ready;
> In one house we are sternly stopped
> To say we are vexed at her brown study,
> Lying so primly propped.
>
> John Crowe Ransom,
> "Bells for John Whiteside's Daughter"

In this stanza about the death of a little girl, the "brown study" is death, and being "vexed" is being grieved. The words seem insufficient; in order to complete the poet's meaning, the reader is compelled to imagine the scene and give of his own feelings.

UNITY—The coherent relationship of all the parts of a work to the whole, with nothing essential omitted and nothing irrelevant included. The *"three unities"* of the drama are those of action, time, and place. During the Renaissance, French and Italian critics who derived the "unities" from Asitotle's *Poetics* insisted that a play should be the imitation of a single action taking place within a single day in a single place. However, the only unity that Aristotle himself had insisted upon was unity of action.

VEHICLE—See TENOR.

408

VERS DE SOCIÉTÉ–French for "society verse," brief epigrammatic or lyrical light verse concerning polite society. It is usually witty and highly polished, using a conversational tone and one of the intricate French fixed verse forms, such as the rondeau or villanelle. It may be gently satiric or elegantly amorous, paying a witty compliment to a lady.

VERS LIBRE–See FREE VERSE.

VERSE–1. Any individual line of a poem. 2. Strictly metrical language; verse as distinguished from prose. Verse is not necessarily poetry, however; it may be mere doggerel.

> A rhymer, and a *poet*, are two things.
>
> > Ben Jonson, *Timber*

VERSE PARAGRAPH–A group of lines, frequently in blank verse, considered as a rhetorical unit similar to a prose paragraph, and indicated as such by the indentation of the first line.

VERSIFICATION–Synonym for *prosody*.

VICTORIAN PERIOD–The period dated from either 1832 (the first Reform Bill) or 1837 (the accession of Queen Victoria to the throne) until the Queen's death in 1901. Much of the writing of this period reflected contemporary social, economic, and intellectual problems, such as the Industrial Revolution, pressures for political and economic reforms, and the impact of the Darwinian theory of evolution. Tennyson, Browning, and Arnold were the more prominent poets. Arnold, Carlyle, and Ruskin were influential essayists. Among the novelists were Dickens, Thackeray, George Eliot, Meredith, Trollope, Hardy, and Samuel Butler.

VILLANELLE–A French fixed verse form of six stanzas (five tercets and a quatrain), characterized by the use of only two rhymes and the repetition of lines as refrains. The opening line is repeated at the ends of the second and fourth stanzas, and the third line at the ends of the third and fifth. The two refrain lines conclude the poem. The rhyme scheme is *a b a, a b a, a b a, a b a, a b a, a b a a*. The form was originally used for pastoral subjects (the name derives from *villa*, a farm or country house), and later used for light verse. See "The Waking," p. 312.

VIRELAY—A name applied to two verse forms derived from old French poetry, neither of which is strictly fixed in form or common in English. The short one has only two rhymes and alternates the first and second lines as refrains. The other has an indefinite number of stanzas with one rhyme in long lines and the other rhyme in short lines. The short lines always provide the rhyme for the long lines of the next stanza, and the short lines of the last stanza rhyme with the long lines of the first.

VIRGULE (SLASH)—The short slanting line used to divide a line into feet, or to mark the division between one line and another:

> Now / my charms / are all / o'erthrown.

VOICE—T. S. Eliot has described "The Three Voices of Poetry":

> The first voice is the voice of the poet talking to himself—or to nobody. The second is the voice of the poet addressing an audience, whether large or small. The third is the voice of the poet when he attempts to create a dramatic character speaking in verse; when he is saying, not what he would say in his own person, but only what he can say within the limits of one imaginary character addressing another imaginary character.

See PERSONA.

WEAK ENDING—At the end of a line of verse, a syllable which, though it is stressed metrically, would be unstressed in ordinary speech, and leads right on to the following line:

> Thy mother was a piece of virtue, and
> She said thou wast my daughter.
>
> Shakespeare, *The Tempest*

WIT—1. Intelligence or wisdom (Renaissance usage). 2. Fancy or nimbleness of thinking (seventeenth-century usage, often applied in discussion of metaphysical poetry). 3. The ability to see similarities, as opposed to "judgment," which was considered the ability to see differences (late seventeenth-century usage). 4. In the eighteenth century, according to Pope,

> True wit is Nature to advantage dressed,
> What oft was thought, but ne'er so well expressed.

5. In the twentieth century, wit is associated with humor in original, clever remarks.

Z E U G M A—A Greek word literally meaning "yoking," and applying to the use of a single word standing in the same grammatical relationship to two other words, but with significant differences in meaning:

Or *stain* her honor, or her new brocade.

Pope, The Rape of the Lock

Index of Authors and Titles

413

414

Acknowledgments and Copyrights

Reprinted by permission of Little, Brown and Company:

"After Great Pain" from *The Complete Poems of Emily Dickinson,* Thomas H. Johnson, ed. Copyright 1929, © 1957 by Mary L. Hampson.

Reprinted by permission of Harvard University Press and the Trustees of Amherst College:

"The Soul Selects Her Own Society" and "Success is Counted Sweetest" from *The Poems of Emily Dickinson,* Thomas H. Johnson, ed., Cambridge, Mass.: The Belknap Press of Harvard University Press, Copyright 1951, 1955, by The President and Fellows of Harvard College.

Reprinted by permission of The Macmillan Company:

"Her Immortality," "Drummer Hodge," "The Darkling Thrush," "The Homecoming," and "Afterwards" from *Collected Poems* by Thomas Hardy. Copyright The Macmillan Company, 1925.

"The Lake Isle of Innisfree" from *Poetic Works* by William Butler Yeats. Copyright The Macmillan Company 1906, renewed 1934 by William Butler Yeats. "Paudeen," a portion of "September, 1913" and "The Magi" from *Responsibilities* by William Butler Yeats. Copyright The Macmillan Company 1916, renewed 1944 by Bertha Georgie Yeats. "Sailing to Byzantium" from *The Tower* by William Butler Yeats. Copyright The Macmillan Company 1928, renewed 1956 by Georgie Yeats. "Byzantium" from *The Winding Stair* by William Butler Yeats. Copyright The Macmillan Company 1933, renewed 1961 by Bertha Georgie Yeats. "Lapis Lazuli," "A Crazed Girl," and "Long-Legged Fly" from *Last Poems and Plays* by William Butler Yeats. Copyright 1940 by Georgie Yeats. Yeats' poems are also reprinted by permission of A. P. Watt & Son and M. B. Yeats.

"The Bonnie Broukit Bairn," "Crowdieknowe," a portion of "The Kind of Poetry I Want," and "Crystals Like Blood" from *Collected Poems* by Hugh MacDiarmid. © Christopher Murray Grieve 1948, 1962.

"The Jerboa" from *Collected Poems* by Marianne Moore. Copyright Marianne Moore 1935, renewed 1963 by Marianne Moore and T. S. Eliot.

Reprinted by permission of Oxford University Press:

"Pied Beauty," "The Windhover," "Binsey Poplars," and "No Worst, There is None" and a portion of "That Nature is a Heraclitean Fire and of the Comfort of the Resurrection" from *Poems of Gerard Manley Hopkins,* third edition, W. H. Gardner, ed. Copyright 1948 by Oxford University Press, Inc.

Reprinted by permission of Holt, Rinehart and Winston, Inc.:

From *The Collected Poems of A. E. Housman:* "On Forelands High in Heaven," copyright 1936 by Barclays Bank Ltd. Copyright © 1964 by Robert E. Symons; a portion of "Spring Morning," copyright 1922 by Holt, Rinehart and Winston, Inc. Copyright 1950 by Barclays Bank Ltd. Housman's work is also reprinted by permission of the Society of Authors and Jonathan Cape Ltd.

"Mending Wall," "Stopping by Woods on a Snowy Evening," and "De-

419

420